THE
LOST
FOUNDING
FATHER

JOHN QUINCY ADAMS (CA. EIGHTY)—ENGRAVING BY UNKNOWN ARTIST

The

LOST FOUNDING FATHER

—

JOHN QUINCY ADAMS *and* *the* TRANSFORMATION *of* AMERICAN POLITICS

—

WILLIAM J. COOPER

LIVERIGHT PUBLISHING
CORPORATION
A Division of W. W. NORTON & COMPANY
Independent Publishers Since 1923
NEW YORK | LONDON

For information about permission to reproduce selections from this book,
write to Permissions, Liveright Publishing Corporation,
a division of W. W. Norton & Company, Inc.,
500 Fifth Avenue, New York, NY 10110

For information about special discounts for bulk purchases, please contact
W. W. Norton Special Sales at specialsales@wwnorton.com or 800-233-4830

Manufacturing by Quad Graphics Fairfield
Book design by Barbara Bachman
Production manager: Lauren Abbate

Library of Congress Cataloging-in-Publication Data

Names: Cooper, William J., Jr. (William James), 1940– author.
Title: The lost founding father : John Quincy Adams and the transformation of
American politics / William J. Cooper.
Other titles: John Quincy Adams and the transformation of American politics
Description: First edition. | NEW YORK : LIVERIGHT PUBLISHING
CORPORATION, a division of W. W. NORTON & COMPANY, 2017. |
Includes bibliographical references and index.
Identifiers: LCCN 2017036932 | ISBN 9780871404350 (hardcover)
Subjects: LCSH: Adams, John Quincy, 1767–1848. | Founding Fathers of the
United States—Biography. | Statesmen—United States—Biography. | United
States. Constitution—Signers—Biography. | United States—History—
Revolution, 1775–1783. | United States—Politics and government—1783–1789. |
Presidents—United States—Biography.
Classification: LCC E377.C675 2017 | DDC 973.5/5092[B]—dc23
LC record available at https://lccn.loc.gov/2017036932

Liveright Publishing Corporation, 500 Fifth Avenue, New York, N.Y. 10110
www.wwnorton.com

W. W. Norton & Company Ltd., 15 Carlisle Street, London W1D 3BS

1 2 3 4 5 6 7 8 9 0

For Patricia

CONTENTS

PREFACE

JOHN QUINCY ADAMS OCCUPIES A CAMOUFLAGED POSITION in U.S. history. With his public career lodged between the grandeur of the American Revolution and the drama of the Civil War, he has been overshadowed. Son of a major Founding Father, John Adams, the second president, John Quincy knew personally the giants of the founding generation, including George Washington, Benjamin Franklin, Thomas Jefferson, Alexander Hamilton, James Madison, and James Monroe. And from the mid-1790s to the mid-1820s, he held important diplomatic posts, culminating in his service as secretary of state in Monroe's cabinet. In that office he was the chief architect of a foreign policy that made his country a continental nation and asserted American preeminence in this hemisphere. Then in 1825 he became the sixth president of the United States. That path alone should have secured him a prominent place in the national pantheon.

Yet, that elevation did not take place. Just as John Quincy entered the presidency, a mighty upheaval began to revolutionize American politics. A new, popular politics energized by sharply increasing numbers of voters along with the growth and maturation of political parties was supplanting an arena in which a restricted electorate coupled with personal loyalty predominated. The politics of our time really began at this moment—a combination of parties directed by political professionals, vigorous, even raucous, campaigns, legions of voters demanding attention, and candidates striving to connect with those same voters.

That momentous shift became identified with Andrew Jackson, who defeated John Quincy when he tried for reelection. A military hero of the War of 1812, Jackson was the first president from west of the Appalachian Mountains. He was also emphatically the first not intimately associated with the Founders. Furthermore, he and his partisans became equated with the broadening franchise that underlay what can legitimately be called the democratization of American politics for white men, the political universe at that time. In spite of Jackson's recent condemnation by some as a slave owner and warrior against Native Americans, no doubt can exist about the political transformation that accompanied his ascendancy. It fundamentally altered the political world. And in that world John Quincy never felt comfortable. He clung tenaciously to values and an outlook much closer to those of the Founders. He was the link to a political world that could not hold.

Driven from the presidency, as he saw it, an embittered John Quincy believed that he had been wronged by political pirates. He viewed himself as an artifact, as did many contemporaries. For years most historians agreed.

John Quincy declined to remain in isolation, however, a man politically dead communing with the physical dead. Refusing to conform with his presidential predecessors in their retirement from public life, he entered the national House of Representatives in 1831 and would abide there until his death seventeen years later.

John Quincy Adams began his congressional career as a vehement opponent of Jackson, whom he thought unfit for the presidency and leading the country in the wrong direction. John Quincy envisioned a dynamic central government dedicated to active involvement in economic and financial policy and to funding internal improvements (roads and canals), education, and science. But his dream became submerged under a cascade of voters fearing federal power.

Although John Quincy never surrendered his vision, while he served in Congress his concern with southern political power mounted. Both the policies it pursued and the evil institution of slavery it defended alarmed him. Secure in his House seat, John Quincy led the congressional fight against what he deemed to be an essentially un-American South. Successfully battling against southern opposition, he maintained the right of citizens to petition for what they wanted, especially antislavery measures. Even if he disagreed with certain of their requests or found them divisive, John Quincy still felt the Constitution guaranteed citizens the prerogative to make them. Yet, he failed to halt the westward advance of slavery and the onset of the war with Mexico, a clash he denounced as a proslavery gambit. In these efforts he came publicly to doubt whether the country could continue with both slave and free states. He stood as the first major public figure to reach that conclusion.

But his death in 1848 occurred a few years before the advent of the sectional Republican party, which was bent on halting the march of slavery and curbing its political impact. The success of the Republican cause and especially the rise of Abraham Lincoln with his twin triumphs over disunion and slavery dimmed John Quincy's memory.

Although John Quincy Adams does not loom large in the American imagination, he has attracted numerous biographers. The initial biography, written by an ardent political admirer, came out just a year after his death. Since then, both earnest scholars and popular writers have chronicled his life, in short books as well as long ones.[1]

First among these must stand Samuel F. Bemis's magisterial work published in two volumes, in 1949 and 1956, respectively. Primarily a student of American diplomatic history, Bemis made his most significant contribution in his first volume, mostly a detailed treatment of John Quincy's diplomatic record. From that time on, John Quincy has been ranked among America's foremost diplomats and perhaps his country's greatest secretary of state. Even today that dimension of his life gains the attention of careful historians.[2]

In the late twentieth and thus far in the twenty-first century, acclaim for abolitionists and antislavery activists has drawn increased attention to John Quincy. His vigorous action against slavery as a congressman has led not only to recognition but also to accolades. In *What Hath God Wrought: The Transformation of America, 1815–1848*, which spans the bulk of John Quincy's public life, Daniel Walker Howe awarded his dedication "To the memory of John Quincy Adams."[3]

Lately two fat biographies have appeared. The first of these, Fred Kaplan's *John Quincy Adams, American Visionary*, concentrates on John Quincy's family life and relations, though it does offer birth-to-grave coverage. Without a comparable focus, albeit with an explicit present-mindedness, James Traub's *John Quincy Adams: Militant Spirit* provides massive factual detail on his protagonist's life. His subtitle, *Militant Spirit*, clearly, however, conveys his perspective.[4]

Yet neither of these lengthy tomes does what I have set out to do. I have no intention of replicating their massiveness. My chief goal has been to understand John Quincy in his time. In my judgment doing so requires discussing him in the context of the developing forces and changing values taking place in American politics during his lifetime. In his responses and reactions he held fast to the verities of the Puritan heritage powerfully bequeathed to him by his parents, even though he often struggled with its sometimes conflicting tenets. At the same time, he both embraced and resisted the transitions swirling about him. Living through tumultuous times, John Quincy clung to the old while he clasped the new.

In the course of a long public life of more than a half century, the same man was at once the last of the Founders both in his sense of politics and his valuing the Union above all. He was also the first of those who rejected the Union with slavery. How these contradictory elements influenced him and how the last gave way to the first compose my story.

In the early chapters of this book, I use John Quincy to distinguish him from his father, John. But later, when his father has a less important role, I employ for him the surname Adams. That shift occurs in chapter 4 when he returns to the United States from Europe to become secretary of state.

PART ONE

—

1767–1817

PREPARATION—
DIPLOMACY
and
POLITICS

—

JOHN QUINCY ADAMS
(TWENTY-NINE)—
PORTRAIT BY
JOHN SINGLETON COPLEY

CHAPTER 1

"To Bring Myself into Notice"

JOHN QUINCY ADAMS'S LIFE DIFFERED SHARPLY FROM THAT of the men with whom he would come later to share the national stage. The son of John and Abigail Adams, he was in so many ways a Founding Father by extension, his travel and education so unique that he would have been more companionable with figures of the eighteenth-century European Enlightenment than with the bruising politicians who would come to occupy the nation's capital in the 1830s and 1840s. No one else in his generation of American leaders—not John C. Calhoun, Henry Clay, Martin Van Buren, Daniel Webster, and certainly not Andrew Jackson—experienced Europe as a youth accompanying his father in the 1770s and 1780s on diplomatic missions. While he traveled in countries like France, Spain, England, Holland, and Russia, even translating French at the court of Catherine the Great, most of the men who would become his political contemporaries gained their own formative life experiences on the frontiers of rural America, often joining the country's relentless advance westward. John Quincy's education at Harvard, where he studied subjects like Greek, Latin, and moral and natural philosophy, would come to distinguish him as well, separating him from most of these individuals who had limited formal schooling. Moreover, he was directly exposed to the ideas of the Enlightenment that so influenced his father and other Founders, chiefly their embrace of reason and the conviction that human beings could fashion a better world.

Furthermore, as the son of the second president, John Quincy from an early age came into contact with this entire generation whom we now call the Founding Fathers, men like Benjamin Franklin and Thomas Jefferson. While still in his twenties, John Quincy impressed the most notable Founder of them all, President George Washington, who named the young man to an important foreign post. No other future political leader of his generation could present such a formidable résumé.

John Quincy Adams was born on July 11, 1767, in Braintree, Massachusetts, a few miles southeast of Boston. The Adams homestead was in that part of Braintree which would later become the town of Quincy. He was the second child and first son of John and Abigail Smith Adams. The Adamses would have two more sons, born in 1770 and 1772, respectively, who lived into adulthood and a daughter who died in infancy. The ancestry of both John and Abigail dated back to the beginning of the Massachusetts colony in the 1630s. Their household found the Puritan cultural heritage in full flower—devotion to religion, to the family, to duty, to self-improvement, including education, to a stern moral code, and to doubts about inherent individual worth.

John, the son of a farmer, aged twenty-nine, married Abigail, daughter of a minister, aged twenty, in 1764. An ambitious young attorney at the time of his marriage, John strove to improve his status, economically and socially. With his business increasing in the early 1770s, he moved to Boston. Almost immediately John became caught up in the growing conflict between Great Britain and its North American colonies stretching along the Atlantic seacoast from Massachusetts south to Georgia on the border of Spanish Florida. The unrest centered on a dispute over the legitimate authority the British government could exert over its colonists, who especially objected to what they termed illegal and unconstitutional taxes imposed on them from London. By the time John began residence in Boston, talk of possible armed conflict between mother country and colonies began to spread. The most ardent opponents of Great Britain's policy phrased their position as affirming local liberty against British tyranny. Some even began to speak of revolution, of independence.[1]

No colony outpaced Massachusetts in the increasing tension and in the determination, if necessary, to confront British authority with force. British officials in London and Boston responded in kind, committed to upholding what they believed imperial rights and prerogatives, which they equated with law and order.

John Adams found himself not only in the midst of this developing quarrel but also thrust forward by it. He took a leading role in opposing the Stamp Act passed by Parliament in 1765, arguing that the British government had no right to levy a tax on Massachusetts because the colony had no representation in that body. Then in 1770 he defended British soldiers accused of killing four Massachusetts inhabitants in a confrontation that became widely known as the Boston Massacre. Although in this instance he seemingly took the side of the imperial master, to many in the city and the colony his stand denoted moral courage. In 1771 he was elected to the colony's House of Representatives.

Three years later he was chosen as a member of the Massachusetts delegation to the Continental Congress, where he served until 1778. In the Congress, which met in Philadelphia, men from throughout the colonies came together in an attempt to fashion a unified stance toward Great Britain. From the outset Adams had influence. Vigorously supporting independence, in 1776 he was named to the committee assigned to prepare a document declaring the thirteen American colonies independent of Great Britain. And on July 4, 1776, the Continental Congress adopted its handiwork, the Declaration of Independence, drafted chiefly by Adams's fellow committeeman Thomas Jefferson of Virginia, who would have a major part in his future.

By that time the fledgling United States had become engaged in a shooting war with the mother country. In April 1775 the first bullets had been fired in the village of Lexington, Massachusetts, just north of Boston. In 1778 Adams was sent to France to complete negotiations for a treaty of alliance with that country. The newly independent United States was at war with the greatest military power of the age. Confronting an invasion, the hard-pressed American government needed an ally to compete with overwhelming British strength. France, Great Britain's chief adversary in Europe, seemed a likely prospect. The French had continued to chafe at their defeat by the British in 1763 in the French and Indian War, a war that had cost them the loss of most of their North American colonies. Moreover, France still possessed a navy that could challenge British might at sea. But by the time Adams arrived, a treaty had already been concluded. Thus he returned home. Back in Massachusetts, he attended as a delegate the state constitutional convention. There he was the principal author of the first Massachusetts constitution, adopted in 1780. Yet he quickly returned to Europe as a member of the American commission charged with negotiating a treaty of peace with Great Britain. His diplomatic duties kept him in Europe until the end of the Revolution in 1783, concluding as the first American minister to Great Britain, from 1784 to 1788.

The American Revolution and his father's participation in it were thus critical in the life of young John Quincy Adams. He often remarked that his memories began with events of the Revolution. When asked at age sixty whether he remembered that at about the time of the Battle of Lexington a company of militia had spent the night in his family's property in Braintree, he replied that he distinctly did so. He furthermore specified that his father had placed him in the midst of the citizen soldiers where he "went through the manual exercise of the musket by word of command from one of them."

He recollected other memorable events and occurrences. Even before the shots at Lexington his family had moved back to Braintree from Boston, which had been turned into a fortified town garrisoned by British troops. From a hill on the family farm in June 1775, he saw the fires and heard the guns associated with struggle on Bunker's Hill just across the Charles River from Boston. He never forgot the tears his mother shed upon her receiving news that a close family friend had fallen in that fight.[2]

Additionally, from his seventh to his tenth year, he grew up with a largely absent father, who was away in the cause of the Revolution. During those years his mother had assured the boy that his father had accepted his patriotic duty carrying out the wishes of his fellow citizens in the holy crusade of the American Revolution. Moreover, she took charge of his early education, having him tutored by a law clerk of her husband's. She was confident that he was in caring hands, though she worried that a regular school might provide better instruction. Yet she comforted herself with the conviction that "less harm" would come to him.

At that moment youthful John Quincy also began reading the titans of his own language with several of Shakespeare's plays, though he later admitted to understanding them only partially. In addition he tackled John Milton's *Paradise Lost*, which proved even more intractable for the lad to comprehend. Not all attention was devoted to his studies, however. Aware that smoking tobacco gave his father great pleasure, he tried it for himself, in the process making himself sick several times.[3]

The young boy did spend more time with his mother and her direct tutelage. Still, his father, though often geographically distant, was considerably more than an absentee parent. Abigail Adams surely strove to keep her husband a living presence in her son's experience. Even during absence, however, the father and the son retained contact through correspondence. Almost ten, John Quincy informed his father that he preferred to receive letters than to write them. His thoughts, he admitted, kept "running after birds eggs plays and trifles, till I get vexed with myself." He confessed that his mother had to keep him on task. From his father he asked for advice and instruction on reading and play.[4]

John was never reluctant to supply what his son requested, especially regarding study and reading. He especially wanted the boy to understand the causes of the American Revolution and to compare it to previous ones that had occurred in Europe. To help with that task he appended an extensive reading list, including the European legal theorists Grotius and Samuel Pufendorf, a heavy dose for a boy of ten, he acknowledged. He knew that John Quincy would wonder at his introducing such a weighty topic to one so young, but he believed that, in the future, his son would thank him. This youthful reading list, even though only partly comprehended, connected him more with his father's generation than with the presidents who followed him.

This history of comparative revolutions did not push aside all other subjects. Father urged him to read Thucydides in the original Greek. But until John Quincy had mastered that language, reading a translation would suffice. John went on to specify the one by Thomas Hobbes, which the boy would find in his father's library.[5]

But most important, when John Quincy was between ten and eleven, his father launched him into an unbelievable world for a youngster who had been kept so close to home in a Massachusetts village. His later description of his childhood and youth as "an Arabian tale, strip'd of the marvelous" focused here. In 1777 John was deputed by the Continental Congress to cross the Atlantic to help arrange an alliance with France. The newly appointed diplomat decided to take along as a companion his eldest son, who very much wanted to go. Initially Abigail, who would remain in Massachusetts, had serious misgivings about her young boy going on what could be a perilous journey. Despite them she finally consented.[6]

The senior and junior Adamses departed Boston on February 13, 1778, on the frigate *Boston* mounting twenty-four guns. The North Atlantic winter and the threat of the British navy made for a treacherous crossing. Storms pummeled the ship, which did encounter British vessels, but escaped conflict with any enemy warships. After a tumultuous voyage of six weeks, the *Boston* sailed into Bordeaux. The Adamses arrived in Paris a week later.

For John the end of the journey proved anticlimactic. The

much-desired treaty with France that he had been dispatched to help negotiate had been concluded by the American delegation already in Paris. Although maintaining diplomatic relations with the new ally was essential, that effort did not require a team. Moreover, relationships among the three Americans who had preceded Adams were less than harmonious. His arrival did not change that fact. All were eager to further the American cause, but personalities and ambitions created difficulties.

The most prominent among the Americans, the Pennsylvanian Benjamin Franklin, was well-known in Europe before the Revolution for his scientific experiments with electricity and by his residence in London advocating the interests of his home colony. While Franklin welcomed Adams, inviting him and his son to stay in his lodgings in Passy, on the edge of Paris, the two men had different temperaments and outlooks. Franklin got along easily and amicably in the society of monarchical France, whereas Adams found himself quite uncomfortable with that same society and with Franklin's general approach to the royal government.[7]

For father and for son, Paris was, of course, a marvel. Neither had ever seen anything comparable. John was conscious of a great city, its culture and monuments. As for John Quincy, he had entered an incredible world—the avenues, the monuments, the buildings, the theater. This opened up a heady time for a young boy. He reported on his sightseeing, often in his father's company—including Versailles, both palace and garden, the cathedral of Notre Dame, the theater, which at times his father let him attend on his own and which became a lifelong pleasure.[8]

Reveling in the sights and entertainment did not occupy all of his time, however. Almost immediately John Quincy began attending a boarding school in Passy. There he pursued his study of Latin and undertook fencing, dancing, and music as well as French. And he took to the last. Urging his two younger brothers back in Massachusetts to study the language, he even sent them details on French grammar books. His father noted that he chattered away in his new tongue.[9]

Even with John Quincy in a foreign land three thousand miles from Braintree, Abigail's presence leapt across the ocean. Before the *Boston* had made landfall, she wrote her husband to remember her most affectionately to her son. Accompanying that affection came a reminder of his filial duty: "Injoin it upon him never to disgrace his Mother and to behave worthy of his Father."[10]

In a letter to her son she instructed him that his acquiring knowledge must ever "render you an ornament to society, an Honour to your Country, and Blessing to your parents." He must always listen to his father: "he is your natural Guardian, and will always counsel and direct you in the best manner both for your present and future happiness." She pressed upon him the need to guard himself against "temptations and vice of every kind," which in her mind abounded in his new abode. Do not, she admonished him, permit what she defined as "the odious monster" to lose "its terror, by becoming familiar to you." Abigail left no doubt about his duty to follow the precepts and guidance of his parents: "I had much rather you should have found your Grave in the ocean you have crossed, of any untimely death crop you in your Infant years, rather than see you as immoral profligate or a Graceless child."[11]

Ever dutiful, John Quincy did not fail to let his mother know that his gratitude matched her solicitude. Shortly after reaching Paris, he penned a letter "to so kind or Tender a Mamma which you have been to me for which I believe I shall never be able to Repay you." He assured her that he would never forget God's goodness in protecting him and his father through their danger-ous weeks at sea.[12]

He also apprised her of his activities. Terming his school in Passy a good one, he reported that his daily schedule began at six in the morning, with the day filled with classes and play. He even sent her a brief note in French, a language she did not read. Still, he knew that he did not write so often as his mother desired. Defending himself, he declared that he was not a gifted letter writer.[13]

In another instance he introduced a subject that remained central to him for the rest of his life. To Abigail he related that his father had spurred him to keep a diary or a journal in which he could maintain a record "of the Events that happen to me, and of objects that I See, and of Characters that I converse with from day to day." Although John Quincy viewed this exercise as valuable, he did not think that at this point he possessed the patience and perseverance to succeed as a diarist. But John had assigned even more than a diary. He had also given his son a blank book in which to preserve copies of his letters. Accomplishing these two assignments, the boy realized, he would have "the mortification a few years hence to read a great deal of my Childhood nonsense." Yet simultaneously he could write, "I shall have the pleasure and advantage, of Remarking the several steps, by which I have advanced, in taste, judgment, and knowledge." The powerful drive to keep this record never disappeared, nor did the unending struggle to sustain it.[14]

Perhaps most important to his mother, he emphasized that neither the attractions nor the perils of his new life endangered his basic, tame self. Even though he liked his situation, he informed Abigail that he would really prefer his hometown.[15]

The epistolary conversation between the mother and her young son contained nothing surprising. Abigail Adams's moralizing fit her heritage and the practice of her time and place, though she may have been more demanding. In turn, John Quincy dutifully responded as she wanted and expected. That pattern would continue through his youth and into his early manhood. Later, by the mid-1790s, with John Quincy an adult, their correspondence revealed the two dealing with each other more as equals. Still, however, the mother-son relationship never disappeared. Instructing and warning remained key for her; for him aiming to please and evincing respect abided.

In Paris the youngster first came into contact with American notables beyond his local environs, the colleagues of his father. The great man Franklin, whose grandson was a schoolmate, was benevolent toward him. And he did not become involved in the deputation's squabbles, such as personal rivalries. His diligence obviously impressed one, for he gave John Quincy a volume on natural law translated from Latin into French.[16]

For the father this stint led to different professional and personal consequences. Professionally this was not a happy time for John. Not only did he not get along with his associates; he had little to do. The negotiations were over, yet on a personal level for the first time he had the regular company of his eldest son, whom he described as a great comfort. "My little son gives me great Pleasure," he related to his wife, "both by his Assiduity to his Books and his discreet Behavior." A proud father also noted that their son impressed those who came into contact with him. The son, in turn, was identifying with his father. In describing to his mother the impact of a harsh letter from her to John, he stated directly, "It really hurts him to receive such letters."[17]

The initial Adams sojourn in the French capital lasted just over a year. With no clear job John was determined to return home. In June 1779 father and son sailed from France on a French ship back to Boston. It seemed that their pre-Paris days would resume. John would once again become immersed in state and national politics, and John Quincy would continue his education, either with a tutor or in a school in Braintree or close by.

Yet before the two could settle into familiar roles, the Continental Congress made a decision that again aimed John back toward Europe. Receiving word from the French about the possibility of a treaty with Great Britain, the Congress in the fall designated John as minister plenipotentiary to negotiate treaties of peace and commerce with the former mother country. He was directed to return promptly to France.

As the senior Adams made his plans for another transatlantic voyage, the family weighed whether John Quincy should again accompany his father. This time the boy did not want to go. The joys and pleasures of home and friends enticed him, as well as his desire to prepare for admission to Harvard College, his father's alma mater and the destiny both Abigail and John intended for him. This time she intervened to influence her son, telling him he would benefit immensely from joining his father a second time. Her tender urging, as he remembered her coaxing, persuaded him. He would go. In her view a repeat sojourn to Europe would enhance his larger education and better equip him for his life's work. "When a mind is raised, and animated by scenes that engage the Heart, then those qualities which would otherwise lay dormant wake into Life, and form the Character of the Hero and the Statesman."[18]

John and John Quincy would once more cross the Atlantic together. On their trip they had company, John's younger brother Charles and his former tutor John Thaxton, as his father's private secretary. A fifth member of the group was Francis Dana, also of Massachusetts, who went as the secretary to the American Peace Commission.

On November 13, 1779, the Adams party sailed from Boston on the same French frigate that had brought John and John Quincy home three months earlier. Adverse weather plagued the passage; never did they witness a cloudless sunset. The buffeted and tossed ship sprang several leaks, which became so threatening that all aboard had to take turns at the pumps. Land was a most welcome sight, even though it was Spain, not France. That did not matter to the beleaguered captain, who brought his wounded vessel into port on December 8 at El Ferrol, on the Atlantic coast of northwestern Spain. By that time Spain, the ally of France, had entered the war against Great Britain.[19]

On European soil but far from his destination of Paris, John had to choose between waiting for the arrival of a ship that could carry his band northward to the French coast or striking out over land. With no knowledge of how long he would have to wait for such a ship, he chose the land route. This journey would require traveling hundreds of miles through the rugged, even mountainous, terrain of northern Spain.

After a week John and his retinue departed El Ferrol, stopped initially at the nearby town of La Coruña, then plunged into the

Spanish countryside. John Quincy kept a brief record of their progress. On the *Sensible* he had begun the daily journal that his father had earlier urged upon him. Maintaining this journal or diary would engross him emotionally and physically for much of his life. At the outset he recorded chiefly names of people and places he encountered. Later, consideration of motivation, his own and that of others with whom he interacted, occupied more space as did musings about himself, his family, his ambition, his principles, his strengths and weaknesses. He also provided substantial detail about major events in which he was directly involved.[20]

The journey across Spain proved arduous. Mules, tended by teamsters, whom John Quincy termed "muletiers," along with carriages aided the travelers. According to John Quincy, they alternately walked, rode in carriages, or rode on muleback. To him they resembled Don Quixotes and Sancho Panzas. The youth cataloged abominable roads and lodgings often barely fit for animals, on one occasion a place where hogs had seemingly been the preceding guests. He found most Spaniards "lazy, dirty, nasty" as well as poor and in thrall to priests. The size of cathedrals in the larger towns impressed him, while the number of religious structures amazed him.

After a laborious month on the road, including coping with mountains, the entourage again reached the Spanish coast, at Bilbao, where they remained a few days. Thenceforward the trip was much less onerous. Resuming the trek, they took just three days to cross the French frontier and arrive in Bayonne. From there they headed to Bordeaux, and finally on to Paris, reaching their destination on February 9, 1780, two months after landing in Europe.[21]

The day after his arrival in Paris, John Quincy entered the same school in Passy that he had attended during his initial stay in the city. The regimen differed little: his day began at seven with study and play until bedtime at nine in the evening. Confronting an imposing array of subjects, from the classical languages to writing and drawing, the twelve-year-old boy asked for his father's advice. As always, John instructed his son to concentrate on Greek and Latin. Writing and drawing he considered "Amusements," which "may serve as relaxation from your studies." Time on any other disciplines should await John Quincy's eventual return to his native country.[22]

The youthful scholar did not only receive guidance from the nearby parent. From across the Atlantic his mother continued her striving to inculcate in him the qualities she believed essential for his development as well as her expectations for him. "These are the times in which a Genius would want to live," she wrote him. "Great characters" did not arise, she continued, "in the still calm of life, or the repose of a pacific station." "Great necessities call out great virtues," from which came "the Character of the Hero and the Statesman." After charging her son to contemplate the purpose of his life, she provided her maxim. "It is not to move from clime to clime, to gratify and idle curiosity, but every new Mercy you receive New a Debt upon you, a new obligation."

Abigail went beyond a general maxim. Her catechism spelled out her guidance. Only religion, belief in the one God, guaranteed a secure foundation for the kind of life she wanted for him and that he should desire for himself. Then she emphasized duty. He had a powerful duty to country, to parents, and to himself to become the man his heritage, position, and opportunity made possible. For that man to appear would require his studying himself. In her view, self-love loomed as the great hazard because it could permit one to deceive oneself. John Quincy must zealously guard against that menace.

Additionally, he had to manage his impetuosity. Governing this did not mean, however, to permit serious injury. When perceiving that, he must repond vigorously, for a man failing to do so "is deficient in point of spirit." After Abigail detailed such stern commandments, her maternal softness appeared in the final sentence of a long letter: "In the mean time be assured that no one is more sincerely interested in your happiness than your affectionate Mother."[23]

From taking in his mother's quite heavy dose of life-path perceptions to heeding his father's curricular advice, the young man
had much to contemplate and digest. There was also, of course,
attending to his school work. His response: "I am your dutiful
and affectionate Son," to his father; the same "dutiful son" in a
later reply to his mother.[24]

The dutiful son accompanied his father when in late summer
1780 John headed to the Netherlands in search of financial aid to
the American cause. His mother hoped that the neat and clean
Dutch would teach him "industry, economy, and frugality." Upon
arriving in Amsterdam, John promptly enrolled John Quincy as
a boarding student in the Latin School, whose instruction took
place in Dutch, which he had just taken up. Because John Quincy
did not yet know the language, he was placed among the younger
students, a status that displeased both him and his father. After a
few months and following a disagreement with school authorities
about John Quincy's standing, John withdrew him.[25]

That withdrawal did not end John Quincy's formal education
in Holland, however. By the beginning of 1781, less than a year
after being put with the younger students in the Latin School,
he matriculated at nearby Leiden University, an institution open
to both younger and older students. Guiding John Quincy on
his academic course, John as before urged the centrality of the
classical languages, specifying the Greek New Testament, Eurip-
ides, and Sophocles. In the classical masters John Quincy must
become adept and eventually be able to judge them critically, but
never imitate them. Rather, John Quincy should look to nature
and study it for imitation. A focused pupil reported working on
Homer and the Greek New Testament. Moreover, he met his
Greek tutor twice daily.[26]

At the same time John advised him not to forget his native language; he especially recommended reading the English poets. But
he did not think the stay in Leiden should entail only work. He
thought skating, dancing, and riding worthy, telling John Quincy
"to be always attentive to this Grace, which is founded in natural

Principle, and is therefore as much for your Ease and Use, as for your pleasure."[27]

In addition to his formal studies, John Quincy engaged in other activities of the mind that would remain with him throughout his life. He resumed his journal, which had lain dormant during his months in Paris. Mostly he recounted factually whom he saw and where he went, without embellishments or discussion. In his diary he related his translating from different languages to which he would always devote time and attention. Then reading periodicals, including the English opinion magazines the *Tatler* and the *Spectator,* began a lifelong and time-consuming habit.[28]

After a year in the Netherlands, John Quincy's European adventure turned in a new and unexpected direction. The Adamses' traveling companion Francis Dana received orders from his government to travel to Russia in an effort to gain recognition of American independence from the empress of Russia, Catherine the Great. Because Dana needed a secretary and because he knew little French, the language of diplomacy at European royal courts, he and John decided that John Quincy, then fourteen years old, would make a superb companion, in no small part because of his greater fluency in French. John also certainly assumed that in the Russian capital of St. Petersburg his son could continue the education he had begun in France and the Netherlands.

In early July 1781 John Quincy left with Dana for Russia, some two thousand miles to the east. His diary charts their course, specifying the route and where they stopped, with few comments. He did note where important battles had been fought and the crossing of frontiers. He made an exception in his description of Berlin, which mightily impressed him, designating it as more handsome and well laid out than any other city he had ever seen.[29]

Finally, on August 27, after six weeks of arduous travel, the little party reached St. Petersburg, the capital of the Russian Empire. The Americans' stay there was uneventful for John Quincy as well as unsuccessful for Dana. Without official diplomatic status and with Empress Catherine the Great uninterested in his mission, Dana was unable to accomplish anything. According to John Quincy's journal the only notable event was attending in July 1782 a grand duke's masquerade ball.

The youngster found continuing his education frustrating. No schools like those he had attended in France and the Netherlands existed. Even so, on his own he maintained his quest for learning. An English subscription library, which Dana joined, offered him the opportunity to check out books. In addition, from booksellers he bought books. His reading and purchasing included David Hume's history of England and Voltaire's of Russia, along with Adam Smith's *Wealth of Nations* and Frederick the Great's works in French. He continued his practice of translating the classics, and he began studying German.[30]

Although John Quincy was in a faraway and literally foreign land, the distance did not deter paternal advice and direction. John applauded his son's taking up German, saying he thought learning new languages highly worthwhile. Yet academic subjects did not head his father's concerns. Make it a rule not to waste time, he instructed; no moral precept had more importance. "Make it the grand Maxim of your Life, and it cannot fail to be happy, and usefull to the World." In John's mind, however, morals had still another and ever more crucial dimension. "My dear boy," he wrote, "above all things preserve your Innocence, and a pure Conscience. Your morals are of more importance, both to yourself and the World than all the Languages and all the Sciences." John stressed, "The least stain upon your Character will do more harm to your Happiness than all Accomplishments will do it good."[31]

His mother also wanted to make sure he did not fritter away his time in his new country. Expressing her unhappiness at his not writing more often, she asked, "Has the cold Northern Regions frozen up that Quick and Lively imagination which used to give pleasure to your Friends?" In her view Russia must provide a large canvas for his comment. While she did not expect in his account "the Elegance" or "the Eloquence and precision" of mature writers, she did want to know what he had gained by careful attention. She reminded John Quincy of his special circumstance—that his father's status set her son apart from the average traveler.[32]

The boy did reply. He wrote his mother that he would have corresponded more often, but the scarcity of vessels sailing directly for America meant expensive postage. Moreover, he told her, letters might be opened and might not even arrive. Ultimately, he sent her a missive about Russia, penning a lengthy account of the social order, in his opinion composed of "Nobles and Serfs" or "Masters and Slaves." The empress controlled the nobles, who dominated all others. He characterized a completely despotical government. His father received brief notices of his educational efforts.[33]

John Quincy did not have an extended stay in Russia. Fourteen months after his arrival, he headed back to western Europe. Few duties and his father's concern about the lack of educational opportunities prompted his departure. The return to the Netherlands, with a long stop in Sweden, required six months. By late April 1783 he was once again on familiar ground in The Hague.

The first surviving likeness of John Quincy dates from this time in The Hague, a small portrait in pastel or crayon by the Dutch artist Isaak Schmidt. It shows the youthful face of a fifteen- or sixteen-year-old lad, with a powdered head of soft contours. These contrast sharply with the direct gaze of his dark eyes. Arched eyebrows with a slight cast in one eye create an impression that is more than pleasant. It intrigues.

In The Hague, with his education so central, the boy came under the tutelage of a close and respected friend of his father's. Born in Germany and long a resident of Holland, Charles F. W. Dumas was a man of letters, especially well versed in languages, both classical and modern. John called him "a Walking Library." Not only did Dumas instruct him; John Quincy also resided in the Dumas household. While there he developed a fondness for Mademoiselle Dumas, with whom he sang duets and played the flute. Three decades later he would record in his diary, "It was the precise time of my change from boy to man, and has left indelible impressions upon my Memory."[34]

Even though Charles Dumas was John Quincy's schoolmaster, John left no doubt that he felt both qualified and duty bound to expound on his son's course of study. Writing from Paris, he declared "the Art of asking Questions" the key to learning. "Never be too wise to ask a Question," he instructed. He did not hesitate, however, to give particular guidelines. John Quincy must not skip a single day with his Greek and Latin exercises. He also urged turning to mathematics, specifying algebra and even a textbook. While he thought John Quincy's handwriting respectable, he advocated constant attention to its improvement.[35]

Study should not occupy every moment, however. "You Should always have a Book of Amusement, to read, along with your Severe Studies and laborious Exercises," he told his son. Then he went on to identify what he considered appropriate, advising against plays, romance, or history. Instead, for relaxation he recommended books on morals as lifelong companions. He listed several authors who would enlighten John Quincy on the "science of Morality."[36]

The father did not omit central Adams maxims. "A regular Distribution of your Time, is of great Importance. You must measure out your Hours," he directed, "for Study, Meals, Amusements, Exercise and Sleep, and suffer nothing to divert you, at least from those devoted to study." All the while John Quincy must watch his behavior and "Remember [his] tender Years and treat all the World with Modesty, Decency and Respect."[37]

The young scholar remained in the Netherlands only until late summer, when once again he joined his father in Paris. There he served as secretary to his father, who was one of the American commissioners charged with signing the definitive peace treaty with Great Britain. John also took on oversight of his son's schooling, as always classical languages and mathematics. But the boy did not spend all of his time with lessons.

John Quincy luxuriated in the sights and opportunities offered by the city. He marveled at the ascent of a lighter-than-air balloon, which he described as "a flying globe." He took in the art displayed at the Louvre and continued his lifelong love affair with the theater, filling his diary with the names of plays he attended. His fluency in French aided these experiences immensely.[38]

Late in October, John became ill and decided on a trip to England for his health, with John Quincy as his companion. Their visit focused on London, which John Quincy found astounding, notwithstanding the charm of Paris. He informed a cousin that he found the city both more beautiful and more convenient than Paris. "Awe and Veneration" characterized his reactions to Westminster Abbey. The size of St. Paul's Cathedral impressed him, though not its beauty. He described it as too heavy a building. He also visited the British Museum and Sir Ashton Lever's museum of natural history, to him utterly fascinating. The Tower of London, with its array of historical artifacts, and Buckingham Palace were also on his itinerary. He was a regular at theaters, where he saw a variety of plays, including several of Shakespeare's.[39]

Although the first trip to England and London lasted only a few weeks before he returned with his father to the Continent, John Quincy soon revisited, in May 1784, this time to await the arrival of his mother and sister from America. While biding his time, he attended the courts of justice and sessions of Parliament. He took special note of the proceedings and debates in the latter. Sir Edmund Burke, William Pitt the Younger, and Charles James Fox particularly impressed him, though he did attribute his admiration to their generally pro-American position.[40]

When John received his son's news about his presence in Parliament, he was quite pleased. He encouraged his son to go there every day, for "it is a great and illustrious school." At the same time he cautioned John Quincy not to permit "the Eloquence of the Bar and of Parliament" to turn his head: "You will find Livy and Tacitus, more elegant, more profound and

Sublime Instructors . . . ," he concluded, adding additional ancients, including Cicero and Demosthenes.[41]

Mother and sister landed in England in July, and in the next month the family was together in Paris. Back in the French capital, John Quincy resumed his regular theatergoing. His diary, at this point still chiefly jottings, details dinners and meeting noteworthy persons, among them the Marquis de Lafayette, whose exploits during the American Revolution still resonated with Americans.

Most important among these individuals for John Quincy was the new American minister to France, Thomas Jefferson of Virginia, who had been a colleague of John's when both were members of the Continental Congress. The teenager and the Virginian took to each other. Jefferson befriended the youngster, whom he judged quite promising. He saw in his young friend "abilities, learning, application, and the best of dispositions," as well as "more improved by travel than could have been expected." An equally impressed John Quincy deemed Jefferson "a man of great judgment" with "universal learning and very pleasing manners."[42]

By the end of the year John Quincy had begun contemplating a new direction for himself. Writing a cousin in December, he admitted he wanted to return to America. He confessed that his country had an attraction for him he could not fully comprehend. It must be that loyalty to one's country was "distinct from all other attachments." He drew that conclusion because he had spent so much time in Europe.

Yet he had another powerful reason propelling him back to his native land. He very much wanted a degree from Harvard, he informed a kinsman. He wanted to follow his father at the college, always a goal of both parents as well. Believing that his touring about Europe had deprived him of a regular educational course, he expected to spend some time in America preparing for entrance into Harvard. Even so, he and the family felt that he would eventually enter at least the junior class.[43]

In the following spring, at age seventeen, John Quincy

addressed his ambitions and anxieties to his diary. By that time that journal had evolved from being chiefly a catalog of people, places, and events to being a place where he often recorded his musings about himself as well as his reaction to others and to circumstances.

He considered remaining in Europe, for he foresaw his proximate future in America as difficult and trying. The news of John's appointment as the first American minister to England made extending his stay in Europe a real possibility. He saw accompanying his father to his new post as providing greater momentary satisfaction than going back home.

Home meant Massachusetts and Harvard. Travel through much of Europe along with the company he had kept made the prospect of a year or two in a college, where he would have to abide by rules and discipline that to date he had avoided, appear dismal. But there was more, for after Harvard he anticipated three additional years devoted to "the Dry and Tedious study of law." Then he would face the struggle of making a name for himself, or in his words, "to bring myself into Notice."

Considering everything, he envisioned "a Prospect somewhat discouraging for a youth of my Ambition (for I have Ambition, though I hope its object is laudable)." Despite the obstacle he constructed, he was determined to make his own way, with no dependence on his father or anyone else. On this point he invoked Shakespeare:

> But still . . . Oh! how wretched
> Is that poor Man, that hangs on Princes favours.

In his view he would have to rely on his own efforts because his father's public service had severely limited his fortune. Still, John Quincy trusted that his ability and his commitment to proper conduct would enable him to live as an independent man. Otherwise, "I would wish to die, before that time, when I shall be left at my own Discretion."[44]

With this combination of hopes and burdens, the young man set sail for America in May 1785. Two months later he landed in New York City, where he remained for several weeks, frequently in the company of members of the national Congress meeting in the city. From there he traveled on to Boston and Cambridge in his quest to become a student at Harvard. Even though his father had written on his behalf, emphasizing his European experiences, he was denied immediate admission. Because he had not read all the requisite Latin authors, the president of the college advised him to make up his deficiencies and reapply in the spring. Though disappointed, John Quincy set out upon that task.[45]

While doing so, he resided in the nearby town of Haverhill with his mother's sister Elizabeth Shaw and her husband, the Reverend John Shaw. The Reverend Shaw oversaw John Quincy's intensive immersion in Greek and Latin. His aunt reported to his mother that she and her family were quite pleased with her nephew, whose ability she never doubted. To Abigail she stressed his commitment to his studies, which too often deprived the family of his company. She feared that his studying so much by candlelight would ruin his eyes. She also praised his modesty and politeness in company, but she noted that in private he could be opinionated and too sure of himself.[46]

Finally, in March 1786, the fledgling scholar once more presented himself for admission to Harvard. The president, three professors, and four tutors examined him in the classical languages, with additional questions covering logic, geography, and John Locke. After the examination the president informed John Quincy that he had been admitted to the junior class. He could enroll immediately and live on campus. This he did. His admission to the junior class was not the norm, but at that time students did not all matriculate as freshmen for the regular four years.

The classics, of course, constituted the central part of the curriculum, which also included mathematics and various humanities and scientific disciplines largely grouped at that time under the subjects of moral, natural, and experimental philosophy. Class-room recitations along with lectures occupied many hours. Chapel attendance also took up time. Ever purposeful, he concentrated on his classes. He feared that devotion to studying was adversely affecting his health, particularly his eyes. In his diary he mulled over the virtue of industry, which he concluded could neither con-fer immortality nor enable one with less ability to equal one with more. Yet he decided history taught that industry had produced more positive results than any other virtue. He also pressed this conviction upon his younger brother Thomas, who intended to follow his elder to Harvard.[47]

A fall and winter of dutiful attention to his studies impacted more than his classroom performance. When another sister of his mother's, Mary Cranch, saw him in the spring of 1787, she wor-ried that his health had suffered because his concentration on his schoolwork had deprived him of proper exercise.[48]

Despite this diligence, he did not neglect other opportunities offered by the college. Within the first few months, he accepted election to two elite campus groups, Phi Beta Kappa and the A. B. Club, a local Harvard organization. Diversions also engaged him. Enjoying music, he played the flute. In his view music distin-guished man from dumb animals and lay at the heart of "all the passions in the human breast." He even found time to pursue his lifelong affection for writing verse.[49]

Although John Quincy described himself as basically con-tented at Harvard, he did express a few reservations. Like so many undergraduates of all times and places, he had little good to say about the college administration. He remarked that it treated its students "pretty much like brute Beasts." Confessing his difficulty in having to submit to it, he still considered doing so possibly use-ful, for if anything could teach him humility, it would be to find himself subjected to commands from a person he despised. While he cast aspersions upon the administration, the faculty generally pleased him. He excepted the tutors, however. Too many were too young to gain respect from the students. Moreover, he regarded some as less than masters of their subject matter—for example, the mathematics tutor who often revealed his ignorance.[50]

As a college student, John Quincy participated in an active social life. In his diary he recounts attending numerous dinners and teas in private homes. Card games were popular, as were dances and sleigh rides. In almost every instance he commented on the presence of young ladies. Invariably he recorded his opinion of their physical appearance. Those he judged beautiful most captivated him. Beauty was quite important to him, for without it a young lady could charm men only by her sweet disposition. At the same time he opined that a woman's chief attributes were love for her family and "a humane and benevolent heart for the rest of the world."[51]

Even though responsibly occupied with his studies and pleasurably engaged in extracurricular activities both on and off campus, John Quincy not surprisingly took note of major current events in his country and pondered the nature of republics. Thinking about Shays's Rebellion of 1786, in which debt-ridden farmers of western Massachusetts organized protests against foreclosures on their property and the state's policy on currency, he opined that, if handled sensibly, such unrest could be advantageous. He turned to medicine for an analogy, writing that potions like certain drugs could by themselves be poisonous, but "if properly tempered may be made, highly medicinal." Leadership would matter, and on that topic he seemed hopeful. He maintained that republics would breed sagacious leaders because in them all citizens, not just a select few, have the chance of reaching high office and most would strive for that honor.[52]

The summer of 1787 found John Quincy on the verge of graduation, though he had spent less than two years as a student. Even in that short time, however, he had been a success at Harvard. For the commencement exercise held on July 18, he was named a class orator, awarded the second honor in his class of forty-eight. By all accounts his address—"Upon the Importance and Necessity of Public Faith to the Well Being of a Community"—was well received. Adams later remembered the occasion as "one of the most memorable events of my life." Following the ceremony, his aunt Mary Cranch hosted a reception with cake and wine for some four hundred guests.[53]

Reflecting on his Harvard days, the new graduate rejoiced that he had left Europe for college. Despite his spending only fifteen months as a student, it had been a most productive and worthwhile experience. Not the least, he admitted that college had forced him to reduce his opinion of himself and to face his future realistically. He never lost his devotion to his alma mater. More than three decades after his graduation, he wrote a friend that Harvard had his "most ardent attachment and deepest reverence." Both intellectually and socially the institution had been utterly central for him. Later in his diary he recorded that all the good fortune he had known stemmed from his time at Harvard.[54]

Contemplating his future after Harvard required him to confront the magnitude of his ambition. The humility he claimed to have learned in college did not significantly alter the scope of his aspirations. He identified with two lines he inserted in his diary from Shakespeare's *King Henry V*:

> If it be a Sin to covet Honour
> I am the most offending soul alive.

He worried that his talents would not carry him as far as he wanted to go, and he had no interest in what he termed "small Distinctions." In fact, he despised those who had the chance for a first station, but settled for less without reaching for the pinnacle. That someone else should ever read these sentiments concerned him, for he feared they would think him stuffed with vanity. That trait he struggled to control, though he could never suppress his charging ambition.[55]

While John Quincy cherished the memories and benefits of his Harvard education, he looked ahead with uncertainty, even foreboding, for ambition and reality collided. Following his father into the legal profession entailed three additional years of study with a practicing attorney, an ordeal in his mind. Yet he understood he had to pass through that trial before he could become an independent man in the world—at twenty years of age his great goal. Success, he realized, would demand immense patience. He prayed for it.[56]

John Quincy would pursue his study of the law in the coastal town of Newburyport, some forty miles northeast of Boston. During his senior year in college, he and his father discussed where he would do so. Unless John returned from Europe and took on his son as an apprentice, John Quincy wanted to avoid Boston. He feared squandering his time in the city. It was ultimately decided that his legal career would begin in Newburyport in the law office of Theophilus Parsons. Parsons would charge £100 per annum for the three years John Quincy would spend with him studying for the bar. For financial support he still depended on his parents.[57]

Being a law student did not stimulate the young man, who had so often expressed interest in literary studies. He found the essential texts for law studies decidedly dull. Plodding through dry legal tomes, including Sir Edward Coke's *Institutes* and Sir James Burrows's volumes on English cases, failed to excite him, though he excepted Sir William Blackstone. He contrasted most of these jurisprudent savants with his nonlegal readings. The marvelous Shakespeare remained a favorite; among others he commented favorably on David Hume's essays and Voltaire's *Louis XIV*.[58]

Even in the midst of his studies, political matters not surprisingly captured his attention. By the late 1780s the wartime government that had been established under a framework known as the Articles of Confederation was floundering. Bonds sold to investors here and abroad to finance the war were coming due, a debt the Confederation could not pay. And without the power to tax, the Confederation Congress could only requisition funds from the states, any one of which could veto any measure proposed in the Congress. The fragile, new nation seemed on the verge of defaulting. The government grew increasingly fractious and unstable. Social unrest plagued parts of the country, with Shays's Rebellion a prime example.

In New England during the 1780s, hard-pressed farmers struggled with debts and high taxes that they believed benefited those in Boston and other towns already wealthy. In western Massachusetts a number of these farmers, many among them veterans of the Revolution, joined with Daniel Shays, a former captain in the Continental army. Shays demanded a moratorium on debts, moving the state capital from Boston to the interior of the state, and eliminating imprisonment for debt. In the summer of 1786, Shays and his men focused on halting the collection of debts and employed force to keep courts closed and sheriffs from selling confiscated land. In winter these rebels advanced on the town of Springfield, hoping to obtain weapons stored in the arsenal there. In January 1787 state officials fearing a new revolution dispatched a force of the state militia, which confronted and dispersed the Shays band. This event would have an encore whenever American farmers became convinced that distant political and financial interests threatened to harm them. In his presidency John Quincy would confront such a conviction from southern and western farmers.

In this precarious environment a group of leaders emerged who were determined to form a truly national government, one with real power, including the authority to tax. Delegations of these concerned nationalists from twelve of the thirteen states met in Philadelphia in 1787. With a burst of political creativity and amid a spirit of compromise among competing groups, these men set up a new national government. They called the document delineating their vision the Constitution of the United States.

This Constitution did not excite John Quincy. He worried that it would increase the power of those who already possessed it. Instead, he wanted to hold on to the system in place, which he had been taught to cherish. Yet, being branded an Antifederalist, the appellation given to opponents of the Constitution, did not please him. When news reached Newburyport in February 1788 that the Massachusetts constitutional convention had voted to ratify the new form of government, he announced he was "converted, though not convinced." The majority had spoken. As he interpreted American politics, the majority ruled. Thus he would either have to acquiesce or become a rebel just like those who had spurred Shays's Rebellion. A rebel he would not become.[59]

Then, in late 1789, when the first president of the United States under the Constitution visited Massachusetts, John Quincy reported with delight being in the company of George Washington. He was grateful to the men who ensured that he would actually meet the great man. Moreover, with pride he informed his mother that he had drafted the address presented to Washington by the town of Newburyport. A Virginia planter, large slave owner, and military hero, Washington had a background that contrasted drastically with the young law student's. Yet his stature as the ultimate American hero captivated John Quincy as it did most of his countrymen.

The tedium of his legal education and his connection with politics did not occupy all his time and thoughts, however. In Newburyport he led an active social life. He enjoyed dances and parties. Late hours and the consumption of spirits were commonplace; "big bellied bottles" led to headaches and hangovers. He applauded "Bacchus and Momus join[ing] hands to increase the festivity of the company."

Young ladies always adorned these affairs. And John Quincy was quite conscious of his propensity to be attracted to them. Succumbing to it must be avoided. Even when studying for admission to Harvard, he fretted in his diary about the dangers of "Passion," which could overpower reason. He averred that falling in love would be the most unfortunate predicament that could befall a young man.[60]

Yet that is precisely what happened to him. In 1790, his final year with Theophilus Parsons, he fell in love with sixteen-year-old Mary Frazier of Newburyport. Despite sketchy details the

evidence makes clear that he and she even contemplated marriage. Word that he had become engaged in a serious relationship
reached his mother, then residing in New York City as the wife
of the first vice-president of the United States. Distraught, Abigail remonstrated with her son that prior to any consideration of
marriage he must establish himself and settle down in his chosen profession, that is, become financially independent. Otherwise
disaster loomed. John concurred. Eventually, John Quincy backed
away, concluding that he could not marry until he had achieved
his independence. That would mean an engagement of indefinite
length, to which Mary objected. To a friend John Quincy wrote
that he needed to get away from Newburyport. Only distance and
time would permit him to get over Mary.

Even though he left Newburyport in the summer, he did not
easily relinquish his love for Mary. In November from Boston
he informed his mother that forty miles separated him from that
plum. Never did her name enter the correspondence. That distance, he continued, meant he would have no opportunity "to
indulge a weakness, which you may censure, but if you knew the
object, I am sure you would excuse."

That powerful youthful passion never totally disappeared,
however. Almost a half century later when visiting Mt. Auburn
Cemetery in Cambridge, he happened upon her grave. She died
in 1804 at age thirty. To his diary he confided that his emotion
brought forth tears. He even imagined the outcome of his having
married Mary. He would have lost her so early in life. Still, he
remembered "how dearly did the sacrifice of her cost me, voluntarily as it was." He recounted "four years of exquisite wretch-
edness." Not until his return to Europe in 1794 with the wide
Atlantic Ocean between them did "the wound in my bosom heal."[61]

Grappling with a frustrating legal curriculum along with
a thwarted love affair, John Quincy often felt his spirits sink.
The punctuation of a lively society could not keep them revived,
though he told his mother he was fine. His correspondence with
his sister Abigail, or Abby, leaves no doubt that he struggled with

sadness. Describing his gloom in his diary, he approached melo-drama in spelling out his anxiety about himself and his dilatori-ness regarding his studies: "God of Heaven! if these are the only terms upon which life can be granted to me, oh! take me from this world before, I curse the day of my birth." He went on to pray that he would fulfill his duty even if others neglected and despised him. Then he would know he did not merit their scorn.[62]

He worried about his future, which to him appeared forbid-ding. Although he chided himself for his indolence, he seemed unable to break its grip and spring toward the goals he had set for himself. Even his joy at reaching twenty-one, which freed him from the bonds of parental dominion, did not spur him, for he suspected his own feet would not have sufficient strength to sup-port him. In an invited address he gave before the Phi Beta Kappa Society at Harvard in September 1788, he pictured the road to the future "rugged with thorns." Only major effort could yield sub-stantial reward. He insisted that sensible boundaries must govern ambition. One must not allow unrealistic hopes to end in mortify-ing disappointment. Only in literature and science should anyone strive for prominence, he asserted. He still apprehended that his own abilities and exertions would leave him short of the success to which he aspired.[63]

By August 1790, when he opened his law office in Boston in a home owned by his father, a powerful melancholy had settled over him. He wrote his mother that he felt "alone in the world without a soul to share the few joys I have, or to participate in my anxieties and suspense, which are neither few nor small." He continued to hope, however, that he would overcome his lamenta-tions, an embarrassment for a vigorous young man. Even before his departure from Newburyport, his father had cautioned him not to indulge his anxiety too much. As always John urged his son to remain steadfast and hold to his "Honor and Integrity," no matter the price. His father instructed, "You will be miserable without them whatever might be your success."[64]

The young attorney discovered that building his legal practice was difficult. Clients did not rush to his door, though some did find their way to him. In his initial address before a jury, he had to grapple with a liability. He found speaking extemporaneously nerve-racking. Recounting that incident to Abigail, he noted that he learned the circumstance of his case only three hours before his appearing in court. He reported himself too agitated to think clearly. A family friend transmitted that lack of self-confidence to his father. Even though his performance in these circumstances improved, many years would pass before he felt at all comfortable speaking without considerable prior preparation.[65]

His practice did grow. He even represented a governmental entity. Making the closing argument in that case, he worried about having only twenty-four hours with the relevant facts. Though not satisfied with his presentation, he informed his brother that he kept the audience with him. He argued before both the Court of Common Pleas and the state Supreme Court. After three and a half years of toil, he admitted to his father that he had no legitimate reason for complaint. His practice provided a living. It concerned him, however, that by becoming quite satisfied he would descend into indolence. Yet he chafed that the eminence his ambition craved still eluded him.[66]

While trying to get on his feet as a fledgling attorney, John Quincy did not live as a social recluse. Even though continuing to cope with his break with Mary Frazier, he often commented in his diary on the young ladies with whom he came into contact. As before, he always remarked on their physical attractiveness; feminine beauty certainly captured his attention. No serious relationship developed, however. Shortly after settling in Boston, he had assured his mother that neither his desperation nor a wealthy woman could push him toward any consequential connection. He emphasized that he would never request her consent in such a matter until he had become totally independent.[67]

In Boston, John Quincy was not simply another aspiring young lawyer; he was also the son of a Massachusetts luminary, now the vice-president of the United States. Politics surrounded

him. At this time the keen differences in national politics, especially over the appropriate American reaction to the French Revolution and the subsequent Anglo-French conflict, were taking
concrete shape. These disagreements wrecked the unity in President George Washington's cabinet.

That harmony had already been threatened by clashing visions
over the direction of the new federal government. Secretary of
State Thomas Jefferson and Secretary of Treasury Alexander
Hamilton of New York articulated the discordant desires. Hamilton and his group championed a strong national government
that with central authority would oversee the building of a complex commercial economy, including the growth of industry and
financial capital. In contrast, Jefferson and his loyalists envisioned
a central government with limited power. They believed the
country should remain mostly rural and agrarian, not aspire to
become commercial and urban. The Hamiltonians became known
as Federalists, then the Federalist party; the Jeffersonians took
the name Republican, then the Republican party. Moreover, the
two political organizations had a sectional dimension. Following
Jefferson, the Virginian, the Republicans dominated in the South
while the Federalists behind Hamilton, the New Yorker, held
sway in the Northeast, particularly in New England.

The same two sides lined up on the leading foreign policy
issue. Jefferson and his supporters wanted the country to support the former wartime ally, France, while Hamilton and his
group, anxious about what they saw as the excesses of the French
Revolution, favored neutrality. The Washington administration,
including Vice-President Adams, stood where Hamilton did.
Accordingly, the administration adopted a policy of neutrality,
declaring the United States would not take sides in either the diplomatic or the armed struggle between the two antagonists. John
Quincy kept his father apprised of how the sharpening division
affected politics in Massachusetts, such as increasingly scurrilous
newspaper attacks on opponents. Still, he said neither side paid
him attention. In his estimation he was insufficiently important.[68]

John entreated his son to become more involved in politics. John Quincy replied that, though he did so a bit, he did not relish going to town meetings, attending caucuses, making speeches, or joining political clubs. Even though he admitted that acting as his father wished might make him a better politician and boost him in the public eye, he still expressed trepidation. Becoming a political person would make him dependent on others, those who would give or deny him office. He went on saying that he preferred to remain in obscurity a little longer and to make his future as a lawyer before he rallied "out in quest of fame or of public honors."[69]

Definitely at this stage not a man of action, John Quincy took his most significant political actions with his pen. In the summer of 1791 eleven letters were published under the pseudonym Publicola in the Boston *Columbian Centinel,* a weekly newspaper. After reading Thomas Paine's *The Rights of Man,* in which the famous pamphleteer praised the French Revolution with its doctrine that the absolute rule of the majority deriving from direct democracy formed the best government, John Quincy on his own initiative responded. That Thomas Jefferson had sponsored the American edition of *Rights,* with his letter extolling it included in the introduction, meant to John Quincy that the pamphlet had been injected into the American political debate. In his essays, entitled *The Letters of Publicola,* he declared a written constitution with checks and balances far surpassed unfettered direct democracy as the cornerstone of fair and good government. Thus, because of the design of government that it had heralded, the American Revolution enjoyed both moral and political supremacy over the French. According to him, the unwritten constitution of Great Britain, even with a hereditary monarch, was superior to the French model. The *Letters* achieved great success. Reprinted in the United States and in Great Britain, they were widely read. Because John Quincy's argument resembled his father's writings on government, many readers assumed the elder Adams to be the author. Soon, however, John Quincy was recognized as Publicola, even by Jefferson's close associate James Madison, who lauded the style.[70]

John Quincy found that mode of political action congenial. He directed his next effort at a local matter. In Boston a dispute arose over the attempt of a theatrical company to stage plays despite a state law prohibiting such performances. A delighted John Quincy relished the prospect of once again going to plays. He had not seen one since his return from Paris. The state, however, moved to close the company. Taking up the pro-theater cause, John Quincy, writing in the *Centinel* as Menander, the comedic playwright of classical Greece, maintained that citizens had a fundamental right to resist an unconstitutional law by peacefully demonstrating against it. He never gave up that principle. In 1793 the legislature repealed the law.[71]

In that same year of 1793 he turned his pseudonymous cudgels to national affairs. In the columns of the *Centinel*, Columbus decried the activities of the new French minister to the United States, Edmond Genet. Upon his arrival Genet injected domestic partisan politics into his diplomatic mission by openly sponsoring an anti-British campaign, a public defiance of the Washington administration's neutrality policy. Despite a recurring eye problem John Quincy took up his pen. Columbus denounced Genet for identifying with a particular group of citizens, those coalescing around Jefferson in opposition to the official stance of the country. He was confident the president had the power to send back home the agent of a foreign country who acted as Genet did. He went on to doubt the validity of political parties, equating them with the passions that caused misery in individuals. Again the administration's loyalists applauded him.[72]

The youthful polemicist took pride in his handiwork. He insisted, however, that ambition did not propel him, for he had no interest in beating any rival for political office. Rather, he wrote his father that his joining the public debate stemmed from his patriotic conviction, not personal ambition. Professing that his country was entitled to his services, no matter how small or insignificant, he claimed he sought only its approval, not a reward.[73]

At the same time he remained committed to the law. His practice was growing as was his stature in the community. An invitation to give the 1793 Fourth of July address in Boston underscored that progression. He prepared it in advance and memorized it. Unsurprisingly, he found it lacking, telling his brother Thomas that during composition he deemed it brilliant, but as time for delivery approached it seemed "a mass of dull common-place, composed of stale facts."[74]

John Quincy gave his address in the Old South Meeting House, located in central Boston. Old South was constructed in 1729, with the congregation dating back to the seventeenth century. Because so many meetings during the momentous events leading up to the Revolution took place in the building, it enjoyed an almost revered status. That John Quincy spoke there stressed the importance of the occasion. His oration was a panegyric of patriotism, in which he studiously avoided any link to partisan politics. Depicting the American Revolution as a defense of liberty, he rejoiced in American unity to defend hallowed rights. In his interpretation Americans took up arms "to repel the insidious approaches of Tyranny," not to jettison the yoke of slavery. In this sense America was unique in the annals of history. America had an unparalleled identity. In his conclusion he called on European governments to follow the American model, to give up monarchy in favor of republicanism. Bostonians reacted positively. To his diary John Quincy confided his gratitude for that response.[75]

When he contemplated an entrance into politics, John Quincy always halted at what he called "the folly of the day." He could not picture himself captured by any fad, which he considered mandatory for a public man's popularity. And his positions on affairs, he informed his father, were not the popular ones. John replied to his son that his views would not always be unpopular. Still, he must not surrender them, stifling hypocrisy at all costs. Do not, the older Adams preached, succumb to "the momentary Fashion," but instead grasp durable principles and hold to them.[76]

John Quincy's epistolary efforts accomplished more than he had anticipated, however. His commentaries on national politics came to the attention of the most important American, George Washington. Even more, they impressed the president. Acting without any inquiries to either the vice-president or his son, the chief executive in the late spring of 1794 nominated John Quincy Adams as the American minister to the Netherlands. The nomination received a unanimous confirmation vote in the Senate. Initially John Quincy, almost twenty-seven, was unsure whether he should accept the appointment. Though flattered, he felt that just as he was making headway in his profession, he would have to give it up. Returning to it would be difficult, for he would lose all that he had gained. A proud father advised acceptance. His country called; merit was recognized. John Quincy decided to accept this summons to public service. Ambition, education, heritage, and opportunity meshed.[77]

CHAPTER 2

"Only Virtue and Fortitude"

JOHN QUINCY'S CONDUCT AND ALLEGIANCE REFLECTED A self-examination unlike that practiced by most of his major political peers. All possessed ambition, and in substantial quantity. Yet John Quincy struggled with the direction his ambition should take. Public service loomed large; as John Adams's son and because of his upbringing, he could not view it otherwise. But thoughts about political advancement did not go unchallenged. He did think about the law. In addition, the possibility of a career involving literature always tantalized him.

Moreover, simply exerting oneself to obtain office violated his sense of himself and his understanding of the new republic. To him merit must triumph over untrammeled ambition. Making the attainment of public office paramount was unthinkable. And he judged harshly those men who placed that goal above all others. Thus, from his appointment by President Washington on through his career, he fought to bridle ambition with the conviction that political reward would result from his own worthiness, not his hunger or striving.

Even though John Quincy had decided to accept the appointment as the American minister to the Netherlands, he continued to mull over its place in his future. Awaiting his final instructions in Philadelphia, the temporary national capital, he confided his ruminations to his father. His duties in the Netherlands, he had learned, would consist chiefly of securing and sustaining loans essential for his country's financial well-being. That task he was confident he could handle, though he saw no great challenge in it. As a result, he considered three years as a sufficiently long time for this diplomatic posting. He also wanted to fix a time frame, for he realized that he served at the pleasure of the president. He preferred to set his departure date, at least in his own mind, before someone else made that decision for him.

Once more he weighed public service against the practice of law. The latter, he repeated, did not excite him. It was respectable, however, and by this time did provide him something he highly prized—independence, not having to rely upon his parents for financial support. Moreover, he had begun to make his mark in the profession. In his judgment turning from the law at this point would mean practically abandoning it, for upon his return from Europe, he could never hope to catch up to his peers. Reverting to the law would be a last resort.

At the same time, the possible consequence of a lengthy absence from his country troubled him. He thought that an American too long in Europe would lose his American character. He did not want that to happen to him. He informed his father, "The attachment which I feel for my native Land, is not merely a sentiment of the Heart; it is a principle dictated by my Reason." No matter his feelings, he continued that he held it as his sacred duty to make his native country the focus of his desires and main object of all his endeavors.[1]

With misgivings, yet with pride that he had been chosen without his or his father's direct supplication, John Quincy again headed eastward across the Atlantic. This time, however, he went not as a son or aide but as an accredited diplomat. Accompanying him as his secretary was his younger brother Thomas Boylston, twenty-two years old. The two young men sailed from Boston on September 17, 1794, and landed in England a month later.

In London, John Quincy experienced his first diplomatic

engagement, and a heady experience it was. John Jay of New York, chief justice of the United States and a friend of John Adams's, had been sent to England by President Washington to negotiate a new treaty dealing with the outstanding issues between the two countries. Jay took the neophyte diplomat into his confidence, briefing him on the negotiations and conferring with him on the contents of the treaty. As for the treaty itself, which became known as the Jay Treaty, John Quincy affirmed that at the moment its terms were the best America could hope for, though he realized that many of his countrymen would find that it provided less than they expected. Most importantly, the British absolutely refused to accept the American position that free ships, or neutral ships, meant free goods. The British navy would interdict American shipping when it chose. John Quincy nonetheless believed the treaty deserved ratification because it maintained "the national honor." He also feared that rejection could lead to war, and massive suffering for his side. In fact, when the treaty reached the United States, it inflamed the already existing political rancor; the antiadministration forces led by Thomas Jefferson and James Madison denounced it as unacceptably pro-British.[2]

With these deliberations concluded, John Quincy, along with his brother, crossed the English Channel to the Netherlands, where he presented his credentials to the Dutch government in The Hague. He began his formal diplomatic service in a Europe convulsed by the French Revolution and the military conflict stemming from it. Europe was basically aligned in two camps, the pro- and the anti-French, the latter championed by the British. Although John Quincy's primary duty concerned American financial arrangements in his host country, he spent many hours contemplating and analyzing the impact of the French Revolution both in Holland and elsewhere in Europe. Long letters containing his assessments, in his phrase an "encyclopedia of politics," went to the secretary of state, to his parents, to fellow diplomats, and to others.[3]

In his opinion the United States had but one safe course in the midst of the European conflagration—neutrality. Taking up arms against either of the major contestants, France or Britain, would lead to disaster, for America was no match militarily for either. The neutral stance proclaimed by President Washington he vigorously supported, desiring no policy that could place his country at war.

Adams did not discount resentments Americans might feel, especially toward Britain. He felt them himself, for he thought the British paid little heed to basic American rights. Yet he refused to adopt indignation as a foundation for a foreign policy. To a friend back in Massachusetts he conveyed his outlook: "But of all the grounds that a nation can follow, passion is the most treacherous, and prudence the most faithful." He wanted his countrymen to be impressed with this reality. Time was on the Americans' side, he was convinced, and he predicted the future would witness their insults satisfactorily redressed.[4]

Just as he deemed neutrality and the prudence on which it was based essential, he believed maintenance of the American Union critical. He foresaw a glorious future for his country whole, but broken apart, he envisioned constant wars among the remnant parts, each probably dominated by European powers. As a result, he insisted that all sectional differences give way to a Union unbroken. When a British official asked him about Virginians and southerners, John Quincy responded, "I consider them all in no other light than as Americans." He underlined his point by declaring he would always think of them in that manner.

He reiterated that theme in letters to his younger brother Charles. Admitting that he disapproved the thrust of southern politics in what he deemed its pro-French and antiadministration position led by Jefferson and Madison, he nevertheless asserted, "I would rather even yield to their unreasonable pretensions and suffer much for their wrongs, than break the chain that binds us all together." He had but a singular touchstone: "All my hopes of national felicity and glory, have invariably been founded upon the continuance of the Union."[5]

Not all of John Quincy's time was consumed with major foreign policy and domestic political matters, however. His daily schedule, which he recorded in his diary, demonstrates that fact. He had a full day, rising at six and not going to bed until eleven. Before noon he had breakfast, read newspapers and serious works, and translated from Dutch. At noon he dressed for the day, wrote letters, and tended to other business until between two and three. Afterwards he walked for half an hour before dining and sitting. Between eight and nine he read for relaxation. Then he took another walk for about an hour followed by a light supper and finally bed.[6]

Not surprisingly, John Quincy said he had much time to himself. He spent many hours translating not just Dutch, which he was trying to master, but also the classics, chiefly Latin. He recorded that he did a page a day from Tacitus, whom he termed the finest historian. As always he had his diary and his books, both of which claimed his attention. He also attended plays put on by a group of French performers; he informed his brother Charles they bore the mark of their revolution. He reported a restricted social life because he had few acquaintances in Holland and did not expect their number to increase.[7]

Having the leisure to pursue practically whatever he chose, John Quincy returned to themes that had long dominated his thoughts. In his diary he spelled out his sense of the requirements for a virtue for which he clearly strove—"the formation of an extraordinary character." To achieve this distinction an individual had to control himself. All other characteristics associated with men he admired, and he included such qualities as judgment and genius, became negligible without that self-discipline. Any man, he wrote, who could not control himself "may be persuaded that ambition does not become him, and that, whatever his lot in life may be, *fortune* will always be the principal ingredient in his success." Not for John Quincy Adams, however.[8]

In letters to his father he also journeyed along well-traveled roads. He professed that his paramount desire was to gain the approval of his parents and simultaneously by his performance in his station confirm the trust placed in him. Although he found his current post generally satisfactory, his future preoccupied him. About one matter he had no doubt; he did not want to go back to the law. He hoped desperately for any other honest respectable occupation.[9]

Despite acknowledging that early advance ensured a following reverse, he still adhered to his benchmark—"to preserve my independence entire." Even with his advantages and parental support, he claimed to care not at all about ambition and fame. What the future held for him, he did not know, but with his independence preserved, he desired a life that permitted time to do what he pleased, especially pursuing his literary studies. He emphasized that for him leisure did not mean idleness. Noting that Americans in Europe had little appreciation of literature, he proposed to render his future service to his country by spending the rest of his life devoted to it.[10]

His diplomatic career was not yet over, however. After a year in Holland he was directed to return to England in order to oversee the exchange of ratifications of the Jay Treaty to which both countries had agreed. He got this duty because the American minister to England, Thomas Pinckney, was away on assignment in Spain. Yet bad weather on the Dutch coast and in the English Channel so delayed John Quincy that by the time he reached London, he had missed the deadline for the exchange. Pinckney's private secretary had substituted for him.

With no task to perform and without specific instructions to return to his post in The Hague, the young man found himself on his own in London. He used the time to indulge in two favorite pastimes, the theater and reading. But as the days became weeks and then months he began to fill his diary with self-criticism, approaching self-loathing. In his mind he had fallen prey to the great sin of idleness. Describing his average day as boring, he went so far as to refer to his debasement. A few months later he recounted falling into indolence amid the depravity of London.[11]

Yet, during the winter of 1795–96, he, almost unknowingly, began moving in a new direction. One location in London where Americans, including John Quincy, gathered was the mansion of Joshua Johnson, the American consul in London. Johnson was a seemingly successful merchant who entertained lavishly. He welcomed his fellow countrymen to his home for dinners and other social occasions. The Johnson household had a special attraction—three musically talented daughters. The young ladies frequently entertained their father's guests with music, playing instruments and singing. John Quincy became a regular at the Johnsons'. With the family he enjoyed dinners, cards, the theater, and balls, often extending past midnight. To his diary John Quincy exulted, "What a life!"[12]

Not long after John Quincy began making regular visits to the Johnson mansion, his diary entries began noting a particular daughter, Louisa Catherine, the middle one. Although the Johnson social scene included all three of them—Nancy born in 1773, Louisa in 1775, Carolina in 1777—only Louisa's name appeared in his diary. When it did, he always mentioned something specific— she sang beautifully; she was ill.[13]

Louisa Catherine Johnson grew up in an unusual family. A member of a prominent Maryland family, her father, Joshua Johnson, not yet thirty, came to England prior to the American Revolution as a partner in a Maryland mercantile firm. Initially quite successful in business, he expanded beyond merchandising. In the escalating crisis between the mother country and her colonies across the Atlantic, he was vocally pro-American. As a result, in 1778 he removed to the seaport city of Nantes, France. There he lived in baronial style and continued his profitable business activities until the end of the war. In 1783 he returned to London and rented sumptous quarters in the Tower Hill section of the city, near the Tower of London. In 1790 Secretary of State Thomas Jefferson appointed him the U.S. consul for the British capital.

Early in his first London stay he met a young English woman, Catherine Newth. Although they began living together, they did not immediately marry. In fact, not until 1785, after the birth of all of their children, did a wedding take place. Evidently, how-ever, from the beginning his peers considered the couple man and wife. There is certainly no evidence that their daughters thought otherwise.

Whether in England or in France, Joshua and Catherine raised their girls in genteel fashion. They lived in lavish homes, with numerous servants. The daughters' education, dress, and social life befitted young ladies of their social class. By the time John Quincy began visiting the Johnson home, all of them had reached marriageable age. And their mother was surely interested in find-ing appropriate husbands for them.

John Quincy met her requirements, as well as her husband's. Joshua definitely wanted American mates for his girls, not English. As a southerner, though, he did have reservations about a New Englander. That blemish did not disqualify John Quincy, however. From the Johnsons' time in France, where they met John Adams, they had known, liked, and respected the Adams family. When John Quincy turned up on their London doorstep in late 1795, he was not only the son of a friend; he was a rising young diplomat whose father had become the vice-president of the United States. Moreover, his regularity at the Johnsons' sig-naled his interest in more than dinners and card games. Noting his attention to her daughters, Catherine initially believed him attracted to Nancy, as did Nancy's two younger sisters.[14]

It became increasingly clear, however, that John Quincy's attention focused on Louisa. Through the winter in the Johnson home, on walks, at dances, he devoted his time to Louisa. Still, he made no declaration of his purpose to her or her parents. Finally, in mid-April, Catherine Johnson took action. Summoning John Quincy, she wanted him to state directly his intentions toward her daughter. On the spot he acknowledged his powerful inter-est in Louisa, a response that satisfied the anxious mother. At the moment neither she nor John Quincy consulted either Louisa or Joshua. When John Quincy called the next evening, he found

Louisa furious. She had learned that he had first declared himself to her mother. He did then make his declaration to her. She told him she needed some time before answering. But within a few days she accepted his profession. Her father also gave his blessing, critical to Louisa for she adored him. She would become Mrs. John Quincy Adams.[15]

Contemporary paintings reveal two attractive young people. A miniature oil of Louisa Catherine done in 1797 depicts her head in three-quarters profile and her dark eyes as her dominant feature. A mass of curls piled on her head trails down her neck and past her shoulders. A suggestion of a smile plays on her lips, but her face overall suggests a demure and very young woman. The portrait of John Quincy by the noted American painter John Singleton Copley in 1796 shows a strikingly handsome young man with an aquiline nose and a generous mouth. His broad forehead is framed by a full head of hair that reaches beyond the nape of his neck. Overall, his is a look of self-conscious composure and aloofness.[16]

The betrothed couple spent the next six weeks in almost constant contact. Theirs was not always a halcyon courtship, however. Along with happy, tender moments came spats that spoiled moods. John Quincy left no doubt that he did not appreciate criticism from his fiancée. In addition, he made clear that there would be no early wedding; he even refused to speculate about a possible date. That pronouncement and refusal distressed both Louisa and her father. John Quincy asserted he would not take a wife until his financial as well as his professional situation was more secure, whenever that might be. And he would be the sole judge. Admitting to his diary that neither his betrothed nor his prospective father-in-law found his stance satisfactory, he averred his conviction about the rightness of his position, which he would not relinquish.[17]

John Quincy did not share his romantic involvement with his parents until he had made his decision to become engaged. Undoubtedly, he could anticipate their reaction. When apprised of their son's and a Johnson daughter's relationship, mother and father were uneasy. Both wanted for John Quincy an American wife, not an English debutante. They, but especially Abigail, worried how a young lady with that background would fit into Massachusetts and American society, and they feared a British-born wife would have an adverse impact on John Quincy's future political career. Abigail even went so far as to suggest that an emotional hangover from Mary Frazier left John Quincy unready to become romantically serious.[18]

John Quincy was adamant, however. Just prior to leaving London, he informed his mother that he possessed the normal desire to marry. His choice, he declared, was final, though consummation yet required "the permission of *Prudence*." Prudence dictated that he return alone to Holland and wait until his prospects improved. Owning that while passion said act now and that delay might cause him to lose Louisa, he affirmed he could not make that choice. "Prudence is inflexible, and I go from hence alone."[19]

Back in Holland by the end of May, John Quincy settled into his former routine, some work, much reading, and little social life. Yet his chief thoughts were centered two hundred miles westward across the English Channel in London. To Louisa he wrote of his love and missing her. He told her that he considered his post at The Hague temporary, that he was eager to return to his native land. To that end, he was writing friends in America looking for an opportunity he could grasp. His great wish was that an occasion would soon occur.[20]

This would delight Louisa. She anticipated the change, which would mean their union sooner rather than later. She professed her love and admiration for her John Quincy, whom she missed terribly. Her letters also revealed a most dutiful fiancée who spoke of herself as belonging to the weaker sex, and would bow before his judgment.[21]

In late summer a momentous change occurred in John Quincy's immediate future and in his and Louisa's courtship. He learned that he had a new diplomatic assignment, minister to Portugal, a promotion. Because of her father's position as consul, Louisa learned of this even before John Quincy. Her letter apprising him of it reached him at almost the same time as official word from the United States. Immediately, John Quincy informed her that wedding plans would have to be postponed. He could not now return to America. Instead, he would remain in Holland until he received formal instructions to depart for his new post. And he made clear to Louisa that he did not know how long that would take, perhaps months.

The delay only grew longer. John Quincy advised her that his holdover in Holland might last until spring. In his letters to Louisa he emphasized the necessity for reason to prevail in their confronting the new situation. He instructed her to prepare herself to cope with their situation, which he could not alter. Additionally, he stressed his love for his country and his duty to its commands, which came before all else. At the same time he assured her of his love, his devotion, and his ardent commitment to their future together.[22]

This news did not please Louisa. Trying to comprehend John Quincy's reasoning and instructions, she echoed his assurance of deep affection. But as weeks and months passed with his continuing refusal to set a date for their reunion, she chafed. She was in limbo. An engaged young lady of her social class could really have no social life without her betrothed. She had been spoken for; she was engaged. Yet she was alone, with no certainty about a wedding date, or even when she would see her fiancé. Moreover, he seemed as content with the uncertainty as she was discontent.

Their prolonged absence from each other along with the requirements that they communicate by letter surely complicated their relationship, especially since the letters took two weeks or even longer to reach their recipient. Missives expressing distress and unhappiness often crossed those filled with endearments and apologies. That both held to their engagement testifies to their love for each other.

At the same time that Louisa had to contend with an elusive wedding date, she had to cope with her father's announcement that in the summer he and the family would return to America. Unbeknownst to her and to John Quincy, he had suffered business reverses that left him in dire financial straits. He felt that only back in Maryland could he raise the funds to meet the demands of his European creditors and recoup his fortune.[23]

This decision by Joshua Johnson put another and seemingly impassible obstruction in the way of a marriage in the near future. A young, unmarried Louisa would, of course, accompany her family to the United States, while at some unknown time John Quincy went to Portugal. No wedding could occur until John Quincy returned to America, whenever that might be. He accepted this eventuality as dutiful and reasonable, given his unchanging stance regarding the timing of a marriage.

Louisa did not share his viewpoint. With her family's impending departure added to John Quincy's inflexibility, she felt trapped, with no escape apparent. To salvage at least a brief face-to-face connection with her husband-to-be, she suggested that her father could sail to America from Holland, offering an opportunity for the engaged couple seemingly plagued by ill fortune to at least see each other. She had begun to doubt that he would honor his commitment. To her suggestion John Quincy responded absolutely not, for in his mind such a visit would be highly inappropriate, without delicacy or dignity.

John Quincy also received a letter from Joshua Johnson advocating even more. Troubled by his beloved daughter's unhappiness and the cloudy matrimonial future, the devoted father proposed that prior to his departure for America, he would come to Holland with Louisa. And there she and John Quincy could marry. John Quincy riposted coldly. He would have none of it. He scolded Louisa for throwing herself at him by entering into a conspiracy with her father to ensnare him in a wedding at a time and place he vehemently opposed.

Outraged at this accusation, Louisa struck back. By this date her letters were no longer those of a dutiful fiancée; instead, she asserted herself directly. Louisa remonstrated with John

Quincy, contending she had not known of her father's letter in advance. Besides, she would never force herself on any man or into any family.

This dispute over the possibility of Louisa's appearing in Holland, with or without a nuptial scheme, placed the engagement on treacherous ground. At this point either John Quincy or Louisa could have said enough, or one could have reacted with sufficient fury to cause the other to end the engagement. Neither did, however. They had formed a bond with a foundation strong enough to withstand this epistolary tempest.

In the midst of this emotional storm with Louisa, John Quincy struggled with what at the close of 1796 he termed a powerful anxiety, occasioned by the two objects he most treasured, his country and his father. They constantly occupied his mind and attention, he confessed to his diary. In a tight electoral contest with Thomas Jefferson, his father was on the verge of becoming the second president of the United States, and his country faced two powerful, frightening forces, France and England. John Quincy described a gloomy future. He prayed to God to remove any potential danger. For himself, he requested "only Virtue and Fortitude. Virtue, to discharge all the duties of life; and Fortitude, to bear whatever destiny awaits me."[24]

Although he had tellingly excluded Louisa from his dearest objects, he had earlier shared with her an underlying cause for his distress. Contemplating his father's elevation to the presidency, he asserted that the more prominent John became, the more he had to prove himself a worthy son. Already, he anguished about the bonds that he carried on that account, and he did not want them increased. He claimed to be not ambitious, but absolutely concerned about his reputation.[25]

To this distraught young man relief came in earlier-than-expected orders for him to proceed to Portugal. They would have him going before the Johnsons left England. Because of the Anglo-French conflict he would have to travel on a neutral vessel. In England, Joshua Johnson could provide such a vessel.

An agreement was reached; John Quincy would stop in London on his way to Portugal. In London he and Louisa would marry. Then Mr. and Mrs. John Quincy Adams would leave for Portugal.

Even with that agreement John Quincy one last time revealed his less than enthusiastic approach to the forthcoming marriage. Before leaving the Netherlands, he offered Louisa a final opportunity to end their engagement. A future with him, he wrote, would be filled with hardship and uncertainty. Because his unconquerable commitment to his country and his lack of fortune could adversely affect her and thus cause him pain, he wanted to give her this option. "Choose, Louisa, choose for yourself," he instructed, "and be assured that [my] Heart will ratify your choice."

Louisa's prompt reply left no room for any further equivocation by John Quincy. With the endearment "my beloved friend," she declared she had made her decision. She had no hesitance. Nothing could deter her from joining him for their journey through life. They would make it together.[26]

Finally, on June 28, 1797, John Quincy departed for London, accompanied by his brother Thomas. Nasty weather on the Dutch coast held them up for more than a week. The future bridegroom did not reach the city until the afternoon of July 12. Yet he did not immediately call on his betrothed. In his diary he simply recorded that he did not go out and retired early. Not until the next day did he appear at the Johnson home. Louisa did not view his delayed appearance benignly, however. She recorded that his delay in coming to her mortified her; she met him with what she described as embittered affection.[27]

When John Quincy did see Louisa, he asked her to choose a wedding day. Having been ready for that event for months, Louisa did not delay. She set the date for only two weeks away. John Quincy seemed a bit taken aback, as did her mother. Still, no serious objections were raised. On July 26, 1797, in the Church of All Hallows Barking, near the Johnson home and the Tower of London, John Quincy and Louisa were married.

Prior to the actual ceremony two events took place that would affect both the immediate and the long-term future of the bride and groom. Even before arriving in London, John Quincy heard that his father, now president of the United States, had changed his diplomatic posting. Instead of Portugal, he would go to Prussia, as the first American minister to that kingdom. In London the American minister to England confirmed the news.

John Quincy was furious. In no uncertain terms he had informed his mother that he wanted no appointment from his father. Such an act would dismiss merit and smack of nepotism. Accepting would degrade and shame him. He thus fired off a letter of protest to his father, telling him he neither expected nor wanted it. He had never desired to experience such anguish.

In spite of his resentment, he reluctantly accepted. But he did so, as he informed John, only because of his respect for his father's authority. Moreover, he asserted that because of the difficulty and inconvenience of his going to Prussia, with no pay increase, he did not believe anyone could maintain that his father had placed him in a featherbed. To his mother he also expressed his reluctance and lamented that hereafter the manner of his appointment would undermine the satisfaction he had thus far felt in his public service.[28]

In time, John replied, disputing his son's opposition and recalcitrance. He condemned John Quincy's stance as the most wrongheaded opinion he had ever known his son to have. In his letter the father made numerous points, for example, that he could relieve John Quincy whether in Portugal or Prussia, that John Quincy would cost the government no more in one country than in the other. He then attested that leading men in government, including George Washington, believed that John Quincy's qualifications matched those of any of his countrymen.

He then branded John Quincy's disapproval of a president's nominating his own son as an unsound principle. The sons of presidents, John announced, possessed all the rights of all other citizens. He rejected the notion that the relationship disqualified the son from serving the government in any office. You are not,

John asserted, "the creature of favor; because you stand exactly as you did, and there is no favor in it." Even though this missive did not influence John Quincy's decision, it lifted the appointment above the muck in which he had placed it.[29]

With John Quincy's new assignment the young couple would head not immediately south to Portugal but at a later date east to Prussia. Because he had to await his formal instructions, their departure for Berlin, the Prussian capital, would not occur for several weeks. In the meantime Joshua Johnson had offered his home as a temporary abode for the newlyweds.

The second notable event concerned Joshua Johnson. His financial standing had been deteriorating rapidly. He did maintain appearances, however, sponsoring elaborate post-wedding festivities for his cherished daughter that included dinners, parties, an excursion in the countryside, and a grand ball. Yet, when he named John Quincy as executor of his will, he divulged that he could not provide even a portion of the promised dowry of £5,000. A ship from America that was supposed to bring funds for his debts failed to arrive, staggering him and leaving him a broken man. He would have to leave for America as soon as possible to stay ahead of those creditors. He and his family actually sailed in early September. But before then John Quincy had secured new quarters for himself and Louisa. Even to their door came men seeking payment for Joshua's debts.

Blissfully unaware of the financial debacle confronting her adored father, Louisa rejoiced in her wedding and the social life that surrounded it. "At the moment everything seemed to combine to make my prospects brilliant," she remembered. When she finally learned that the family situation was not so rosy as she assumed—indeed far from it—she was profoundly affected. First, she had to deal emotionally with her idolized father, now suffering. Even more importantly, she worried that John Quincy would conclude that the desperate Johnsons through less than honorable means had lured him into marriage. He had married the daughter not only without a dowry but with none coming. Joshua Johnson was practically destitute as creditors hounded him. In fact, he left the country to escape them.

This disaster became a burden that she would carry through her life. Decades later she wrote about the trauma. She cried that she could offer no justification for herself. Innocent appearances seemed like purposeful deception. She confessed that any pride she had was gone forever. She was also convinced that her husband would never again have any confidence in her or her family.

As Louisa noted, John Quincy never revealed to her any such feelings, then or later in their long marriage. Even that attitude proved troubling for her, however. Years afterward she stated plainly, "The more kindly and tenderly my husband has treated me, the more bitterly I have felt the pang, that a connection formed under such circumstances was an injustice on my part not to be overcome."

At the time John Quincy described in his diary his reaction to Joshua Johnson's fall, terming it a trial stronger than he had anticipated. Still, confident that he had acted correctly toward his father-in-law and his wife, he asserted that he had done his duty and that no other more self-interested course would have been better for him.[30]

The wedding celebration itself did not apparently engage the new husband. The numerous social events held little charm for him. To his diary he admitted that he would have been delighted not to attend. The weeks following the wedding he spent waiting on his orders did not agree with him. This delay, he grumbled in his diary, led to idleness. He gave thanks that it would not continue for long.[31]

At last his directives arrived. On October 18, 1797, Minister and Mrs. Adams, accompanied by his brother Thomas as secretary and two servants, departed for the new world of Berlin and Prussia.

John Quincy had a double assignment in Prussia. In establishing formal diplomatic relations with countries like Prussia, the government had the long-term goal of building commercial relationships, which would result in increased trade. Accordingly, the State Department directed him to renegotiate a commercial treaty that had expired in 1795. He was also charged to complete that task with Sweden. At the same time his father privately wrote him that he had been wise in his willingness to take on all of Europe. Keep us as informed as you can, the president urged. He wanted John Quincy to write openly to him, but more cautiously to the State Department.[32]

John Quincy and Louisa left London in mid-October and, after an arduous journey, reached Berlin some three weeks later. Travel over rough, sandy roads in a carriage marked the final leg of the trip. That portion proved extremely difficult for Louisa, now pregnant. Arriving in Berlin ill, she became weaker until, before the month was over, she miscarried. From that sad beginning poor health usually connected with pregnancies plagued her for much of their time in the city.

John Quincy found his main diplomatic goal difficult to reach. Although he made a favorable impression at the Prussian court and got along marvelously with the new king, the European political situation worked against him. Because of the Anglo-French conflict, the Prussian government did not want to alienate the two major foes by making any commercial agreement that could antagonize either. And doing so with the United States would undoubtedly displease both. Thus it held off agreeing to any renewal.

With his chief diplomatic mission on hold, John Quincy devoted himself to two other endeavors. He became an active member of the social circle at the royal court. His fluency in French surely assisted, for ever since Frederick the Great had instituted its usage several decades earlier, French was the preferred language of the court as well as of European diplomacy in general. Dinners, receptions, and balls were the order of the day. Initially, because of Louisa's poor health, he attended these events alone. He also spent considerable time on the German language, which he found difficult to master. Undeterred, however, he worked at it, reading poetry, fiction, and history. Finally, employing a tactic he had often used with the classical languages, he began translating. He focused on a long poem, Christoph Martin Wieland's *Oberon*. He wrote his mother that he spent so much time on it that he had precious little for any other endeavors.[33]

Even though his social life was an essential part of his role as a diplomat and his learning German contributed to his success, he censured himself. In his diary he used the word "dissipation" to characterize the social aspect of his job. He grumbled about the time he spent in that manner. He appeared to resent what he described as a kind of luxury that resembled idleness, always a great bête noire for him. It seemed to be a magnet from which he could not detach himself.[34]

Despite his private lamentation, there was no idleness. In addition to his social and intellectual activities, concern about Louisa's well-being continually occupied his attention. The couple quickly moved from their hotel to an apartment near the Brandenburg Gate. They found it disquieting, however. The noise connected with the military exercises taking place there and the corporal punishment meted out to soldiers at the site dismayed them. Soon they were able to secure much more appealing quarters near other diplomats.

Still, Louisa's physical debilities worried him. They found medical assistance from Dr. Charles Brown, a Scottish-born physician who lived nearby. Even more, the Adamses and the Browns became friends. Dr. Brown was always at Louisa's side when she needed him. And that was often. Louisa's regular pregnancies brought almost constant struggle; she had difficulty carrying a fetus to term. From her first miscarriage, in late 1797, until her final one, in early 1800, pain and suffering marked her first four efforts to bear a child. To his diary John Quincy revealed his deep distress: he cried that he had fallen under increasing despair. Although both wanted a child, Louisa's becoming pregnant almost terrified her husband. He wrote of horrible potential prospects that frightened him.

Combatting this ongoing discouragement, John Quincy did not spurn his religion or his God. In traditional Calvinist fashion he accepted that man did not question the acts of Providence. He recognized that thus far in his life he had indeed been fortunate. That brought forth the fundamental question—"Shall I receive good, and shall I not receive evil?" Answering, he recognized the struggle between the mental and the emotional. "The mind at least submits, however the heart will rebel." He depicted his bowing to the will of God, with thanksgiving for blessings and with prayer for the strength to bear whatever the future brought. As always, God's will be done.[35]

While Dr. Brown provided his medical services during these trying times, John Quincy gave Louisa constant attention. She described his affectionate consideration in extravagant language, calling his kindness constant and acknowledging his "perpetual anxiety." Yet she continued her self-criticism, terming her ill health an endless burden on her husband. She also came to see a negative reaction in herself. His anxiousness, she admitted, kept her in a turbulent state. She said she became excessively nervous, and any disturbance upset her mightily, just as her husband feared. Despite her own anxiety, which matched his, these extraordinarily trying months forged a powerful bond between them.[36]

Marital turmoil did not disappear, however. When not housebound, Louisa joined her husband in the diplomatic social whirl. At a ball the queen noticed her paleness, the result chiefly of her maladies. The monarch wanted to give her a box of rouge; Louisa replied that John Quincy would not allow her to wear it. To him the absence of rouge equaled republican simplicity. The queen came back, saying if she provided the cosmetic, he could not refuse. Louisa accepted.

Later, as she prepared for a party, she noticed her face paler than usual. She dared to put on a little rouge, which she thought made her exceptionally beautiful. Wanting to evade John Quincy's scrutinizing, she asked him to put out the lights while she hurried toward the door. His curiosity aroused, he saw what she had done. He told her that the rouge must go, or he would not go. He thereupon took a towel and put his wife on his knee. The outcome, in her words, "all my beauty was clean washed away." She went to the party, her usual pale self.

Not dissuaded, she made another try. Still concerned about her pallor, she applied rouge as she dressed for a court appearance. This time she walked directly toward John Quincy. As before, he insisted it come off. In a huff, Louisa refused. He bolted for the carriage and left her alone crying. Recovering, she composed herself, redressed, and went to the Browns, who never guessed why she had not accompanied her husband. Upon his return, he found her at the Browns' after finding the house empty. The couple returned to their home as friends, according to Louisa. She declared that in those days her anger with him never lasted more than a few minutes. Kisses and making up solved everything. Then all would be forgotten. Yet she recorded that after this episode she never again attended any court festivities. And as she penned her recollections decades later, she obviously had not forgotten.[37]

While she did go, however, she enjoyed the society of the court. Her fluent French eased her way. The queen befriended her, and she discovered some of the Prussian ladies as well as some diplomatic wives to be congenial. She also noted that court etiquette could be amusing. She recounted the impropriety of turning one's back in the presence of royalty. This was a tough rule, for the king and princes walked about the room. "The watchfulness it imposes," she continued, "keeps you in a perpetual fever, lest you commit some blunder, sharply corrected by Officers of the Court." Then there was the supper "consisting of all sorts of meats in great joints and in great abundance very well calculated to produce indigestion."[38]

But neither the court nor his preoccupation with Louisa absorbed all of John Quincy's attention. He never forgot his duty of gaining another treaty. In the summer of 1798 the government signaled that it was prepared to begin discussions on one.

Much to John Quincy's satisfaction the negotiations turned out positively, and in July 1799 he signed a new treaty. Adams never managed, however, to renew the agreement with Sweden. With the Prussian treaty in hand, his main occupation became reporting on European affairs, which, as in the Netherlands, he did in lengthy missives to the State Department and to his parents.[39]

In the summer of 1800 John Quincy and Louisa set off on a great adventure. He had determined to visit the region of Silesia southeast of Prussia toward Austria. It had been made part of the Prussian kingdom by Frederick the Great. The Adamses spent three months touring the mountains, valleys, countryside, and towns. Much that he saw impressed John Quincy, from the magnificent scenery to the quality of the manufactured glass, to the bitter antagonism between Lutherans and Roman Catholics, to Jewish ghettos.

John Quincy did more than simply record his observations and reactions in his diary; he also wrote forty-three long letters to his brother Thomas, who had earlier returned to the United States to study law in Philadelphia. The initial thirty he penned while still on his travels, the remainder after his return to Berlin. The time this effort consumed underscores not only his resolve to complete this particular task but also his determination to maintain a full record for himself of what he was seeing. The keeping of his diary required many hours, and then came the extended epistles to Thomas. But it did not stop there, for he copied those letters in his letterbooks.

This correspondence did not remain in the family, however. Assuming that his brother would not object, and he never did, Thomas turned the letters over to the editor of *Port Folio*, a fledgling weekly literary magazine published in Philadelphia. In the year 1801 all forty-three appeared in its pages. Even so, this serial-like appearance of the letters did not conclude their publishing history. An unknown person took them to London, where they came out in a 387-page book as *Letters on Silesia . . .*, by "His Excellency John Quincy Adams." Within the next three years, the volume was translated into both French and German. No other leading political figure of his time could match that publishing feat.

John Quincy himself had nothing to do with any of these three versions. Upon learning about them, he expressed reservations. If he ever decided to become a published author, he informed Louisa, he would produce a more elevated volume. He did hope at some future time to publish that kind of book.[40]

During the months John Quincy finished his final letters on his Silesian travels, he confronted two consequential events—one making him rejoice, the other saddening him. Both would resonate in future years.

In late fall of 1800, he learned that his father had been defeated for a second term as president. The victor was John Quincy's older friend from long-ago Paris days, Thomas Jefferson, who in the 1790s had led the Republican opposition to the Federalist party of the Adamses. The election was quite close; Jefferson had 73 electoral votes, to Adams's 65. A critical element in the Virginian's victory was his sweeping the slave states, taking 80 percent of their electoral votes. In those states the three-fifths clause of the Constitution, which counted a slave as three-fifths of a person for representation, added to southern members in the national House of Representatives and to southern votes in the Electoral College.

John Quincy wrote his father that the loss should not have an undue adverse impact on him. With John's years in political life, John Quincy went on, he had to know that eventually he would have to bear the rejection that his labor and sacrifice inevitably returned. The son had every confidence that their country's most loyal supporters would feel the pain of the father's defeat more than would the father. Moreover, spared the burden of office, John could now devote himself to farming and literature, avocations he loved. They would take up his time and preclude any embitterment that could make his life miserable.[41]

Writing to his brother Thomas, John Quincy concentrated on the sectional aspect of the election. He denounced southern political principles, which he denoted as "principles of unlimited democracy." According to John Quincy they produced Jefferson and triumph. He saw a dark southern future, however. In his mind the planters, the slave owners, had not yet discovered their inconsistency in proclaiming the rights of man while holding a lash for their slaves. He pronounced "slaves better logicians than their masters."[42]

While coping with the disappointment of his father's failure to win reelection, he also worried about Louisa, once more pregnant. Again John Quincy underwent the trial of her physical debilitation. This time, however, the setbacks did not continue. Louisa succeeded in carrying her baby to term. On April 12, 1801, she gave birth to a son. John Quincy named him not after his own father, but after the father of his country. The arrival of George Washington Adams brought joy to both father and mother. To his diary John Quincy expressed his thankfulness: "I have this day to offer my humble and devout thanks to almighty God for the birth of a son." Louisa remembered her exultation: "I was a *Mother.* God had heard my prayer."[43]

The newest Adams heralded a fresh turn in the life of his parents. John Quincy's assignment in Berlin had been completed; there was no pressing reason for him to remain in the country. Moreover, his father did not want his son recalled by the new president. Before he left office, President Adams called John Quincy home.

Although the recall letter reached him in April, John Quincy did not leave with his family until midsummer. He had to make his formal departure known to the Prussian government. Even more important, Louisa had to regain her strength after giving birth to their first child. During this time John Quincy, in good Adams fashion, thought about the education of his newborn son. Of course, it would begin at home. As part of his contemplating this subject, he read the sermons on educating youngsters by the well-known English minister John Tillotson.

Finally, in July the Adamses left Prussia. After a transatlantic voyage of almost two months, they landed in Philadelphia, where his brother Thomas met them. Louisa made her first steps on American soil. She and her husband promptly separated. John Quincy journeyed northward to Massachusetts to see his mother and father, while Louisa and baby George Washington Adams headed south to the new national capital, Washington, District of Columbia, where her entire family had resettled.

In his native land for the first time in seven years, John Quincy was impressed with what he saw. To a friend he wrote that he saw considerable improvement in the appearance of the country since he had departed in 1794. He found peace and prosperity everywhere. What he described as impressive mansions especially struck him. They seemed to have appeared as if by magic.[44]

He reached Massachusetts and his parents' home in Quincy on September 21. Relating his joy at once again being with them, he used the phrase "irrepressible delight." There was a caveat, however. He noted that they had aged, with his mother's poor health rendering her frail and unwell. He reported that they welcomed him most affectionately. Back on familiar ground, he also celebrated renewed connections with friends and relatives.[45]

Even so, he missed his wife and son. Two weeks after arriving in Quincy, in a letter to Louisa he left no doubt about his feelings. "Our dear George—how I long to kiss even *his* slavering lips!" For Louisa his ardor did not diminish: "As for those of his mother I say nothing—Let her consult my heart in her own and all that pen can write or language express will shrink to nothing." He would leave for Washington to fetch them, he informed her, within a week.[46]

Their reunion in that city was a happy one. Having her husband present meant a great deal to Louisa, for her mother and father were not as she wished. Joshua remained a broken man, severely impaired physically and in ruinous financial circumstances. The elder Johnsons lived on the margin. In Washington, John Quincy along with Louisa dined with both President Jefferson and his secretary of state, James Madison.

After a brief stay, John Quincy returned to Massachusetts with his family. In Quincy, Louisa had her initial meeting with her in-laws. She did not feel comfortable, recollecting that she could never suit them, no matter how hard she tried. She described herself as "an aparté in the family." Abigail did not hide her lack of enthusiasm for her daughter-in-law. Even the presence of her heretofore unseen new grandson did not seem to mellow her. Earlier the naming of the baby for George Washington rather than his grandfather, her husband, had displeased her. Louisa's father-in-law reacted differently. "The old Gentleman took a fancy to me," she stated, and he was the only one who did. They got along famously, becoming fast friends.[47]

Not lingering in Quincy, John Quincy after a short stay moved his family to Boston, where once more he would practice law. That prospect did not please him. "The commencement of my old profession again is attended with difficulties somewhat embarrassing and prospects not very becoming," he confided to his diary. Still, his determination to overcome what he defined as adversity had not lessened. "But I thank God, I can yet struggle with the ills of life allotted to me." He had no choice but to return to the law, for he had no other means of supporting his family. And business did come. Moreover, he was appointed a commissioner of bankruptcy, which brought him a small income he could add to his fees from clients.[48]

Both he and Louisa were accepted into elite Boston circles. Louisa noted with pleasure this social world, with dinners, parties, and balls. She liked many of the ladies who called on her, including Mary Frazier, now engaged to be married. According to Louisa, on their passage to America John Quincy had informed her about Mary and himself. No evidence indicated why he did so at that time. Perhaps, he realized the two women would likely meet.

Having heard about Mary, Louisa was eager to see her. At that same time in almost melodramatic fashion she demeaned herself. She remembered what she had heard of Mary's extraordinary beauty, her accomplishments, her elegance—which made her feel inferior to the imposing Mary. She felt no jealousy, however; she just could not deal with being compared with Mary. While she had no doubt about her husband's love, she admitted, vanity prompted her attitude. She painted herself as "that poor faded thing that I was." When she and Mary did meet, Louisa stated simply that she found her everything that had been said about her.[49]

An active social life and a new start as an attorney did not satisfy John Quincy, however. After only a month in his new life, he ruminated in his diary about being tempted to leap into politics. Nevertheless, he wavered, afraid he would have to become a party man because no politician could otherwise succeed. Being a partisan was not for him, however—"I would fain be the man of my whole country."[50]

John Quincy's family and experience abroad made him a desired political commodity. The Federalist leadership in Boston viewed him as a valuable asset. Despite his private avowal that he did not embrace a party, those men assumed that he shared his father's and their partisan loyalty. John Quincy never said publicly that he did not. There was talk about a seat in the U.S. Senate or on the Massachusetts Supreme Court. Nothing happened in those instances, but the Federalists did nominate him for the state senate. Although in his diary he professed that he had little interest in that post, because it would interfere with other, preferable pursuits, he did not refuse the nomination. In the April 1802 election he won.[51]

In that same month he received a noteworthy speaking invitation. He was asked to give the speech at the anniversary commemorating the landing of the Pilgrims at Plymouth in 1620. For loyal citizens of Massachusetts few events in the state's past matched this one in importance. The first English settlers in the state, the Pilgrims were revered as noble and God-fearing ancestors. John Quincy accepted the invitation, and with the date for the ceremony not until December, he had ample time to prepare.

He proceeded to work on his address as he practiced law and served in the legislature. Still hoping to capitalize on his name, Federalist leaders pressed him to stand for the U.S. House of

Representatives. Reluctantly, he agreed. He came up short in an extremely close race, losing by only 59 votes out of 3,800. In his diary he defined defeat as relief; victory would have meant his being burdened with a task offering no rewards.[52]

That defeat did not interfere with his commitment at Plymouth. There on December 22 he presented his interpretation of the Pilgrims' achievement and legacy. He began by connecting generations, identifying among the most powerful human traits those of venerating our forefathers and of loving our posterity. The settlers of the country, including the Pilgrims, were people their descendants could honestly exalt. That meant a unique ancestry, for all other nations had beginnings in various shades of barbarism. Our forebears who landed on this very spot possessed courage and endurance, he declared. Those qualities "have a magic talisman before which difficulties disappear and obstacles vanish into air." They paved the way for an unprecedented phenomenon, "shooting up to maturity and expanding into greatness with rapidity which has characterized the growth of the American people."

At Plymouth occurred, John Quincy observed, "perhaps the only instance in human history, of that positive, original social compact," which he defined as "the only legitimate source of government." Everywhere else colonists looked to England and a royal charter, but in this holy place a new basis for legitimacy was created, "the instrument of voluntary association," the Mayflower Compact.

He also applauded the Pilgrims for bringing civilization to the wilderness. Here he introduced the topic of Indian-white relations that would remain a constant throughout his career, albeit with different themes. The natives—in his words variously Indians, savages, and aboriginals—had no particular right to possess the immense territory on this shore. God did not form it for "everlasting barrenness." Farms, harbors, towns, and commerce should spread over its vastness and cause "the wilderness to blossom like a rose." Moreover, he asserted, the Pilgrims treated kindly and justly the Indians they encountered.

He told the citizens of Massachusetts that they had the duty of maintaining a reverent respect for their forefathers. They must carry on in the same spirit and with a similar determination. All must join in praying to the God who builds worlds that the vision of the Pilgrims be kept alive for all time. The result of doing so was a foregone conclusion: "the destinies of this empire, as they appear in prospect before us, disdain the powers of human calculation."[53]

Despite this evidently successful endeavor, John Quincy ended the year with negative reflections. As was his wont, he doubted that his actions measured up to what they should have been. The bar he set for himself in his mind consistently seemed a bit beyond his reach. Of course, he could have placed it so high because in his judgment self-satisfaction came dangerously close to sinfulness. Then self-doubting could be a salve. As usual he cataloged his thoughts in his diary. His accomplishments had not met his goals, he commented, even though he recognized that he had been more fortunate than he could have reasonably hoped. For his predicament he blamed an old nemesis, unconquered indolence, which undermined his resolutions.[54]

Shortly after these melancholy meditations, two notable events took place. In February 1803 the Massachusetts legislature elected him to a full six-year term in the U.S. Senate, beginning in the fall with the first session of the Eighth Congress. With this designation John Quincy would for the first time occupy a substantial position on the national political scene. Then, on July 4, Louisa gave birth to a second son; this time John Quincy followed the expected family pattern, naming him John Adams II.

These happy occurrences were tempered, however, by serious financial reverses that fell upon both himself and his parents. He had placed the greater portion of his funds as well as theirs, which he had begun to manage, in a London banking house. In the spring it failed, wiping out John and Abigail's savings and severely hurting John Quincy. Conscious of his responsibility for their hardship, he confided to his diary that he felt responsible for their catastrophe. He would share in the suffering. He sold homes he owned in Boston and moved back to Quincy. He also sold stocks. These sales, along with loans from friends, enabled him to cover the debts incurred by the insolvency of the London bank.[55]

In October he set out for Washington to assume his duties as a U.S. senator. No matter his private musings against political parties, he had been elected as a Federalist, the party of his father and at that moment the dominant one in his state. In both houses of Congress the Federalists were a minority, however. Their opponents the Republicans controlled them. The president, Thomas Jefferson, the man who had sent John Adams home after a single term, led their party.

Traveling with Louisa and the children, John Quincy on October 20 reached Washington, where they would stay in the home of Louisa's sister Nancy and her husband, Walter Hellen. The session of Congress had already begun. In fact, the day before his arrival, the Senate had already acted on the most important measure to come before it during the session. It ratified the treaty acquiring Louisiana known as the Louisiana Purchase, an agreement in which France agreed to sell this immense territory to the new nation. Spanning identical boundaries claimed by its previous French and Spanish owners, which totaled 828,100 square miles, and stretching from the Gulf of Mexico in the south to Canada in the north and from the Mississippi River in the east to the Rocky Mountains in the west, Louisiana doubled the size of the United States. The new acquisition also included the major port of New Orleans, which by the Mississippi River connected a vast hinterland to the sea.

The Louisiana Purchase was the major triumph of the Jefferson presidency. And his Republican party stood unanimously behind it. The Federalists provided foursquare opponents, however. Because of his late arrival Senator Adams did not cast a vote on the treaty. Even so, in all probability, he would have voted aye because subsequently he made clear his support. He saw the purchase as a major augmentation of American strength, only adding to the greatness he foresaw for his country.

While he never evinced any doubt about obtaining Louisiana, he believed a constitutional amendment essential to legitimize it. In his judgment the Constitution nowhere authorized expanding the original territorial limits of the country. Soon after he got to the capital, he expressed this view to Secretary of State Madison, who agreed with him. President Jefferson shared that opinion. For Madison and Jefferson this judgment stemmed naturally from their long-held principle of strict construction of the Constitution—no policy could go beyond the document's specific language. For such a prize as Louisiana they would violate the creed, but then validate that action with an amendment, the method sanctioned by the Constitution for altering any provision. John Quincy said if the administration did not propose such an amendment, he would gladly do so.

Yet, for political reasons, the administration never sent to Congress any amendment. Some Republicans perceived no need for one. More importantly, Republicans feared that such an amendment would provide ammunition for the opposing Federalists. Constitutional theory did not drive the Federalists' resistance. Centered in the Northeast, especially in New England, they recognized their political weakness in the current southern and western states, almost all preponderantly Republican. Louisiana simply projected that weakness, ever increasing, into the future. The result would mean diminishing even further Federalist strength and influence in national affairs. Federalists could envision the political burial of their party and particularly of New England.

In this partisan conflict the new senator from Massachusetts did not side with his fellow Federalists. While he concurred with them that the interests of New England must be protected, he viewed the national benefits as outweighing any parochial fears. His confidence in a country growing more and more powerful did not necessarily entail the ultimate overpowering of his native soil.

John Quincy's backing the Louisiana Purchase signaled that he was not a lockstep Federalist, but neither had he donned a Republican uniform. When the Republican majority in Congress moved to organize a territorial government for the new possession, John Quincy spoke against any such action. According to him Louisianians must be consulted and heard from prior to any congressional legislation. In his view, under the Constitution fundamental power rested with the people; thus for Congress to impose any government on Louisiana before its citizens consented to it contravened both the Constitution and the basic rights of Americans. He did not prevail, however. Congress did create a territorial government for Louisiana.

In the debate over Louisiana, John Quincy first addressed publicly a topic that would absorb him in later life: slavery. The Louisiana Purchase permitted slavery because it allowed residents to retain their property, and property in the territory included slaves. The institution had been legal under both the French and the Spanish.

John Quincy, of course, supported the treaty. Certain Federalists introduced a bill that would prohibit bringing any additional slaves into the territory. John Quincy opposed the proposed antislave legislation. He did consider the institution a moral evil. At the same time, he observed it had important commercial benefits. He gave two reasons for his opposition to antislavery measures. First, he stood against any legislation for Louisiana until its citizens had a voice. Second, he thought the antislave men were going too fast on such a vital matter. On another slavery-related question he supported the majority who wanted to receive a petition from Quakers in Philadelphia urging Congress to restrain the growth of slavery as far as constitutionally possible. At this early period his stance revealed a man with firm convictions tempered by circumstances.[56]

On a different major issue he aligned with the Federalists. Republicans did not like the federal judiciary. Judges on the federal branch, including the Supreme Court, had all been appointed by Federalist presidents. Moreover, a number of Republicans, led by President Jefferson, objected strenuously to the lifetime appointment for all federal judges stipulated in the Constitution. Jefferson and the Republican congressional majority intended to use their power to transform the third branch of the federal government by removing judges via the impeachment process. They began in late winter of 1804 by moving against a federal judge in New Hampshire. They picked as their target a man all recognized as mentally unstable and unfit for the bench. Even though his family did not resist his removal, they sought some honorable way out. The Republicans refused; they wanted to set a precedent. The House duly impeached; the Senate tried and convicted. John Quincy was appalled at the process. To him it was nothing but a rank display of political muscle.

Next the Republicans targeted a Supreme Court justice, Samuel Chase of Maryland—an avowed Federalist. Chase brazenly pronounced his political opinion from the bench. Once again the House impeached. As the Senate prepared to try Justice Chase, leading Republicans in that body argued that impeachment simply meant that Congress would determine whether someone else might better fill an office than the incumbent. To John Quincy such politically motivated reasoning flouted the constitutional meaning of impeachment. As he saw it, the Republican maneuver meant simply that they wanted to put their own in office, and to do so would use any means to remove opponents. Because some Republicans had become uneasy with their leadership's tactics, the two-thirds majority required for a conviction could not be attained. Chase was not convicted. This outcome both surprised and pleased Senator Adams.[57]

In Washington he kept a busy schedule. He rose at seven, then wrote in his room until nine, when he had breakfast and dressed. At ten he left, usually on foot, for the Capitol, a forty-five-minute walk. From around eleven until two or three, the Senate was in session; afterwards he returned home. If the Senate adjourned early, however, he listened to debates in the House. In the evening he spent time with the extended family, going to bed at eleven. He attended worship on Sundays, often in the House chamber. He also devoted an hour to reading the Bible; in a lifelong habit he would read it through and begin again.[58]

His reading was, as always, impressively wide-ranging. He read American history and consumed official documents, including congressional journals and federal statutes. Authors on his list included Michel de Montaigne, Edward Gibbon, and Blaise Pascal. He never forgot the ancient classics. There was the Greek New Testament, Plautus, and Juvenal, many of whose satires he translated. In addition, he maintained his French and German.

He also continued to grapple with his constant psychological companion, self-reflection. Noting "the errors, imprudences, and follies" in his conduct, he allowed that discovering them did not always lead to improving them. Yet his examining himself did lead to self-awareness. "Pride and self-conceit and presumption lie so deep in my natural character, that, when their deformity betrayed them," he admitted, they made every effort to mask themselves from his heart. Even though he claimed that he often recognized and condemned his failings, he thought a sanction essential to correct them. But voluntary punishment, he declared, had been deemed superstitious and banned from our moral system. He had not tried it, at least not to this point. Still, he believed it essential to make self-discovery worthwhile.[59]

In the Senate he had to deal with practical matters, and he did not find contending with partisanship his only difficulty. He feared that he spoke too often, which he feared would make him look ridiculous, or worse. Even more importantly, he decried his ineffectiveness in speaking on the Senate floor. Describing what he called his shortcomings, he employed such phrases as *"miserably defective"* and "without order and without self-collection." "I never speak without mortification," he lamented. To his satisfaction he understood why: he felt he did not think rapidly enough for continuous speaking. His initial confused thoughts required time before becoming shaped into articulate speech.[60]

Senators who exhibited the talent he lacked—among them he highlighted James A. Bayard of Delaware—he praised extravagantly. According to John Quincy, Bayard spoke with such facility that he was never embarrassed, nor were others for him. Describing Bayard's speaking style, John Quincy used admiring adjectives: "clear, forcible, and overflowing with illustration." In the midst of this praise, he inserted a caveat, however. He judged Bayard's "moral and political knowledge [not] very profound."[61]

Senator Adams also believed that often his intensity in debate contributed to an outcome the very opposite of his wishes. He became convinced that because of antipathy toward him personally and his performances, some of his counterparts voted against measures he supported. The views of colleagues, even friendly ones, suggested that his personality could affect reactions to him and his causes. He was spoken of as honest and quite well informed. Yet his vehement opinions and rigid manners came to define his temperament. Moreover, he was "too tenacious of his opinions" and "incline[d] to be peremptory."[62]

Although he did not always, as already noted, stand with Federalists in the Senate, he had few good words for Republicans. Even before his election as senator, he faulted them for lacking moderation. He posited that they knew that only a porous foundation supported them. In constant fear that the Federalists would regain favor, Republicans concentrated on uninterrupted slandering of their opponents. He found no reason, no prudence. Yet, he sadly concluded, their efforts succeeded.[63]

Still, he perceived more than slanderous rhetoric propping up the Republican party. In a series of five lengthy articles published in October and November 1804 in a weekly Boston newspaper, the *Repertory*, using the pseudonym Publius Valerius, he returned to a familiar bugbear. In them he denounced the three-fifths clause of the Constitution, which enhanced southern and thus Republican political strength. This unfair system penalized all the free states, especially in New England. It placed them in an insulting status. He had company in his opposition to the three-fifths clause. Northeastern Federalists overwhelmingly shared his contempt for that constitutional provision. John Quincy did more than denounce this nefarious constitutional provision, however. He went on to advocate its repeal by amending the Constitution to eliminate it. Evidence exists that he contemplated addressing the Senate on such an amendment, though he apparently never did. And the record does not reveal why.[64]

In his onslaught against what he saw as constitutional injustice, he did not attack solely on legal and political grounds. Lacerating both slave owners and the institution of slavery, he strove for the moral high ground. Here there was no tempering. The masters of slaves he castigated as "a privileged order of slave-holding Lords," who profited from a system grounded in "the infamous traffic of human flesh." That salvo underscored his barrage against the inhumanity of slavery itself. The number of slaves, he asserted, already bestirred genuine alarm among all compassionate and thoughtful people. Thus, early on, Adams expressed these anti-slavery views, which would become dominant in later years.

That he depicted the three-fifths clause diminishing and, with Louisiana and southern expansion, threatening to strangle the influence of New England in the nation did not mean that he directed his entire bombardment at the slave states and slave owners. He reserved particular venom for Republicans in his own state. The Massachusetts partisans of Jefferson, in his scenario, betrayed their state and its citizens by supporting a party whose national dominance depended upon the notorious three-fifths clause. For him it did not matter whether personal or partisan motives prompted these men. He thundered they had allied with a party that penalized the legitimate interests of their own commonwealth. In fact, they were aiding a party whose success portended the annihilation of New England in the country. In spite of those dire pronouncements, he expressed confidence that in time Massachusetts would regain its force in the Union, which some of its own had unashamedly colluded to take from it.

In these essays John Quincy presented himself not as a Federalist but rather as a New Englander, as a man from Massachusetts. Never did he overtly raise the Federalist flag. Yet his argument meshed perfectly with the views of Federalists in his state and section. Thus, despite his favoring the Louisiana Purchase, he did not break with the Federalist party, which sent him to the Senate. Nor, at this point, did the Federalist leadership in Massachusetts identify him as a traitor to party or state.

Even though he was a sitting U.S. senator, John Quincy had another enticing offer presented to him. In June 1805 his alma mater tendered him a professorship of rhetoric; he could become the first Boylston Professor of Rhetoric and Oratory. He had long told himself that his ideal entailed a life of learning and study. Even with an academic berth in the offing, though, he would not or could not turn his back on politics. While he desired the chair, he would not give up the Senate. In fact, he wanted both.

In order to keep his Senate seat and become a professor, he strove to arrange the terms of his professorial appointment to accommodate his political career. Initially the requirements of the Boylston chair included the stipulations that he live in Cambridge and be available during the entire academic year. John Quincy told Harvard officials that he could agree to neither. Most important, he refused to commit his services for the year. Following negotiations, the two sides reached an agreement that greatly favored him. His academic duties would necessitate his presence only part of the year, and he would not have to reside in Cambridge. In fact, his course would commence in the summer and conclude in the fall. He would begin in the summer of 1806. Thus, in winter and spring, when Congress usually met, Senator Adams could assume his post in the Senate chamber. Among contemporary politicians his academic appointment was unique. None of them was on the Harvard faculty.

Although he demanded and received what might be termed a part-time appointment, he devoted himself to preparing for his class. He would create it, for such a course had not been previously taught at Harvard. He took a long view of his situation. He wrote Louisa that, given political reality in Massachusetts, he would most likely serve just one term. In his diary he called getting his course in order a major undertaking, and he prayed for the ability to accomplish it. Only with God's favor could he succeed. He spoke of seven years as a time frame for meeting his goal of making a significant contribution.[65]

His official installation as the Boylston Professor occurred on June 12, 1806, with his initial class and his lectures following. He thought his first one well received, which encouraged him. Yet he found the preparatory work of research and writing time-consuming and difficult—in short, "troublesome." He read widely in the classical giants, including Demosthenes, Aristotle, and Cicero as well as more modern European writers on rhetoric. Sermons and speeches also occupied him.[66]

His labor did not lessen with time. In 1807 he confided to his diary that preparing the lectures resembled the labor of Sisyphus, a figure in Greek mythology condemned to roll a large stone up a hill in Hades, only to have it when nearing the summit roll down again. He reported that it took two weeks of hard work for a half-hour class. A year later he moaned that the work that went into his lectures represented more time than he had ever spent on anything else. Accordingly, his exertions called for perseverance and stamina, which required him to embrace adversity as a virtue. Acknowledging his struggle, he stated that his struggle in composing the lectures almost overpowered him.[67]

Although by all accounts his efforts yielded positive results, Professor Adams had a short stint in the classroom. Chiefly because of his ambition for a public life, three years after his initial lecture, he gave his culminating one. The attendance at his last lecture and the actions of the students testified to his achievement. Not only those in his course but students from across the university as well as others crowded the chapel for his concluding performance. A student committee expressed disappointment at his departure and requested that he publish his twenty-four lectures. Pleased, John Quincy replied that he had not thought about doing so, but would consult with the university leaders about it. He received their blessing.[68]

In 1810 the lectures were published in Cambridge in two volumes—*Lectures on Rhetoric and Oratory Delivered to the Senior and Junior Sophisters in Harvard University*. With his usual self-deprecation and self-protection, the author wrote his brother that he anticipated nothing positive for his reputation, but most likely the opposite. He nonetheless trusted they would "excite the genius, stimulate the literary ambition, and improve the taste of the rising generation." While he expected vigorous criticism, he hoped that his volumes might assist the development of American literature. He even contemplated improving his productions in future editions.[69]

No future editions appeared; nor did *Lectures* have significant impact. Yet John Quincy could absorb himself in reading through them. He wished they could have that effect on at least one other person. Doubting this outcome, however, he prayed that he might "be duly prepared for resignation to their fate, whether of total neglect, of malicious persecution, or of deserved condemnation." He anticipated the last two, though not the first. Even that negative reaction, he told his diary, might help him learn humility, which he felt he sorely needed.[70]

While John Quincy performed his professorial duties, he, of course, continued as a senator. When in Washington he and Louisa participated fully in the social life of the capital, which blossomed during the congressional sessions. The events included parties, receptions, and dinners, with the Executive Mansion among the venues. Both Adamses also formed and expressed their opinions about major personalities of the dominant Jeffersonian Republican party.

John Quincy did not look favorably upon President Jefferson. His judgment about the Virginian whom he had admired as a youth had changed. Without question the pain of his father's failed bid for reelection influenced his attitude. Yet more was involved. He reacted strongly to certain of the president's remarks in social gatherings. In particular he felt the president had far too great a penchant for what he labeled exaggerations. He deemed fanciful Jefferson's claim that during a transoceanic crossing of nineteen days he had learned Spanish, with the aid of only a grammar book and a copy of *Don Quixote*. Commenting on Jefferson's insistence that in Paris he had seen the thermometer at twenty degrees below zero and for six weeks never saw it reach zero, John Quincy noted that Jefferson knew better but liked to stir up his audience. He summarized his take on the man by asserting that Jefferson could not love history. "There are important traits in his character, and important actions in his life," John Quincy wrote, "that he would not wish should be delineated and transmitted to posterity."[71]

For John Quincy, Jefferson's theater called excessive attention to the performer. Jefferson he saw as a man who had to occupy center stage by upstaging his guests. In his judgment this conscious self-aggrandizement equaled vanity, which for him characterized individuals who had too great an opinion of themselves. His Calvinist heritage and teaching instructed that he reject any such personal display. Wild stories and fanciful reports about supposed experiences he simply disdained. Moreover, he would grant Jefferson no license for playful hyperbole or harmless tall tales. Dignity and decorum must govern all, especially a president.

Louisa Adams shared her husband's negative opinion, though she employed more slashing language. She had arrived in their country thinking approvingly about Jefferson because of her adored father, an avid Jefferson partisan. Her contact with the president changed her mind, however. She depicted him as a cunning hypocrite. When he mingled with guests, she observed a restless man worried that his visitors would scan him more closely than he liked. She did not hold back, denouncing him as "the ruling Demagogue of the hour."[72]

In contrast, she admired and respected Secretary of State Madison. His conversation and pleasing, unassuming manners impressed her. His intelligence wowed her. "I never saw a man with a mind so copious, so far from the pedantry and mere classical jargon of University Scholarship." And Mrs. Madison was his match. "She is the cynosure of all eyes—a really charming woman," Louisa marveled. In her view, Dolley Madison exercised great social influence, and not a little in politics.[73]

Regarding a powerful, provocative, at times notorious, Republican legislator, husband and wife did not totally agree. John Randolph of Roanoke, a Virginia congressman, fascinated Louisa. "The lyon of the day," she recollected, "a man perhaps the most extraordinary of his day." In his actions and speeches he could be extreme, she admitted. He was "at times a delightful companion, or an insolent bully." She posited that his personality "ruled the timid and amused the weak." "To sum up the whole," she concluded, "he was to congress what Shakespeare's *Fool's* were to a Court."[74]

Other than conceding Randolph's sporadic brilliance, John Quincy had nothing good to say about this Virginian, who embodied the antitheses of Adams's virtues. He judged Randolph fundamentally a wild man, an individual devoid of self-control. Reflecting on a speech Randolph made in Congress, John Quincy characterized it as without form, consisting chiefly of hackneyed topics, combined with praise and invective about different people. He did admit, however, that it had "a few striking figures, much distortion of face and contortion of body, tears, groans, and sobs, with occasional pauses for recollection."[75]

John Quincy's service in the Senate did not draw Louisa to politics. She wrote about her husband's absorption in Senate business and politics. When the Senate met, he had little time for his family. Diverging from the social life that she loved, Louisa confessed, she did not interfere with politics, for she could not abide them. No matter how "hot"—her word—the political world became, she kept herself apart.[76]

Although Louisa Adams clearly did not embrace the role of political wife, John Quincy's years in the Senate did no permanent damage to their marriage, though they had to cope with difficulties and disagreements. At times during the months Congress did not meet, she and the children remained in Washington with her sister's family while John Quincy returned to Massachusetts and his parents. When she did go with him, she did not care for life in Quincy. John Quincy, however, was determined to spend time there every year. And after accepting the Boylston Chair, his residence in Massachusetts was required. Even though neither of them enjoyed their separation, they endured it while missing each other mightily. The children also caused a disagreement. In the winter of 1806 John Quincy, against his wife's wishes, decreed that both boys, George now four and John just two, would remain in Quincy for the winter. Despite the discord occasioned by separations and disagreements about their sons, their bond remained powerful.

An occurrence in the summer of 1806 testified to its strength. In that summer a pregnant Louisa in Washington was carrying to term what would have been their third child. With her husband in Massachusetts, Louisa Catherine delivered a stillborn baby. She reported that sad news to him. John Quincy replied that the letter had been handed to him in the presence of company. The news so affected him he had difficulty retaining his composure. In private, he related, he "could include the weakness, which the bitterest of sorrows is forbidden to discover to the world." "If the tears of affliction are unbecoming a Man," he continued, "heaven will at least accept those of gratitude from me, for having preserved you to me."[77]

The following year Louisa Adams's next pregnancy had a more auspicious outcome. In Massachusetts in August, with John Quincy present, she gave birth to a son. Initially it seemed a reprise of a year earlier, for at first the infant did not breathe. According to Louisa, the trauma lasted half an hour before the baby's lungs began functioning. Still, they worried for two days, until the infant Charles Francis started to thrive. The mother made clear that because her husband was present during the ordeal, he had viewed suffering he could not previously imagine. Now their sharing went even deeper.[78]

While presiding over a growing family and teaching Harvard students, John Quincy continued his senatorial duties. In 1806 he found himself in a difficult political situation that grew ever more onerous over the next two years. The basic cause was the great conflict engulfing Europe, with Great Britain and France leading opposing forces. Confronting and reacting to a European maelstrom was not a new experience for the United States. Back in the 1790s the country had faced the same scenario.

This time America became so entangled because both Great Britain and France, locked in a death struggle, interfered with and disrupted American trade whenever they chose. Although the United States assumed a neutral stance and insisted that neutrality guaranteed the right of American commerce to ply the ocean without restraint, neither of the European powers recognized any such claim. But because the powerful British navy ruled the seas, for America the British became the great malefactor. Moreover, the British warships went much further by stopping and boarding American merchant vessels in order to impress, or to force into British service, their seamen, claiming they were English subjects. Some were, others were not, but the key for America was that this practice ridiculed and undermined the independence and integrity of the United States.

This time President Jefferson and Secretary of State Madison had to devise a policy that would protect their countrymen on the high seas and uphold the honor of their country. The administration's demands that the British respect American rights and the American flag went unheeded. Unwilling to resort to war, Jefferson and Madison opted for economic pressure. They based their policy on the belief that England needed American trade. By placing restrictions on that trade, they hoped to persuade the British to respect American rights.

Congress passed its initial effort in the winter of 1806, the Non-Importation Act. This legislation prohibited the importation from Britain of specified articles. The Republicans in Congress backed their president and his policy. The Federalists did not. Jefferson's commercial diplomacy would cause hardship for American merchants and shipowners, activities critical to New England, the center of Federalist strength. In opposing Jefferson's strategy, Federalists argued that basically it aided the French while harming both the British and their constituents. They saw no neutrality.

When the Non-Importation Act had no effect on British practices, Jefferson advocated more stringent measures. At the close of 1807 the Republican-controlled Congress passed the Embargo Act, which banned imports and exports, shutting down virtually all commerce with foreign nations, whether by land or by sea. Federalists strenuously objected to it, albeit unsuccessfully. The Embargo Act did lead to widespread distress, particularly in mercantile areas, again focused in New England, most especially in Massachusetts, where shipping occupied a critical place in the economy.

As the Federalist party almost unanimously condemned Jefferson's approach, Senator Adams found himself in a most uncomfortable position. He was the only Federalist in the Senate to vote for both the Non-Importation Act and the Embargo Act. He did so, in part, because he thought keeping American ships in port would halt impressment, the chief cause of Britain's quarreling with his country. More importantly, he believed the United States had to affirm and protect its rights as a neutral country or forfeit its independence and honor. He saw as the only alternative to Jefferson's program a declaration of war against England, and that he did not want. In his undoubtedly correct view his country was not prepared for a military confrontation with Great Britain. The risk was too great. Defeat, in his mind likely, could mean the end of American independence. Thus, despite enormous political hazard, he took his forthright stance. His conviction about the right policy overrode all other considerations. He would stand where it placed him, even if he stood alone. This would not be the last time.[79]

His endorsing Jefferson's diplomacy led to a bitter divorce between him and the party that had sent him to Washington.

Responding to an inquiry from a Federalist congressman from his state about his motives, John Quincy detailed them. According to John Quincy, his questioner replied that those who sent him to Washington would not thank him for his commitment to unadulterated principles. In turn, John Quincy said he did not care about their gratitude or about whether they valued him. "My character, such as it was," he retorted, "must stand upon its own ground, and not upon the bolstering of any man or party."[80]

The Federalist leadership in Massachusetts considered Senator Adams a political traitor who had betrayed their interests and trust. Rumors abounded that John Quincy voted as he did only to curry favor with the Jefferson administration, hoping for some political plum as reward. When, in late January 1808, he accepted an invitation to attend the Republican congressional caucus to select that party's presidential nominee, rumor turned into rage, even though he did not vote. "His apostasy is no longer a matter in doubt with anybody," railed one Federalist. Even his mother was incensed, writing, "I have considered it as inconsistent both with your principles, and your judgment, to have countenanced such a meeting by your presence."[81]

John Quincy countered. In March he published a pamphlet addressed to a prominent Federalist chieftain. In it he attacked the Federalist party for putting party ahead of country, for placing provincial and selfish concerns before national priority. To him the Federalists seemed willing to tie the United States to England in a subordinate role. In his view, doing so would jeopardize American independence. Nationalism must be the watchword, not provincialism or sectionalism.[82]

As for his angling for reward from the Republican party, John Quincy vehemently denied any such intention. There was no quid pro quo. He wrote his father that he had no communication with the Jefferson administration except in his official capacity as a senator. When a prominent Republican senator asked what he might want for his support, John Quincy said he answered nothing. He added that his assistance to Jefferson's or any other administration would be governed by his judgment about the national welfare, and nothing else. Informed by the same senator that a Federalist colleague had offered to assist the Republicans with appropriate inducement, John Quincy asserted that individual's stance did not have a moral foundation.[83]

With Massachusetts Federalists and Senator Adams at such loggerheads, no reconciliation occurred. To express their displeasure, the Federalists who dominated the state legislature, six months earlier than usual in early June, chose a replacement for John Quincy when his term expired in March 1809. Determined that he would control his future, John Quincy within a week reacted to his rejection by submitting his resignation from the Senate. In it he defended himself by repeating his assertion that he had acted "to vindicate the rights essential to the independence of our country, against the unjust pretensions and aggressions of all foreign powers." Looking back two decades later at this eventful period, John Quincy discovered no reason for regret. In fact, the review satisfied him about his conduct. In his diary he penned his final assessment: "I find little to censure in what I did; nothing in what I intended."[84]

Yet at that moment a fundamental pessimism governed his outlook. Early in his time as a senator, he had written his father that he did not expect stability in public affairs. "As *change* is the only permanent characteristic feature in our governments and constitutions," he had to adjust to it. Unlike John, however, he envisioned no change for the better in the offing. He could foresee nothing but worsening change for many years to come. His only hope was that the country's development rested on so firm a foundation that "the vice and follies of the people" could not undermine it. Even so, he still depended upon the grace of God despite having so little confidence in the good sense, even the goodness, of his fellow citizens.[85]

His years in the Senate did not change his frame of mind. In January 1808 he portrayed his Senate tenure as "a fiery ordeal that I have to go through. God speed me through it." Writing to his father later that month, he stated plainly that, because of what he saw as the dismal prospects in the nation, he had no desire for public office. He went on to predict a quite different future. Revisiting a constant theme, he spoke of his return to his books and commitment to literature. This instance revealed a dialectic of opposing external and internal interests with which he grappled throughout his life. That endeavor and educating his children, he declared, would fill his time with honorable duties. He also mentioned returning to the law, though without enthusiasm.[86]

Politics did not immediately disappear, however. Upon his return to Massachusetts from Washington, he faced both political and social ostracism by notable Boston Federalists. Being treated as an outcast by them made John Quincy ever more attractive to local Republicans. Even though he never indicated any desire to affiliate with them, they approached him to run for the national House of Representatives. He refused. Later they tried to get him to make a run for the governorship. Again he refused. He did not desire to become a partisan, and he could lose. Confiding his conviction to his diary, he recorded in a particularly Shakesperean mood that he would never "suffer my feelings to be sported with, or my imagination to be deluded, by the electioneering intrigues of any party. In the dreams of other fancy's, may the reality of my own situation still be present to myself, and teach me the steady possession of myself."[87]

CHAPTER 3

"Let There Be . . . No Deficiency of Earnest Zeal"

MUSING IN HIS DIARY AS 1808 DREW TO A CLOSE, JOHN Quincy termed it a more momentous year than any other he had previously experienced. During the past months he had been removed from office, ending up with the public opinion of Massachusetts Federalists against him. Only his conscience approved his course, he wrote, "and the conviction upon my own mind of having done my duty at every hazard." His private affairs had also suffered. He pronounced them embarrassing with gloomy prospects. Still, he anticipated the future, for he had no doubt that God, who could bring forth good from evil, would do so for himself, his family, and his country. But no matter, "His will be done."[1]

In committing himself to God's will, John Quincy acted in character. His faith in an active and personal God never wavered, though he admitted he did not always fathom the immediate meaning of the result shaped by that will. But if God's will spurred another call from his country, he stood ready to hear it. His diplomatic and political experience had become so thoroughly imbued in him that he could never dismiss the prospect of public service.

Despite that fundamental truth, he could not bring himself to say openly that he wanted office. His desire surely matched that of his political peers, yet he differed in a notable way. Persuaded that the Founders such as Washington and his father, excepting Jefferson, whose motives and conduct he had grown to distrust, waited for office to find them, he felt he acted similarly, following in their steps. That conviction helped him keep his ambition in check. Of course, this approach also enabled him to guard against disappointment if no summons occurred.

Still, accepting the call could not be an end in itself, no matter the privilege and pride. For John Quincy incumbency must be accompanied by giving genuine benefit to his country. Thus, whenever he received the invitation, he would serve wherever he was wanted, with but a single caveat—that he considered himself temperamentally and intellectually qualified. As both diplomat and legislator, he believed that he had performed capably and, even more important, dutifully. He consciously tried to follow the example he perceived set by his founding elders. No one else in his generation so consistently attempted to imitate that model.

Practically, John Quincy's immediate post-Senate future meant a return to the law and to his professorship. His practice would not be constrained to Boston and environs, however. He would also appear before the U.S. Supreme Court. He had been admitted to its bar back in 1804 and had advocated before it while a senator.

In early 1809 he returned to the capital to argue before the high court. He was counsel in one lawsuit that would give rise to a major constitutional decision, *Fletcher v. Peck*. The case involved a claim growing out of a grant of state land to private companies by the Georgia legislature, a number of whose members had been bribed. A succeeding legislature had voided the sale on grounds that fraud and corruption had tarnished the legislation. John Quincy's client, John Peck, who had sold some of his land obtained under the original act, wanted the court to validate the legality of that transaction. The state of Georgia wanted the cancellation affirmed, maintaining that the land grant was not a contract as defined in the contract clause of the Constitution. Furthermore,

Georgia asserted that, as a sovereign state, it possessed the authority to decide such matters, not the U.S. Supreme Court.

On March 2 John Quincy spent five hours before the court
contending that the contract clause did in fact govern and should
inform the justices' ruling. Assessing his appearance, he gave
himself poor marks. Once again it was his inability to speak in
public. Notwithstanding all his preparation, he still judged that
his remarks lacked clarity, with a ferociously dull exposition. He
did note, however, that the court heard all he had to say. For technical reasons, the court at that time did not render a decision.
But the next year, when it did, it upheld John Quincy's position,
affirming that the constitutional contract clause did control the
case. Moreover, in *Fletcher v. Peck* the Supreme Court for the first
time struck down a state law as unconstitutional, declaring that
the court, not a state, had the final word on constitutionality.[2]

While in Washington in the winter of 1809, John Quincy visited
and conferred with many notables, including President Jefferson,
Secretary of State and President-elect Madison, solons, Supreme
Court justices, and diplomats. On March 4 he attended President
Madison's inauguration and that evening the inaugural ball. The
next day the new president asked John Quincy to call on him.

At that meeting Madison offered John Quincy a new diplomatic post, minister plenipotentiary to Russia. There had not
previously been one. The chief executive told John Quincy that
the Russian tsar Alexander I had suggested this new relationship
between the two countries. For the United States the ultimate
goal would be increased trade. Though surprised, John Quincy
accepted on the spot. He did so without consulting either his wife
or his parents, all of whom were in Massachusetts.

It was not to be, however. Within a week the Senate rejected
the proposed mission, not simply the minister. With that information in hand, John Quincy wrote Louisa, recognizing the news
would not disappoint her. He admitted that for their children and
themselves the assignment would have been more troublesome
than advantageous. He had certainly not expected that appoint-

ment, or any other. In the end, while he was grateful to the president for it, he informed his wife that he really preferred staying at home to going to Russia.[3]

In summer with John Quincy back in Massachusetts, the subject of Russia returned. In June, President Madison renewed his request that Congress authorize a Russian mission, with John Quincy in charge. This time he got it. When the news reached John Quincy, he again immediately said yes.

Why John Quincy Adams? While rumors of political payoff were heard, no evidence exists to indicate any direct reward for his having voted in the Senate for Republican measures. John Quincy certainly did not lobby for the job. The president was aware of his qualifications; no other American was better qualified. On two previous occasions, he had served ably as the country's representative in European capitals. Moreover, his fluent French, the language of European diplomacy as well as the Russian court, would ease his way into this new posting. Yet Madison had firsthand knowledge of John Quincy's support as a senator for Jefferson's and his commercial diplomacy. All in all, John Quincy was a logical choice.

Still, John Quincy was at pains to explain why he agreed to take this situation in a far-off land—to his diary and himself as well as to others. He emphasized that he really did not desire the post. Family, particularly the youth of his children and the age of his parents, gave him reason for remaining in the United States. He asserted, too, that he would break his academic connection with Harvard most reluctantly. He also claimed that he could benefit public service more as a private citizen than as a diplomat in a foreign land. According to him, all personal interests tugged him to decline the offered undertaking.[4]

Yet the tug did not hold him. He cited numerous motives for his decision. But ambition was not one of them. Foremost among them, he avowed, was the call to serve the country coming directly from the president. He made clear to a friend that what he viewed as "the spontaneous and unsolicited" act of Madison powerfully influenced him. In his judgment he had been chosen solely because of merit. In his acceptance letter to the secretary of state, he underscored his conviction that the president's chief goal was the well-being of the country. To that end he expressed a great wish to give all the assistance he could. He yearned for nothing more. His country required his service—selfless duty for the good servant. He had to accept the call. In doing so, he beseeched Almighty God for favor. He prayed for his country's safety in a perilous world and for himself "the continued consciousness of purity in my motives, and, so far as it has been or may be deserved, the approbation of my countrymen."[5]

John Quincy's family did not welcome his prompt acceptance of the Russian post. As on the earlier occasion in Washington, he decided unilaterally, without consulting his wife or parents. Neither his mother nor his father thought he made the right decision; he was exiling himself. More importantly, his choice stunned Louisa Catherine, who believed her husband had deceived her.[6]

She had to cope with even more appalling news, however. Fearing for their schooling in Russia and worried about playmates and weather, John Quincy, again on his own, decided that the two older boys, George and John, ages eight and six, would not accompany their mother and father. Instead, they would remain behind in Massachusetts, boarding in Quincy with John Quincy's aunt and uncle Richard and Mary Cranch, with his parents responsible for their general supervision. Even though this plan meant that Louisa Adams would be separated from her sons for three or more years, she had no voice in her husband's decision. Of course, in that time husbands usually had total control of such decisions. Realizing how wrenching his judgment would be for his wife, John Quincy deputed his brother Thomas to inform her. "Oh this agony of agonies!" she wailed. She would have only two-year-old Charles Francis with her. A powerful melancholy enveloped her: "And from that hour to the end of time life will be to me a suscesion [sic] of miseries only to cease with existence."[7]

Upon notifying the secretary of state that he would go to Russia, John Quincy moved quickly. On August 5 the ship with him and his party aboard sailed from Boston. In addition to Louisa and Charles Francis, his entourage included a nephew employed as a private secretary and Louisa's younger sister, Catherine, known as Kitty, as a companion for his wife. As in all other matters involving this undertaking, Louisa had no say in inviting her sibling. It was solely John Quincy's doing. There were also two servants, one each for husband and wife as well as two additional young men as unpaid, unofficial secretaries.

The passage all the way across the Atlantic and through the Baltic Sea to Russia took eighty days. Changeable weather marked by violent storms in the Baltic and interference from British warships and Danish privateers characterized the difficult voyage. Finally, in late October, John Quincy with his group set foot in St. Petersburg, the Russian capital. Twenty-seven years had passed since as a boy of fifteen he had left the city.

Promptly upon his arrival John Quincy presented himself to the host government in the person of Count Nikolai Rumiantsev, chancellor and foreign minister and principal adviser to His Majesty Tsar Alexander I. A week later the tsar received the American envoy at the Imperial Palace. Adams's instructions were general rather than specific—to create goodwill, to watch over the interests of the United States, to gain favorable treatment for American trade. He was also to report back to the secretary of state and the president his observations on Russia and European affairs. Although his charge did not specify negotiating a commercial treaty, he was told that if the possibility arose, he was to request guidance from Washington.

From the outset John Quincy met with a favorable reception. To his father he commented on the marvelous welcome with which he had been received. He established an excellent relationship with Count Rumiantsev, the official with whom he would work most closely. He was also a success at the imperial court, where his fluent French served him well. Though a student of languages, he never mastered Russian. He even developed a personal relationship with Tsar Alexander himself. Because both men often exercised by walking in the city, they frequently encountered each other, which led to private conversations.[8]

Russia, of course, was part of Europe and occupied an influential position in the strife convulsing the Continent. Although war between France and various European powers had engulfed the Continent since the 1790s, the advent of Napoleon increased the intensity and scope of the conflict. A military genius with boundless political ambition, Napoleon had become the leader of France in 1799 and five years later declared himself emperor. By 1810 the French dominated most of Europe, from the Baltic Sea to the Mediterranean Sea and from the Atlantic coast to the Russian frontier, except for the Balkan Peninsula.

In many ways Russia served as the pivot, first an ally then a foe of Napoleon, whose ambition and military prowess made him master of most of Europe. Through it all John Quincy always proclaimed American neutrality, his country's policy of not taking sides with either the French or their opponents. As he had since the 1790s, he wholeheartedly embraced America's neutral position in the European wars.

In the summer of 1812 Napoleon invaded Russia, making that country the epicenter of the fight against the French conqueror. Attention was riveted on the person of Napoleon; even John Quincy was not immune. It appeared that all Europe thought the future of mankind depended solely upon the French emperor, he noted in his diary, and as a result many hoped for his death. Napoleon did not fall on a Russian battlefield, but the massive defeat inflicted upon his grand army by Russian defensive strategy and an early, brutal winter sent him reeling back toward France with but the shell of his forces about him. The disaster in Russia left him unable to restore himself and his cause to primacy. He ultimately confronted a coalition of all the major European powers, with Russia a leader. Forced to capitulate in the spring of 1814, he abdicated his throne, retreating to an island domain in the Mediterranean Sea granted him by the victors.[9]

John Quincy interpreted the fallen emperor's career as history informed by theology. As Napoleon fled from Russia, John Quincy wrote his mother, "It has pleased heaven for many years to preserve this man and to make him prosper as an instrument of divine wrath to scourge mankind." But with the Russian debacle "his race is now run, and his own turn of punishment has commenced." To his diary he later confided, "I believe the man is abandoned of God, and that Heaven is breaking one of the instruments of its wrath." Yet, with his doubts about the human condition still vibrant, John Quincy prayed that worse horrors would not replace the fallen emperor.[10]

Official business, even adding the whirlwind of Napoleon, did not take up the bulk of John Quincy's time. The social life surrounding the imperial court and the diplomatic corps made serious demands upon him. During the season Minister Adams recorded in his diary an array of almost unending balls, card games, dinners, and receptions. In each venue his French made him a congenial guest. With so many diversions offered at these soirees, John Quincy often had to choose among them. He admitted that at some parties he had to dance in order to avoid card games of chance, though he occasionally found himself at card tables. He always paid close attention to the guidelines governing court etiquette, which required gentlemen to wear wigs. At a celebration of the tsar's birthday Alexander noticed that John Quincy was without his. John Quincy replied that he had seen the tsar without one and accordingly followed His Majesty's example. Alexander replied that he liked the comfort.[11]

In his diary John Quincy recorded sights that amazed and occasionally amused him. The pervasive opulence of rooms, decorations, attire, and jewelry exceeded anything he had ever known. The quantity of medals adorning diplomats, members of the nobility, and military officers astounded him. He observed of a princess that she was "venerable by the length and thickness of her beard," which he reflected was "no uncommon thing among ladies of this Slavonian breed." In the Academy of Science he had

seen a portrait of a deceased woman with a beard matching Pla-
to's. At an evening occasion with numerous titled people and their
secretaries, his thoughts turned to the Old Testament. The diners
reminded him "of the resurrection of dry bones in the Prophet
Ezekiel."[12]

The late hours of the events along with the available refresh-
ments often gave rise to aftereffects that John Quincy decried.
Many diary entries list functions lasting past midnight, at times
until four or five. To cope with such marathons, he resolved to
observe temperance, which he made an extraordinary effort
to keep up. That commitment did not always hold, however. As
his diary makes clear, those late nights always meant not rising
until late morning and then slow days. Such festivities, he noted,
always left a day of dissipation, with more of idleness following.
Bemoaning a lengthy series of invitations, he confessed they had
kept him from spending time where his best judgment said he
should. No matter these lamentations, John Quincy never faltered
in his social duties.[13]

His wife proved to be a superb sociable partner. Her French
helped her immensely as did the fact that almost all other diplomats in St. Petersburg were without wives. Much more important,
the imperial family warmed to her, particularly the tsar and his
mother. He even danced with her and with her sister Kitty, whom
he found quite charming. To them both the tsar issued an invitation to his private theater at his palace the Hermitage, an unusual
privilege for any foreign woman. Louisa termed it "one of the
greatest honors" bestowed on foreign ladies. She attributed the
tsar's generosity to his delight in Kitty as well as to his partiality
to her husband. Despite her triumph in society, Louisa grumbled
that the family finances precluded her always being able to dress
as she thought she should, in her opinion a severe disadvantage.
Still, she more than held her own on these lavish occasions. And
she certainly aided John Quincy's standing with Alexander I.[14]

Despite their undoubted social achievement, the Adamses'
life in St. Petersburg did not begin altogether smoothly. As in

Berlin, they initially experienced difficulty in finding a suitable abode. Eventually, however, they located comfortable living quarters. At the outset their most critical problem concerned money. John Quincy quickly learned that his official allowance fell far short of covering the cost of living in St. Petersburg, especially given the seemingly requisite ostentatious display of wealth by Russia's aristocrats and ambassadors from European nations and courts. Although he never attempted to emulate the wealth of either natives or diplomats—utterly unrepublican in his view—he feared that even so he would have to call on and deplete his personal assets just to get by. His resulting anxiety he shared with his mother, telling her that his limited resources caused discomfort and made him desperate to escape his irritating situation. Yet, by curtailing costs and with careful accounting, by the end of 1810, he had managed to bring his expenses in line with the funds provided by his government.[15]

While he did reconcile income and outgo, he never got used to the weather. The winters were unlike anything he or Louisa had ever known—interminably long, ferociously cold, with just a few hours of daylight even in fair conditions. Taking note of the short span the sun shone, John Quincy commented that he could only see to write from ten until two. The brutal cold did not deter him from his walks, however, for after writing he usually took to the streets. One winter he recounted seventeen successive days when the temperature never rose to zero. In a letter to his mother, he said that even stoves and double windows could not keep the cold from penetrating into their living space, remarking that when he wrote he could barely hold his pen. "It is certainly contrary to the course of nature for men of the south to invade regions of the north," he concluded. His final judgment: he and Louisa were thoroughly disgusted with the climate.[16]

The climate never kept John Quincy from two of his treasured indoor pastimes, his diary and his reading. His determination had him entering in his diary the events of a given day on the following day. That effort could take hours, especially after an interview with Count Rumiantsev. The time spent with his pen caused him to wish he knew shorthand, which would have made his task much easier. But he resigned himself to the conviction that it was too late for him to learn the technique. At times, of course, he could not stick to his preferred schedule. Although interference could come from outside incidents, he admitted that when he had much to record, he was prone to postpone the work that he knew he must do. Inactivity then spawned sluggishness and an increasing backlog. As a result, he acknowledged that sometimes he did not record instances that he should have remembered.[17]

Even though diary keeping often preoccupied him, he did not neglect his reading. He generally started the day with chapters in the Bible. He also gave attention to newspapers and periodicals, stating in 1811 that for the past twenty years he had spent at least two hours daily with them. In Russia he continued his habit of ranging widely in books. His list included works of Sir Walter Scott, Lord Byron, and Thomas Malthus, books of sermons, and William Paley's *Natural Theology*. Toward the end of 1813 he confided to his diary that the time spent reading enjoyable books took him away from other, more essential tasks. "The rule of not too much is essential to all things," he reminded himself, "but I have not learned to observe it."[18]

In his Russian years he substantially increased the volumes on science. They became part of his embrace of what he saw as a captivating subject. In this matter, as in others, John Quincy was quite unusual for his generation. He said he pursued such studies not only because he so enjoyed them but also because he wanted to help with his children's education. In one exercise he calculated the circumference of the earth, specifying his calculations in his diary. Astronomy especially enthralled him. He conversed with a professor at the Imperial Academy of Sciences about Johannes Kepler, the great German astronomer. He also made his own astronomical measurements and observations. He noticed the precise times of the rising and setting sun and keenly observed the entire sky, detailing what he saw in his diary.[19]

In addition, he focused on what was close by on the ground, exhibiting his usual interest in his host country. The fairs and festivals in St. Petersburg appealed to him as avenues to study and understand popular customs. To learn about the Russian version of Christianity, on religious holidays he attended Russian Orthodox churches. Although he judged the message of Orthodoxy to be as Christian as his own Congregationalism, he did not take to the numerous festivals and elaborate ceremony and ritual. To him they seemed more appropriate for slaves than for free people.[20]

Not only culture and folkways attracted his attention. As in Prussia, he found manufacturing establishments fascinating. Visiting both a textile factory and a glassworks, he commented that he wanted to spend several hours in a manufacturing establishment every week. If nothing else, doing so would give him a powerful lesson in humility by making him conscious of his ignorance. He did not, however, duplicate one Prussian venture; he never undertook anything like his Silesian travels. Instead, throughout his almost five years in Russia, he never journeyed beyond St. Petersburg and its environs.[21]

Even with his many activities, John Quincy's attention regularly returned to the sons he had left behind in Massachusetts. Less than a year after his separation from them, he expressed the sentiment that he never forgot his dear boys. And nothing about those boys concerned him more than their education. In his view a parent had no more sacred mission than guiding children in a manner that would prepare them for living worthy lives in the world. At the same time, however, he acknowledged soon after the birth of his eldest, George, that he could not mold a child as a potter did a piece of clay. Even so, for him it was of paramount importance to provide a moral foundation for his sons, which would begin with their proper education.[22]

His general instruction commenced with a memorandum he prepared while sailing across the Atlantic to Russia. This missive looked to his determination to prepare George and John for the world of adulthood. That young boys, ages eight and six, could comprehend the contents of this document is more than problematical, but John Quincy obviously felt compelled to spell out the principles essential for them to follow the path he believed would lead to fulfillment and accomplishment. In this task he emulated what his mother and father had done for him. In fact, these ruminations repeated precepts that had long since become dogma for him. No doubt, he envisioned himself as the potter who, despite his explicit reservations, could successfully mold his sons.

He began by declaring that each boy should "consider [himself] as placed here to act a part—that is, to have some single great end of object to accomplish, towards which all the views and all the labors of your existence should steadily be directed." That guideline he emphasized "as one of the directing impulses of life, that you must have some one great purpose of existence." When selected, that object "should be as much as possible within your own control."

With that admonition, he warned that it would be dangerous to combine that chief end with political office. Placing the primary goal as gaining such a station could bring little happiness to oneself and none to others. Moreover, one's time in office might end abruptly, even involuntarily. Thus one must always be prepared for a return to private life.

Yet he charged that a patriot must be ready to heed his country's call. When it comes, it must surely modify what a man decides to make most important in his life. While an officeholder had to discharge faithfully his duties, he also had to ponder how to become of more benefit to his country. The father wrote that public office "may be wanted but can never be desired."

Beyond office, he instructed, cultivating the arts and sciences is always fulfilling. Even more important, it is a most honorable path for a man with leisure to follow. He cautioned, however, about a lurking temptation, the peril of wandering without direction. The real and only difficulty to be overcome is focusing on a particular and special object. His summation: "Let the uniform principle of your life . . . be how to make your talents and your knowledge most beneficial to your country and most *useful to mankind.*"[23]

John Quincy did not restrict his ardor about his sons' education solely to general principle. Writing to his brother Thomas in Quincy, he discussed specific topics. Of course, he addressed academics. For classical studies, the languages included, he would rely on regular schools. He counted on Thomas to make sure they had instruction in French, public speaking, and writing. He also hoped they would have lessons in drawing and fencing, both of which he deemed valuable. In addition, he wanted his brother to teach his nephews to use and care for firearms because accidents usually occurred from ignorance about weapons. Finally, he advocated relaxing and sporting activities as became their age, naming ice skating and horseback riding.[24]

While what happened with his two boys in distant Massachusetts clearly had his attention, he had his youngest, Charles Francis, in St. Petersburg with him. The father took direct charge of the lad's schooling, though the child was just two when the family arrived in Russia. With the youngster at four, John Quincy recorded that only by using apples and sugarplums could he entice Charles Francis to read. Even at that age, however, the lad was learning to speak French and German. The father identified his young scholar's greatest problem as focusing his attention, for almost anything from the sight of a boat or a fly flitting about would draw him from his book.

By the time Charles Francis had reached six, the father-schoolmaster had him reading chapters in the English New Testament. He was also drilling the boy in arithmetic. It bothered him that the child had difficulty with the principles of addition, but he was equally pleased that his pupil had learned the multiplication tables by heart and had taken up the same task in French. Moreover, a tutor provided lessons in writing and Russian. The dedicated parental pedagogue did recognize the tender age of his charge, however. He tried his best, he wrote, not to press too hard upon the young mind; he made his lessons easy.[25]

Although John Quincy's engagement in his sons' education seemingly consumed him, his wife was never out of his mind. Far from elated about the Russian posting and despondent about departing from her two older boys, Louisa rallied to become stalwart in St. Petersburg. Her social triumph certainly did not hamper John Quincy's success at court, which aided his overall mission. Still, she contended with her own struggles. She never embraced the climate, and ill health plagued her. As before, difficulties with pregnancy contributed significantly to her physical problems, including fevers and headaches. The regularly prescribed bleeding with leeches did not add to her well-being. In the spring of 1810 she once more miscarried. By the beginning of 1811 she was again pregnant, however.

In the summer of 1811 John Quincy reflected on his marriage. On his fourteenth wedding anniversary he thanked God for the happiness stemming from his union with Louisa, which he described as more than he deserved. He felt that way despite the difficulties and disagreements confronting them. In his catalog he listed the education of children, temper, and money. Yet the greatest tribulation concerned his wife's delicate constitution, and the maladies resulting from that condition. At the same time he praised her for her faithfulness and affection. And he complimented her as a loving mother. His final judgment: "My lot in marriage has been highly favored."[26]

Both husband and wife experienced true joy in that same summer of 1811 when on August 12 Louisa gave birth to a healthy girl, a relief after her customary troublesome pregnancy preceding delivery. The father named the infant Louisa Catherine in honor of her mother. In less than a month he had her baptized by an Anglican minister in the absence of any Congregational clergy or churches, asserting that of those available the Anglican service came closest to the Congregational of his tradition. He did not want to delay the rite that he cherished, dedicating his daughter to God. The mother rejoiced in her newborn: "O she grows lovely. Such a pair of eyes! I fear I love her too well."[27]

In just over a year that delight descended into overpowering grief. Shortly after her first birthday the small girl, heretofore healthy, contracted dysentery followed by high fever and convulsions. Nothing could relieve her; in the early morning of September 12 she died. Her death devastated both parents. A distraught mother could not attend the funeral. A month later, still overcome with sadness, she begged God's mercy to give her strength to cope with the horror He had visited upon her. She was convinced she was being punished for her own transgressions. If she died, she wanted to be buried beside her adored child. In the next year, contemplating a return to the United States, she unbosomed to her diary, "My heart is torn at the idea of quitting forever the spot where my darling lays and to which my soul is linked."[28]

Still worried about his wife's emotional and mental stability eighteen months after the baby's death, John Quincy pressed upon her a book by one of America's most eminent physicians, Dr. Benjamin Rush of Philadelphia—*Medical Inquiries and Observations, upon the Diseases of the Mind* (1812). After reading it, she declared, "It produced a very powerful effect upon my feelings . . . and occasion'd sensations of a very painful kind since the loss of my darling babe." Since that awful event, she admitted she was aware of a great change in her, even to her questioning her sanity. Even though Dr. Rush's volume had a notable influence, it did not lift the gloom that had enveloped her. She struggled in vain against her deep anguish, fearing she would never be rid of it. Nearly thirty years later she could still cry out, "My child is gone to Heaven."[29]

Opening his heart to his own diary, John Quincy shared with her the sorrowful visit of heaven upon his family. While he mourned losing his precious gift from God, he tried to reconcile his sorrow with his Christian faith: "Yet in this fallen Condition of man so much of unavoidable bitterness is mingled up in the cup of human being on Earth that we ought perhaps to be no less grateful for the Death of a tenderly beloved Child than for its life." To be sure, he could not wall off all doubt. To his mother he wrote that for the first time in his life he contemplated distrusting God's goodness. Like his wife, he worried that perhaps he and she were being chastised for some terrible sin. Hope still broke through, however: "If there be a moral Government of the Universe, my child is in the enjoyment of blessedness, or exists without suffering, and reserved for unalloyed bliss hereafter."[30]

The Christian religion and thinking about it had always been central in John Quincy's adult life. Yet in Russia, and even before his baby daughter's death, he devoted considerable energy and effort to trying to understand what he believed. In both his diary and several letters to his son George, which like his epistle on education to his Massachusetts-bound sons he wrote fundamentally about himself for himself, John Quincy pondered the depths of his faith.

His commitment to daily Bible reading underscored the importance of religion in his life. In order not to permit his busy schedule to interrupt that practice, most often he read his Bible during the first hour after waking. His goal, which he usually met, was to get through the entire book in twelve months, and then begin again in the new year.

He admitted that he found much of the Bible difficult to understand. To assist him he regularly turned to commentaries by biblical authorities. Moreover, he read it in different languages. He could utilize the Greek New Testament, but he lamented his ignorance of Hebrew, which could have helped him with the Old. He also turned to French and German translations for comparison with the English. In his diary he noted that many passages murky and even impossible for him to understand in his native language became clearer in French and German. In his judgment German had the least cloudiness.[31]

As a man deeply imbued with the Calvinist tradition of New England and simultaneously infused with the rationality of the Enlightenment, John Quincy struggled at the intersection between faith and reason. He wrestled with distinguishing the portions of the Bible that should be taken literally from those to be understood as symbolic. After discussing chronology in the Old Testament and the genealogy of Christ in the New, he commented, "I believe it best not to attempt consulting the Bible and Herodotus together." He rejected the proposition that authority, whether clerical, institutional, or traditional, not reason, must rule the human response to religion in general and to the Bible in particular. Still, he never accepted that reason alone could or should suffice to govern man's approach to scripture or his relationship with God.[32]

John Quincy did not doubt that the Bible represented "a Divine Revelation." According to him the basis of morality rested on three truths elucidated in it: God's existence, the soul's immortality, and an afterlife with punishments and rewards. The fundamental moral truth taught by the Bible instilled the chief human virtue, obeying God's will.[33]

As a practicing Christian, John Quincy pondered his reason-faith question when considering the person of Jesus Christ and the events surrounding his life. Refusing to embrace the dogma that much should be received as religious mysteries existing beyond rational thought, he listed several verities of the Christian faith, including the divinity of Christ, the Trinity, the doctrine of atonement, and miracles. In his mind all seemed opposed to human reason. In his ruminations about religion he seemed more of a philosopher than a political man. No other political figure of his generation spent so much time and effort trying to comprehend and explicate the bases and even the mysteries of Christianity. But for John Quincy the strenuous undertaking to understand matched the commitment he felt.[34]

Religion he defined as "one of the *wants* of human nature—an appetite which must be indulged, since without its gratification human existence would be a burden rather than a blessing." Reason should thus "serve as a guard and check upon the religious appetite." Reason could not triumph, however. He would not refuse to accept a particular doctrine just because it appeared unreasonable. He asserted, "I must appeal to a higher tribunal, and believe what I want to believe, am taught to believe, and may believe, without injury to myself or others."[35]

From that position he meditated upon the divinity of Christ, confiding in January 1811 to his diary that he hardly knew how to escape doubt when he contemplated it, chiefly because as a layman he had never had the opportunity to research the subject thoroughly. Yet he found especially convincing a sermon on the question by Jean-Baptiste Massillon, an eighteenth-century French bishop. Reviewing the clergyman's argument, John Quincy repeated its evidence. The scriptural declaration by Christ himself and others in the Gospels and Epistles of the New Testament made a persuasive case, which became even more powerful when contrasted with the care taken by prophets in the Old Testament and apostles in the New never to make any such claims. He summed up with the statement that he would surely return to Massillon's exposition.[36]

John Quincy wrote that the purpose of Christ's earthly life was to emphasize immortality. For him this mission was critical, for "if the existence of man was limited to this life, it would be impossible for me to believe the universe under any moral government." In his interpretation Christ replaced all temporal sanctions with a future spiritual life in which punishments and rewards would be bestowed. Preceding that immortal state, the doctrine of Christ was a moral system for mankind on this earth—in his judgment a system superior to all others. He quoted Christ's charge to his disciples that they strive for perfection. "Be ye therefore perfect, even as your father in heaven is perfect."[37]

In a letter intended for his son George, John Quincy summarized his sense of Christian morality: "piety to God and benevolence to man." Formal rites and burnt-offering sacrifices were not required. In their stead he listed the Christian virtues, which included repentance, obedience, humility, and worship of God from the heart. He emphasized Christ's new commands to humans to love each person, even enemies. Yet this creed did not mean for his son, or for himself, to be too yielding, to allow himself ever to be led astray from what his conscience told him was good and right.[38]

Though some four thousand miles from St. Petersburg, Abigail Adams did not relinquish her active role in her son's life. She certainly did more than merely correspond with him. Without John Quincy's permission she placed in Boston newspapers parts of his letters explaining his effort to obtain favorable treatment for American commerce from the Russian government. These pieces were widely reprinted. Not pleased when he learned what his mother had done, he asked her to get his prior agreement before she made public any additional information from his correspondence.[39]

She went beyond attempting to boost him in the public eye, however. Upon getting word early in John Quincy's residence in St. Petersburg about his worry about his finances, she took forthright action. Again without consulting her son, in August 1810 she wrote directly to President James Madison asking that he allow John Quincy to come back home because of the financial ruin that faced him and his family.[40]

President Madison took her request quite seriously. He brought up the matter with his secretary of state, who advised that no action be taken until they had heard from John Quincy himself. Madison felt that justice would necessitate permitting a return if that is what it took for his diplomat to avoid financial disaster. At the same time he hoped the depth of the mother's anxiety did not represent her son's.[41]

Having made that determination, the president in October sent to John Quincy a private letter stating that his worthy mother had informed him about a precarious financial condition. As a result, John Quincy would receive an official document authorizing his leave and providing for the handling of the government's business until the appointment of a successor. Yet, because he had not received any comparable news of application from John Quincy, the president wished that the emergency specified by Abigail was not his but hers. He went on to tell John Quincy that he desired

him to continue his able service unless confronting an unreasonable sacrifice. Concluding, Madison said he relied upon John
Quincy's patriotism to make the correct decision.[42]

Replying, after the five months it took for the president's communication to arrive in St. Petersburg, John Quincy thanked
Madison for his kind confidential letter. He did not dodge the role
of his mother, who during his life had been his "guardian Angel"
as well as a parent. Alarmed at the news of his financial anxiety, she acted, he assured the president, from the best of motives,
obviously believing that tactfulness had kept her son from peti-
tioning for a recall.

John Quincy then turned to Madison's open-ended permission
to leave Russia. He let the president know that he had informed
Count Rumiantsev of it, but he did not anticipate an early departure. He found his financial burden much less onerous than he
had initially feared. Moreover, the winter season and family
concerns—Louisa's condition, which he did not specify—made
such a move implausible anytime soon. He could easily wait for
more detailed guidance and would assuredly act upon the government's direction. Finally, he declared that he concurred with
the president's reasoning for his staying on for the time being. He
would stand by his duty.[43]

At about the same time John Quincy penned his letter to Madison, the chief executive acted to offer him a new and significant
position as well as a superb reason for leaving Russia. He nominated John Quincy to fill a vacancy on the Supreme Court; on the
day after receiving the nomination the Senate voted unanimously
to confirm him as an associate justice. The president chose John
Quincy because New England was due a seat on the high court, and
from all angles John Quincy appeared to be an excellent choice.[44]

News of his February appointment reached St. Petersburg in
June 1811. A flattered John Quincy wrote the president that he
deeply appreciated the appointment. He also informed his father
that the Senate's unanimous support for him gratified him more
than anything else ever had. His father was supremely pleased,

as was his mother. Both considered the court a worthy place for their son, and because of it the son would come home.[45]

John Quincy nonetheless declined the honor. His response to President Madison gave two reasons. The first, his family situation; Louisa's pregnancy, again unspecified, made immediate travel impossible. And the early onset of the Russian winter meant another year would go by before he could get to America. That delay being unavoidable, he certainly could not expect the president to keep such a vital office vacant for that long. He also informed Madison that he had never found the legal world gratifying. Moreover, because most of his career had kept him away from courts of law, he seriously doubted his fitness for the bench.[46]

Even before he learned about the Supreme Court, he had been quite frank to his brother Thomas about himself and the law and the judiciary. "As for the law, the little metal I ever had of it has gathered such an inveterate rust, that it will never take an edge of polish again," he revealed. He also stipulated that he was too much a political partisan to become a judge. He hurried to add, however, that even though he knew how to adopt a nonpartisan stance, he would not care to place himself where he would have to do that as regularly as his perception of his duty would require.[47]

Aware of his parents' wish that he accept Madison's offer, John Quincy took great pains to assure his father that throughout his life he had given foremost consideration to how any of his actions would reflect upon his parents. No office or award from anyone, he avowed, could offset any pain he would give them from any voluntary choice he made. He closed by stating he had every confidence that after weighing all his father would approve his decision not to become a member of the Supreme Court.[48]

Although family and personal matters required John Quincy's attention, he never neglected his diplomatic assignment. That he got along famously with both Count Rumiantsev and Tsar Alexander, and gained their respect, surely aided his professional task. From the outset he worked successfully for his country. Within weeks after his arrival he persuaded the tsar to use his influence with Denmark to secure the release of captured American ships held in Danish ports. He then prevailed upon Alexander to permit American vessels and cargoes detained in Russian waters to leave. John Quincy succeeded chiefly because the tsar was moving away from his close ties to Napoleon. He had been adhering to the French emperor's Continental System, which banned from the Continent all goods from the British Empire and subjected neutral shipping suspected of carrying such cargo to capture and detention. In 1810, however, he formally announced Russia's separation from Napoleon and his policies. Yet John Quincy's own diplomatic talent undoubtedly contributed to his achieving a positive outcome for the United States.[49]

With Alexander's rejecting the Continental System, the prospect opened for a formal commercial agreement between Russia and the United States. In January 1811 John Quincy reported to President Madison not only that the Russians desired a regular and permanent diplomatic relationship but also that he had been repeatedly led to believe they wanted a commercial treaty with the United States. He received instructions to proceed with negotiating such a treaty. Additionally, his guidelines directed him to include in it an agreement on trade along the northwest Pacific coast of North America where Russia had set up trading posts. Serious negotiations never got underway, however. Russia and France seemed headed toward war, which would place Russia in England's camp. Simultaneously, increasing tensions between England and the United States made very uncertain the continuance of peace between them.[50]

On the issue of hostilities among European powers, as always John Quincy insisted that the United States would not become involved. As he informed Count Rumiantsev, the cornerstone of American policy was to refrain from taking sides in any European clashes. Still, in the midst of confrontation among the European powers, his goal and that of his country was to keep open the seas for commerce carried in vessels of neutral countries like his own. The neutrals should have the right to trade unmolested by the antagonists. Although he did not deviate from his insistence on neutral rights, he became more and more troubled about the direction of America's relations with England.[51]

From his time in the U.S. Senate, John Quincy had worried that his country could not escape war with England. He dreaded the potential contest, fearing that the United States had little chance of gaining anything and could very well lose that which was most precious, its independence. Although he kept hoping that conflict could be avoided, by the spring of 1812 he concluded that eventual armed struggle could not be averted. In his judgment America had to counter England's conscious insults to its rights, particularly impressment and the interdiction of American vessels by the British navy. Never doubting the legitimacy of the American cause, he proclaimed to his brother, after the fighting had commenced, that if ever Almighty God saw a valid cause for war, it would be the American position in this instance. He summarized that Britain pushed oppression while the American side stood for *"personal liberty."*[52]

Nothing so disturbed him as the possibility that war with England would exacerbate the partisan strife that had ended his Senate career and made him a pariah among Federalists in New England. According to him, in the turmoil of war the stubborn pro-English among the New England Federalists might cause the dismemberment of America. That outcome would create in place of a single American nation "an endless multitude of little insignificant clans and tribes at eternal war with one another for a rock or a fish pond, the sport and fable of European masters and oppressors." He had a sharply different desire and vision: "The whole continent of North America . . . destined by Divine Providence to be peopled by one nation." For the success of the United States, the federal Union had to be maintained.[53]

Shortly after war had been declared by the United States in the summer of 1812, and even before John Quincy had received official notification of the declaration, Count Rumiantsev informed John Quincy that Tsar Alexander offered to serve as a mediator. Now an ally of England against Napoleon as well as a friend and trading partner of the United States, the tsar wanted to halt hostilities between the two combatants, if possible. John Quincy replied that although he had no guidance on that subject he was confident his government would gladly accept Alexander's tender. And in the summer of 1813 word reached St. Petersburg that the Madison administration had indeed responded positively. England's agreement appeared uncertain, however.

With the military contest going quite badly for their side, President Madison and his new secretary of state, James Monroe, had not hesitated to embrace the initiative coming from Russia. Madison appointed Secretary of the Treasury Albert Gallatin, Swiss born and French speaking, along with Senator James Bayard, Federalist from Delaware, to act as commissioners with John Quincy in the hope for forthcoming discussions with England mediated by Tsar Alexander. Gallatin and Bayard promptly departed for Europe. Arriving in England, they learned that the English government had little interest in any Russian-brokered mediation. Even so, they journeyed on to St. Petersburg, which they reached in late July. There the three commissioners awaited developments. And for six months they waited without any official information about what was or was not going to happen. Tired of sitting with nothing to do, Gallatin and Bayard departed in January 1814.

Finally, news came from London that England would be willing to engage in direct talks with the United States at Göteborg, Sweden. Receiving instructions to proceed to the Swedish city, John Quincy in April bade farewell to Louisa and his son Charles Francis and headed west.

During his years in St. Petersburg, John Quincy maintained his usual regime of rigorous self-examination. Never did he relax these musings. None of his political contemporaries equaled him in this effort. This investigation of himself formed part of his philosophical bent, which also underlay his penetrating analysis of his religion. This determination to understand and articulate himself contributed massively to his uniqueness among his peers. He believed that in Russia he had ably performed his official duties. In addition, he told himself he could not indict himself for any intentional wrong in his personal life. Even so, as always, he mourned his idleness. He chastised himself for not using his leisure more profitably because he had not focused on any subject. Comparing himself with possible competing contemporaries, he noted the gravest error rested in his overrating himself, a temptation he must guard against.[54]

Yet measuring himself against the ideal would lead to an estimation that would rightly lead to humility. He had, however, to avoid underrating himself because that would be beneath his dignity. He had to shun the excessive humility that could result in surrender to the wants of others. Admitting that throughout his life he had found this difficult, he closed his analysis of this continuing quandary with the conclusion that he must rely on Almighty God.[55]

He expressed great concern about the anxiety that gripped him, observing that it too often burdened him. The effort to hold to "the perfect line between self-denial and self-indulgence" consumed him. It led him to conclude that temperance, which to him meant self-denial, even in excess was superior to the opposite.[56]

The attempt to identify, achieve, and maintain this emotional balance created immense struggle for John Quincy. It was made vastly more difficult because of his ambition to reach the pinnacle both he and his parents had set for him, whatever and wherever that might be. Its identity and location were so unclear because neither he nor they had ever been specific about it. In 1812, on his forty-fifth birthday, he confided to his diary that after two-thirds of his life had gone by he had done nothing notable for his country or for humanity. Again, this self-deprecation set him apart. Because he believed that he had fallen short of self-set goals, he would only strive harder to find that sense of success so elusive for him. He hoped that he had lived with a commitment to his duties to society and a determination to fulfill them.

His shortcomings, however, had at times caused him to deviate from the path of right. He cataloged them as "passions, indolence, weakness, and infirmity." He thanked his Maker for all the blessings He had showered upon him and entreated Him for future kindnesses. Still, he declared, it was past time for making useless resolutions.[57]

A month after his departure from St. Petersburg, his trip delayed on land and sea by the palpable remnants of winter, John Quincy arrived in Stockholm. Following a short stay he continued westward to Göteborg. Even before leaving Stockholm, he learned that the negotiations would not take place in Sweden. In Göteborg he received word that the site had been moved to Ghent, in present-day Belgium. With that news John Quincy turned south. Traveling through the Netherlands stirred memories; in his diary he recorded that it appeared that he had returned home. Approaching The Hague, he admitted he felt pulsing sensations. That city he remembered as the location where he had grown from youth into manhood, leaving an unforgettable imprint on his mind. Finally, on June 24, he entered Ghent.[58]

Within a short time all of his fellow commissioners had reported to the small city. President Madison had appointed five commissioners, adding two to the original three he had designated following Tsar Alexander's offer of mediation. The individuals composing the group made for an unusually strong contingent. The president could not have put together an abler and more inclusive group. Named to preside was John Quincy, the most experienced active American diplomat, well versed in European diplomacy and politics.

Joining him were the two holdovers, Albert Gallatin and James Bayard, both of whom had spent time with John Quincy a year earlier in St. Petersburg. There Gallatin had impressed John Quincy. The senior among the five, Gallatin was even more well-known in Europe than John Quincy and had a larger reputation. After immigrating to the United States from his native Switzerland and finally settling in Pennsylvania, he rose rapidly in the

Republican party until he became Jefferson's and then Madison's secretary of the treasury. His foreign birth meant, however, that the presidency was beyond his reach. He vacated his cabinet office for this foreign duty. He brought not only recognition in Europe, along with knowledge of European culture and manners, but also an urbane outlook and a moderating temperament heightened by the use of humor. The third original member, the reasonable, thoughtful Bayard, a former Federalist senator from Delaware, ensured that his party had representation in Ghent, though he did not line up with the antiwar zealots dominating New England Federalism.

The two new appointees brought different strengths. Without question the more notable was Henry Clay of Kentucky, an extraordinarily talented politician, Republican leader, and ardent champion of the war, who had become Speaker of the House of Representatives and probably the most influential member of Congress. He stepped down from the speakership to accept Madison's invitation to go abroad. Ten years younger, Clay had impressed John Quincy when both sat in the Senate. He was quite a figure, John Quincy then wrote, "an orator—and a republican of the first fire." Completing the group, and its youngest and least distinguished member, Jonathan Russell of Massachusetts, though not a native of the state, had occupied diplomatic positions in both London and Paris and had just been named the first American minister to Sweden. At Ghent he attached himself to Clay, becoming practically an acolyte of the Kentuckian.[59]

For John Quincy working intimately with these four would mean a new experience. As his country's chief diplomat in the Netherlands, Prussia, and Russia, he operated mostly on his own, with basically a free hand in how he carried out instructions from the government back in the United States. He had not had to interact with colleagues of real ability and equal rank. In the Senate he had surely belonged to a larger body, but senators basically remained on their own. Although committees did exist, senators were not separated into small units charged with the sole responsibility to find a solution to a complex problem. Even so, John Quincy discovered himself essentially an outlier, finding it hard to become a congenial and cooperative member of the club. Having to associate closely with other able, strong-willed men on such a critical mission was unprecedented for him, and the assignment would test his ability to manage his strong opinions and rein in his temper so that he could contribute to harmony within the group.

John Quincy fully grasped the gravity of the task at Ghent. Failure to negotiate an honorable end to the war could result in disaster for the United States, already reeling from a dismal military performance and with government finances in a shambles. Yet, as he assured his father, he would never countenance submitting to Great Britain, nor would his colleagues or their superiors back in Washington. That all five commissioners were of one mind on this topic signaled a unified approach to the most critical issue.[60]

In John Quincy's view three of his fellows would pose no serious difficulty in maintaining unity of outlook and collegiality among them. He recognized real strength in both Bayard and Gallatin, though unsurprisingly he found neither without shortcomings. Bayard he considered capable and judicious. The worldly, talented Gallatin would make every effort to effect a cordial team endeavor. The most junior of all, Russell, who had traveled from Sweden with John Quincy, would defer to his seniors, originating no disputes.[61]

For John Quincy, Clay was the unknown quantity. From his observations in the Senate, he initially had a positive impression of the personable, tall, lanky Kentuckian. Still, the two men were both alike and different. Supreme ambition drove both. Each evinced self-confidence and self-importance as well as a volatile temper. Profound differences marked them, however. A social lion, Clay relished convivial occasions, imbibing alcohol, smoking cigars, and playing cards late into the night—a tonic for him. John Quincy barely tolerated such events and practices. A superb student of practical politics, Clay had little interest in intellectual pursuits. Regarding social and intellectual matters the two men were exact opposites. Each, however, counted himself an ardent patriot who would steadfastly guard the fundamental interests of his country.

Although the American delegation had gathered in Ghent, negotiations did not begin right away, for their British opposites had not yet arrived, and would not for another month. While locating suitable quarters and getting settled, the Americans discussed their mission among themselves. John Quincy reported that despite different backgrounds and temperaments they got along amazingly well.[62]

John Quincy's assessment of the mission rang true, but he overstated the harmony. His own predilections and conduct contributed to a gap in sociableness. The smoking and drinking, led by Clay, put him off. He noted in his diary that they suited neither his habits nor his health. As a result he separated himself and dined alone. He asserted that such socializing took too much time, especially keeping him away from his writing, which always consumed many hours. In Ghent his normal practice differentiated him even more sharply from his colleagues, for each of them had a secretary to assist in their copying and correspondence. John Quincy had none; moreover, he had his diary to maintain. Displeased by John Quincy's removing himself, the gregarious Clay expressed regret about the withdrawal. Accepting Clay's intervention as a positive overture, John Quincy decided that hereafter he would dine with the others. That he did.[63]

The three British commissioners arrived in Ghent in early August. Although they did not match the Americans in prestige in their own country, they had ability and made for a solid team. With Ghent so close to London, the British government, most importantly the foreign minister, Lord Castlereagh, wanted tight control over its men. While the deliberations in Ghent obviously mattered, for Great Britain was fighting a war with the United States, European affairs remained primary. Napoleon had been defeated; British and other allied troops occupied Paris, with the great British warrior the Duke of Wellington in command. To fashion a new order following the end of the Napoleonic Wars, the victorious powers had decided to meet in Vienna. That assembly and its outcome were much more crucial to the British than what transpired in Ghent.

Still, at Ghent the initial British strategy aimed at determining just how stalwartly the Americans would stand. The proposals the British first presented to end the fighting treated the United States as a foe already defeated. The major points were these: the United States must relinquish control of the Great Lakes, meaning American demilitarization, as well as portions of Maine; a new independent Indian state must be created between the Ohio River and the Great Lakes, a sine qua non for a treaty; maritime rights and impressment were off-limits; the special fishing privileges awarded to the United States at the end of the Revolution would not be renewed without a forthcoming equivalent. The British would consider their side triumphant if the Americans either agreed or indicated they would have to obtain further instructions from their government. The former, of course, would leave a measurably weaker and geographically hemmed-in United States; the latter would allow time for additional British military successes, which could lead to an even more draconian settlement.

The Americans were horrified by what they considered a harsh and utterly unacceptable proposal. To John Quincy the British initiative "opened to us, the alternative of a long, expensive and sanguinary War, or submission to disgraceful conditions, and sacrifices little short of Independence itself." His fellows shared his bleak outlook, except for Clay. The inveterate gambler surmised that the British might back away somewhat from their extreme position. John Quincy thought that prospect impossible. In addition, the Americans regarded the British delegates as overbearing and insulting, as superiors talking down to inferiors.[64]

Even so, the five Americans had to decide how to respond. After deliberating, they agreed they would reject the British conditions, but not request further guidance from Washington. They had already concluded that Britain would not grant concessions on impressment and maritime rights, the expressed reasons for declaring war in 1812. They simply dropped these two items. On the question of territorial integrity and an Indian state, however, they refused to bend. They would prepare a written response.

Their reply rejected totally the transfer of the Great Lakes to Great Britain and the creation of an Indian state. The former would diminish the United States and leave it vulnerable to British depredations from Canada. In John Quincy's words the latter would turn over an immense territory to "wandering hunters" who could never become "civilized" with "permanent habitations, and a state of property like our own." Harking back to his Plymouth oration of 1802, he declared it completely unacceptable "to condemn vast regions of territory to perpetual barrenness and solitude that a few hundred savages might find wild beasts to hunt upon it." He termed such a proposition "a species of game law that a nation descended from Britons would never endure," denouncing it as inconsistent with moral truth and physical reality. No treaty he and his colleagues avowed could block Americans from immigrating to and civilizing that land.[65]

Although all five commissioners stood firm on American independence, differences did exist among them. Members differed on the lengths of notes to the British and on the language in them. As the chair of the delegation, John Quincy started out drafting the American papers. His compatriots applied a heavy editing hand to his prose, however. He did not welcome this kind of rejection, but he acquiesced in it. Eventually, with John Quincy's consent, Gallatin, the peacemaker within the group, took over the drafting duties. Yet John Quincy felt it necessary for him to make drafts as if he were solely responsible.[66]

He also noticed that neither Gallatin's drafts nor anything else written by others encountered the disapproval that his did. If anyone objected to his production, he observed, all the others agreed, meaning he could not prevail. In contrast, his objections tended to be dismissed. No matter this discrepancy and slight, John Quincy accepted with good grace both Gallatin's primary authorship and the criticisms his own efforts received.[67]

Throughout the autumn of 1814 the two parties sent notes with proposals and responses back and forth. Events on the battlefields in America surely affected the talks in Ghent. In August, British troops had successfully assaulted Washington, burning the presidential mansion and the Capitol, actions John Quincy condemned as "Gothic barbarism." Even though that news, which they possessed by October 1, depressed him and his colleagues, they did not retreat on what they interpreted as American independence. Later, in September, a British advance southward from Canada had been turned back by American army and naval forces at Plattsburgh and on Lake Champlain, in northern New York State, thwarting the British effort to sever antiwar New England from the rest of the United States. In November, when intelligence of that outcome reached across the Atlantic, the British rethought their stance and the Americans took heart.[68]

During the course of the negotiations John Quincy and Clay stood out as the most forceful members of the team. Despite their shared commitment to preserve their country's independence, their perceptions of Great Britain's basic negotiating strategy differed sharply. From the outset Clay believed that the British were running a bluff, that they would pull back their most onerous demands if the Americans held firm. He never gave up that conviction. In contrast, John Quincy was convinced that the British were deadly serious, determined to insist on tough terms that would weaken and diminish the United States. Like Clay, he clung to his belief.

Clay made his point in early December by urging that his side play "*brag*" with the British. According to John Quincy, he argued that the British had been doing so since the beginning and that now the Americans should respond in kind. He asked John Quincy whether he knew how to play the game; John Quincy replied that he had forgotten. Clay then gave a tutorial: "He said the art of

it was to beat your adversary by holding your hand, with a solemn and confident phiz, and outbragging them." Part of the conversation, James Bayard agreed that Clay correctly described the
game. But he injected that you could lose by bragging once your
opponent detected your weakness. John Quincy recorded that
then Bayard spoke directly to him: "Mr. Clay is for bragging a
million against a cent." This exchange changed no one's makeup
or outlook.[69]

Not only did Clay and John Quincy read British diplomatic
strategy differently; they also clashed on two serious substantive
matters—British access to the Mississippi River and America's
ability to catch fish in Canadian (that is, British) waters and dry
them in Canadian territory, combined as the fisheries issue. In less
than a decade this contention would have repercussions for John
Quincy. According to the treaty ending the American Revolution,
both countries enjoyed freedom of navigation on the Mississippi,
and Britain granted to America the "right" of the fisheries. An
adamant Clay made clear that he would sign no treaty that permitted the British to reach the Mississippi, the great artery of the
American West. At the same time he would give on the fisheries.

John Quincy, in turn, announced that he would put his name
on no treaty that abrogated in any way the "right" of the fisheries, central to the economy of New England, especially Massachusetts. Regarding the Mississippi, he would compromise, allowing
the British limited access through a single route with customs
duties charged.

Even though deeply held beliefs led to vigorous discussions,
John Quincy reported them as occurring with good humor. Clay
claimed that John Quincy was obdurate on the fisheries only
because his father had obtained that specific "right" in the earlier
treaty. John Quincy admitted that his father's accomplishments
influenced him, but he insisted this was not central. He spoke
of two crucial matters. First, in 1783 the British had granted a
"right," not simply a privilege, and in his mind the current war
could not eliminate a "right." Second, as a Massachusetts man

and New Englander, he could not stand by and countenance the destruction of an essential segment of his state's and section's economy.[70]

On the Mississippi, he maintained that his compromise really gave Britain nothing consequential. Reminding his fellows that no water route connected Canada to the great river, he observed that any British traders would have to travel a considerable distance overland to reach it. Moreover, he would allow them to enter United States territory at just a single point and require payment of a customs duty. He foresaw no threating British traffic.

The arguments of neither man persuaded the other. Yet Clay clearly prevailed. He had support on his Mississippi position, while John Quincy had none on the fisheries. Jonathan Russell did indicate he would side with John Quincy, though not if doing so would torpedo a treaty. Confronting their standoff, the commissioners decided to press neither issue. Instead, they would see how the negotiations developed.

Even though occupied with arduous tasks, John Quincy strove to maintain his personal schedule. Following his standard practice, he detailed his routine in his diary. He usually rose between five and six, lit his fire, then wrote, including letters, until breakfast at nine, and for an hour or two afterwards. The mission met regularly at two in the afternoon, a session that normally lasted until four, though special meetings occurred when needed. At four the group dined, remaining at table for two to three hours. In the evening he engaged in a little reading or writing. He either took walks or joined his colleagues in various activities.

He had one notable complaint. He failed to maintain his habit of exercising. It was a fault he declared he had to correct, for it had led to his gaining too much weight, with the result "that industry becomes irksome for me." His final judgment came in familiar form: he urged himself not to fall into an indolent state.[71]

In the midst of strenuous debates among themselves and vexing encounters with their British opposites, the American commissioners did enjoy an active social life, in which John Quincy fully participated. A company of French actors performed several times a week. John Quincy was critical, terming them the worst French performers he had ever seen. There was also a group of English players. Concerts and galas took place twice each week. Outings to public houses occurred. The townspeople were congenial hosts; in response the Americans on one occasion hosted a tea-and-card party attended by 130 people. At this affair John Quincy rebuffed neither the dancing nor the games of whist. He admitted that even while coping with their heavy workload, he and his fellows could enjoy themselves as much as they desired.[72]

As the autumn weeks passed, the two parties sent notes back and forth. Details changed, but the British kept pushing and the Americans kept holding on. Wanting to benefit from the army's successes on the ground, the British pressed for language that would stipulate *uti possidetis*, meaning that each side would retain the territory it held at the signing of the treaty. Rejecting that approach, the Americans clung to the *status quo ante bellum*, no territory lost.

The last month of 1814 opened with little fundamental movement. Both sides seemed entrenched. The two most vocal Americans had not changed their minds about British intentions. John Quincy remained convinced that the British intended to humble the United States. Henry Clay was still persuaded that the British would back away from their most onerous demands.

Yet change, swift change, was about to occur. The combined reverses at Plattsburgh and on Lake Champlain prodded the British government to reassess its war aims and negotiating strategy. For more than two decades Britain had been battling France. The defeat of Napoleon brought enormous relief to a weary populace, who had grown tired of the mobilization and taxation essential to carry on the extended conflict. More of each would be required to continue the struggle in America. The government worried about public support. Moreover, British merchants were eager to reopen the profitable trade with America, long curtailed by policy and war.

There were additional considerations. Trying to decide whether to pursue its undertaking across the Atlantic, the British government asked the country's greatest military hero to take command in America. The Duke of Wellington replied that as a professional soldier he would go if ordered. But he told his superiors that he saw little chance for real success unless the British navy could gain superiority on the Great Lakes, a goal that would require additional resources. He added that he did not believe the British military position on the ground supported the exacting of major territorial concessions from the Americans.

Finally, meeting simultaneously with the conference at Ghent, the Congress of Vienna was deciding on the future of Europe. The major European powers once united against Napoleon now advanced their own interests. The American war complicated Britain's relations with its peers in Vienna, who had their own commercial and territorial objectives. Continuing its belligerent American policy could easily end up jeopardizing Britain's agenda on the Continent and at sea. All these influences combined led the British government to decide that the American war had to end. It would not wait for the outcome of a major thrust underway that targeted the southernmost part of the United States, the coastal area along the Gulf of Mexico, including the city of New Orleans.

Having reached that decision, the British government determined to reach a quick agreement at Ghent. It would retreat from thorny issues like territorial acquisition, accepting the American position of *status quo ante bellum*. Other difficult questions, such as navigation on the Mississippi, the fisheries, impressment, and neutral rights, would simply be omitted from the document. Postwar commissions would be set up to handle other contentious matters like the precise boundary between northern Maine and Canada.

On Christmas Eve of 1814 the negotiators signed what became known as the Treaty of Ghent. Although the American commissioners had gained nothing on the stated reasons for going to war, impressment and neutral rights, they had not wilted under British pressure. The United States emerged whole, with no

loss of territory. When the treaty reached Washington in mid-
February 1815, a delighted and relieved President Madison immediately placed it before the Senate. On the very next day that body
voted unanimously to ratify it. Of course, the treaty was signed
in Europe prior to the major American victory over the British
at the Battle of New Orleans on January 8. While that triumph
lifted American morale, it did not cause any reconsideration of
the treaty negotiated by John Quincy and his companions. The
United States desperately wanted no more war.

With good reason John Quincy and his colleagues believed
that their country had done as well as it possibly could have at
Ghent. On the night of the signing, John Quincy confided to his
diary that he thanked God for permitting the success of the negotiations. He also prayed that the peace would benefit his country.
A week later he declared that 1814 had been the most exceptional
year he had known. Writing to a friend, he acknowledged that
Ghent had not gained the stated reasons for going to war, but,
most importantly, the treaty did not disgrace the United States.[73]

In the immediate aftermath both delegations appeared
delighted with their handiwork. A festival atmosphere prevailed
in the small city. Dinners were held, with bands playing "God
Save the King" and "Hail, Columbia," and toasts given, the British to America and the Americans to Great Britain. John Quincy
even raised his glass to the king of England, still George III, and
still an infamous name to Americans. Henry Clay thoroughly
enjoyed these celebratory social occasions, though he never mentioned prayers.

John Quincy also relished a less formal celebration. The daughter of a resident with whom he had become friendly sang couplets
to honor him. In response he wrote four verses for her. To present
them, he recorded in his diary, he "went to a bookseller's shop,
purchased three small volumes of Etrenne's Géographiques, with
colored plates, packed them up with [his] song," and addressed
them to the young girl with a note to her mother requesting that
they be presented in his name.[74]

He had one other self-assigned task to tend to prior to leaving Ghent. Early in January he agreed to sit for the Flemish artist Pieter van Huffel, who had already done pencil sketches of Bayard, Clay, and Gallatin. He persuaded John Quincy to permit him to paint an oil portrait. Although the painting had not been completed when John Quincy left, he liked what he saw, remarking to his wife that the artist had indeed captured the way he looked. In van Huffel's portrait, John Quincy has the same dark eyes and eyebrows as the younger man painted by John Singleton Copley back in 1796, though he now has less hair and more jaw. This older man looks directly at the painter or the viewer, smiles quizzically, and holds a furled document, surely meant to be the treaty. He projects the self-assurance of a man of accomplishment, an emotion he certainly felt at the time.[75]

Within a month after completing their work, the American commissioners began exiting Ghent. They had decided that while awaiting news of the treaty's final ratifications, they would decamp to Paris. Upon his own departure John Quincy mused in his diary about his stay in Ghent. He noted that he had resided there for seven months and two days and that it had been "the most memorable" period of his life.[76]

He left for Paris on January 26. Although he did not know how long he would be in that city, he had two great desires. First, he did not want to go back to the perpetual Russian winter. Second, and more importantly, he anticipated a reunion with his wife and son, whom he had not seen for nine months.[77]

Toward the end of December he had written Louisa, inviting her to join him in the French capital. He informed her that he did not believe he would return to Russia and that he had asked President Madison to recall him from that post. Additionally, he alluded to the possibility that he might get assigned to London. As a result he wanted her to close down their quarters, disposing of the furniture as she saw fit. Then she and Charles Francis should set out for Paris, where he would be eagerly awaiting them.[78]

En route John Quincy made a stop in Brussels, which provided a preview of what awaited him in Paris. After the arduous months in Ghent, he eagerly embraced the opportunity to visit an extensive private art collection and library. In this place he spent hours devouring paintings by the Dutch and Flemish greats, including Holbein, Rembrandt, Rubens, and Van Dyck. Italian masters were also represented. There was a Leonardo da Vinci as well as one about which John Quincy commented that if it were his, he would not trade it for all the rest—*The Holy Family* by Guido Reni. This delightful interlude would have held no interest for John Quincy's Ghent partner Henry Clay.[79]

On February 4 he arrived in Paris and took an apartment in a house. Describing his feelings in a later letter to his mother, he rhapsodized about "the great city where all the fascinations of a luxurious metropolis had first charmed the senses of my childhood and dazzled the imagination of my youth." He remembered that then he "was at an age when the hey-day of the blood is tame, and waits upon judgement." Now he had observed much of the world and could better assess the attractions of what he called "that fairy land."[80]

Yet the temptations of that "fairy land" remained strong. He remarked in his diary that he did not seem able to resist tending toward dissipation. Even at forty-seven he was not immune. "There is a moral incapacity for industry and application, a 'mollesse' against which I am as ill-guarded as I was at twenty," he admitted.[81]

He feasted on the bounty of the city. He walked the boulevards, visited the courts and the National Museum, enjoyed the opera. His special delight the theater captured him; he attended night after night, no matter the quality of the plays or the performers. Works by Molière, the seventeenth-century French playwright, particularly engaged him. Then he visited men he had known in former times, notably the Marquis de Lafayette. He was also introduced at court to Louis XVIII, placed on the throne by the victorious powers. The king inquired whether he was related to the famous Mr. Adams.[82]

During his initial weeks in the city he awaited the arrival of his wife and his son. While John Quincy had a tranquil, even pleasurable, trip to Paris, Louisa Adams was embarked on a harrowing and hazardous overland trek of nearly three thousand miles across eastern and western Europe. And she traveled in the midst of winter, leaving St. Petersburg on February 12 with Charles Francis and three servants. Determined to make as much time as possible, she pushed on day and night through lands still reeling from months and years of warfare. Finally, after forty days on the road, she reached her husband's lodgings in Paris at eleven in the evening on March 23.[83]

John Quincy had returned from the theater just prior to her arrival. Nothing else could have so dramatized the difference in how they had spent the previous five and a half weeks. John Quincy luxuriated in the offerings of a magnificent city; Louisa Catherine heroically traversed the war-ravaged, still dangerous European continent. John Quincy's diary provides no glimpse into his emotions on rejoining his long-absent family. Nor does her journal detail hers. What does seem evident is that he exhibited little interest in her remarkable journey, though she did indicate that her odyssey amazed him.[84]

Once reunited, the couple appeared to enjoy the Parisian attractions together. Louisa Adams showed no ill effects from her dramatic adventure. They went on walks and frequented museums, with Charles Francis often along. Nighttime found John Quincy and Louisa in the theater, where they saw almost every kind of performance, from opera to pantomime. She also occasionally accompanied him on visits to acquaintances and associates, though she did not hesitate to decline invitations.[85]

John Quincy was in Paris at a tumultuous moment—the return of Napoleon. The defeated emperor refused to stay in exile on the Mediterranean island of Elba. Escaping from Elba, he landed on the southern French coast on March 1 and by the twentieth had made it to the capital. Along the way the populace hailed him, and old soldiers lined up alongside him. Even troops dispatched to capture him refused to do so, instead joining his ever-growing band. The cry "Vive l'Empereur" resounded through the countryside and eventually in the city.

A fascinated John Quincy occupied a box seat for this extraordinary occurrence. Making every effort to view the great man, he succeeded, even though he never really got close. And he never received an introduction. He did observe the emperor in church, at the theater, and in a window appearing before a cheering crowd of French citizens. He reported that on one occasion he had a good look at the great man's face. During John Quincy's residence in Paris this wondrous character once again captured the attention of all of Europe.[86]

Napoleon both captivated and repelled John Quincy. The enthusiasm of the French for their returned leader impressed him. According to him Napoleon had gained more power on the Continent than anyone else since Charlemagne back in the eighth and ninth centuries. But he had also done more harm than any other living man. Later, after Napoleon's death, John Quincy continued to think about him. In his estimation the emperor was undoubtedly a military genius, who also possessed an extraordinary imagination and did some good. He had a great failing, however—no moral principle guided him. John Quincy's final assessment: "Napoleon and his preternatural power have crumbled into dust, and now he becomes the moral of a sermon against selfishness."[87]

While an onlooker at the resurgence of Napoleonic France, John Quincy waited on news about the official ratification of the Treaty of Ghent as well as about his new assignment. He learned in mid-March that his country had ratified the treaty; Great Britain had done so earlier. In early May he received notification of his commission, as minister plenipotentiary to Great Britain.

On May 16 he and his family left Paris for the French coast and the short voyage across the English Channel to his new diplomatic home. In his diary he mulled over his sojourn in the French capital. His reflections revealed his unending struggle with his sense of duty. He wrote that in Paris he had spent three leisurely and agreeable months, but had accomplished nothing useful.[88]

John Quincy and Louisa, with Charles Francis, arrived in London on May 25. They found waiting for them at their lodgings the two sons they had left behind in Massachusetts almost six years earlier. John Quincy observed that George, fourteen, had grown almost beyond their recognition, while John, nearly twelve, remained small for his age. Except for the phrase "my dear sons," their father's diary maintains silence on the emotion he undoubtedly felt upon seeing the boys from whom he had been apart for so long. The drama of this reunion he kept to himself.[89]

During the summer he engaged in a variety of activities with his sons. They took walks in London parks, went to theaters and museums. He and Louisa were unfamiliar with rambunctious boys of George's and John's ages who created much commotion in the household. Still, on July 11, his forty-eighth birthday, John Quincy recorded his joy in his diary. The past year, he wrote, "has in relation to public affairs been the most important year of my life, and in my private and domestic relations one of the most happy years."[90]

Of course, John Quincy's professional responsibilities required his attention. Two of his negotiating partners from Ghent, Henry Clay and Albert Gallatin, had preceded him to London. They had already begun work on the commercial treaty the three of them had been charged to complete. Because Clay and Gallatin had done so much, John Quincy did not take a major part in the discussions with British officials. It became clear, however, that a meaningful treaty was beyond their reach, for the British would compromise on neither critical trade matters nor impressment. Finally, both sides agreed upon a narrower convention that basically restated existing conditions, with a key added provision prohibiting discriminatory provisions on exports, imports, and port charges by either party. Castlereagh shifted the major issues to Washington, where additional Anglo-American talks would take place.[91]

Although deliberations among the Americans on what eventually became the convention were generally amiable, a sharp disagreement erupted over the order of signatures. The final document listed Great Britain ahead of the United States on every occasion. John Quincy insisted they should alternate, arguing that in treaties between European powers such alternation—the principle of *alternat* in diplomatic usage—always occurred. Neither Clay nor Gallatin thought the order mattered. They believed it of no importance, even though Secretary of State Monroe had set it as a guideline in his instructions.

An adamant John Quincy vowed he would not sign the convention without the *alternat*. He saw it as an essential signal of British respect for an equal power. American prestige required it. According to John Quincy, a heated exchange took place, in which Gallatin told him not to lose his temper. John Quincy replied that his two companions might sign, but he never would. In the end John Quincy prevailed, with the British acquiescing. Afterwards he reported that he and Gallatin remained composed and in good humor with each other. Immediately thereafter Clay and Gallatin exited the British capital, leaving John Quincy in sole charge of American affairs in the country.[92]

On August 1 the Adams family moved to the village of Ealing, only eight miles west. Finding their lodgings too small and London rental prices too high for a suitable house, Louisa searched elsewhere and discovered a delightful house in Ealing. It already had a most appropriate name, Little Boston House.

After moving, the parents made it a priority to find a school for their boys. Grandmother Abigail counseled John Quincy to use a light hand with her grandsons. You must realize that you cannot treat children as if they were adults, she advised. Her son determined, however, to adhere to the formula that he was convinced had succeeded with him. Only a mile from Little Boston House, he and Louisa found a boarding school, the Great Ealing School, that met their approval for John and Charles Francis. George would be kept at home, where his father would take charge of preparations for entering Harvard.[93]

John Quincy established a strict regimen for his eldest. To ensure that his role as tutor in Ealing would not interfere with his job as diplomat in London, John Quincy roused George from bed by six for their lessons to begin. He had his son read from the French Bible while he followed in the Latin, after which they exchanged Bibles. Then, of course, there were the essential Latin assignments. Lamenting in his diary that George was proving an indifferent student, John Quincy realized a change had to occur. After only two months of this home schooling, George joined his brothers at Great Ealing School, though as a day student.

Even so, John Quincy kept his hand in the boy's education. Because George had to be at school at seven, early morning lessons remained the norm. He had George continuing in the French Bible while adding the Greek New Testament and the Latin Vulgate Old Testament. Moreover, every day George recited fifty lines of Homer for his father.[94]

Although nothing mattered more to John Quincy than his son's education, in the autumn of 1815 he had to cope with two serious health issues. In mid-October while firing a pistol bought to teach the boys the proper use of firearms, he suffered a serious accident. When he pulled the trigger, the weapon, overloaded with powder, flew from his hands. His right hand was wounded in several places, including the forefinger, which became infected. Complete healing took months.[95]

Later that same month his left eye became inflamed. Heavy discharge flowed from the eye; he could barely open it. The treatment prescribed by his physician included applying leeches. "I was nearly delirious," he recorded. With the leeches "it seemed to me as if four hooks were tearing that side of my face into four quarters." For weeks he could not leave a dark room. By early November he had improved. Then infection struck the right eye, though not with equal ferocity. By midmonth his vision had almost returned to normal, but daylight still caused some pain. Although his physician claimed responsibility for saving his sight, John Quincy gave more credit to a natural remedy—the passage of time.[96]

These afflictions affected John Quincy mightily. With his right hand incapacitated, he anguished over his changed lifestyle. He worried about when he could resume his duties, since with his eye disorder he could not read. At the end of November he noted that in the previous thirty years he had never read or written so little in a single month. So compulsive was he about his reading and writing during the month that his wife stepped in as reader and writer. She took dictation for his correspondence and diary, and she started reading to him, particularly novels by Maria Edgeworth and Sir Walter Scott, who at that time was all the rage in England. By the end of the year he was up and about and slowly beginning to read and write once more.[97]

By early 1816 he had fully returned to his official tasks. From the outset of his time in London, his chief contact with the British government was the foreign minister, still Lord Castlereagh. In their initial meeting John Quincy recorded Castlereagh's conduct as gracious. He considered the foreign minister handsome, though with a frosty, albeit not repugnant, manner. Before their meetings John Quincy spent much time preparing a detailed agenda. He took particular care when writing to Castlereagh, confessing that his colleagues' criticism in Ghent had made him distrust his own productions. Even though his experience there had jarred his confidence, he realized that now he had to act in his own way. He told himself that whatever mistakes he might make, "let there be . . . no deficiency of earnest zeal."[98]

His various responsibilities made for a full schedule. The correspondence and reporting with other American diplomats in Europe and with his government back in the United States took up many hours. Almost every American visiting England appeared in his office whenever any questions arose. American citizens who had been released from service in the British navy, into which they had been impressed, came to him for assistance in returning to the United States. In addition, Britons searching for some patronage from the American government crossed his threshold. A harried diplomat fumed, "One would imagine that the American legation at London was the moon of Aristo, or Milton's Paradise of Fools—the place where things lost upon the Earth were to be found."[99]

He spent much time, however, on more serious matters, especially issues that had been passed over or not finalized in the Treaty of Ghent. Most important to John Quincy was the fisheries question. Since Ghent, some difficulties had arisen for American fishermen off the coast of the Canadian maritime provinces. Although Castlereagh would not come to John Quincy's position on the "right" of fisheries, he did repudiate the harassment of American fishermen by the British navy. Moreover, he continued the hands-off policy that permitted the fishing. Finally, as with the trade issue, he transferred the entire subject to Washington to become part of a more thorough settlement in British-American relations.

John Quincy also pressed on the treaty provisions requiring British compensation for slaves taken by the British military during the war—in his words at Ghent those "negroes seduced from their masters in our Southern States by promises of liberty." Castlereagh argued that the British were responsible only for those slaves within British garrisons when the war ended, not for those on board British ships, or on vessels in American territorial waters. Even when the British made a moral case for those slaves, John Quincy insisted that the treaty recognized slaves as private property, requiring the British to compensate their owners. With the two sides unable to agree on how to resolve this dispute, John Quincy suggested arbitration by a third party. The British concurred.[100]

John Quincy and Castlereagh discussed another slavery-related topic. An article in the Ghent treaty pledged both governments to make their best effort to end the African slave trade. The British had eliminated the trade to their colonies, and the United States in 1808 had outlawed the trade to its shores. Nevertheless, the trade continued to destinations in the West Indies and South America. The British wanted all maritime powers, including America, to join in a program that would allow naval ships of all to board any vessel suspected of transporting African slaves. With memories of Britain's impressment policy so fresh, John Quincy could not endorse any plan permitting the British navy to stop and search American ships. This subject would recur.

During his months as minister plenipotentiary, John Quincy and Castlereagh grew to respect each other. John Quincy was always thorough and diplomatic in his dealings, while Castlereagh adopted a conciliatory posture toward his former enemy. That John Quincy could make little substantive headway on serious concerns did frustrate him. He could not achieve anything tangible, he informed his father. He adopted an overriding goal—to advocate peace, he told his father in another letter. He was absolutely convinced that peace served the best interests of both countries.[101]

Business did not totally occupy John Quincy when he was away from Little Boston House. He and Louisa experienced a social life that was simultaneously active and inactive. As a fully credentialed member of the diplomatic corps, John Quincy received invitations to many affairs in London, which he and Louisa attended. In fact, he complained that frequent calls to London interfered with his keeping up his diary and correspondence. On one occasion during dinner in Ealing, a card arrived inviting him to a party in the city later that same evening. He changed clothes and went to London, not returning home until almost daylight.

At the same time, the Adamses did little socializing with the British upper classes outside of official functions. Although John Quincy well understood "the benefit to a public minister of associating with people of rank and consequence in the country where he is accredited," he had to contend with two facts. First, invitations from the upper classes did not flow to Little Boston House. Second, he was always aware of his financial limitations. As a result he did not seek out such bids, because he did not want to appear "only as a retainer, receiving unrequited favors, and not as an equal, sharing and dispensing by turns the interchange of social good offices." He felt strongly, "If I cannot join in the chorus of the convivial song, and let *him* spread the table tomorrow, I would fain not be listening to it at the table of another." To his diary he confided "the perpetually mortifying consciousness of inability to return the civility in the same manner."[102]

His attendance at official social events placed him in situations that both perturbed and amused him. His old struggle with extemporaneous speaking reappeared when he was called upon to respond to a toast at a London dinner. According to him he made a gushing response that left him greatly embarrassed, though he asserted his remarks were well received. At another dinner when his blunt comments about the weather in Russia offended the Russian ambassador and his wife, John Quincy felt acute discomfort. On still another occasion the noted British chemist Sir Humphry Davy held forth on his travels and chemical discoveries. Describing this dinner table lecture, John Quincy quipped, in his diary of course, "If modesty is an inseparable companion of genius, Sir Humphry is a prodigy." In general these functions did not suit John Quincy's temperament. To his diary he identified himself as stodgy in these circumstances. Based on his own record of his behavior at numerous such affairs, he surely exaggerated. At the same time this description allowed him to indulge his penchant for self-deprecation.[103]

He met another notable Englishman with whom he had an interesting relationship. Jeremy Bentham, an originator of modern social science and an advocate of political reform in his country, initially called on John Quincy. The two men saw each other often at meals and on walks. They discussed politics in America and Great Britain as well as numerous other subjects, including religion. Bentham's learning along with his originality and kindness impressed John Quincy, though his feeling that his friend was an atheist did not. Later the Englishman stated that their friendship had become intimate.[104]

John Quincy spent many of his private hours involved in the activities that had always engrossed him. He composed a multitude of poems in various forms on a variety of topics. In doing so, he gave in to a self-proclaimed and all-consuming ambition. To his diary he admitted that if he could have chosen his calling he would have been a great poet. Even so, his self-awareness made him recognize that he fell far short of that goal. He understood that he had written much mediocre verse. Even more, he judged the time spent on his versifying as time wasted.[105]

Books and the theater were always available. He did not neglect his constant companions, the Bible and Shakespeare. He also read a recently published canto of Lord Byron's *Childe Harold.* Sir Walter Scott's new novels occupied him, whether he did the reading or, while ill, listened to Louisa. Although he praised Scott's delineation of characters and style, he considered the incidents overly romantic and unrealistic, and he disclaimed the credence awarded superstition. At the theater he relished Shakespearean productions. He did manage an unusual diversion, a visit to an exhibition featuring a rhinoceros, an animal that fascinated him.[106]

No matter his myriad tasks and entertainments, John Quincy never forgot his commitment to his diary. In the summer of 1816 he noted that maintaining his diary put him under constant pressure. It was not only keeping his journal up-to-date that concerned him; he also worried about its inclusiveness. Following several engagements in London, he mourned his inability to record everything of consequence occurring in conversations. Ultimately, he noted that he became discouraged and gave up. Late in July 1816 he penned in his diary a history of it, in which he specified format and fallow periods. He also commented on his determination to prepare an index for each volume. Doing so would substantially increase the hours the diary required. He stated that he had to allot five days in the current month to make the index for the previous month.[107]

Serious thinking about religion occupied him as well. In correspondence with his parents John Quincy became caught up in the religious turmoil racking Massachusetts. In the old Puritan commonwealth the new doctrine of Unitarianism was rocking the foundation of Calvinism that had been institutionalized in the

Congregational Church. Unitarians denied the divinity of Christ as well as the Trinity. Instead, they portrayed Jesus as a superior human being and stressed toleration and benevolence. This new creed attracted a substantial portion of the Massachusetts elite, including John and Abigail Adams. Their son did not share the new inclination, however. He wrote his mother that he did not think Unitarianism and true Christianity harmonious, and he did not hesitate to spurn it. To his father he made clear that he aligned with the doctrine propounded by the Trinitarians and Calvinists.

In another long letter to his father, he spelled out in more detail why he held to what he termed "real Christianity." First, to his mind the Bible provided indisputable evidence of Christ's divinity. And he detailed the various languages and translations he had utilized. Replying to John's assertion that believing that an omnipotent God could be crucified was blasphemy, John Quincy avowed, "God is a spirit." That spirit, he went on, had not been crucified; rather, only the body of Jesus. For him "the Spirit whether eternal or created was beyond the reach of the cross." Jesus's Sermon on the Mount dominated and commanded his faith. It directed him to put his faith in heaven, not upon earth. Professing that Christ's gospel provided the foundation for his belief in an afterlife, he declared, "I cannot cavil or quibble away, not single words and ambiguous expressions, but the whole tenor of his conduct, by which he sometimes positively asserted, and at others countenanced his disciples that he was *God*." Despite their differences, John Quincy assured his father that they stood united for tolerance and "the doctrine of toleration and benevolence."[108]

While residing in Ealing, John Quincy and Louisa Catherine had their portraits painted. They chose a young artist, Charles Robert Leslie, born in England of American parents. Both subjects indicated their approval of the results, especially the painter's depiction of John Quincy; even he thought his likeness better than hers. According to Louisa, Leslie's effort captured the most vivid likeness of her husband, who looked better than he ever had. Since his stay in Russia, John Quincy, standing five feet seven inches, had, as a diplomat who had known them there noticed, put on weight, evidently to good effect.[109]

Leslie painted the seated John Quincy with a three-quarter profile and with the same aquiline nose captured by John Copley in 1796. This painting portrays a man less of action than of reflection. He gazes into the distance, appropriately with a finger marking his place in a book. John Quincy's expression here is not so bold as in the van Huffel portrait of the preceding year. He appears, however, more content but more than a year older.

In Leslie's portrayal of Louisa, she also gazes into the distance. She has her own aquiline nose and the soft chin and dark eyes of a young matron. Her fashionable Empire gown and the elegant glove she is holding convey sophistication along with a worldly air. She has a smile on her lips and a faraway look in her eyes.

The Leslie portraits caught the Adamses at a special moment, for both enjoyed their interval at Little Boston House. In a real sense these months were the happiest of their marriage. For the first time in six years, they had their family together. John Quincy did have his work, which could be hectic, but it was less burdensome than it had been. He described their abode, its setting, and their life as a "little Paradise." Upon his departure, he depicted Ealing in his diary as a delicious location, one of the most delightful in which he had ever lived.[110]

Louisa Adams's idyll ended early in 1817, however. Another pregnancy dealt her health its usual blow. Now forty-two, she had experienced as many as eight miscarriages and a stillbirth; this, her final pregnancy, promised more difficulty. She spent much time in bed, with doctors attending with their leeches and bleeding. Social life was out of the question. By spring she was better. Though still weak, she had not lost the baby.[111]

Even while relating the delights of Ealing, John Quincy was contemplating an uncertain future. He would not remain in England forever. In his diary he underscored his uncertainty and anxiety about the future. He focused not only on a probable and desired return to the United States but on what awaited him in his native land. Before the end of 1816 rumors reached him that the new president would name him secretary of state. James Monroe, the man John Quincy had reported to from St. Petersburg, Ghent, and London as James Madison's secretary of state, had been elected president in November. Writing his father early in January 1817, John Quincy said he would make no comment about the whisperings until he received official notification, if that ever came.[112]

His diary revealed his hopes and doubts. Although he considered the possibility of that offer still doubtful, he pondered whether he should accept. Sincerely questioning his ability for the post, he concluded that skepticism should end the matter. Still, he told himself, he could reasonably justify taking it. He, of course, had not and would not engage in reaching for it.[113]

President James Monroe did indeed offer the position to John Quincy, who received Monroe's letter of March 6 on April 16. As the third consecutive Virginian to be elected president, Monroe decided that making anyone from the South or West secretary of state would be a political liability. That cabinet office had apparently become an unofficial stepping-stone to the presidency— Jefferson had held it, and both Madison and Monroe had moved directly from it to the nation's highest office. The assumption would follow that Monroe's choice would be in a most advantageous spot to succeed him. And as Monroe informed Thomas Jefferson, when he looked to the northeastern states he found John Quincy, "who by his age, long experience in our foreign affairs, and adoption into the republican party, seems to have superior pretensions to any there." In choosing John Quincy, Monroe made a calculated and thought-through political decision.[114]

Upon receipt of the president's letter, John Quincy wrestled emotionally. He assured himself that Monroe made his choice without any pressure from himself or any of his friends, at least that he knew about. John Quincy decided the president acted purely in the public interest. Satisfied about the purity of his appointment, he reflected upon the severe blows that would come with the job. And he questioned his ability to do it, writing his mother that he had never questioned so seriously whether or not to accept any previous appointment. But he did overcome all his doubts and decided to accept. He told her and himself that he would rely on God's favor, which had carried him through all the ordeals of his life. Moreover, he was convinced his doing so ensured his safekeeping.[115]

The very next day after he got Monroe's invitation, he dispatched a letter of acceptance. He would become secretary of state. Moreover, he would depart for the United States as soon as he could get all his affairs in order. He would leave without regret. He recorded in his diary that he wanted to spend the rest of his life in his own country.[116]

A VISION

of a

NATION—
REALIZED

and

THWARTED

—

ANDREW JACKSON,
ALLY TO ANTAGONIST

CHAPTER 4

"Perhaps the Most Important Day of My Life"

A
S JOHN QUINCY ADAMS PREPARED TO DEPART FOR HOME, he would take with him a fully formed vision of his country and its virtues as well as his own convictions about the political world. Having represented his native land abroad and successfully defended its vital interests at Ghent, he had no doubt that his country's values and principles exceeded those of all others. Its commitment to fundamental rights of freedom and liberty contrasted sharply with the situation in monarchical Europe. In his mind the United States upheld a new moral standard in government. Moreover, the outcome at Ghent reinforced his belief in American exceptionalism. He now saw his country as a growing power, one with which the Europeans would have to reckon.

As secretary of state he would find himself well located to articulate and defend America's place in the world. To that task he would bring certainty about his own moral and political position. He was an American convinvced not only of American uniqueness but of his determination to maintain, even to advance, his country's stature in the world.

Doing so, of course, would necessitate keeping the American Union strong. He would strive to make sure that internal disagreements and squabbles did not endanger what he saw as the future glory of his country. None would be more threatening than the sectional jealousy and suspicion he saw revealed during the War of 1812 and at Ghent. Politics, for him, meant first of all conducting himself in a fashion that would enhance unity. Even if he as a New Englander shared certain of those feelings, he must bridle them, lest he assist national division. Following that path would be a moral act, for the United States was a moral as well as a political entity.

The Adams family sailed from England for the United States in June of 1817, three months after James Monroe's inauguration as president. Except for Adams, seasickness plagued all, especially Louisa, who also exhibited additional serious symptoms. Fortunately, among the passengers was a prominent Scottish physician who attended her, treating the ill woman with the usual palliatives, laudanum and bleeding. Late in the month, still in great distress, she experienced violent pain. Ultimately relief came; she miscarried for the ninth time. The unborn child was buried at sea.[1]

Finally, after a voyage of just over seven weeks, the Adamses landed in New York City, then experiencing a period of considerable growth as it began to emerge as the great international port city it became later in the century. The political and business notables of the city celebrated Adams's arrival with a dinner held in his honor. He also took in museums and other attractions, including his initial observation of a steamboat that had come down the Hudson River from Albany. At the Brooklyn Navy Yard he went aboard his country's first steam frigate as well as the USS *John Adams*.

Then via steamboat and stage the family traveled to Massachusetts. In Quincy, Adams felt great joy upon greeting his parents after an absence of eight years. For their ages he thought them in remarkably good health. In Boston he was feted yet again at a public dinner, which even some of his former political foes attended.[2]

After a brief stay he and Louisa departed for Washington. Before then, however, he planned for their boys' schooling.

He placed John and Charles in what would become the Boston Latin School. Mother and father expected George to enter Harvard immediately, but replicating the father's experience three decades earlier, the admissions committee found his preparations deficient. Though disappointed, Adams arranged for the tutoring that would prepare his eldest for admission.

On September 20 they arrived in Washington. Two days later at the State Department, Adams took the oath of office. He was now secretary of state. Upon accepting this position, he expressed his usual trepidations about his ability to perform this new task. He worried that both President Monroe and the country at large had overestimated not his dedication but his ability. The road ahead he described as thorny, and he worried that he would be unable to traverse it to the end.[3]

At the same time he reflected upon the status of his country and his own stance toward it. The war experience troubled him. It had revealed to him a nasty factionalism, which drove part of the country pell-mell toward sectionalism and disunion and even hinted at civil war. He pinpointed his native New England, especially his own Massachusetts, as the great malefactor. He thought harshly of certain fellow New Englanders, the Federalist antiwar zealots, who not only attacked national policy in opposing the war with England but also contemplated extreme actions, such as dismembering the Union and forming a northern confederacy.

One occurrence especially disturbed Adams, a meeting in mid-December 1814 in Hartford, Connecticut, that became known as the Hartford Convention. Called by antiwar Massachusetts Federalists, the conclave attracted Federalists from all the New England states. But neither the country at large nor the men gathering in Hartford knew that as they convened the treaty ending the war was being finalized. At the time it met, the convention spurred fears that the delegates might call for rash action, such as treating with Great Britain for a separate peace or even disrupting the Union. The proceedings produced nothing radical, however.

With more moderate men leading its deliberations, in mid-January the convention issued a report that did little more than repeat long-standing complaints of New England Federalists about the war and southern domination of the national government. It did complain that the Madison administration failed to provide adequately for the defense of New England, but mostly it proposed constitutional amendments aimed at curbing southern power in order to shield what the attendees perceived as New England's waning influence in the nation. These included eliminating the three-fifths clause and requiring a super congressional majority for declaring war and enacting a commercial embargo. Only one item posed a potential danger—a call for another New England convention if hostilities continued into June.

Of course, events rendered that possibility moot. Even though the Hartford Convention never really threatened either the war effort or the Union, it acquired among many Americans the stigma of endangering both. In essence, it became almost a synonym for treason. Adams denounced these New England Federalists for placing partisanship ahead of patriotism, charging that becoming a minority propelled them into what he termed "hypochondriac fits." Such convulsions drove these narrow-minded men into parochial and venomous corners. As Adams put it, their myopia caused them to contemplate the end of the world because their leadership had been rejected.[4]

He stood in the precisely opposite position. Though a proud son of Massachusetts, he emphasized even before he left England his devotion to the Union, to the country whole. "But the longer I live," he informed his father, "the stronger I find my national feelings grow upon me, and the less of my affections are compassed by partial localities." His conclusion: "My system of politics more and more inclines to strengthen the union and its government." To make his point even more graphically, he contrasted himself with the well-known Virginian John Randolph of Roanoke, who extolled state governments. Adams declared that his outlook was just the opposite.[5]

As secretary of state, Adams moved into an office previously held by some of the most illustrious members of the founding generation, including Thomas Jefferson, James Madison, and James Monroe, his immediate predecessor. Even though the secretary of state was considered the premier cabinet officer, Adams in 1817 and throughout his tenure presided over a small staff, unbelievably so by today's standards. He had only ten clerks, along with a chief clerk, to assist him in carrying out the myriad responsibilities of the department.[6]

Adams's Department of State had a multitude of duties. First, it had responsibility for handling the foreign relations of the country, which ranged from formulating fundamental policy, always with presidential approval, to preparing instructions for American agents sent abroad, to dealing with foreign diplomats accredited to this country. In Adams's time, however, the department also had a substantial domestic agenda. It had charge of the decennial censuses mandated by the Constitution. Other duties included operation of the patent office, distribution of the acts and resolutions of Congress, and preparation of an alphabetical index to congressional legislation at the end of each session.

When Adams took over, he discovered administrative chaos. "All is disorder and confusion," he recorded in his diary. No procedure existed for keeping a record of letters received each day; he instituted one. Looking for documents of any kind proved a vexing trial, which beset his labors every day. In addition to lax administration, the department's records had suffered from fires and the sack of governmental buildings by Britain's army in 1814.[7]

The omission of documents in packets prepared for Congress particularly distressed him. Again the absence of an administrative system agitated him. He also faulted his chief clerk for incompetence. Additionally, and as usual, he blamed himself for his own shortcomings. Yet his own tendency to self-criticize made him compassionate toward the weaknesses of others, at least to a certain point.[8]

Adams found his effort to get ready for the 1820 census particularly onerous. He searched for the instructions for the 1800 and 1810 counts but could find none. Finally, he did turn up a volume of departmental archives for 1800 that had a record of the instructions for that year. He learned that the originals had been destroyed by the British.[9]

Confronting this disorder and charged with seemingly unending requirements, Adams devoted countless hours to his task. Although the department's listed office hours went only from 9 a.m. to 3 p.m., they bore little relation to his workday. He was often in his office past closing time; he even noted in his diary an occasion when the watchman locked him in. Moreover, at home he regularly labored on departmental papers at night. He described many of his days as topsy-turvy, which he defined as marked by continuous interruptions and volumes of mail.[10]

He specified as perhaps his most arduous tasks the preparations of instructions for ministers going overseas. He had to keep in mind all the particulars of his country's relations with every power in Europe. That required him to have the foresight to advise an individual envoy on his course to promote the interests of his country. He did strive to standardize the guidance by advance accumulation of certain materials germane to all. Still, each necessitated individual attention, for particulars differed with each country. Contemplating this labor, he recalled Roman history, noting that Julius Caesar reportedly dictated letters to four secretaries simultaneously. Adams applauded "an achievement which every statesman deeply involved in business finds it necessary to accomplish."[11]

Then, of course, there were the state papers—treaties, responses and reports to Congress, replies to communications from foreign governments, and letters to them. They took much time, and Adams wrote most of them himself. He remarked that his pen never stopped moving across paper. While writing such documents, he "constantly fel[t] like the Grecian orator who said he had not time to make a speech short."[12]

Adams's job did not always involve writing. An assignment he deemed distinctly annoying was dealing with supplicants for political appointments. He stated that nothing else bothered him so much as contending with stubborn office seekers, especially those who kept returning even after their rejection. Continuing to say no civilly required an effort beyond herculean. Moreover, he found it terribly painful when he had to relay a presidential decision against a person's desire.[13]

He also had to defend his budget against members of Congress always eager to slash what they considered extravagant spending in executive departments. In defending salary increases, which made up most of his budget, he pointed out that his own compensation— $6,000 annually in the 1820s—fell short by some $4,000 to $5,000 of covering his individual and domestic expenses. In 1821 he informed a senator that while he was prepared to make such a financial sacrifice, he insisted that his subordinates should not have to do so. Furthermore, he declared that the workload in the department had increased substantially since his arrival.[14]

Even while trying to cope with his many-faceted job and regularize administrative practices as well as protect his departmental budget and staff, Adams engaged in the serious work demanded of him. During his initial year in office a notable commercial convention was concluded with Great Britain. It built on the April 1817 agreement with the British known as the Rush-Bagot Treaty, which authorized the demilitarization of the Great Lakes and Lake Champlain, scenes of much conflict during the War of 1812. The Commercial Convention of 1818 had even more significance because it resolved or placed on the road to resolution critical issues left unsettled in the Treaty of Ghent. Its provisions granted America the right to fish in the ocean off the Canadian maritime provinces, set the U.S.-Canadian border from the Lake of the Woods to the Rocky Mountains along the forty-ninth parallel, opened the territory beyond the Rockies for joint settlement and development for the next decade, and provided for the arbitration of American claims regarding slaves held by British forces at the end of the war. This convention clearly signaled that America and Great Britain were heading away from the antagonism and actual war that had dominated relations between the two countries since the American Revolution.[15]

On the domestic side Adams began research on a report on weights and measures assigned to him in 1817 by the Senate. The Senate wanted the report to assist it in meeting the constitutional directive that Congress legislate a uniform system of weights and measures, which had not yet been done. The topic did interest him. During his Russian mission he had made comparisons between American and Russian practices. In October 1817 he confided to his diary that he spent hours thinking about the subject. Early on he thought he would propose the metric system utilized by France. He shared that view with Thomas Jefferson, who as secretary of state had studied the matter and come to that conclusion. He, too, in 1790 made a report to Congress, though it had not led to action.

Before arriving at a final decision, Adams would, however, conduct a thorough investigation that included a survey of practices in the states and in Europe. By the end of the 1810s his research was taking up so much time that he worried about his lack of progress on the report itself. The more research he did, he wrote, "the deeper and darker appears the deep beneath." He knew that his deadline of 1821 for a completed report would soon force him to finish without ever reaching that bottom. At the same time he admitted that the area now fascinated him so much that he neglected essential business.[16]

As secretary of state, Adams was responsible directly to the president of the United States. The fifth man elected to that office, Monroe, was the fourth Virginian and third in a row following his mentors Thomas Jefferson and James Madison. Basically an eighteenth-century man, the fifty-nine-year-old Monroe was the last veteran of the Revolution to become president. Moreover, with his powdered wig and buckled knee breeches, he maintained the dress of an earlier age.[17]

As president, the Republican Monroe had an overriding goal. Given his large margin of victory in 1816—he carried all but three states—the once formidable Federalist party was no longer a viable threat to win a national election. Monroe wanted to forestall renewed partisanship, to prevent the rise of a new round of organized, opposed parties. As did most of the founding generation's leaders, he did not view party or partisanship as a good. Instead, he saw danger of national division. Toward the close of his second term, he informed Adams that "it had been a great object of his Administration to consolidate the people of the Union towards one another and to mitigate the asperities of party spirit." During Monroe's first four years John Quincy judged his goal successful, calling it the most peaceful period in the nation's history. Yet during the second term he feared the quest for the presidential succession would torpedo that tranquillity and explode Monroe's dream.[18]

President and secretary set out to work together. Having deliberately selected Adams, Monroe had every reason to desire a positive relationship. Moreover, with diplomatic experience rivaling his foreign minister's—assignments to London, Paris, and Madrid as well as six years as Madison's secretary of state—Monroe understood both foreign affairs and the office he gave John Quincy. For his part, Adams perceived it his duty to stand behind the president. As he told his chief, department heads like himself had responsibility only as a presidential subordinate. At the beginning Monroe set the tone for their interaction by telling Adams that he would set a time for their regular meetings. In addition, he had given orders that he would receive his foreign minister at any time. Thus Adams had practically unlimited access to the president.[19]

The secretary from Massachusetts and the president from Virginia did establish a good working relationship. The two men shared a sense of America's position in the world, especially vis-à-vis the European powers. Illustrating this confluence, Monroe had Adams prepare the foreign affairs portion of his annual messages to Congress. In addition, John Quincy usually drafted the papers regarding foreign policy for other presidential communications

with Congress. Although Monroe generally exhibited more caution than his secretary did, the more forceful Adams usually
got Monroe to stand where he did. While he most often ended
up where Adams wanted him, Monroe left no doubt about his
authority. On important documents he approved Adams's drafts
before final copies were made.

Adams understood the president's concern about ultimate
authority along with his propensity to place his own imprint on
papers. He learned to include paragraphs with language more
vigorous than Monroe preferred. The chief executive would tend
to soften the words, but not alter the meaning. With that tactic
he kept the thrust of his document at the same time the president
exercised his prerogative. What Adams called "the pure metal"
would remain.[20]

While Adams considered the president a fair man, he thought
him prone to make hasty judgments. Yet he generally felt that
Monroe's shortcomings inclined toward the positive side. More
seriously, Adams worried that the president too often feared popular prejudices. Subserviency to popular opinions would never
do for Adams, however. Contrasting himself with his superior,
he declared that he would always face them directly. Even so,
he asserted that he had more confidence than the president in
the thoughtful assessments of the people. That appraisal he had
rarely expressed, and in a critical sense his customary outlook
and reactions contradicted it.[21]

One aspect of Monroe's management style troubled him. In
making appointments to foreign posts, the president did not normally take Adams into his confidence. In 1818 the president asked
him to recommend a person for the Spanish mission. Upon hearing his secretary of state's recommendation, Monroe immediately named someone else, whom, in Adams's estimation, he had
already selected. And it bothered Adams that the president would
make such a request when he had already made his choice. An
identical incident had taken place previously. Adams described
such occurrences as having the "character of a cabal," undoubt-

edly connected with presidential politics. It smacked of "a back-stairs influence" and "the worst features of elective monarchies."[22]

Although the secretary of state might be considered primus inter pares among cabinet officers, especially because by the late 1810s the office appeared to offer the surest road to the presidency, no line of authority existed. Adams had four colleagues in Monroe's official family—the secretaries of treasury, war, and navy along with the attorney general. As at Ghent, he would have to work with others. His influence would depend on personal and political matters more than on his office.

Of course, all cabinet officers reported to the president. Although Monroe often held cabinet meetings and regularly encouraged deliberations among the members, he made the final decisions. Thus Adams's sway with him would count for more than his ability to bring his fellow department heads to his side. Still, his engagement with them would undoubtedly have an impact on his effectiveness with Monroe.

Adams's cabinet fellows ranged from notable national figures to men with considerably less prestige and visibility. Without question the two most outstanding were William H. Crawford, secretary of the treasury, and John C. Calhoun, secretary of war. Benjamin Crowninshield of Massachusetts, who headed the Navy Department, was a holdover from the Madison administration, in which he occupied that same post. Completing the lineup, William Wirt, a Marylander who had moved to Virginia as a young man, assumed the role of the nation's chief law officer as attorney general.

A native Virginian who as a boy had migrated with his family to Georgia, where he practiced law and rose to prominence, William H. Crawford at the outset of Monroe's presidency clearly possessed more political stock than any of his associates. Although his name is virtually unknown today, Crawford in his time was a potent political force. Called by some "a giant of a man" in an age when men were much smaller—he was six feet three inches tall and weighed well over two hundred pounds—the Georgian had been a U.S. senator and minister to France before joining Madison's cabinet in 1815 as secretary of war. He transferred to the Treasury in 1816, a position in which Monroe retained him. Even more important, he had in that year been a serious challenger to Monroe for the Republican presidential nomination, losing by only 11 votes out of 119 cast in the party's congressional caucus, its nominating body. Crawford and his supporters promptly backed Monroe. His performance left him assuming that he occupied the first spot in the line to succeed Monroe. He also had the backing of Virginians and other southerners dedicated to preserving what they considered Jefferson's political legacy. Thus, from the outset of Monroe's presidency, he occupied the front-runner's post.[23]

Almost rivaling Crawford on the national stage, John C. Calhoun of South Carolina stood out among the younger Republican luminaries. Only thirty-five in 1817, he had been a significant influence in the U.S. House of Representatives since his arrival in Congress in 1811. Recognizing his ability and intelligence, all observers considered the tall, angular, strong-jawed, self-confident Carolinian to have a bright future in American politics. Although not Monroe's first choice for the war slot—in fact, he was the third—he took on his task with characteristic determination and energy.[24]

Early on Adams formed an opinion of these two men, one favorable, the other not. Over time the former would turn sour, while the latter remained unchanged. He had met Crawford before, but not Calhoun. He identified Crawford's "point d'honneur" as disagreeing with him in cabinet deliberations. Crawford was consumed by an ambition for the presidency that, according to Adams, had been prematurely aroused by his near loss to Monroe.

In his appraisal Crawford had little knowledge of finance and could barely manage the normal business affairs of his office. Rather, he was an extremely talented intriguer. At the same time Adams did not condemn the Georgian as a bad man. Crawford did not totally lack principles, but his ambition overpowered them. Adams did allow that Crawford might be unaware of the fundamental motive behind his actions. Adams's final word: "Oh, the windings of the human heart."[25]

Adams held an entirely different view of Calhoun, whom he had not previously met. After observing his new colleague in the cabinet, he recorded in his diary, "Calhoun thinks for himself, independently of all the rest, with sound judgment, quick discrimination, and keen observation." Then with a powerful mind he backed his opinions. Building on that estimation, Adams averred that he anticipated from Calhoun, a Yale alumnus, more positive contributions to the country than from any other of their contemporaries. Convinced that it would add to his qualifications, he urged Calhoun to spend some time in Europe. Although Calhoun concurred on the value of European experience, he regretted that his finances would not permit it. To Adams the secretary of war was the only true intellectual in the administration, indeed an accolade coming from the secretary of state.

In 1821 Adams gave his measured assessment. "Calhoun is a man of fair and candid mind, of honorable principles, of clear and quick understanding, of cool self-possession, of enlarged philosophical views, and of ardent patriotism," he wrote. This applause continued. He found Calhoun less bound by sectional and partisan prejudices than any other political man with whom he had ever dealt. No one except George Washington and his own father ever received such acclaim from Adams. Yet even this exceptional man had a particular Adams-identified flaw—he paid too much attention to public opinion. To underscore that fault Adams took pains to point out that he did not suffer from it.[26]

Adams's approbation of Calhoun and condemnation of Crawford had much to do with his view of the electioneering taking place to succeed Monroe during his initial term. Because of the Virginian's overwhelming victory in 1816 plus the demise of the Federalist party, except in local bailiwicks, politicians and political observers expected him to easily win reelection in 1820. In doing so he, of course, would follow the path of his two immediate predecessors in the Executive Mansion. Both Jefferson and Madison served two terms; neither tried for three. Again all assumed that Monroe would do likewise.

That tradition of only two presidential terms, which George Washington initiated, distressed Adams. He pointed out that the Constitution contained no restriction on the length of a president's serving. Even more important, in his judgment, it was no more than a fetish that precipitated the political scrum for the succession. According to Adams the pushing and shoving began just as soon as Monroe took the oath of office in March 1817. For this unfortunate state of affairs he blamed the three Virginian presidents for having forced the acceptance of what he considered the nefarious two-term fixation upon the country. In contrast, he believed a president should be able to remain in office as long as the people wanted him there.[27]

During Monroe's first term Adams depicted Crawford and Henry Clay, his erstwhile colleague at Ghent, as the great transgressors. While Adams believed he had discovered the key to Crawford in his insatiable ambition for power, he also discerned that characteristic governing the treasury secretary's conduct toward him in the cabinet. He asserted that Crawford's chief end was to differ with him. That perturbed Adams, and he claimed Monroe agreed with him.[28]

Although Clay was not a member of Monroe's administration, he was a powerful player in Washington and national politics, thanks to his seat as Speaker of the House of Representatives. Not that he had not coveted a place in the cabinet, for he surely had. He had set his goal, however, on the secretaryship of state, which he and almost everyone else identified as the stepping-stone to the presidency. He thought that place of honor his due. But Monroe did not agree, turning to New England and Adams to fill that position. Still, he offered Clay the War Department, which the Kentuckian refused.

That disappointment coupled with his ardent desire for the presidency caused Clay from the outset to strive to embarrass Monroe and his administration. In his drive he used two weapons,

the first being the revolutions in South America against Spanish rule. By the 1810s a vastly weakened Spain was losing control over its empire in the Americas. Clay argued that the country
should exhibit brotherhood with rebels against colonial authority.
In Congress he pushed for American aid for and recognition of
the new, self-proclaimed republics. The Monroe administration
balked. Attuned to Europe and hoping to negotiate the cession
of Florida from Spain, it was cautious, refusing to rush American
involvement.

Clay also prodded the president on internal improvements,
the designation at the time for the federal government's spending money for roads, canals, and river improvements. Holding to
his Virginia and strict-construction heritage, Monroe maintained
that such expenditures were unconstitutional because the Constitution did not specifically authorize them. To overcome that constitutional barrier, he urged Congress to initiate a constitutional
amendment that would legitimate the use of federal funds. Clay
rejected Monroe's reservations and his advocacy of an amendment. He simply urged Congress to pass internal-improvements
legislation.[29]

For Adams, Clay was as besotted with ambition as Crawford.
At Ghent he had certainly noted Clay's ambitiousness, but here for
the first time he witnessed the Kentuckian in electoral politics. In
Adams's mind, Clay was striving to build a political opposition,
which he would lead, and hoped to thrive upon the wreck of Monroe's administration. When Clay's moves against Monroe failed
to generate the political momentum he desired, Adams detected
Clay's concentrating his antagonism on him.[30]

To Adams the sense that all of Clay's and Crawford's machinations aimed at 1824, not 1820, made them even more appalling. As for himself, he would stand behind the president and shun
any politicking. When a friend from New Hampshire approached
him with the suggestion that to boost his chances for 1824 some
electors in his state were willing to cast their vice-presidential
ballots for the secretary of state, Adams rebuffed him. He would

have none of it. He wanted Monroe and his vice-presidential mate elected unanimously.[31]

The results of the 1820 presidential election surprised no one. With no real opposition, Monroe carried every state; even Federalist electors in Massachusetts voted for him. It underscored the magnitude of his triumph that Monroe would have been the only president except Washington to win the electoral vote unanimously, save for a single elector in New Hampshire. That lone dissenting vote came from the same friend who queried Adams about shifting some vice-presidential votes. And he cast his presidential ballot for John Quincy Adams. Learning about it, Adams expressed in his diary his "surprise and mortification."[32]

While deprecating the political swirl surrounding him, Adams had to cope with an immense personal loss. At the beginning of November 1818 he received a letter from his son John informing him that a few days before, on October 28, his mother had died. When he had last seen her, during his visit to Quincy the past summer, she had seemed in reasonable health for her seventy-four years, though she had endured bouts of serious illness. Upon his departure for Washington in early October, apparently nothing had changed. Soon after his return to the capital, however, he got word that she had weakened seriously. Thus the sad news that she was gone did not come as a total shock.[33]

Yet its emotional and psychological toll was considerable, a cost he elucidated in his diary. She had been such a force in his life. Deeming her "an angel upon earth," he remembered her as "the real personification of female virtue, of piety, of charity, of ever active and never intermitting benevolence." She was always "a spirit from above watching over me for good, and contributing by my mere consciousness of her existence to the comfort of my life." With "that consciousness . . . gone, and without her the world feels to me like a solitude." Still, as always he bowed before his God, intoning that God's will, not his own, be done.[34]

A month later he poured out his sense of her meaning for him. "The silver cord is broken," he wrote. His life would never be the same. When she was alive, he continued, his return to Quincy brought forth joyful memories of youth, which made him happy. Yet, as he told his father, he hoped that now his mother's sanctified spirit existed in a better state.[35]

These deep feelings lasted. Upon visiting Quincy almost a year after her death, he confided to his diary that his entire existence had been altered. In the old home place he experienced the desolation occasioned by her absence. Even more than a score of years later, reading some of her letters brought forth falling tears. Upon hearing extracts from them read by another, to his diary he unbosomed, "I actually sobbed as he read, utterly unable to suppress my emotion." It was powerful: "Oh, my mother! Is there anything on earth so affecting to me as thy name? so precious as thy instructions to my childhood, so dear as the memory of thy life?" He answered no.[36]

Despite the trauma of his mother's death, Adams never wavered in his attention to his duty, one of the chief lessons she had drilled into him. The world of reality in which he operated certainly did not disappear. At the outset Adams focused on Spain. The revolts in South America against Spanish rule had become a political issue. Moreover, Spanish Florida on the southeastern U.S. border had long been a prize much desired by many Americans.

Even before Adams left England, the Spanish minister there had approached him on those two topics. He indicated that Spain would cede Florida to the United States; in turn, Spain would expect the United States to shun any involvement with the South American insurgency. In his diary Adams noted that he did not have time to pursue this initiative before his departure. He did conclude, however, that with the overture the Spanish intended to engender his excitement without offering anything concrete.[37]

At the same time the British foreign minister Lord Castlereagh brought up the possibility of Great Britain's using its good intentions to help settle American-Spanish differences. Adams responded warily because at the time he did not trust British motives. At Ghent the British had seemed antagonistic toward the United States regarding Spain.[38]

Yet he had no reservations about the general attitude of European governments toward his country. Before leaving England, he wrote his father that those governments were hostile toward the United States, because all the monarchies loathed Americans as republicans. Since taking office, he had not changed his opinion. Conversations in Monroe's cabinet covered what all considered the negative attitude toward and treatment of the United States by both Britain and Spain.[39]

Adams forcefully expressed his opinion that the negativity from both came from their view of the United States as little and insignificant. The country could do nothing to change that perception, he held, until the world recognized that it would dominate all of North America. He argued that a natural law decreed that the British possessions on the northern border and Spanish on the southern should become American just as the Mississippi River empties into the sea.[40]

While Secretary of State Adams spoke directly in the cabinet, he engaged in negotiations with the Spanish minister to the United States, Luis de Onís. In these discussions Adams had two goals: the cession of Florida and the fixing of a western boundary between the Louisiana Purchase and Spanish claims, a border that had never been formally finalized. Under instructions to deliver Florida, Onís demanded as a quid pro quo an American pledge to keep hands off South America. In addition, the Spanish wanted the southwestern boundary of Louisiana set as far east as possible, keeping the United States far away from its jewel, Mexico. Holding firmly to his conviction that America must retain independence of action, acting when and where it chose, Adams would not agree to any stipulation on South America, nor to any restrictions on American conduct. His overriding goal was to assert American power and extend his nation's boundaries.[41]

Then, in the summer of 1818, unexpected developments in Florida fundamentally altered the course of negotiations. In July,

Major General Andrew Jackson, the victor of the Battle of New Orleans in 1815, was placed in command of American troops in the border region between the state of Georgia and what in 1819 would become Alabama and Spanish Florida. That porous boundary allowed slaves of American farmers and planters to escape into Florida. Simultaneously, it enabled Seminole Indians, at times with their black allies, to cross it, attack American settlers, and carry off slaves. Those settlers clamored for escapes as well as raids to be halted. Andrew Jackson was just the man for that job.

The first American military hero since George Washington, Jackson not only had bested the British at New Orleans but had earlier decimated the Creek nation, opening an immense territory in southwestern Georgia and Alabama to American settlement. When not leading an army, Jackson was a slave-owning cotton planter in Tennessee. A tall, spare man with ferocious energy and an iron will, Jackson had a deserved reputation as a hard-driving commander who placed punishing his enemy and achieving success above all else. His instructions from the War Department permitted him to cross the international frontier in pursuit of Indians, if necessary. At the same time, should he find his foe sheltered in a Spanish fort or by Spanish authorities, he was to contact Washington for guidance.[42]

A determined Jackson led his force into Florida, where he routed Indians along with their black confederates and burned their villages. When they retreated into and occupied a Spanish fort, he captured them and the fort. During his assault Jackson also took as prisoners two British citizens, whom he accused of aiding the Indians. He had them court-martialed and executed. Confronted by Jackson's campaign, the Spanish governor in Pensacola declared he would drive the American invaders out of Florida. Thereupon Jackson marched on Pensacola, seizing the town and the governor.

While a rousing military success, Jackson's action caused a diplomatic explosion. Unsurprisingly, Spain was irate, demanding the restoration of Spanish authority in Florida. Onís made that point clear to John Quincy, telling him his government would not negotiate until that demand had been met. Likewise Great Britain did not take lightly Jackson's harsh treatment of its two subjects. Yet, despite popular outrage, Castlereagh exercised restraint. American-British relations did not deteriorate.

The uproar reached into Monroe's cabinet, where Adams had to deal with his colleagues and the president. With one exception Monroe's officers wanted Jackson and his actions condemned. Moreover, a public outcry, with Henry Clay a leading spokesman, demanded that the president disavow the general's high-handedness and discipline him. In the cabinet Secretary of War Calhoun took a hard line, asserting that Jackson had exceeded his orders and needed to be called down. While those men saw a rogue general who had run amok, Adams perceived opportunity. He wanted to use Jackson's exploits to prod Spain not only to give up Florida but also to agree to an expansive western boundary for the United States.

Adams constructed an inventive argument. Admitting that he pushed his principles to their extreme limit, he concluded that the United States should be wrong with strength, not with weakness. He would back Jackson, who had rendered exceptional service to the American cause; to not do so, in Adams's argument, would be akin to backing the country's enemies. According to Adams, Jackson had not conducted an unauthorized offensive. Rather, the general had acted on the defensive, because he had simply responded to American citizens crying to their government for help against marauding Indians. Defining his position in writing for the president, he employed diplomatic language: "We could not suffer our women and children on the frontiers to be butchered by savages, out of complaisance to the jurisdiction which the King of Spain's officers avowed themselves unable to maintain against those same savages." Moreover, he continued, when the Spanish governor in Florida threatened to use force to eject Jackson from the territory, Jackson had no alternative but to move against him.[43]

Adams argued that because Spain had proved too weak to police its border, the United States had not only the right but the obligation to do so in order to defend basic interests. His unyielding stance got results. Asserting American authority and power meant for him that Spain would have to give way. Executive prerogative also concerned him. His placing Jackson on the defensive ensured that the executive as commander in chief could authorize his actions. If Jackson was on the offensive, however, then the legislature would have precedence, for only Congress could declare war. Adams worried that any "disclaimer of power in the Executive is of dangerous example and of evil consequences."[44]

Although Adams never brought his fellow cabinet members all the way to his side, he did persuade the president to back him most of the way. Monroe refused to disavow Jackson's actions, though he did direct him to restore Spanish authority in Florida and withdraw from the territory. He also moderated Adams's language in the secretary of state's communications with Spain. Yet he did not alter his top diplomat's thrust.

The most important document was a letter dated November 28, 1818, to the American minister in Madrid, who was to convey it to the Spanish government. While addressed to that official and a single nation, Adams had it sent to every other American representative in European capitals. In addition, it appeared in American newspapers. It was his and his country's bugle blast about ambition, determination, and power. He wanted all Europe as well as his fellow citizens to hear it. The core of this lengthy dispatch essentially covered the same ground Adams had laid out before the president and cabinet as well as Onís. Noting that Monroe would neither punish nor censure Jackson, he declared that the general acted as a pure patriot, defending innocent American citizens who had been horribly assaulted by Indians. Every principle of international law and natural law endorsed Jackson's and America's vindication—self-defense.

Adams broadcast that Spain should look not to America for an apology or recourse but to the incompetence of its officials in

Florida. He drove home his paramount point: Spain must understand that the United States would tolerate neither treachery nor
impotence. He gave Spain advice—either place a force in Florida
adequate to protect the territory and meet its obligations or cede
to the United States a province over which it exercised merely
nominal authority. This situation provided a perfect opportunity
for Adams to emphasize the rise of America as a power.[45]

This missive had a powerful impact. Americans generally
cheered. Writing Adams, Thomas Jefferson called it and a later
letter to Onís the most powerful state papers he had ever read. It
muted calls in Congress for resolutions disapproving the administration's handling of Florida and Jackson. In Europe governments took note of John Quincy's assertions. They especially
noticed Britain's inaction despite the execution by military tribunal of two of its subjects. Europeans had to acknowledge that on
its own continent America's independence and power were apparently beyond challenge.

After Jackson's campaign and Adams's use of it, negotiations
moved forward smartly. In July, Onís had left Washington for his
summer retreat in Pennsylvania and to protest Jackson's foray.
Adams had already informed him that although America abhorred
the evil of war, it was not scared of it. With Onís away from the
capital, the French minister Hyde de Neuville stood in for him
during the tense summer weeks, transmitting messages to and
from the secretary of state. It was quickly decided that Florida
would come to the United States; in turn the United States would
provide five million dollars to cover American citizens' claims
against Spain.[46]

The western boundary of the Louisiana Purchase occasioned
more discussion. An alarmed Spain wanted to brake the westward advance of an expansionist and increasingly powerful
United States; its chief goal was the security of most of Mexico.
As a result, it desired to retain all of the northernmost Mexican
province of Texas as a buffer. Its eastern border with Louisiana
on the Sabine River had in the eighteenth century marked the

dividing line between Spanish and French possessions. In 1818 the Sabine remained the divider between the American state of Louisiana and Spanish Texas.

The Americans initially wanted to move farther into Texas, some even advocating as far as the Rio Grande, hundreds of miles beyond the Sabine, which separated Texas from Mexico proper. Adams himself was prepared to demand the Rio Grande. In addition, various streams between it and the Sabine were mentioned as possible borders. Finally, President Monroe directed Adams to accept the Sabine. The secretary of state did not oppose that decision, though later he stated that he was the last man in the administration to agree to it. Texas was left for another day, when both Adams and the country would have to face it.[47]

Adams accepted the Sabine in no small part because he aimed at a target far to the north and the west. At that time Spain had a legitimate claim to the huge expanse lying west of the Rocky Mountains and south of Canada. Adams perceived and grasped the opportunity to realize his dream of making his country a continental power. He would press Spain to relinquish to the United States a major portion of that territory all the way from the Rockies to the Pacific Ocean. By then the Spanish government and Onís were beyond obstruction. They mainly wanted to salvage as much as they could. He went back and forth regarding possible boundaries with Onís, who in the fall had returned to Washington. They proposed different routes from the Sabine north to the latitude that would then run west to the Pacific. Finally, in January 1819, the two diplomats concurred on a broken northwesterly line from the Sabine along rivers to the forty-second parallel. From there it ran directly west to the Pacific Ocean. All to the east and north of that line would be indisputably American. With this agreement Spain surrendered to the United States its claim to the Pacific Northwest.

With the signing of the Adams-Onís Treaty, also known as the Transcontinental Treaty, on February 22, 1819, Adams had achieved his great goal—his country stretched from the Atlantic to the

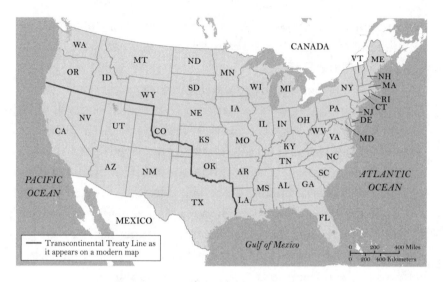

**THE TRANSCONTiNENTAL TREATY BOUNDARY, AS SEEN ON A MODERN MAP OF
THE UNiTED STATES.**

Pacific. In fewer than five years he had witnessed and contributed significantly to an almost unbelievable change in his country's fortunes. At the end of 1814 the United States had barely
escaped humiliation by Great Britain. Now it stood athwart much
of North America unchallenged as a continental power.

Adams had accomplished an amazing diplomatic feat. At practically no cost to his country, he had secured the southwestern
border and obtained a window on the Pacific. The $5 million
assumption of claims was minuscule; moreover, he gave nothing
on the American position on South America. Underscoring the
acclaim for the treaty, the Senate ratified it unanimously a mere
two days after Adams and Onís had signed it.

He had certainly devoted himself to the negotiations. Louisa reported him so invested that he barely took time to eat or
sleep. Adams termed the signing day "perhaps the most important day of my life." While he and President Monroe had col-
laborated smoothly, Adams gave chief credit to the "Disposer
of events, who had brought it about in a manner utterly unexpected and by means the most extraordinary and unforeseen."
Thus he explained Jackson's role. In his view America's future

looked incredibly bright. Now his great hope—may God grant this outcome.[48]

His satisfaction and pride were quickly exploded, however. One article of the treaty voided all land grants in Florida by the king of Spain prior to the initial Spanish proposal to cede the territory. Yet within three weeks after the treaty had been concluded, Henry Clay, of all people, informed the president that the grants had in fact been made on the day immediately prior to the date stipulated in the treaty.

Adams was mortified. He blamed both Onís and himself. He accused the Spaniard of duplicity, of signing the treaty even though aware of the problem with the land grants. As for himself, he deplored his heedlessness in not examining all the documents as carefully as he should have. In his diary he bemoaned his lapse, which gave him the sensation that the treaty was so much a blessing that something had to blemish it. No matter the future, he would always remember his carelessness. If reproach should come his way, he will have deserved it.[49]

There was no disastrous outcome, however. To repair the situation, Adams, with Monroe's concurrence, directed the American minister in Madrid to tell the Spanish government that upon ratifying the treaty Spain must explicitly renounce the disputed grants. At first, the Spanish sought to find some advantage, to no avail. The renunciation and ratification came, but not immediately. Not until February 1821 did the final ratification by the two countries take place.

The interim between the two ratifications gave Adams pause. In March 1820 he said to a senator that the treaty meant little to him. The next month he told a congressman that he had always placed much less value in it than assumed. Yet that self-proclaimed reservation did not hold. Once the final treaty had been ratified, he repeated his initial assessment. On the day after the Senate reaffirmed its ratification, he recorded it as "the most important event of my life." More than two decades later he rendered his final judgment: "The Florida Treaty was the most important incident in my life and the most successful negotiation ever consummated by the Government of this Union." He did not exaggerate. Almost two centuries after the fact, most historians award the Adams-Onís Treaty a privileged place in the pantheon of American diplomatic history.[50]

Adams had attained a magnificent trophy for his country, for which he was justifiably proud. He saw his achievement as a national blessing—in his words, "every part of the Union was equally dear to me." Yet he admitted that he harbored a substantive qualm. During the interim between ratifications, he talked with a senator about the question of the Sabine River boundary. In the conversation he declared that as an eastern man he would have opposed the acquisition of Texas or even of Florida without a restriction on slavery. He went further, avowing that if he were in Congress, he would urge rejection of the treaty without a prohibition against slavery. Moreover, he expressed surprise that no eastern member had done so. In a great irony, the ardent nationalist who professed devotion to the entire Union stated explicitly that on sectional grounds he would have opposed his own handiwork.[51]

Adams's statements about how he would have reacted to his treaty had he been a member of Congress were undoubtedly influenced by an uproar in domestic politics that occurred simultaneously with his Spanish negotiations. In 1818 Congress began seriously to consider the application for statehood from the Territory of Missouri. Although the Missouri petition did not specifically mention slavery, the territory held a number of slaves. In fact, slavery had been legal in Missouri under both the French and the Spanish, and the Louisiana Purchase also guaranteed the legality of slavery in the territory. As a result, it was generally assumed that Missouri would be a slave state. That fact alone did not initially cause any alarm. Since the adoption of the Constitution, four new slave states had joined the Union—Kentucky, Tennessee, Louisiana, and Mississippi. And in 1819 Alabama would increase that number to five. No excitement accompanied those admissions, which made for a total of eleven slave states. At that moment there were also eleven free states.[52]

Yet Missouri sparked the first great national crisis over slavery. Many in the North regarded Missouri as different from any of its predecessors. In the first place, it would upset the balance of slave and free states, giving the former an advantage. Moreover, and much more important, people saw in Missouri the future. It would become the first state admitted from west of the Mississippi River as well as from the Louisiana Purchase. Yes, the state of Louisiana had come into the Union in 1812, but that area had a long history centered on the city of New Orleans. And unlike Missouri, Louisiana was viewed by few as heralding anything new. Not only did Missouri represent the future; most of the territory lay above the Ohio River, heretofore the dividing line between slave and free states west of the Appalachian Mountains.

In this view a slave Missouri would carry the institution west and north, greatly expanding its domain and adding to the political power of the slave states. For people, especially in the Northeast, who were concerned about the place of slavery in the nation and southern political potency, Missouri therefore sparked alarm. Becoming known as restrictionists, they fought to restrain the spread of slavery by denying admission to a slave Missouri.

Increasingly rancorous and bitter congressional debates over Missouri lasted from 1818 until 1820. During those months Congress divided fundamentally into two contending forces. Attacks on Missouri stemmed from the North, chiefly the Northeast, while southerners in phalanx defended Missouri and their major social and economic institution. Finally, the adoption in March 1820 of the Missouri Compromise seemingly settled the difficulty. With Speaker of the House Henry Clay a key in its passage, the compromise had two components. First, Missouri would join the Union as a slave state, but in tandem with Maine, which separated from Massachusetts and would come in as a free state. With both slavery and freedom getting new states, the balance between them would remain unchanged. Second, a line was drawn along the southern border of Missouri, 36 degrees 30 minutes of latitude, and extended to the western limit of the Louisiana Purchase. Below this line slavery would be permitted, but not above it, the vastly larger body of the purchase.

Although the compromise settled the dispute over statehood, Missouri created a second furor when its proposed state constitution reached Washington. It contained a clause making illegal the entry of free blacks into the state. To many northerners, particularly the restrictionists, this provision clearly violated the privileges and immunities clause of the U.S. Constitution, which specified that the citizens of every state were entitled to the privileges and immunities in each state. Some northeastern states did grant citizenship to their blacks. Thus congressional members from these states correctly denounced the Missouri prohibition as unconstitutional discrimination against a portion of their citizenry.

The restrictionists, in a second effort to stymie Missouri's entrance into the Union, demanded the removal of this patently unconstitutional limitation prior to admission. Defenders of Missouri insisted that Congress could not dictate terms to a sovereign state. This contest resulted in another sectional settlement. Congress would accept the constitution, but at the same time direct that the state legislature declare publicly that no citizen of any state would be denied the privileges and immunities guaranteed by the federal Constitution. The passage of that agreement in February 1821 finally put to rest the Missouri problem.

Throughout the Missouri controversy Adams participated as a vigilant observer. The debates and the legislative outcome raised in his mind critical issues about the character of his country and its future. They also caused him to reflect upon the relationship among sectional loyalty, political parties, and the future of the Union. The juxtaposition in his mind of morality and the Union forced him to ruminate about utterly fundamental questions.

Adams first mentioned the Missouri crisis in his diary in

July 1819. That entry set the tone for his future deliberations concerning it. He condemned both southern and northern congressmen and senators. The former he slammed for their bellowing and browbeating. Berating them as "slave drivers," he mocked their din about downtrodden workers in the North, dissolution, and bloody conflagration. In turn, he scorned the latter because they cowed before "the slave-scourging republicanism of the planters."[53]

As for the Missouri Compromise itself, Adams favored it. He based his support on four reasons. First, slavery had long existed there under both French and Spanish rule; second, the Louisiana Purchase had validated that slave owning; third, because of slavery's history in the territory, Congress had no right to demand that the state of Missouri abolish the institution; fourth, he did not want to endanger the Union.

At the same time he considered the 36 degree 30 minute line vital. In his mind that provision severely restricted the future growth of slavery. Additionally, he had no problem with Congress's asserting its authority to prohibit slavery in federal territories. In fact, when the legislation reached Monroe's desk, the president polled his cabinet on that article. They all held the restriction valid. But on a second question the president posed, Adams differed with his fellows. Monroe wanted their opinion on whether the restriction applied only to the territorial phase, or whether it also applied to any state that might grow out of the territories. And he desired the responses to both questions in writing so that they would be preserved in the archives of the State Department.

In his declaration that the restriction also included future states, Adams found himself alone. While his colleagues agreed that a sovereign state clearly had the privilege of making its own decision regarding slavery, Adams countered that because of the Declaration of Independence it could not. According to him the Declaration's proclaiming the equal creation and entitlement of all men meant just that; thus no state could establish slavery de novo. At Calhoun's suggestion and to preclude division among his advisers, Monroe specified that they would only have to say whether they considered that section of the compromise consistent with the Constitution. Once the issue was put that way, all five men could answer affirmatively.[54]

Adams's diary makes clear the profound impact Missouri had on him. Noting a conversation with Calhoun in late February 1820 about the crisis, he began to reflect in earnest. He stated the issue had so grasped his mind that he felt compelled to commit his thoughts to paper so that he might organize them. He admitted that he had views that no one had yet publicly expressed, and he did not think the time appropriate for him to do so. He had no doubt that the Missouri crisis was but a preface to "a tragic volume." Although silent at present, he expected that in time he would have to make his opinions known. On Missouri he disagreed with the president, who believed a compromise would satisfy all parties. Adams was not sure, opining that his chief did not comprehend the depth of the dispute.[55]

In his view the debate over Missouri brought forth a heretofore unseen formula for organizing parties. He acknowledged that efforts to do just that with both South America and Florida had failed, but this basis he defined as qualitatively different. This new party formed in the free states would be potentially lethal for the South. And it would ultimately lead to the breakup of the Union. That divorce would take place to separate formally slavery from freedom.

To reach that conclusion, the destruction of the Union, Adams had to envision positively destroying what he had been taught to revere and had served so ably and loyally and in fact was continuing to do—the United States. He had come to this surprising and unprecedented place because he was making up his mind that the evil of slavery made it impossible for the Union to continue while harboring such a barbaric institution. Calling for a leader to rise with the skill to "lay bare in all its nakedness that outrage upon the goodness of God, human slavery, now is the time, and this is the occasion, upon which such a man would perform the duties of an angel upon the earth." He did not see himself as that man, however.[56]

In his mind the occurrence of the separation would not lead to peace between the separated parties. Slavery would again be the precipitating force. "If slavery be the destined sword in the hand of the destroying angel which is to sever the ties of this Union, the same sword," he predicted, "will cut in sunder the bonds of slavery itself." He foresaw a servile war in the slave states combined with the same between North and South. That conflict would lead to the elimination of slavery from the entire continent. Additionally, following emancipation, he foretold that because of racial intermixing when whites predominated, the African race would gradually disappear from the continent. Emancipation, though terrible in its consummation as all great political and religious revolutions are, would end gloriously.

The battle to eradicate slavery would indeed be horrendous. Yet calamitous as he conceived this event, Adams did not waver. Because he defined the institution as "the great and foul stain upon the North American Union," he regarded its death as absolutely worth any price. Although he envisioned a bloody Armageddon ravaging his country, he doubted whether the most ardent resrictionists in Congress could even imagine the ultimate consequences of their goal.[57]

Focusing directly on the congressional debates, Adams lamented the performance of the restrictionists, even though he cherished their agenda. He judged the South much more ably represented than the North, in both oratorical and parliamentary talent. Only Senator Rufus King of New York could contend successfully with men from the slave states like Clay or John Randolph of Roanoke. Regrettably, he acknowledged that the slave men had the most effective speakers. A fatal liability he called it. It chagrined him that so many free-staters revealed themselves to be too feckless or insufficiently committed to their objective.[58]

He thought he knew why. In the free states people knew the

slavery question as only theoretical; they did not feel it emotionally or financially. On the southern side, however, "it comes home
to the feelings and interest of every man in the community." To
him the slavery men had a more profound commitment, with
their feelings and interests more aroused. They saw their society
at stake, whereas most restrictionists concentrated on slavery's
influence on the power relationship between North and South.
He deplored that distinction, which in his view illustrated how
much personal interest overpowered all thoughts of benevolence
or human decency.[59]

On that matter Adams had long expressed his view. The bargain in the Constitution between freedom and slavery had conveyed to the South far too much political influence, its base the
notorious three-fifths clause, which immorally increased southern power in the nation. And in his opinion the past two decades
had witnessed a southern domination that had ravaged the Union.
Now, however, he emphasized what he saw as the moral vicious-
ness of that founding accord. It contradicted the fundamental
justification of the American Revolution by subjecting slaves to
oppression while privileging their masters with about a double
representation. This arrangement meant that the representatives
of slave states had controlled the Union, a dominion that had
led to everything negative in the country's history. In contrast,
Adams asserted, almost everything positive they have opposed.[60]

He did discuss his stress on the universal rights pledged to men
in the Declaration with one southerner, the cabinet associate he
most admired, John C. Calhoun. Following a cabinet meeting in
which Adams had extolled that founding document, the two walked
home together. Adams reported that Calhoun agreed on the nobility and justice of the case he had just elucidated, but the South Carolinian stated the South had long considered the language of the
Declaration regarding universal rights as affecting whites only.

Calhoun went on to argue that confining "domestic labor" to
blacks made for many advantages. He hurriedly added that his
phrase "domestic labor" did not include all work, especially not

farming. He himself had often walked behind the plow, as had his father. Nor did it refer to "manufacturing and mechanical labor," but only "manual labor—the proper work of slaves." Calhoun maintained that racial slavery guaranteed equality among whites because it placed all of them above blacks. "It not only did not excite," he professed, "but did not even admit of inequalities, by which one white man could domineer over another."

Adams said he fundamentally disagreed, for Calhoun's exposition conflated labor with slavery and dominion with freedom. Commenting on the conversation, he wrote in his diary that when probed on slavery, southerners revealed vanity and pride in their masterhood. In his opinion they looked upon themselves as "more generous and noble-hearted" than "plain freemen who labor for subsistence." Furthermore, "they look down upon the simplicity of a Yankee's manners, because he has no habits of overbearing like theirs and cannot treat negroes like dogs." In sum, slavery "establishes false estimates of virtue and vice," especially making "the first and holiest rights of humanity" dependent upon race. In his judgment slavery "perverted human reason," notably in claiming that Christianity sanctioned the institution and that "mutual affection and attachment b[ou]nd master and slave."[61]

Adams's fulminations did not let up during the second phase of the Missouri crisis. Railing against the article in the Missouri constitution barring free blacks, he pronounced it not only unconstitutional but also immoral. In his diary he averred that if he were in the Massachusetts legislature, he would move for an act to declare that so long as the anti-black prohibition remained in the Missouri constitution, the white citizens of Missouri would not enjoy any rights of American citizens when in Massachusetts. This action would only redeem the U.S. Constitution. And if Missouri should retaliate, the result would be the de facto breakup of the Union, initiated by Missouri.[62]

These ruminations, ponderings, and outcries remained largely private. Even in his conversation with Calhoun, he constrained himself, expressing his deepest feelings about slavery and free-

dom and their manifestations only in his diary. Three years after
the final settlement of the Missouri crisis, he discussed the entire
affair with a South Carolina congressman. He told the lawmaker
that his opinion on slavery in general and the Missouri restriction in particular had been falsely presented in the South, with
the goal of hurting him politically. He went on to make clear that
on the first question, the admission of Missouri, he had opposed
the restriction on slavery. On the second, the article in the Missouri constitution, he granted his opposition, but claimed he did
so because it violated a specific clause in the U.S. Constitution. In
the South, Adams said, the two had been erroneously conflated.
The South Carolinian replied that he understood the explanation,
which pleased him immensely.[63]

In this exchange Adams did not disclose the concerns about
slavery that he had mentioned in his diary. His motives for keeping to himself his beliefs, opinions, and predictions about slavery were undoubtedly complex. He admired President Monroe, a
slave owner. Additionally, he believed that as secretary of state he
was engaged in important work for his country. He surely realized that public advocacy of strong antislavery views would mean
his ouster from the cabinet. He would no longer be able to honor
the high calling of serving his country. Even more, any chance
for his advancement to the presidency would end. That goal was
always there, though difficult to acknowledge. He recognized that
the Republican party provided the only political conveyance capable of transporting a man to that office. He was also quite aware
that it would never accept a vigorously antislavery passenger.
He knew full well, as the fulminations in his diary make clear,
that the South occupied a powerful place in it. For the foreseeable
future his national aspirations would require his public silence on
his antislavery convictions.

Clearly at this point Adams was not prepared to sacrifice his
place in Monroe's cabinet and his ambition in the nation on the
altar of antislavery. And he did not disclose his genuine sentiments
on slavery until his career as a national politician had ended. Yet,

through his thorough communion with himself between 1818 and 1821, he began marking his probable path if and when he gave up his ambition for national office.

While surely the most searing, Missouri was not Adams's only contact with a slavery-related issue during his secretaryship of state. In these years Great Britain stepped up its effort to halt the transatlantic slave trade from Africa to the Americas. The United States had outlawed the trade to its shores in 1808, and in 1819 Congress passed new legislation giving the federal government control over the disposition of Africans taken from ships trying to smuggle them into the United States. Great Britain, however, wanted closer cooperation from the United States in blocking that traffic.

The British minister in Washington, Stratford Canning, appealed to Adams to obtain that collaboration. Specifically, the British wanted the United States to agree to a treaty that would enable warships of all signatories to stop and board vessels on the high seas when suspected of trafficking in slaves. Though a staunch opponent of the slave trade, Adams refused to accept this proposition. He also made clear to Canning that he spoke for the Monroe administration as well as for himself.

Remembering the struggle over impressment leading up to the War of 1812, Adams could not support any policy that would permit the British navy, or that of any other nation, without war to stop and search American ships. When Canning spoke of the horror of the trade, asking the secretary of state whether he could imagine a greater evil, he had a ready rejoinder: "I said, Yes: admitting the right of search by foreign officers of our vessels upon the seas in time of peace; for that would be making slaves of ourselves."[64]

Even before the British proposal on the slave trade, Adams had concerned himself with the American Colonization Society. Founded in 1817, the American Colonization Society planned to transport free African Americans to a colony established for them on the western coast of Africa. There would be no compulsion;

the society anticipated that large numbers of free blacks would volunteer. Though not an abolitionary organization, the society hoped that by removing a substantial portion of the free African American population, in the South a subordinate, unwanted group not admitted to citizenship and in the North a people subjected to a powerful prejudice, its efforts would encourage masters to manumit their slaves and prompt some states to adopt a gradual emancipation plan. To accomplish its goals, the society sought funds from Congress, from state governments, and from private individuals. It obtained some funding from all three and gained the support of many prominent political leaders, slaveholders included, such as President Monroe, former president Madison, William Crawford, and Henry Clay.[65]

Adams, however, expressed grave doubts about the society and its program. He had several reservations. He thought the blacks would suffer more in Africa than they did in America; besides, he believed their emigration would deprive the country of their needed labor. He also worried that the creation of an American colony in Africa would inadvertently make America an imperial power, with citizens unaware of the possible effect. He wanted no transoceanic American empire.

Furthermore, he could not find in the antislave trade legislation any provision that would permit funding for this sort of purpose. He judged such an interpretation of the law as "an Indian cosmogony: it was mounting the world upon an elephant, and the elephant on a tortoise, with nothing for the tortoise to stand upon." Moreover, he regarded the project as utterly impractical, on par with traveling to the North Pole underground.[66]

At the same time, he respected the motives of the American Colonization Society and esteemed many of its members. That he held both views did trouble him. His admiration for their views forced him to question his own. He concluded, however, that he should hold to his own. He never became a member or financial supporter of the society.[67]

Moreover, another group living apart in his country attracted his attention. At least since his address at Plymouth back in 1802, he had contemplated the place of Indians in American society. In that oration he certainly did not depict them as exalted stakeholders meriting special treatment. Defending Andrew Jackson's campaign in Florida, he branded Jackson's Indian opponents as savages who had no home in his country. Later, at the Executive Mansion, he witnessed a deputation of Indians from six different tribes given an audience by President Monroe. He portrayed them as "among the most savage of the desert, part of them all naked." In addition, he did not think they knew what was happening.[68]

Yet when he attended meetings between the president and representatives of the Cherokee tribe, he had a quite different reaction. He termed the Cherokee "the most civilized of all the tribes of North Americans Indians." He described them as dressed as Americans dress and with an excellent command of the English language. He also reported that they gave an account of their present institutions, which he labeled most promising.

When on another occasion four Cherokee chiefs met with Monroe, Adams found himself impressed. Their conduct did not differ from that of "well-bred country gentlemen." He noted that in Washington they had attended evening parties, visited drawing rooms, and even appeared at Louisa's receptions. He also held that they had the advantage in a written contest with the Georgia congressional delegation. Clearly, he had not come to a single vision of the Native Americans and their future in the United States.[69]

Wrestling with the Spanish negotiations and the potential repercussions of Missouri, Adams sought to refine for himself the meaning of his country and its future direction. The proper place of free blacks and Indians also occupied his attention. An opportunity for him to articulate his thoughts about his country and his hopes for it came with an invitation to address the celebration in Washington marking the anniversary of American independence, set for July 4, 1821.

Adams began his oration with a history lesson underscoring his understanding of the fundamental reason for the migration of certain Britons from their homeland to colonies that would become the United States. Although he admitted that Great Britain had a noble history, he argued that the overpowering authority of church and state had given rise to such pervasive conflict that freedom faltered. As a result our ancestors willingly left a country they treasured more than their lives. They departed because they esteemed liberty and conscience even more than their native soil.

Despite their immigration to this side of the Atlantic, Adams said that these colonists remained loyal to their native land until the British government's assertion of a right to absolute power compelled them to separate themselves from their mother country. Even before the separation, however, all along they had suffered because the mother country had treated them harshly and unjustly. For Adams the final blow came when the British Parliament decided to benefit the British people by taxing unrepresented Americans.

He insisted such oppression had prompted overt American resistance. When Americans had conveyed to Great Britain their sincere belief about the wrongs they had suffered, the British government coldly rejected them. In Adams's interpretation Britain responded aggressively, "insultingly obliging the Americans to cling to their unyielding rock of human rights."

This stance led directly to the Declaration of Independence. That document, according to Adams, spoke to the world in the first public pronouncement by a nation that civil government had no other legitimate foundation for existence. In his view that truth became the basis of a new truth to spread over the world. The Declaration must stand perpetually, he proclaimed, "alone, a beacon on the summit of the mountain, to which all the inhabitants of the earth may turn their eyes for a genial and saving light till time shall be lost in eternity, and the globe itself dissolve, nor leave a wreck behind."

With this moral standard America confronted Great Britain during six years of war and subsequently in a hostile world. Never did Adams's Americans waver; with a slingshot they confronted the Goliath of Great Britain. Continuing his biblical metaphor, he averred that when they dispatched the rock guided by heaven, with a thud "the giant monster fell."

With their new position in the world, Adams maintained, Americans had first and foremost to secure their independence. But they also had three additional objects to attain—first, to celebrate and make for all time their Union and posterity; second, to organize governments in the several states; third, to arrange for friendship and commerce with foreign nations. Striving to guarantee and shield these goals, Americans moved quickly to establish a federal Constitution, and their delegates, all chosen upon precepts affirmed in the Declaration, did so peacefully.

In his judgment Americans had succeeded. In the four decades since prevailing over Great Britain, the country had gone through modifying its own government and through the hardships of peace and war. And, absolutely central for him, "never for a moment have the great principles, consecrated by the Declaration of this day, been renounced or abandoned."

In the larger world, Adams described America as announcing "to mankind the inextinguishable rights of human nature, and the only lawful foundations of government." Yet its calls had been contemptuously dismissed. During the almost half century of its existence, without exception his homeland had respected the independence of others while upholding its own. "Wherever the standard of freedom and independence, has been or shall be unfurled, there will her heart, her benedictions and her prayers be." Simultaneously, he made clear, "she does not go abroad in search of monsters to destroy."

Adams wanted most for his country to retain absolute control of its independence and freedom of action. As he saw the world, his country must never sign up under any other flag, for then it would put itself in an inextricable position. For Adams such involvement would entail moving "from *liberty* to *force*." His country must spurn any semblance of an imperial canopy. It must never deviate from its inherited spirit and always maintain control over its own actions.

His conclusion reiterated his credo that America's "glory is not *dominion*, but *liberty*." His country did brandish weapons, but never abandoned this core value. This credo, he broadcast, had been its testament, and as far as possible its practice with all others. On its own continent, however, as emphasized in his dealings with Spain, dominion and liberty went hand in hand. Moreover, in its sphere peace meant its freedom to act independently, when required.

In his final affirmation he declared that if the God ordaining the Revolution, the God cherishing the pure heart, could at this moment descend from heaven and speak in words mankind could hear, His charge to all here and everywhere else in the world would be "GO THOU AND DO LIKEWISE."[70]

In his July 4 address Adams spoke eloquently about the appropriate conduct of the United States, albeit theoretically. Since he was his country's chief diplomat, his views assumed concrete form in his policy toward the crumbling Spanish Empire. By the time he became secretary of state, Spain no longer had the power to hold it together. In fact, it had to contend with open revolt in several colonies in South America. Yet, despite its weakness, Spain was not prepared to relinquish voluntarily its possessions on the western side of the Atlantic.

Though an opponent of European imperialism, Adams had no doubt that his country had to take a neutral stance in the Spanish colonial contest. At the same time he continued to believe that the United States had to oppose adamantly any other European power replacing Spain as colonial master in the Western Hemisphere. As far back as his Russian mission, he asserted that Spain could not sustain its empire.[71]

Secretary of State Adams did not function in a vacuum, however. The striving for independence in South America spurred a strong positive reaction in the United States. Many Americans expressed their eagerness to assist others struggling to throw off a colonial yoke. After all, those who were doing so were only emulating the American example. These voices of Americans cried for the United States to support the rebels diplomatically and with aid, including arms.[72]

Unsurprisingly, this sentiment had political manifestations. A number of men in Congress urged the Monroe administration to be proactive on behalf of the South Americans fighting for their freedom. Solons already opposed to the administration, with Speaker Clay in the forefront, took an especially strong stand. Adams found himself in the midst of the political turmoil; as secretary of state he became the flash point. When the administration did not act as the opposition wished, the opposition struck at him both as the architect of foreign policy and as a potential successor to Monroe.

Even facing the domestic squabble, Adams kept his attention focused on how Europe might react to events in South America. Of course, with domestic and foreign affairs so intertwined, they could not be divorced. He doubted that France would intervene, even though the country had a new royalist government installed by the victorious powers following the fall of Napoleon. Moreover, an army of France had successfully invaded Spain to put down an insurgency against the Spanish crown.

He worried only about Great Britain's intervening. That country had not merely the strongest navy in the world, which could bolster a new colonial effort, but also flourishing Caribbean colonies nearby. Yet he never wavered in making clear to Great Britain that neutrality remained America's policy as it should Britain's. In December 1818, however, he informed the British minister that when Great Britain decided to acknowledge one or more of the South American governments, the United States would go along but not with any formal agreement.[73]

By the early 1820s the growing rapprochement between the two countries led to a British diplomatic initiative that prompted Adams to formulate a major foreign policy principle. In the late summer of 1823, the British foreign minister, George Canning, proposed to the American envoy in London an alliance to counter any effort by continental European powers to intervene in South America.

When this proposal reached Washington in October, it occasioned both excitement and debate in the administration, which lasted until the beginning of December. Impressed with the British offer, yet cautious, Monroe shared it with his two Virginian mentors, Jefferson and Madison. With Jefferson the most enthusiastic, all looked favorably upon Great Britain's seeming willingness to treat the United States as an equal, not an inferior. Discussions in the cabinet generally took that path, with Calhoun forcefully arguing for acceptance. Ultimately, in the cabinet unity prevailed, with one notable exception.

Vigorously disagreeing, Adams advocated a different approach. In his judgment the United States should act alone, announcing its policy as its own, and tied to no one else's. It would be more honest as well as more dignified, he professed, to spell out our principles ourselves "than to come in as a cock-boat in the wake of the British man-of-war."[74]

During the deliberations two diplomatic notes from Tsar Alexander I helped Adams press his case. He saw them as providing a marvelous opportunity to make a bold statement to all of Europe. In both the notes, speaking for the Holy Alliance, the concert formed by the monarchical powers after their defeat of Napoleon, as well as for himself, Alexander proclaimed the virtues of royal government and even of despotism. He exulted in the failure of rebellion against monarchs in Europe and asserted the determination of the alliance to suppress incipient republican regimes anywhere.

Adams felt the United State had to reply. Because in 1822 the United States had already recognized several of the new South American republics, he wanted no doubt to exist about his country's view of any prospective European move toward that continent. He thought his paper should begin with a resounding statement about the virtues of republican government. Then it should make plain the resolve that the United States would not accept any European intervention on the western side of the ocean. He wanted two documents carrying the same message, one to Great Britain, the other to Russia.

He broached his idea to the president and cabinet, in oral presentations and in written drafts. Lively discussion ensued, at first most of it negative. There was fear that Adams's wish for a powerful statement could antagonize its recipients, causing strong negative reactions from them, possibly even a military one. Adams forged ahead, maintaining that their own interests would temper any overreactions from the Europeans. Monroe wavered, changing his mind more than once. Finally, however, he gave Adams authorization to send tough messages; because of John Quincy's insistence, he even agreed to a stern paragraph that really worried him.

Adams considered this missive to Russia the most notable paper he had ever written. His language left no doubt about where his country stood. And although the words were his, he spoke for his country. He proudly pronounced it republican and that the United States would maintain its independence, with neutrality its watchword and peace its goal. Those three qualities—independence, neutrality, peace—he proclaimed as the American maxim. While the United States would, as heretofore, avoid any involvement in European politics, Adams affirmed that his country could not look with indifference at any effort by any European power to interfere with force on this side of the ocean to restore Spanish power, or to transfer any possession of Spain to any other European country, or to introduce a monarchy in any of them.[75]

He left unsaid whether the United States would react with force should such intervention occur. In fact, he did not regard that eventuality as a realistic possibility. Still, he unmistakably declared that the United States considered both North and South America its particular sphere of influence. And within that realm the United States would make the rules; there would be no partners. Commenting on the possibility of a South American country's becoming part of an American system, Adams did not mince words. Regarding any system in this hemisphere, he thundered, "We have it; we constitute the whole of it; there is no community of interests or of principles between North and South America." In his mind the concepts of independence, neutrality, and peace obviously did not preclude that of power. He stood foremost among Americans in his unswerving determination to assert the hegemony of his country.[76]

While going over Adams's messages to foreign powers, the president and his cabinet also conferred about what his annual message to Congress, due when that body convened at the beginning of December, would contain on this issue. Initially Adams wanted the entire matter restricted to diplomatic messages, thus kept basically private within the administration. Monroe, however, wanted to make a public statement of the policy he had approved. And he did so in his message dated December 2, 1823.

The principles enunciated in that document carried his signature, yet they conveyed Adams's thinking, even his words. Closing this portion of his message, the president announced, "The occasion has been judged proper for asserting, as a principle in which rights and interests of the United States are involved, that the American continents, by the free and independent condition which they have assumed and maintained, are henceforth not to be considered as subjects for future colonization by any European powers."[77]

That ringing declaration publicly proclaimed this hemisphere the distinct province of the United States, a fact that European powers must understand and accept. The United States would not abide any future European colonization or intervention. This creed, which became known as the Monroe Doctrine, carried the president's name, but his chief diplomat's concepts.

Throughout this decision making, Adams insisted that attention remain riveted on the Western Hemisphere. When President Monroe wanted to include in his message reproof of the French invasion of Spain and support for the Greek effort to break away from the Ottoman Empire, Adams urged reconsideration. He pointed out that the United States had always asserted that it would not interfere in European affairs. To do otherwise now, he argued, would both appear to defy all of Europe and undermine his assurances to Europe that America would always follow a neutral path regarding internal European affairs. As with the specific reaction to Great Britain and Russia, in this instance he also prevailed. According to him, American policy must never vacillate, but stay fixed on what he perceived as the critical object, authority in the American continents.[78]

While Adams found himself deeply involved in developing and expounding major foreign policy decisions, his dealings with European diplomats accredited to the United States stimulated him to make observations about them personally as well as about diplomats and their craft generally. He considered Stratford Canning, who came from Great Britain in 1820, a most troublesome partner. Although he admired Canning's sincerity, he faulted him for lacking suppleness and complained about his stubbornness. Adams recorded that he had to employ provocation to get anything from the Englishman. In contrast, he prized the "moral qualities" of Hyde de Neuville. Even though the Frenchman was touched with royalism and at times indiscreet and irritable, Adams lauded his commitment to the critical virtues, such as honor, justice, even liberty. Unable to forget his duplicity regarding the Transcontinental Treaty, the secretary of state reserved his harshest evaluations for the Spaniard Luis de Onís, describing him as unscrupulous and decrying his untrustworthiness and deception. In sum, he charged Onís with immorality and dishonesty.[79]

The foreign representative Adams most esteemed, Sir Charles Bagot, the British minister with whom he dealt from 1817 to 1819, forced him to reassess his criteria for a successful diplomat. Amazed, he attributed much of Bagot's success to what he viewed as the Englishman's mediocrity. In his diary Adams admitted that this realization undermined his conviction that the most talented made the best diplomats.[80]

Secretary Adams zealously guarded his perception of himself as the chief foreign policy spokesman of the administration. It distressed him when other cabinet officers as well as members of Congress conversed about policy with foreign representatives. In his mind, those discussions, by possibly divulging information that should be confidential, could adversely affect his dealings with those men. Relishing his almost unlimited access to the president, he believed he stood foremost upon any topic of foreign affairs, and should be so recognized.[81]

Even before the events immediately leading to the Monroe Doctrine, he wrote to Louisa that everything notable and all that would be historically important had been handled by the secretary of state. The United States had gained Florida, had become a continental nation, and would soon affirm supremacy in the Western Hemisphere—all had been gained by himself, he asserted in confidence. This boast indicated that he had succumbed, at least for the moment, to the sin of pride, against which from his youth he had been warned, especially by his mother. Yet it contained a fundamental truth. He not only saw the opportunity for his country presented by a decaying Spain; he seized it. Recognizing the unique position given the United States by the broad Atlantic, he forcefully proclaimed America's dominion on its side of the ocean, but always with the addition that it would claim special prerogatives only within its self-defined orbit.[82]

Even in the midst of his trying, albeit exciting, diplomatic life, Adams kept toiling away on his Senate-mandated report on weights and measures. In late 1819 he bemoaned his inability to escape from the maze of research. More than half a year later he recorded that the writing was difficult and went slowly. On the last day of 1820 he acknowledged that he had been working constantly for six months on that project, but had not quite completed it. Taking the report and the continuing Spanish negotiation together, he described the year 1820 as possibly the most grueling he had ever known.[83]

Finally, in February 1821, almost concurrently with the Senate's re-ratification of the Adams-Onís Treaty, he announced he had finished what he termed a herculean task. Louisa's exultant "Thank God we hear no more of Weights and Measures" reflects the impact of the work on him and his household. When he presented his manuscript to the Senate, it had been seen only by the departmental clerks who copied it and his most intellectual colleague, Secretary of War Calhoun, who liked it, but considered it a book more than a report. He also made a few suggestions, which Adams incorporated.[84]

His finished product totaled 245 pages in its published format as a Senate report. Typically, he deprecated it as less than perfect. Still, he did not anticipate that he could "ever be able to accomplish any literary labor more important to the best ends of human exertion, public utility, or upon which the remembrance of my children may dwell with more satisfaction." Expectant, he yearned for the realization of his hopes.[85]

The Senate received a document based on exhaustive research that discussed the history of weighing and measuring down through the centuries. His study led him to advocate that the United States adopt the French metric system. In fact, he desired it to become universally used. That would, he predicted, advance the cause of peace in the world, helping to fulfill Christ's mission on earth. At the time his effort had little impact. The Senate accepted it, ordered it printed, and tabled it. Congress did not adopt the metric system. Indeed, the report disappeared. Even so, close students of the subject judge it one of the finest scholarly treatments of the topic ever written.[86]

Although Adams never stinted on his diplomatic responsibilities and pushed himself to complete on time the report on weights and measures, he also found himself caught up in the swirl of presidential politics. Even before James Monroe's second inaugural, on March 4, 1821, angling for the succession had begun. Then, from the outset of his second term, the jockeying became a whirlwind if not a gathering maelstrom. Adams knew he could not escape the turbulence, and he would not choose to do so.

He realized that no matter what he did or did not do, his post in the State Department thrust him directly into the path of the onrushing torrent. His position as secretary of state, he wrote, made it the interest of all the candidates' supporters to try and turn public opinion against him. With that statement he acknowledged that attacks on him originated in the aspirations of men who perceived him as an obstacle to their paladins' march to the presidency.[87]

Early on Adams concentrated his attention, as well as his disdain, on two men he identified as scheming candidates. Henry Clay, he believed, had for years seen him as his chief rival to become Monroe's successor. In Adams's mind, Clay's antiadministration stance in Congress on everything from Jackson's expedition into Florida to aiding South American rebels aimed at embarrassing both the president and his secretary of state. Clay did resent Monroe's not naming him secretary of state, and he was determined to succeed his nemesis. That led him to spur and aid anti-Adams initiatives, because he saw the secretary of state as a major roadblock to his reaching his goal. As secretary of state, Adams seemingly was next in line for the presidency. Moreover, he had a distinguished name, an exemplary diplomatic record, and an assumed base in New England. For Clay, making Adams a target made good sense, and he went after the secretary of state where he could. Although his ambition matched Clay's, Adams's political creed would not permit attacks on an individual.[88]

From the outset of his service in Monroe's cabinet, Adams had branded William Crawford with just a single talent—conspiracy. In his judgment Crawford was really a traitor to the president because he placed his own ambition ahead of loyalty to his chief. Adams saw Crawford making use of all possible venues to give himself an advantage. He especially denounced his colleague for putting forth appalling opinions, their main object being to harm him.[89]

Even though he did not have precisely the same opinion of both men, he did find one trait in common. Both had been born in Virginia, though Clay had moved west and Crawford south. Virginians still viewed the Union as their particular province. And with no actual Virginian a serious possibility, Adams assumed that one of the two native sons would receive the backing of that still powerful state. For that matter, even though Monroe had assured John Quincy of his neutrality in the race, he worried that Virginia nativity could influence the president's choice. He even opined that Crawford would be the man.[90]

Preoccupied with Clay and Crawford through Monroe's first term, Adams at the beginning of 1822 confronted the appearance of an additional contender when the one cabinet associate he really admired entered the fray. Secretary of War Calhoun permitted friends to put forward his name. Adams was informed that the Carolinian's main objective was to stop Crawford. He had nothing against Adams, whom he really preferred. Yet information coming to Adams had Calhoun asserting that his intelligence indicated the secretary of state did not intend to become a candidate.

Calhoun's entry quickly affected John Quincy's relations with him. Attacks on Adams promptly appeared in pro-Calhoun newspapers, as they had been coming from those favoring Clay or Crawford. From the moment Calhoun came in, Adams said that assaults on him from Congress, state legislatures, and newspapers increased tremendously. He confided to his diary that he and Calhoun now had a tricky relationship. Now their friendship could be only civil, not confidential. He discerned Calhoun's looking only to his self-aggrandizement, in Adams's catechism a major transgression.[91]

In the summer of 1822 yet another name was put forward to join an already crowded field. In August the Tennessee legislature placed General Andrew Jackson's name in nomination. No one knew exactly how to take this action, for Jackson did not possess a notable political record, though he had been a U.S. senator. His fame was military; the country had not seen such a man since George Washington. And no one knew whether a second military man could reach the nation's highest office. As for Adams, he looked upon Jackson differently from the other three. At this point, having vigorously supported the general in Florida, he saw Jackson as a valiant soldier who had done great service for his country. Jackson, in turn, expressed gratitude to Adams directly and to others for the secretary of state's ardent defense of him. To a friend he described Adams as the most intelligent American civilian and a man deeply attached to republican government. He further professed that he would never combine with anyone else against Adams.[92]

Although Calhoun, Clay, and Crawford viewed Adams as a formidable opponent, he placed himself in a quite different spot. Those three men were all involved in overt activities promoting themselves that he would never consider appropriate for him. As early as March 1818, when a friend asked whether he planned to do anything to bolster his presidential chances, he answered negatively, declaring his duty was to attend to his responsibilities as secretary of state and not plot additional personal advancement. His remonstration did not end there. Averring he had never even hinted to anyone that he desired any office, he said he would not start now, especialy not with the presidency, which should be conferred freely. That profession he repeated regularly.[93]

He did more than profess, however. He refused to use patronage when doing so would have placed supporters in advantageous posts. Nor would he work with members of Congress in requesting or granting favors. He even rejected his wife's suggestion that he treat civilly all those seeking office. Admitting the excellence of her advice, he discerned a fatal flaw, telling her with a Homeric epithet "there is a Scylla as well as a Charybdis" in her recommendation. According to him, those people wanted most of all a promise, and he found many willing to go to any extreme to obtain one. Some ask openly, while "others like elderly maiden ladies costume a civil word and even a smile into a promise, and then if not on the first possible occasion gratified, charge one with giving delusive hopes and expectations." Then he said of himself he would prefer that people think of him as severe rather than disingenuous. "It is the best of my nature to be rather more willing to be thought hard than insincere."[94]

He castigated all these activities as "caballing," "purchasing," "biding," or "bargaining"—in none of which he would participate. He would have "no ticket in that lottery," he informed a Pennsylvania friend. He had neither ability nor interest in intrigue, and he would do nothing for himself or to counteract others. Building up himself while tearing down others, never—"For this, if I had the talent, I have not the will; and if I had the will, I have not the talent."[95]

Similarly, he rejected any program to rebuff the constant attacks on him in the press. He was certainly aware of the assault from all across the country, condemning it as slanderous. Still, he believed any general effort of rebuttal foolhardy, "for every amputated head of the hydra there will always be two new to shoot up."[96]

He did, however, make one prominent exception. In late 1821 the House of Representatives passed a resolution calling on the president to forward to the House all correspondence relating to the Treaty of Ghent. When the packet reached the House, it included a letter written after the conference to Monroe by Jonathan Russell, one of the American negotiators, now a congressman from Massachusetts. Russell claimed that John Quincy had violated instructions from the secretary of state and offered to give to the British navigation on the Mississippi River in order to guarantee fishing privileges for New England.

Adams exploded. He blamed Clay, a charge with which Clay's major biographer concurs. Clay desired to destroy Adams in the West and much of the South. What made it even worse, Adams considered Russell a friend who had betrayed him. It especially galled him that Russell charged him with breaching the public trust. Confident that Russell had altered his letter, marked "duplicate" rather than "copy," sent to Congress, Adams compared it with the original held by the president in his personal file. He discovered deliberate alteration leading to the prevarication.

Reacting to the perfidy, Adams composed an overpowering written statement highlighting Russell's editing. It demolished Russell's false claim. In the fallout Clay abandoned Russell and in a public letter tried to distance himself from the entire plot. An onlooking Andrew Jackson applauded the deserved thrashing given Russell, whom he denigrated as a proficient villain. Adams's cannon blast destroyed its target; his exposure of the duplicity ended Russell's public career.

Adams had taken great pains in preparing his riposte because in his mind Russell had attempted to undermine not only his integrity and patriotism but also his very sense of himself. Spring 1822 found him diligently working on his initial message. Then, in overkill, he prepared a massive document, complete with appendices containing corroborating papers. It took him the entire summer of 1822, causing him to forgo his traditional seasonal return to Massachusetts. This labor yielded a volume of 256 pages, which he had privately printed. It was as long as his report on weights and measures, a testament to the depth of his anger and his feeling of betrayal.[97]

Setting himself apart from the grasping office seekers, Adams presented himself as a public servant doing his very best and as loyal to the president he served. Only his holding the office he did made him a candidate; certainly nothing he did indicated otherwise. He simply relied on his country and would never retreat from the perils in any position in which it had placed him. People, including his wife, who thought he was "panting to be president" were utterly wrong. He even told himself that he did not want the presidency, informing Louisa that he dreaded becoming president more than he wanted the office.[98]

Yet he would make no public declaration denying his candidacy. To Monroe he did offer to withdraw from consideration if the president thought his withdrawal would serve the country. Monroe did not, a response that surely pleased the questioner. In a letter to Louisa he directly addressed the matter of withdrawal. "Decline publicly to be a candidate?" he asked. His answer was definitive: "No. That would be political suicide." Even more, "it would be to distrust myself and my country."[99]

At the same time he made denials to himself as well as to others, he engaged in several activities that belied those disclaimers. He suggested foreign posts for Calhoun, Clay, and even Jackson, which would of course, if accepted, remove them from contention. That no acceptance transpired does not negate his effort. Additionally, he authorized supporters in Congress and out to work toward increasing their number. On two occasions he even dispatched long letters to both Virginia and South Carolina defending his career in public service. The former went to voters in a congressional district whose representative had been attacking him in Congress on his record as a U.S. senator. It also appeared in the *Richmond Enquirer*, the most important newspaper in the state, and arguably in the South. The latter he addressed to an editor in Charleston.[100]

His concurrent denials and admissions led a frustrated Pennsylvania backer to invoke Shakespeare's *Macbeth.* Terming Adams's yes-no stance a "Macbeth policy," he declared in a letter to Louisa that it would never work. "The man who sits down to be crowned, either by chance or just right, will go bareheaded all his life." Adams countered in a lengthy memorandum that his and Macbeth's situations were totally different. Macbeth lived in a monarchy; chance would never make him king. Moreover, if Macbeth had waited for chance, he never would have been king, and there would have been no tragedy, and no play. Thus the goal of the playwright required Macbeth to act. To his mind, the issue was simple: the pure principle of the Constitution directed that the presidency go to the ablest and most meritorious man. He must rely solely on his country. "*Merit* and *just right* in this country *will be heard*," he pronounced. "And in my case," he continued, "if they are not heard *without my stir* I shall acquiesce in the conclusion that it is because they do not exist." In that event, as he informed Louisa, he relied on himself, with God's blessing of course, and hoped he had the strength to cope with rejection, should that occur.[101]

In sum, Adams was both unable and unwilling to profess openly that he would make a concrete effort to win the presidency. He had to camouflage his ambition. Publicly avowing his desire for the office would place him squarely in the den of politicians he disparaged as grasping and self-seeking. Such an avowal would also violate his sense of decorum as well as his desperately held conviction that his countrymen should perceive his merit and reward it. Furthermore, to announce publicly that he wanted the office would open the door to potential embarrassment and humiliation, both public and private, should he lose. That hazard required that he guard against the eventuality.

Yet in one area he engaged in a most successful strategy, with Louisa as willing partner. At the same time, no doubt can exist that Adams perfectly understood his and her roles. During James Monroe's presidency the social center of the capital was not located in the Executive Mansion. Unlike Dolley Madison, her predecessor as first lady, Elizabeth Monroe was not a social lioness. She evinced little interest in making the president's home the hub of Washington society. Into that vacuum stepped Louisa Catherine Adams. The Adams home on F Street just east of the Treasury Building, which he purchased in 1820, became the social headquarters of the city.

That Adams's home became such a destination was in a basic sense astonishing. He was certainly no social lion. Even his wife noticed an off-putting manner, which she attributed to his focus on studying. He did not disagree, describing himself as a "man of reserved, cold, austere, and forbidding manners." Admitting this character defect, he said, "I have not the pliability to reform it." He detected a key reason as his deficiency as a conversationalist. He conceded that he had never mastered that art of engaging others in a way that "once the ball is set in motion, it will roll." Reflecting upon his performance on social occasions, he reproached himself for various faults, such as saying things that should have been left unsaid, talking too little, or telling jokes in poor taste.[102]

The British-born Louisa Catherine made up for all those shortcomings. "Delicacy through every state of life is the greatest charm a Woman can possess," she wrote. That quality meshed with her upbringing, which taught her the value of sociality and exposed her to numerous social venues. She recognized that she had always wanted men to admire her, no matter their political orientation. And she surely triumphed in this role. To her diary she confided that she feared becoming too popular because she had visitors from every political direction.[103]

Moreover, she greatly admired her husband, whom she thought "a great man." In her view his conscientiousness had brought him to high office, and he merited the recognition he had obtained. She wanted her boys to emulate him and strive to succeed in the manner he had. As the year 1823 drew to a close, she proudly declared that John Quincy deserved his recognition and his country's thanks more than any other man in the United States. In him, along with her three sons, she expressed enormous pride. "I may raise my head in thankfulness to my maker just for having been so greatly blessed," she exulted in her diary. She would stand with and for him.[104]

During the months that were in Washington labeled the season, December until March, she hosted countless gatherings, often several in a single week, ranging from small receptions, often termed drawing rooms by contemporaries, to dinner parties, to larger assemblies, sometimes with dancing. The dinner parties were often all male, but the others included women as well. The diplomatic and political elite came often and in numbers that could range from around a dozen to more than a hundred. By early 1823 the occasions had become so numerous that because of the expense she had to curtail providing music.

Louisa Adams was both a dedicated and an observant hostess. She would not even permit illness to keep her from joining her guests. Yet even she could not always prevent sharp political repartee, especially at what she called a "snarling dinner" composed of intense political opponents. At times, however, John Quincy's cellar helped. After one dinner party she recorded, "The Gentlemen enjoyed themselves apparently very much and testing the strength of Mr. A-s old Madeira the strength of which was not found wanting by the merriment it produced." By the end of 1823 no one else had expended more energy or effort in keeping John Quincy in the political forefront.[105]

According to Louisa Catherine, her husband commended her for her success as a hostess. She reported on one occasion he was so pleased that after the guests' departure, he danced a reel with her and their boys, much to the amusement of the servants and musicians. Generally, she appreciated his not complaining, especially regarding what she termed "my follies." That characteristic, she related, made her extremely grateful.[106]

Although Adams made no specific reference to politics, he expressed great praise for his wife. On their twenty-fifth wedding anniversary, July 26, 1822, he recalled his married years as the most glorious of his life. Finishing a letter to Louisa on that day, he recorded in his diary, "Looking back—what numberless occasions of gratitude!"[107]

While secretary of state, Adams had several portraits painted of him and Louisa. Between 1818 and 1824 he had his done by the notable artists Gilbert Stuart, Charles Willson Peale, and Thomas Sully, as well as by the less well-known Charles Bird King. He certainly showed no aversion to sitting to have his likeness taken. He mentioned that in late September 1818 he sat seven times for Stuart. In the portrait, devoid of details like buttons and books and with only one eye highlighted, he looks straight at the viewer, appearing self-possessed but not austere. Peale's similar pose in the same year gives Adams a longer, more oval face and eyes that gaze into the distance. While the face is warmer, it lacks distinction. The next year King's effort accentuated his subject's long, chiseled nose and broad brow. A lowered chin and downcast eyes give him a preoccupied, almost pensive, look. In Sully's 1824 portrait, as in Stuart's, Adams appears in a three-quarter profile, but the artist has cast the far side of his face in shadow, thus softening the aquiline nose and rendering the secretary of state quite handsome.

Two were done of Louisa, and they provide a sharp contrast. Unlike his of Adams, Stuart's of her, done in 1821, pays greater attention to detail, especially in the lace of her collar and the ribbons of her cap. Her face is enigmatic, either pensive or scornful, and the eyes seem to be looking inward rather than outward in any direction. Charles Bird King's large portrait of 1824 contrasts strikingly with Stuart's, not only in size and brilliant color. Here Louisa is literally costumed, in elaborate dress and turban, and posed sitting with a harp and book of music. Reportedly this portrait pleased neither Louisa nor some of her family. She worked to have it "new dressed" and made an offer to King to defray the cost. No evidence suggests that the alteration ever occurred.[108]

Both husband and wife continued to take seriously their roles as parents. They showed a remarkably similar approach. Louisa granted that since the death of her infant daughter she had never been able to fill the void left in her heart. While she declared that she did love her sons, she had always thought of them as satisfying her pride rather than fulfilling her need for affection and empathy. Yet she craved their company and thought their father too often treated them far too sternly.[109]

Adams no doubt felt great affection for his sons, but in his mind being human meant difficulties would surely come with them. Although he usually noted that when with the family the boys brightened it, he saw himself as needing to imbue them with the same sense of responsibility and duty that his mother and father had pressed upon him. Furthermore, he would hold them to the same high standard he had been expected to meet. Any failure to reach that standard would certainly disappoint him. Of course, their academic education was central, and that meant Harvard for all of them, but he also ensured that in Washington he placed them in the presence of political luminaries. He wanted them to see the most notable.[110]

In his diary Adams reflected on his "cares for the welfare and future prospects" of his sons. Those concerns at times troubled him so much that they interfered with his sleep. By 1820 both George and John were enrolled at Harvard, and Charles Francis was preparing to enter. None had shone as a scholar, however. Admitting he had hoped one of them would have striven for that distinction, he confronted his conviction that all had instead revealed tired minds. He did not hold back: "It is bitter disappointment."[111]

Sharing his displeasure, Adams in 1821 forbade them to come to Washington for a winter break, including Christmas. In his judgment they had not earned that vacation. Their absence distressed their mother. Still, she held her feelings closely; it was her husband's decision to make.[112]

In the fall of that year Adams had visited Harvard and spoken with its president. Although George's and John's low scholarly standing mortified him, a positive report on their moral conduct provided substantial relief. Even though George graduated at the August commencement, both son and father thought that at the ceremony the college had discriminated against him by assigning him an inferior part. About that the father complained unavailingly to the president.

Despite his less than stellar academic performance, George had become an alumnus; his younger brother John would not follow him. In his senior year a few months prior to graduation John was expelled along with some forty other students for violating rules of conduct, probably connected with alcohol. A distraught father wrote two letters to Harvard's president trying to obtain a lessening of the sentence. He did not succeed; John did not receive a diploma. Displaying his disapproval, Adams for the first time declined the president's invitation to attend commencement.[113]

That same summer twenty-two-year-old George, preparing for the law, requested his father's consent to become engaged to a fifteen-year-old niece of Louisa's. When John Quincy asked how long his son expected the engagement to last, George answered five or six years, until he had established himself. Consent was given when George agreed to certain conditions, which Adams did not specify in his diary.[114]

The triumphs and trials of fatherhood did not distract Adams from his continuing embrace of his Christian creed. In the fall of 1819 he finally decided on a church to attend regularly. Before then he had not done so, chiefly because among its many churches Washington did not have an Independent Congregational church, the church, in his words, in which he had been raised and expected to die. He said he could go to any church without embracing its specific doctrine. He ended up choosing the Episcopal Church because he preferred its minister to any others he had heard, though on occasion he still went elsewhere. On one Sunday he heard a sermon by the chaplain of the House in the Capitol. His assessment: "the text was too mighty for the Doctor's talent, which does not consist in preaching."[115]

Attendance at Sunday services failed, however, to satisfy Adams's relationship with his faith. He continued to wrestle with what he perceived as perplexing complexities in traditional Christian doctrine. The fall of mankind through the sin of Adam and his subsequent redemption through Christ on the cross—Christian atonement—he thought utterly unfathomable. Regarding the former, he said he could answer the question of the purpose of a beneficent Creator's placing his own creation in a garden of good and evil only by pointing to the inscrutable ways of God. But when Adam chose evil and in so doing cursed subsequent generations, Adams had to conclude that the absurd became the cruel.

Turning to the New Testament teaching that the death and resurrection of Christ redeemed fallen mankind for all time, he could find no reason, only mystery. He advised Christian ministers to say little about this topic to any listeners prone to use their rational minds. His final judgment: for mankind it is sufficient to know that the Almighty made implausible the wisdom of the world. Struggling with doctrine did not, however, cause him to turn from the faith of his fathers. He identified Christianity as the only religion that posits humility as virtuous and an obligation, which defined Jesus's morality.[116]

His conviction about the excellence of Christian morality made him contemplate requiring that belief for federal service. Conversing with President Monroe about an individual who had one government job yet wanted another, Adams told an undecided chief executive that the man in question was an unbeliever and had published on that subject. He added that some people equate infidelity to Christianity with immorality. He admitted that he had considered doing so, but could not adopt that view generally. He knew the person in question, had taught him at Harvard, and had never heard anything dishonorable about him. Still, he was unsure about his future employment.[117]

Even with his busy schedule Adams made time for physical exercise—sporadic horseback rides, walking, and especially swimming. Swimming had two great advantages over any other form of physical exertion—"cleanliness and muscular exercise, without being heated." He claimed that he had always considered swimming good for his health and thought that learning to swim was so important that it should become a requirement in education.

In Washington he took the Potomac River as his spot. When in the capital during the warm months, he swam regularly, usually with his valet, who would bring a boat along for any emergency, and on occasion with a son. He would disrobe at a favorable place on the banks of the river and spend an hour or more in the water, at times swimming across the river and returning by the boat.

Even though he enjoyed swimming, he conceded one drawback. The pursuit of his favorite pastime carried with it, he admitted, risking his life. To him that liability explained why so few people learned to swim. Friends cautioned him, and he deliberated about giving it up because of that advice. Yet he decided on discretion in his practice, not abandonment. Swimming he would hold to for many more years.[118]

Aside from his seasonal swimming breaks, Adams while in Washington fought for time to relax. He decried the hours he spent on newspapers and materials concerned with official business, for they kept him from reading for pleasure. At moments he would turn to his old and favorite companions Cicero and Tacitus, in the original Latin, of course, whom he sorely missed when those moments were so fleeting. He could even steal an instant to translate lines from Horace. At times he had to abstain from all reading because of inflamed eyes, but nothing so serious as what he had experienced in England afflicted him.

There were other escapes. He retained his attachment to the theater, to which he informed Louisa he had always been devoted. For more than forty years the stage had delighted him. During its season he went when he could. Occasionally at home with a guest he indulged himself in the card game Boston, which, according to Louisa, greatly amused him. In the game the terms used referred to the siege of Boston during the American Revolution. Then the return visits he made most summers to Massachusetts rejuvenated him. He visited with his father and other relatives as well as friends. Fishing trips and swimming in the waters off Quincy harbor he also enjoyed.[119]

Those journeys to and from Massachusetts caused him to celebrate the material progress of the country, exemplified by the improvement in transportation since his Senate days more than a decade earlier. He ascribed the chief advance to the steamboat, a marvel to him. He detailed one 1819 trip in his diary. From Boston all the way to Washington took only one week. Previously it had taken that long to get from Providence, Rhode Island, to New York City. Moreover, the steamboat had beds to rival those in inns, and the periodicals on board amazed him. He noted a single drawback, the noise of the engine, but for him the convenience overpowered it.[120]

No matter the press of official business, the demands of social life, or even the hours taken for exercise and escape, Adams strove to fulfill a self-imposed duty—the keeping of his diary. Upon taking office in 1817, he worried that he would have difficulty making the time for his personal record. And at times he fought to maintain it, and not always successfully. Gaps did appear, once in 1821 for five months. Yet, even when despairing that he could do so, he would find a way to make up the missing record. On April 1, 1822, for example, he noted he had given up any attempt to keep

a full diary, but on June 14 he recorded that he had brought it up
to date. In the lean periods he would usually jot down brief notations, which he would later flesh out into more complete accounts,
but some of the gaps were never filled.[121]

He realized that the diary took precious hours and a great deal
of energy. Yet he persevered. The document did have practical
value for him, as a reference for what had transpired in cabinet
meetings and especially for what he and others had said. To illu-
minate past events he even shared excerpts with the president.
There was more, however. He did not want to sever the binding
that had tied him to his journal since his youth. Furthermore, he
wanted to have a detailed record of his activities in the Monroe
administration. He thought his journal might be the best source
for a history of that presidency. And it certainly did not perturb
him that the history would have an Adams perspective.[122]

At the same time he granted that maintenance of his chronicle came at a high price. Once more he remarked that his grand
ambition was to make some lasting intellectual contribution. "Had
I spent upon any work of science or literature the time employed
on this diary, it might perhaps have been permanently useful to
my children and my country." A few months earlier, after calling
literature "the charm of my life," he avowed his highest ambition
would have been to write a magnificent work of literature that
would have honored him and his country and, just as important,
earned him the gratitude of future generations. Those fervent
aspirations aside, he lamented that he had spent too much time on
his diary. Even so, he could never bring himself to turn away from
his combined narration of his country's and his own history.[123]

His tenure in the State Department would make up, of course,
part of that history. Evaluating it as early as 1821, a proud Adams
reflected with satisfaction on his performance. For that he offered
total thanks to Divine Providence. He intended to look optimisti-
cally toward the future, focused on pursuing his duty and with no
regard for his public reputation. That would come, if it did, from

his hard work and merit, certainly not from any effort on his part to cultivate it.

"The reputation which must be pampered and cosseted" he shunned. His credo he penned in a letter to a friend: "Give me that which is spontaneously bestowed by strangers. Give me that which is reluctantly extorted from rivals. Give me that which the whole nation shall sanction and after ages shall ratify, or give me none." He desired to stand as a moral hero, anointed and blessed by his nation. Looking forward, he exclaimed, "Let my heart be grateful for the past, and prepared with resignation and resource for the future!"[124]

CHAPTER 5

"To Meet the Fate to
Which I Am Destined"

As JOHN QUINCY ADAMS COMPLETED HIS TENURE AT THE Department of State, he found himself immersed in the contest to succeed James Monroe. He would know some success, but would prove unable to sustain it. Between 1824 and 1828 the political world of the Founding Fathers, which Adams idealized and to which he paid fealty, underwent wrenching transformation. In this rapidly changing universe Adams felt uncomfortable. He usually could not bring himself to work actively in his own behalf or to support energetically others wishing to do so. He even refused to employ political patronage for his own benefit. In short, the old political order that he cherished was in its death throes, and Adams was unable or unwilling to escape from its paroxysms.

The highlight of the Washington social season took place at the Adams home on F Street on January 8, 1824, the anniversary of the Battle of New Orleans, when the Adamses hosted a gala to celebrate the victor, General Andrew Jackson, now a sitting U.S. senator. The decision to put on this extravaganza had been made little more than two weeks earlier.[1]

Characteristically Louisa Adams took charge. Her first task involved the preparation of invitations—she ordered five hundred printed. Those invited included almost all members of Congress, executive department heads, and the capital elite. Then she hand delivered most of them herself. Many who did not receive one called on her hoping to be added to the chosen. A marveling, and perhaps political, Louisa Catherine noted in her journal, "The number of persons who came to be invited on this occasion exceed belief."[2]

Contemplating her event, she recorded that she had "a beautiful plan in my head which I shall endeavor to be executed." She transformed her home. Taking doors off hinges, clearing out furniture, rearranging rooms, she made space for the expected throng. Adams's library and study became the ballroom. She had her own design of spread eagles, flags, and the greeting "Welcome to the Hero of New Orleans" chalked on the dance floor. For the music she hired members of the U.S. Marine Band. Worried about the weight of the crowd on the second floor, where the late supper would be served, she went to the trouble of having pillars installed for additional support. To camouflage them she would "make some sort of ornament," which she feared would "occasion more talk than I like." She did not hesitate, however: "I must take my chance and brave it as well as I can."[3]

The elite of Washington political and social society began arriving at seven thirty, with their passage to the home lit by bonfires placed as far as two blocks away. She in an elegant ball gown and her husband in his usual working attire stationed themselves at the front door to greet guests. As expected, hundreds arrived. At nine the guest of honor appeared. Louisa escorted him through the crowd, guiding him up the stairs and to the head of the supper table, while Adams escorted an honored lady to the foot. At the bountiful table the general drank to her health. Although he departed after the meal, the festivities lasted until the early hours of the next morning.

The ball was such a huge success that it became known as the Adams Ball. Louisa observed that it generated lots of talk and "a great deal of nonsense in the Newspapers." The press did give it much attention. A doggerel by an editor caught on:

Belles and matrons, maids and madams
All are gone to Mrs. Adams.

The soiree was widely hailed as a phenomenon, both social and political. Plaudits aplenty came Louisa's way. One observer even asserted that she now rivaled the long-recognized doyenne of Washington society, Dolley Madison.[4]

The dazzling evening permitted Adams to reap the rewards that stemmed from a broadly publicized and admired event designed not to benefit himself but to recognize and exalt the contributions to the nation of another. Yet that he paid a warmly received tribute to Jackson could only redound to his credit. Moreover, his doing so made abundantly clear his positive connection with the man already identified as the "Hero." An Adams-Jackson alliance seemed within the realm of possibility.

While the Adams Ball surely had the intention of advancing his candidacy for president as well as celebrating Jackson's victory, it underscored Adams's opinion of the renowned general. At least since the Florida episode, he had upheld Jackson as a true patriot who deserved his country's gratitude. Furthermore, he never grouped Jackson with the three men he branded as political intriguers and manipulators—Calhoun, Clay, and Crawford. Still, he considered Jackson a formidable candidate, meritorious as well as strong. According to a friend, Adams preferred the Tennessean to any other possibility, except for making "a tacit reservation in his own favor."[5]

At the same time the extent and depth of Jackson's natural charisma and popular appeal escaped him. Through the winter and spring of 1824 he constantly pushed the general as an ideal vice-presidential choice. "I thought the place suited to him and him suited to the place," he confided to a Vermont senator. Although that statement is telling about Adams's ignorance of Jackson's character, he did have some understanding of it. He told a congressman that "the Vice-Presidency was a station in which the General could hang no one, and in which he would need to quarrel with no one." Most important, in Adams's view, he would restore prestige to the office. Time and time again he let his supporters know that he preferred Jackson for vice-president, urging his friends that whenever they could they should register their preference for him in that office. Mostly left unsaid, he clearly hoped that John Quincy Adams would head the ticket on which Jackson had the second spot.[6]

No matter how often he might decry politicians who paid attention to public opinion, Adams sided with Calhoun and Clay as well as Jackson on one critical issue. By the early 1820s the traditional method for Republicans to choose their presidential nominee, the caucus of all congressional Republicans, had come under increasing criticism. Partly it derived from growing popular demand for a more open nominating process. Additionally, partisans of candidates who feared that their favorite stood little chance in the caucus attacked it as unfair, as violating the rights of the people. Convinced that a majority of both citizens and states opposed the caucus, Adams made up his mind to join those standing against it. He told a New York congressman that he considered the procedure "adverse to the spirit of the Constitution and tending to corruption."[7]

The one candidate whose backers championed the old way was William Crawford. They believed that he had the loyalty of a majority of congressional Republicans and would emerge from the caucus as the nominee. They pressed vigorously for it despite having to contend with a severe liability. In September 1823 while visiting in Virginia, Crawford was felled by a stroke. Even though he still suffered from serious physical disabilities in the new year, his political managers refused to let up in their campaign for him.

One tactic they pursued involved Adams. From numerous pro-Crawford sources he got word that the Georgian wanted him as vice-president. A Crawford-Adams ticket, they maintained, would combine New England with the South and surely result in triumph. Never hesitating, Adams refused, stating that a ticket with Crawford "could have no charm for me." At the same time, he insisted his rejection rested on his objection to the caucus more than to the man. He went so far as to announce that because of his strong antipathy to the caucus, he would never even consider a nomination with himself in the first spot. While no doubt can exist about his genuine aversion to the caucus, it is difficult to imagine under any circumstances his uniting with Crawford, a man he had stingingly criticized since joining Monroe's cabinet.[8]

The caucus did meet on February 14, 1824, and it did nominate Crawford. In fact he obtained all but four of the votes, but only sixty-six Republicans attended, barely over one-third of their total number; others chose deliberately not to be there. That Crawford won overwhelmingly created little excitement. His was a Pyrrhic victory. The opposition had withered the status of the caucus.

Although noting in January that the canvas for the presidency was heating up, Adams, as he saw it, maintained his candidacy on his terms. He wanted nothing to do with what he designated as the "mining and countermining," which he identified "as an admirable study of human nature." The newspapers engaged in "pouring forth continual streams of slander upon my character and reputation, public and private" brought forth little retaliation. He recorded that he even answered few letters calling for his opinion, and should not have responded to any.[9]

Yet he kept in contact with his preferred supporters, in certain instances directing them to act, for example, to oppose the caucus and any union with Crawford and to assist Jackson where appropriate. In addition, he made every effort to assure Federalists that the old antagonisms between him and them, which dated back to his days in the U.S. Senate, had disappeared, at least for him. He assured them that an Adams presidency would not mean "a general proscription of federalists from office." Moreover, concrete evidence of what he viewed as spontaneous support gratified him enormously. A handbill from Rhode Island indicating that twenty-seven of thirty-one towns had nominated him for the presidency, even though he recognized it probably meant little in the larger context, "call[ed] for my most grateful sentiments."[10]

For his quest for the presidency Adams paid a high emotional and psychological price. Given his highly self-critical nature, he constantly dealt with the possibility of failure. "The game is up for him," Louisa commented as early as December 1823. In March 1824 he reported dim prospects. In May he opined to his diary, "We know so little of that in futurity," he wrote, "which is best for ourselves, that whether I ought to *wish* for success is among the greatest uncertainties of the election." He continued, "Were it possible to look with philosophical indifference to the event, that is the temper of mind to which I should aspire; but

> Who can hold a fire in his hand
> By thinking on the frosty Caucuses?

To suffer without feeling is not in human nature," he noted, in Hamlet-like lines, "and when I consider that to me alone, of all the candidates before the nation, failure of success would be equivalent to a vote of censure by the nation upon my past service, I cannot dissemble to myself that I have more at stake upon the result than any other individual in the Union." Left unsaid was that each of his opponents had also rendered past service to their country, albeit arguably less extensive. In his judgment any man aspiring to the presidency "shall be a man proof alike to prosperous and to adverse fortune." Furthermore, he who would be president "must possess resources of a power" to serve the country when the country denies him that goal. As always, he concluded, "I look to wisdom and strength from above."[11]

He had delayed his usual summer sojourn in Massachusetts, but by late August "the bitterness and violence of Presidential electioneering" disgusted him. He complained it took too much time from his public business. As a result he decided to bolt Washington, head for home to visit his father, and "dismiss care."[12]

Two events on that trip illuminated his uneasiness with his candidacy, even at that late date. When the steamboat carrying him from New York City docked in Providence, Rhode Island, he received a request to go to the front cabin. There, he recorded, almost all the male passengers had gathered. They paid him a magnificent personal compliment and requested that he join them in a glass of wine. He gratefully accepted and shook hands with each man.

Yet, when at Quincy, he declined an invitation to a public dinner in Boston given in his honor. Fearing it would seem a political spectacle, he directed the bearer of the invitation to say "in the present agitation of the public mind," he thought his appearance would lead to even more excitement, which he wanted to discourage.[13]

On the way back to the capital after a month's holiday, he prepared himself for what he saw as his uncertain future. He recorded that he was anxiously returning to Washington, where he would "meet the fate to which I am destined by the Disposer, who 'Leads the willing, drags the backward on.'"[14]

Back in the capital, Adams had little additional time to fret about the election. In November, Americans would make their choice. There was no uniform procedure, as there is today, with the popular vote prevailing in every state on the same day. In 1824 the election was held on different days. Moreover, some states allotted electoral votes by congressional district, and in six the legislature decided. That no person could amass a majority of the electoral vote was almost foreordained. With four strong candidates, each claiming allegiance to the dominant Republican party, it would be practically impossible for any one of them to rise very far above all the others. There were four, not five, because Calhoun had for the time being given up his presidential hopes and opted for the vice-presidency, for which he had no substantial opposition.[15]

Both the popular and the electoral votes were spread among the four contenders. Still, the outcome separated the four into two distinct groupings. Adams and Jackson far outdistanced their rivals in both counts. Jackson won 99 electoral votes; Adams 84. Far behind, Crawford and Clay garnered 41 and 37, respectively.

That result meant the election would move to the House of Representatives, for the Constitution stipulated that when no one gained a majority of the electoral votes, the House would make the final choice from the top three finishers. That meant dropping the man with the fewest votes. Accordingly, Henry Clay, the most influential member of the House, would not come before that body. The representatives would decide among Adams, Crawford, and Jackson.

The Constitution gave no role to the popular vote in the House proceedings. Yet in a basic sense it followed the electoral count. Jackson and Adams each had far more than either Crawford or Clay. Traditionally, Jackson has been given a clear lead in the popular count with almost 142,000, while Adams polled just under 116,000. Crawford trailed with not quite 48,000. Recent scholarship, however, including estimates of the popular vote in the states where the legislatures still chose, has reversed that standing, allotting Adams more than 212,000 votes and Jackson almost 178,000, with Crawford still far in the rear with over 139,000.

The voting totals aside, the election had a clear sectional dimension. Adams swept New England and enjoyed an overwhelming electoral majority in New York. In the slave states he managed only six votes from Delaware, Maryland, and Louisiana combined. Though Jackson swept Pennsylvania and New Jersey, his great score was seven southern states, while he split the West with Clay. Crawford managed to carry only his native Virginia and his adult home Georgia, with eight additional votes from three states. Clay took Kentucky and Ohio along with Missouri, as well as four in New York. Thus the House would select between two southerners, who shared the votes of their section, and one northerner, who predominated in the Northeast.

With the knowledge that he would be one of the three contestants before the House, Adams did not, as he so often did, sit on the sidelines and let the outcome be what it may. Earlier he had declared that if he finished third, he would withdraw, but no evidence suggests that placing second would have caused him to contemplate dropping out. The convening of Congress at the beginning of December signaled the start of the final push for the prize, which the House would award in early February. At that point Adams became quite active, meeting and talking with numerous congressmen and senators. In December and January his diary details a host of engagements.[16]

Likewise, Louisa kept up her role as the manager of the crucial social dimension of her husband's campaign. Her dinners and drawing room soirees continued to attract notables, and she did not show favoritism. A participant in the Washington scene commented on an evening at the Adamses where "Jacksonites and Adamsites and Crawfordites all mingled harmoniously together." Bitter political partisanship had not yet triumphed over social civility.[17]

Viewing the upcoming House contest, Adams did express distress about one matter. He noticed that both his opponents had settled on a vice-presidential preference. Calhoun had allied himself with Jackson. For their choice Crawford's partisans turned to the longtime congressional veteran from North Carolina, Nathaniel Macon. That the two southerners aligned themselves with two other southerners especially upset Adams. "The north was having nothing by this double conspiracy, of the south and west, the north was proscribed," he informed a friend. In his judgment the motive was dislike of his section, not of individuals, as if anticipating the political fissures that would cleave the nation in future decades. He predicted change in his section that would eventually lead to success. At the moment, however, he depicted himself standing alone, succeeding solely "upon his own strength." Still, he foresaw victory for himself if his side held firm against the divided opposition.[18]

By the close of 1824 his outlook became unusually positive. On Christmas Eve, Congressman William Plumer Jr., of New Hampshire, a political ally, found Adams in better spirits than when he had last seen him. He was "now entertain[ing] more expectation of success than he appeared then to indulge." On New Year's

Day, in his diary Adams admitted, "There is in my prospects and anticipations a solemnity and moment never before experienced." Unused to thinking he might actually win, he had, of course, to call up his shortcomings, avowing "to which unaided nature is inadequate."[19]

Adams's almost optimism derived chiefly from his conversations with Robert P. Letcher, a Kentucky congressman close to Clay. As early as December 17 Letcher intimated that he would receive Clay's backing. A week later Letcher was even more direct. On January 1 Adams recorded in his diary that Letcher now assured him that the Kentucky delegation in the House would cast its ballot for him. He also wanted Adams to meet with Clay, a request with which Adams readily agreed.[20]

Finishing fourth in the electoral count and eliminated from any possibility that he could become president, Clay quickly shifted from candidate to president-maker. The question for him was which of the three remaining contenders he should get behind. He and Crawford differed profoundly on critical issues, chiefly the role of the federal government. Clay advocated a vigorous government, sponsoring what he termed the American System, which would have the central government active in the country's economy and society. In contrast, Crawford was championed by southern states' righters bent on a weak central government. Moreover, he disliked Crawford, who in any case had finished a distant third. By this time he and Jackson already had great antipathy for each other. Furthermore, Clay had grave reservations about elevating a military chieftain to the presidency. Finally, Jackson, from Tennessee, was a westerner as well as a southerner, as was Clay. His rise would not assist Clay's own ambition to reach the nation's first office.

That left Adams, with whom Clay had not previously been friendly. In fact, at Ghent and during Adams's years in the State Department the two men had often been at odds. And Clay surely had a hand in the Russell forgery scandal, of which Adams was convinced. Yet in this circumstance for Clay the man from

Massachusetts had distinctly positive attributes. They agreed on a vigorous federal government, especially regarding internal improvements. Moreover, the accession of Adams, a New Englander, would provide no impediment either to Clay's stature in the West or to his national aspirations.

Adams was thus Clay's logical choice. The question for Clay then became whether he could bring enough strength to elect Adams. Victory would require thirteen states, a majority of the twenty-four then in the Union, to triumph in the House. The Constitution directed that in this process each state would have one vote, no matter the size of its delegation. Assuming that Adams could hold the seven he had carried electorally and Clay's three would do as he desired, that combination would bring Adams's total to ten, just three short of the magic thirteen. Clay believed that with his influence plus Adams's basic support, he could deliver the needed three additional states. He set out to do just that.[21]

On at least two occasions, January 9 and 29, the political kingmaker and the patrician intellectual met for extended discussions. After going over past disagreements, the two men managed to put aside former hostile feelings. They talked about policy, agreeing that on most basic issues, particularly the role of the federal government, they found themselves in accord. Insisting that his decision for Adams came "without any personal considerations for himself," Clay said he preferred the secretary of state over either Jackson or Crawford.[22]

Adams left no record of what he told Clay concerning any considerations for Clay personally or for anyone else he might bring to Adams's side. Yet little doubt can exist that for Adams these conversations were of high moment. The silence in his diary on this matter testified to his reluctance even to mention what he always considered unseemly politics. A bit earlier, however, after a long meeting with Congressman Letcher on December 23, he concluded his summary of their exchange with a sentence in Latin that illuminated his feelings, feelings that would not abate for the next six weeks: *"Incedo super ignes."* (Translation: I am treading upon fires.)[23]

While he met constantly with members of Congress and conferred privately with Clay, Adams continued to assert that he would not bar Federalists, past or present, from office. This assurance could become important in swaying those men in crucial delegations to back him. He informed a lawmaker from his own state that he would exclude no one based on the old party differences. Instead, he aimed to "bring the whole people together in sentiment as much as possible." He made a similar declaration to a rising star in Massachusetts politics, Congressman Daniel Webster. Webster, like Adams, had been a Federalist, and he wanted Adams's pledge on the Federalist question. Although in Adams's opinion Webster suffered from the fatal flaw of "ambition in the breast," he met with him, making unmistakably clear that he would not proscribe Federalists from participation in his administration. A satisfied Webster conveyed to Federalists, including a representative from Maryland who had a crucial place in his state's delegation, that he was convinced Adams would govern without "excluding Federalists, as such from his regard and confidence."[24]

Two weeks prior to the House vote on February 9 signs pointed toward Adams's victory on the first ballot. Clay publicly announced his support. At the same time the Kentucky and Ohio delegations, with whom he had enormous influence, promised they would vote for Adams, although the legislatures of both states directed them to go for Jackson. Even Adams admitted a prevailing impression that he would triumph. A whirl of politics had enveloped Washington, with Adams's exclaiming just a few days before the House would decide, "The excitement of electioneering is kindling into fury."[25]

Confronting the real possibility of his becoming president, Adams called on his old companion self-doubt. "To me the alternatives are both distressing in prospect," he confided to his diary, "and the most formidable is that of success." He told himself, "All the danger is on the pinnacle." Danger, because "the humiliation of failure will be so much more than compensated by the safety in which it will leave me, that I ought to regard it as a consummation devoutly to be wished, and hope to find consolation in it."[26]

The day of decision came on a snowy February 9. Adams did retain his seven states, and Clay held his three. Moreover, Clay's influence was central in bringing both Maryland and Louisiana into Adams's camp. Illinois became the essential thirteenth state, even though Jackson had won two of its three electoral votes. The lone congressman who would cast the state's vote was a longtime supporter of Adams. He withstood considerable pressure from the Jackson forces to stand by his personal favorite. On the first ballot the House awarded the presidency to Adams. Relaying the day's events to his father, Congressman Plumer reported, "Every thing in this election was conducted with perfect propriety and decorum on the part of the House." Calm prevailed: "There was no noise or confusion—no undue exultation in Mr. Adams's friends and no resentment expressed by those of the other candidates."[27]

One great irony characterized Adams's victory. Despite his deep, though guarded, antipathy toward slave owners and his long history of decrying the political strength of slavery, a slave owner and slave states were utterly critical in his victory. It was most unlikely that he could have prevailed without the vigorous participation of the slave-owning Clay. Additionally, his majority of thirteen states included four slave states—Kentucky, Louisiana, Maryland, and Missouri—almost one-third of his total. The South and slavery provided him with a crucial component of the coalition that generated his triumph.

With all the uncertainty finally gone, Adams rejoiced, "May the blessing of God rest upon the event of this day!" On March 4 he would become the sixth president of the United States. He would follow his father twenty-eight years later into the nation's highest office, vindicating him and reaching the goal, though always unspoken, set by his father and now dead mother as well as himself. Labeling February 9 "the most important day of my life," he wrote his father "asking for his blessing and prayers." In that letter John Quincy Adams related he would close the day as he began it, "with supplications to the Father of mercies that its consequences may redound to His glory and to the welfare of my country."[28]

The protracted tumult now seemed over. Congressman Plumer's description of the House vote emphasizing calm and decorum seemed to herald an end to the political clamor that had pervaded Monroe's second term. A presidential reception honoring the president-elect held on the evening following the election provided an encore to Plumer's assessment. Those crowding into the Executive Mansion included the victor and his closest rival. No unpleasantness took place. Meeting Adams, Jackson extended his hand; the two men shook. The result of the House decision had not altered the friendly relations between them that had spanned Monroe's presidency.[29]

Yet, even before his inauguration, which occurred less than a month after his selection, Adams initiated an action that would not only change forever how he and Jackson viewed each other but also fundamentally affect his presidency. Before taking office, he understandably wanted to settle upon his cabinet. Appointing people to office brought up his hated topic of patronage. Moreover, as Daniel Webster perceived, appointments would have an added difficultly because Adams's situation was "full of embarrassment," in Webster's words. He had not won in an open election and had not even garnered a plurality of electoral votes. Underscoring his antipathy toward what he had long considered an unsavory part of politics, Adams attempted to shield himself from as much of the process of dispensing patronage as possible. He wanted Monroe to make several diplomatic assignments before leaving office so that he would not face that task. Furthermore, even before he was chosen, he divulged to an ally that he had decided he would ask all of his colleagues in Monroe's cabinet to retain their offices, even

Crawford, for whom he had expressed nothing but disdain. That would leave for him to fill only his own post of secretary of state and the slot vacated by Vice-President Calhoun, secretary of war.[30]

The former, of course, was the plum. With his advance to the presidential chair, Adams became the third secretary of state in a row to make that move. As a matter of course whoever he named would be looked upon as the anointed one, at least as the obvious favorite to succeed him.

Three days after his election Adams offered his old stand to Henry Clay. Contemporary evidence does not clearly indicate his thinking, but five years later he spelled out his reasons, specifying three. First, Clay had been a prominent candidate for the presidency; second, he carried several western states; third, he was, in John Quincy's opinion, the "best fitted" man in the country for the job. While all of these surely had validity, there is a notable absence from that catalog. Clay's role in the House selection does not appear, and it is difficult to explain its nonappearance, except in realizing that reward for personal service, or favor, was not among the political acts acceptable to Adams. Reward must come from merit and qualifications, alone. Yet he surely knew that Clay had been essential to his victory in the House.[31]

Clay said he would take the offer under advisement, and after consulting with friends give the president-elect an answer. Recognizing a possible outcry against his appointment, Clay, according to Adams, "made light of the threatened opposition, and thought all the projects of that nature . . . were ebullitions of disappointment at the issue of the election, which would soon be abandoned." Clay obviously foresaw the possibility of aversion to his becoming secretary of state in this manner. As for Adams, he had been cautioned that nominating Clay would be troublesome. Representative Plumer, who enjoyed Adams's confidence, informed his father that everyone expected Clay to get that spot. Yet Plumer discerned the "current peculiar state of things" that would make it "a question of great delicacy to determine what [Clay] might do in this emergency." Should Clay accept, he feared, political enemies would have "an opportunity to represent both Adams and Clay as unprincipled intriguers."[32]

In less than two weeks Clay told Adams he would accept the invitation. He remained confident that his nomination would face little opposition in the Senate, with a maximum of ten senators against him. In fact, there were thirteen; all the other cabinet appointees were confirmed unanimously.[33]

Much more important, the Jackson forces raged. Upon getting the news, an unrestrained Jackson exploded: "The *Judas* [Clay] of the West has closed the contract and will receive the thirty pieces of silver—his end will be the same. Was there ever witnessed such a bare faced corruption in any country before?" Vice-President Calhoun, who before the House election had aligned himself with the general, echoed that judgment, declaring "the power of the people [*sic*] has been set at naught" by "ambitious men with a view to their own interest." The result, he was convinced, has deservedly "caused the deepest discontent in the country."[34]

Across the country Jacksonians took their clue from terms like "*Judas*" and "ambitious men" and raised the cry of corruption. The charge of a corrupt bargain reverberated from the Atlantic coast to the Mississippi River—a diabolical deal had been struck, the presidency in 1825 for Adams and the president-designate for Clay. Did the two men consciously make such a bargain? The evidence does not permit a definitive answer. Each man made a logical, though politically disastrous, choice. Also, both men never stopped denying they had entered into any such agreement. Even after the passage of almost two decades, Adams still felt the yoke of that accusation. In public remarks on a western trip after paying his respects to Clay, he proclaimed, "I solemnly declare that the charges of corrupt bargaining which have been trumped up against him and me are utterly without foundation." Even later, in 1850, Clay was still denying the charge of political corruption, though he finally acknowledged that he had erred in political judgment to become secretary of state.[35]

The real damage to Adams from the uproar against an alleged corrupt bargain was that it gave a rallying call for the rise of a national political opposition. All opposed to him could claim they had a simple and noble goal—to protect the republic and the rights of the people from scheming corrupters. And they had a unique and charismatic man to champion and to lead them— Andrew Jackson.

Since any untoward conduct involving the two men was problematic at best, the question remains why they so massively misjudged the political fallout. Even the superbly talented politician Clay failed to anticipate the maelstrom following his acceptance. Perhaps his ambition interfered with his political antennae, or more probably even he did not grasp how rapidly the popular politics spawned by the campaign and election of 1824 had transformed the political landscape. Without either Clay's political skills or his temperament, Adams never envisioned danger. In his mind, he had awarded the first cabinet seat to the most qualified and deserving person. He believed that the public should understand, as he told himself he did, rewarding merit, expertise, and service to the nation. He could not comprehend what had happened in any other way, nor could he admit otherwise.

With Clay set in the State Department, Adams turned to filling the remaining cabinet positions. Holding to his decision to retain his colleagues from Monroe's official family, he did invite them all, including the detested Crawford, to continue in their posts. Crawford promptly declined, but Samuel Southard and William Wirt agreed to stay on as secretary of the navy and attorney general, respectively. In Crawford's stead as secretary of the treasury Adams selected one of his supporters, Richard Rush of Pennsylvania, who had replaced him in London. For the final vacancy, the War Department, Adams to no avail tried to interest Jackson, who spurned the offer. He then picked a Crawford backer, James Barbour of Virginia, a sitting U.S. senator.

Adams could legitimately present this group as a unity cabinet. Only a strong Jackson partisan was missing, yet Jackson himself had refused Adams's overtures. There was certainly no sectional bias. Three—Barbour, Clay, and Wirt—came from slave states, while two—Rush and Southard—resided in free states. Except for Clay, none of them generated any opposition in the Senate; that body unanimously confirmed the other four.

Adams desired harmony and conciliation as the hallmarks of his presidency. He would build on what he identified as the non-partisanship pushed by Monroe. He wanted no partisanship, political or sectional, past or present, to characterize his administration. His private statements made clear that intention. He informed Senator Barbour, "The ultimate principle of my system with reference to the great interests of the country was *conciliation*, and not *collision*." To a Massachusetts congressman he emphasized his ambition to "bring the whole people together in sentiment as much as possible."[36]

His inaugural address would declare to the public that same goal. He realized the importance of his first pronouncement as president. Not surprisingly he had two sleepless nights prior to his inaugural day that accentuated the anxiety and emotion he felt. Just before noon on March 4 he left his house on F Street for the Capitol, with a militia escort, along with a complement of citizens. President Monroe followed in his own carriage.[37]

In the crowded home of the House of Representatives, Adams took the oath of office. Solemnity marked the occasion. Congressman Plumer described it as "one of the most august and interesting spectacles" he had "ever witnessed." Plumer noted that when John Quincy began his address he "was a little agitated but soon recovered his self possession and spoke with great clearness, force, & animation." The then vastly popular writer James Fenimore Cooper, part of the audience, commented on the earnestness and sincerity that marked his delivery.[38]

Evoking many themes espoused by the Founding Fathers before him, he began by professing a "religious obligation" to perform the duties of his new office. Then he offered a paean to the Constitution, which he defined as the instrument that had guided the country to its present happy state, a success that equaled even the most sanguine outlook of the noble forefathers who had adopted it and put it into operation. The incredible geographic expansion along with the roads and canals that spanned much of the country testified to the current national well-being. The Constitution's ultimate principle, from which no patriotic American could dissent, pronounced "the will of the people" the only authentic cornerstone of government. Proclaiming that all remnants of rancor and discord among Americans must be discarded, he called on all to join together with him in unity and harmony. That aim transcended all others, and he professed that he and his administration would hold it high.

Closing, he addressed the "peculiar circumstances" of his election. He knew that he did not begin with the confidence bestowed upon his predecessors. Yet he pledged he would make every effort to earn that confidence. He fervently called upon his God for favor and blessing. To that Providence he committed his own fate and that of his country.[39]

Following the ceremony both the outgoing and the incoming presidents entertained large numbers of people, Monroe in the Executive Mansion, Adams in his home on F Street. The new president now stood where his father had stood almost three decades earlier. The Adams name and Adams values had both been recognized and vindicated. To succeed in his quest to harmonize and unify his country, he told his inaugural audience, he would zealously bring hard and honest work to his task, but he looked for assistance and guidance from Congress, the states, and his fellow citizens. In his mind his elevation had rewarded his conviction about merit and individual worth. Now, still gripping this persuasion, he expected it to serve him well as his nation's chief executive.

Following his inauguration Adams had to begin thinking about how to formulate and articulate a program he could present to Congress and the country that would advance his professed desire for a united America and permanently jettison all forms of partisanship. His opportunity would come in his first annual message to Congress. In his time those communications received great attention from members of Congress and the general public alike. Americans looked to them not only for a report on the status of their country but also for a blueprint of what their president envisioned for them and their country, especially a newly elected chief executive.[40]

The first session of the Nineteenth Congress would convene in early December. Before that date Adams would prepare drafts of his message, which he would put before his cabinet for comments. While working on the document, he recognized that his relationship with Congress might be fraught. He told himself that he must "be prepared for severe trials." At the same time he reiterated his conviction that human actors, even presidents and congressmen, did not control events. In his diary he quoted from the Bible: "It is not in man that walketh to direct his steps."[41]

In late November he began sharing his handiwork with his official family. He found that in reacting to what he presented, his unity cabinet was not unified. Different members supported and opposed different particulars. Some felt he went too far in proposing a multitude of projects involving the federal government, such as a national university, to him a civilian counterpart to the military academy at West Point, and a national astronomical observatory. The southerners Barbour and Wirt worried that his push for a centralized system of federally sponsored internal improvements would hurt him politically in their section.

Highlighting these specific disagreements, Barbour and Clay gave differing general recommendations. Barbour wanted no proposal that had such inherent popularity that it could win congressional approval without a presidential endorsement. Clay, on the other hand, insisted on excluding any item that might fail because if its unpopularity. Receiving such contradictory advice, the president told his advisers that they put him in the position of "the man with his two wives—one plucking out his black hairs, and the other the white, till none were left."[42]

After a thorough discussion in which the individual officers had their say, Adams decided to retain the basic purport of the document he had placed before them. Their division did not caution him to temper his thrust. Not backing away, he informed them that his thinking went beyond the upcoming congressional session. "The plant may come later," he declared, "though the seed should be sown early." Even so, his divided cabinet should have signaled to him that his ambitious agenda entailed political hazards that might threaten the national harmony he so valued.[43]

On December 6, 1825, he sent it to Congress. As had his predecessors since George Washington's first year as president, Adams had his message delivered to the Capitol, where it was read. He did not appear in person. This document would have far-reaching effects on both President Adams and his country; it reflected a distinct inability for the new president to gauge the political antipathy and discord that lay in his future.[44]

He began with thanksgiving to God for His blessings bestowed on America and Americans. To him abundant evidence demonstrated divine favor. Then he spent a few pages detailing the financial health and the general well-being of the country, emphasizing that peace and prosperity marked the nation's situation.

When he turned to his vision for America, he concentrated on a single concept, improvement. *Improvement* he defined as "the great object of the institution of civil government." His list of what he considered essential improvements included a massively expanded system of roads and canals, planned by and under the control of the central government. Equally important, he advocated using the federal government to improve the citizens' condition through the acquisition of knowledge. Doing so would involve a national university and federal support for scientific investigation. Here astronomical observatories were central; he called them "light-houses of the skies." Adams pointed out that the great European powers had expended considerable sums and effort to expanding knowledge, especially in science, including some 130 astronomical observatories. While asserting that those countries had forms of government greatly inferior to the American, John Quincy insisted that in this area the United States should strive to emulate them.

Having spelled out in concrete fashion the direction he hoped Congress would follow, he acknowledged that the Constitution did limit the power of the national legislature. Thus, if representatives and senators decided that enacting his proposals exceeded these limits, they should not "assume the exercise of powers not granted to you by the people."

Yet, even after such a qualifying statement, he returned to his main theme. "The spirit of improvement is abroad upon the earth," he declared. The moral purpose of the Creator, he sermonized, aimed at improving the lot of mankind. He therefore challenged the solons to join him and not "to slumber in indolence or fold up on our arms and proclaim to the world that we are palsied by the will of our constituents." Not seeming to perceive the contradiction between telling the Congress not to reach beyond the warrant given by the people through the Constitution and simultaneously not to be barred by that same warrant, he hurried on to urge action on measures that would benefit the entire Union and all its citizens.

This message did not end up in a dustbin, unheard and unread. In a howl of dissent that would come to reflect the disharmony of his term, horrified conservatives and states' righters charged that the perpetrators of the corrupt bargain intended to create a gargantuan central government pervaded by corruption that would destroy constitutional liberty. The phrase that members of Congress should not be palsied by the will of their constituents sparked particular outrage. It appeared to mock the very meaning of government by the people. Andrew Jackson, though personally motivated, spoke for the outraged: "I shudder for the consequence—if not checked by the voice of the people, it must end in consolidation, and then in despotism."[45]

Undoubtedly both political naïveté and utter conviction about the rightness of his vision left Adams unprepared for this reaction. Even among his adherents his eloquent appeal to nationalism and national greatness caused concern. Though some did applaud, many feared that he asked for too much, went too far. They worried that a congressional opposition would emerge that could thwart his initiatives and be followed by a national opposition that could endanger his reelection.

A specific item embedded in the message would add measurably to the antagonism toward the administration growing from it. Adams noted that back in the spring the United States had been invited to a conference of Latin American republics to be held in Panama, and that he had accepted the invitation. He did not divulge, however, that his cabinet had been divided over acceptance, even though he had Secretary of State Clay's support.

Because he wanted Senate confirmation of his envoys and House approval of their financing, he sent to Congress three weeks after the message an additional note in which he detailed his reasons for agreeing to the Panama meeting. He pointed out that those nations were sister republics in this hemisphere, though behind the United States in development. Thus this country should extend the hand of friendship and also support, giving guidance on the proper direction for them. He wanted the U.S. delegation to propound the worth of generous commercial relations and the principle of maritime neutrality. Additionally, in accord with his tone in his annual message, he asserted the United States would press upon its southern neighbors the advantages of advancing religious liberty, for some of them still formally embraced the Roman Catholic Church.[46]

In his brief for participation Adams in a significant way moved from his earlier foreign policy principle of keeping the United States out of the internal affairs of other countries. Despite his insistence on his consistency, his proposal for American engagement, especially his upholding moral precepts, did differ from the hands-off maxim he had advocated and promulgated as secretary of state. He obviously desired a direct American influence, which he felt could come only from an American presence on-site.

The congressional reaction to his proposed Panama mission in a fundamental sense mirrored the response to his annual message. It did even more, however, for that answer fueled the increasing resistance to what his opponents deemed an ever-expanding, almost missionary federal government.

Accusing Adams of breaking with George Washington's hallowed doctrine from his Farewell Address of no foreign entanglements, antagonists set about blocking both Senate confirmations and House appropriations. Much of the objection was centered among southerners, who had special reservations about an American presence in Panama. That Haiti, the creation of a successful slave revolt and governed by blacks, would have representation at the conference mightily distressed them. They wanted nothing to do with Americans dealing on any level of equality with Haitian delegates. Congress wrangled for months before finally signing on to Adams's Panama enterprise. Yet the confirming of envoys and appropriating of funds took so long that the conference ended before any American appeared.

Congressional delay and the failure of American participation was not, however, the key result of this ill-fated adventure. The Panama episode provided a powerful catalyst to the unease stemming from the substance of the message. A heretofore formless political force was taking shape or, more accurately, being shaped to stand against Adams and all that he proposed. The danger posed by corruption and consolidation became the watchword of these men.

Of course, the cornerstone of the movement was unhappiness at the outcome of the presidential election. Still, Adams in his vision of an energetic federal government committed to the great moral crusade of improvement provided cement. Experienced politicians who had favored Crawford or Jackson would use it to construct a formidable political organization. This effort had two leaders—Vice-President Calhoun, who had tied himself to Jack-

son even before the House chose Adams as president, and Senator Martin Van Buren of New York, who had led the Crawford
campaign but now, in alliance with Calhoun, turned to Jackson.
With Jackson they had a proven, popular champion to place at the
head of their forming coalition. Jackson, now a fabled hero, had
the fame and charisma that could hold it together. Moreover, he
was eager to avenge the great wrong he claimed had been done
him, the stealing of the presidency from him.

Adams's supporters in Congress recognized the essential
political dimension governing the anti-Adams alliance. Congressman Daniel Webster informed a correspondent that those who
were against the Panama measures intended more than merely to
defeat them. "Various parties, not likely to act together often," he
wrote, "united on this occasion in a close phalanx of *opposition*."[47]

Apprised that those aligning against him denounced him
for taking Caesar as his model and for endangering the liberty
and happiness of his fellow citizens, Adams grasped that a great
undertaking was being mounted against him. And he correctly
identified the Calhoun, Crawford, and Jackson stalwarts as leading the way. He even designated Calhoun and Van Buren as
the two men most responsible. This political landscape, Adams
remarked in his diary, "admonishes me to proceed with extreme
circumspection."[48]

While facing the reality of growing opposition, the president
on July 4, 1826, joined other luminaries in the Capitol to celebrate the fiftieth anniversary of the Declaration of Independence,
of the nation's birth. For him that day was to become even more
meaningful. Two days later news reached Washington that the
chief author of the Declaration, Thomas Jefferson, had died, on
the fourth. The symbolism of Jefferson's death on that special day
touched many. Then, on July 8, Adams received letters from three
different people informing him that his father, almost ninety-one,
was rapidly approaching the end of his life.

The next morning at five in his own carriage and accompanied by his son John, Adams left for Massachusetts. At a stop

halfway to Baltimore, he learned that his father had died, also on the fourth, and eight years after the death of his mother, Abigail Adams. Because of the letters that had prompted his departure, that information did not surprise him. He proceeded onward, arriving in Boston on July 12.

The next day he went to Quincy, too late for the funeral, which had taken place on the seventh. As he entered his father's bed-chamber, where the two had last seen each other, the reality of his father's death powerfully sank in. "That moment was inex-pressibly painful," he recorded in his diary. He felt as if an arrow had penetrated his heart. No longer could he consider that the house possessed a distinctive enchantment. At the same time he experienced a resurgence of his attachment to his homeplace and region, stronger, he affirmed, than ever before.[49]

That his father had departed life on the same national birthday as his Revolutionary partner Jefferson made an indelible impres-sion on both Adams and the country. It seemed that heaven wanted to welcome the last two titans of the founding generation on the same day. Adams also knew that in their later years his father and Jefferson had reconciled their differences through cor-respondence, renewing in a significant way their friendship of an earlier time. Adams remembered those days fondly, when as a boy in France he had first come to know Jefferson. The connection he fathomed between his God and his country upon Jefferson's death on the fourth grasped him even more tightly. The coinci-dence that the lives of the two men ended on such a notable day in his country's history he counted as "visible and palpable marks of Divine favor."[50]

Adams also held dearly to his conviction of his father's great-ness, a belief he never relinquished. He admired much about his father—from his patriotism and public service to the frugality of his old age, which he contrasted favorably with Jefferson's prof-ligacy. He wanted to build a library next to his father's house, which he inherited, to hold his parent's books and papers, as well as in time his own. Some fifteen years later reading his father's letters filled him with awe. He deemed them profound; in his opinion no others in the English language could match them. So taken was he that he confessed he "dare[d] not turn upon them a critical eye."[51]

Always viewing his father's loss to Jefferson in the presidential election of 1800 as a blot on the history of the nation and an insult to his father, Adams could never see that outcome as resulting from anything but the machinations of unscrupulous men. More than to the victor Jefferson, he assigned chief blame for denying his father his deserved second term to collusion between Aaron Burr and Alexander Hamilton. Yet, contemplating the role of the divine in human affairs, he found some solace. That one murdered the other—Burr killed Hamilton in a famous duel—and that the one left alive ended up disgraced he viewed as a "remarkable example of Divine retributive justice." In his mind the scales of justice had never been more evenly balanced. That the final judgment came from "a higher state of being" pleased him immensely. God himself had avenged the injustice done his father.[52]

Adams remained for a time in Quincy to settle his father's estate. During those weeks he made a momentous decision. He determined to join the church of his ancestors and of his parents in which he was raised. Although as an adult attending church services, reading the Bible, pondering religion, and calling on his God all formed a central part of his life, he had never openly professed his faith by becoming a member of a church. At this point he rationalized that he had not done so because of his moving about and his sense of unworthiness. As a result, he had not taken a step he should have taken three decades earlier. He decided he wanted to belong to the ancestral church in Quincy, where he hoped when his time came to be gathered to his fathers.

On October 1, during the morning service, he, a sitting president, made his public profession. In the ritual the minister asked that each person intent on joining the congregation profess his or her faith in the divine mission of Christ and commit to living by the precepts of His gospel. Adams did so and then took communion for the first time in his life. Making this declaration of Christ's divinity was no perfunctory or rote pronouncement for him. He had previously contemplated the matter of Christ's divinity and would continue to do so. Some six months later he confided to his diary that the New Testament did countenance that doctrine. Although in his mind scripture did not clearly reveal that truth, it both directly and indirectly pointed toward it. Still, he acknowledged that the New Testament left the question debatable, "never to be either demonstrated or refuted till another revelation shall clear it up."[53]

Returning to Washington, Adams resumed his busy schedule. As he had for so many years, he rose quite early, usually between five and six, but occasionally at four. Prior to breakfast at nine, he read the Bible, public documents, and newspapers. At times exercise would follow, but sometimes that effort would not come until later afternoon.[54]

From midmorning until around five in the afternoon, his hours were often filled with visitors. During sessions of Congress its members regularly trooped into his office. On one day in December 1826 he noted that thirty-three congressmen and eleven senators called on him. Adams complained that the avalanche of callers had begun to render life burdensome. It emphasized the different age in which he lived that others considerably less distinguished commonly found their way into the presidential presence—the wife of a Baltimore tailor looking for a job, a dismissed West Point cadet seeking reinstatement at the military academy, a young woman hoping to gain a government clerkship for her husband, even a man, termed objectionable by Adams, who announced himself as Saint Peter and spoke violently for fifteen minutes. The president did, however, make use of one of these uninvited callers. When a man identified himself as a dentist, Adams promptly took the opportunity to have him pull a decayed tooth and remove the tartar that for the past four years had been collecting on his front teeth. Although he surely benefited on at least that occasion, the range of people finding their way to his office amazed even him. By early 1828 he considered the increasing number an annoying nuisance.

Between the visits of those from both high and low stations, he attended to the business of the country. Following the example of President Monroe, he held frequent cabinet meetings, where he sought the opinions of his official advisers on foreign and domestic issues. When his annual messages came due as well as responses to specific congressional requests, he usually prepared the drafts by himself. Then he looked to the entire cabinet or individual officers for comment.

After dinner, usually at seven until eleven and bed, he engaged in several occupations. Work was never far away; signing individual land grants and blank patents took up many evening hours. He affixed his signature to every one of them. On occasion, however, he would escape from official duties at the billiard table or with a favorite author, like Tacitus, Plutarch, or even Voltaire. The former, of course, he denounced as idleness, even though it afforded him relaxation. In contrast, the latter was always profitable.

Once Adams had to deal with a threat to his life. Informed that an army surgeon cashiered for embezzlement threatened to kill him, he was urged to be extra cautious, making sure the individual never got in to see him alone. Despite considering the warning credible, Adams asserted that he could not possibly guard himself against a determined assassin. Finally, however, he did receive the desperate man, but only with another person present. Denying that he had ever entertained murder, the disgraced doctor begged for reinstatement. Adams refused. His account ends tersely: "He finally went away." Through this episode Adams contented himself with his oft-stated belief that "a higher power than the will of man" controlled his life.[55]

One aspect of his role as president he clearly disliked, even more than having to face a herd of visitors. In May 1825 the Maryland Agricultural Society requested his presence at its exhibition outside Baltimore. Adams refused. Making what he identified as a public spectacle of the president not only took time away from important tasks but, even more, would set a precedent for him to end up as an exhibit at "all the cattle-shows" in the country. Two years later he declined an invitation to appear at the opening of the Pennsylvania Canal because it did not mesh with his principles or taste. He considered such public showings unsuitable to both his office and his character.[56]

Some occasions he could not escape. In October 1827, after he had toured the Philadelphia navy yard, a crowd of several thousand gathered. He spoke to those closest to him, saying he would shake hands with all who could make their way to him. Some two or three hundred did grasp the presidential hand. When his boat left the wharf, the assembly sent up three cheers. That gesture Adams returned with a bow. Yet he worried that some "vain or unworthy sentiment" might mingle with the grand thoughts and reflections that the experience excited in him.

On July 4 of the next year he participated in ground breaking for the Chesapeake and Ohio Canal, which took place in Maryland just west of the District of Columbia boundary. With some two thousand onlookers he was handed the spade for the initial breaking of the ground. His first several efforts failed because he struck a large stump hidden just beneath the surface. Undeterred, Adams removed his coat and returned to his chore, succeeding in bringing up the first shovelful of dirt. His triumph brought forth a shout from the gathered throng. Following his own brief remarks and a few other incidents, he returned to the Executive Mansion accompanied by the marshals of the day. He invited them in, and all joined in a glass of wine. He reported himself exhausted and also, as usual, bemoaned his awkwardness in crowds. Still, he was thankful he got through the day without notable failure.[57]

In fact, on this occasion as in Philadelphia, he conducted himself admirably. Even so, these situations obviously made him uncomfortable. As in other areas of the new political environment taking shape around him, he found himself ill at ease. This rapidly shifting landscape disturbed him, for he perceived that it called for him overtly to advertise himself. That endeavor he could never bring himself to embrace.

The social events that helped define Adams's stand for the presidency did not disappear when he became chief executive. His diary refers to well-attended drawing rooms as well as dinner parties held at the Executive Mansion during the Washington season. He generally counted them successes, though he occasionally grumbled that the length of the dinners and the dissipation accompanying them deprived him of his usual postdinner commitment to official business.

In one critical aspect, however, these affairs differed from those of the prepresidential years. Although Louisa Adams presided over some of her drawing rooms, she did not exhibit the magnetism and verve that had made her the envy of Washington society. Simply, she seems to have lost her enthusiasm both for her special social role and for political life in general. Even during her heyday as the capital's leading social figure, she did not relish the political future. "I have no ambition beyond my present situation," she confided to her journal; "the exchange to a more elevated station must put me in Prison." She conveyed the same feelings in letters to her sons.

Even though she had demonstrably assisted her husband's elevation to the presidency, those sentiments dominated her time as first lady. Serious illness, including fainting, kept her from the inaugural ball. Sickness continued to plague her, causing her absence from some of her drawing rooms. Moreover, she grew more and more distant emotionally from the political world. No longer did she relish participating in, much less promoting, John Quincy's hopes for reelection.[58]

A trip that she took in the summer of 1826 with her youngest son revealed the change that had occurred in her attitude and outlook. Traveling with his mother in upstate New York, Charles Francis observed that she was wandering about the country with apparently "no fixed purpose and with no intent." In an attempt to boost her spirits, he adopted a forced gaiety, but his effort did little to alter her mood. Finally, he prevailed upon her to return home.

Two years later a distressed son remarked on what had now become her "usual melancholy." According to him she had "lost all elasticity of character," which had previously served her so well. Obviously an emotional pall had enveloped Louisa Catherine Adams; today some would call it a depression. Although concerned about his wife's physical failing and emotional disillusionment, John Quincy could not permit his anxiety to deter him from his duty.[59]

President Adams was the subject of two notable paintings. Shortly after his inauguration he received a request from a Boston friend to permit the renowned Gilbert Stuart, who had done his portrait while secretary of state, to paint a full-length portrait, which the friend would commission. Adams agreed and first sat for Stuart in Boston in the fall of that year. Delay set in, however, and when Stuart died in 1828, he had finished only the head. Stuart's head presents a familiar forceful visage looking toward the artist, with a mostly balding head above a strong nose and chin. Thomas Sully of Philadelphia was engaged to complete the assignment, which he did in 1830. The result was considerably less than successful. Sully's placing Stuart's head on a standing Adams did nothing to enhance the total work. Sully's fully clothed body is indistinctive, as are the surroundings in which he placed his subject. Still, in 1831, Adams himself thought the head bore a true resemblance to the man.

In 1827 and 1828 he sat in Washington for a second portrait by the successful portraitist Chester Harding. Harding painted the president from the waist up. The head, here completely bald, again dominates, with nose and chin once more prominent. In this portrait the eyes focus directly to the front, adding to the strength of character the artist wanted the face to convey.[60]

Having portraits painted did not seriously intrude on the demands of the presidency, but those demands did overwhelm an activity that for decades had been central in his life—maintaining his diary. Almost from the outset he periodically bemoaned the difficulty of keeping it. And the diary itself makes this clear. In the twelve-volume edition of his father's journal that he edited and published between 1874 and 1876, Charles Francis Adams stated directly that it was not continuous for the presidential years. Comparing the coverage in this edition of the years of the secretaryship of state with those of the presidency illustrates the impact of the latter on his diary keeping. The secretaryship gets two full volumes plus all but thirty pages of a third, a total of 1,592 pages, while the presidency has only one full volume along with small portions of two others, a total of 681 pages, more than two-thirds fewer. The manuscript diary confirms that extensive difference. The lengthy discussions that characterized so much of it prior to March 1825 have become much sparser. A great deal of the diary during the presidential years consists of jotted notes or lists of various items, ranging from visitors to the weather to chapters from the Bible he had read.[61]

Although the diary suffered, Adams did not cut back his exercise regimen. Almost daily he engaged in some vigorous physical activity. In the warm months he continued to swim, in the Potomac River when in Washington. Unimaginable as it is today, crowds did not gather to watch the president take to the water. As before, he continued to praise this activity, though he told himself he must discard the motive of swimming just to show what he could do, and instead focus on the physical benefit. During one swim in the Potomac he watched the body of a drowned man pulled from the river. That incident caused him to reconsider the potential hazard in this form of exertion, but he concluded that abstaining would pose an even greater danger to his health. He resolved to be careful but, as always, affirmed that his life rested in the hands of God, to whom he was indebted for every breath he drew.

When the weather turned colder, Adams resumed his walking. He generally alternated his treks, from the Executive Mansion to the Capitol and back or a round-trip from the mansion to Georgetown, each around three to four miles. Usually, walking before breakfast, he was out in the predawn chill, which on occasion could get to him. He recorded one morning, with the thermometer at thirteen degrees, that it took him an hour after his return to regain full feeling in his fingers.

In the spring of 1828 he added a third activity to his customary swimming and walking, horseback riding. At times he would substitute it for one of the other two. He rode as many as fourteen miles in a morning and often noted that the ride left him fatigued. Still, he was confident the effort improved his physical well-being.[62]

Concern about his health was a constant for President Adams. He frequently worried that even his regular exercising was failing to keep him fit. His diary, though terser than usual, contains numerous comments on maladies that struck his body. Catarrh and inflammation of his eye particularly plagued and alarmed him, though the latter did not equal the seriousness of his ophthalmological illness in London. On various occasions he mentioned a vague soreness and pain that so disheartened his spirits that he could not use reason to revive them. In May 1827 he reported his health as "drooping," prompting him to count his career as closed.[63]

Yet in the Executive Mansion he did find a new hobby, gardening. This interest stemmed from a resolution passed in 1828 by the House of Representatives designed to promote the silk industry. And he plunged in with fervor. Botany became a fresh passion; he read voraciously on the subject, utilizing books in both English and French. On his walks he began to notice plants and their characteristics. He devoted so much time to the pursuit that he reiterated his time-honored lament that he spent too much time away from what he should be doing. Furthermore, despite the pleasure he experienced, he reported his almost desperate effort to learn about this newly embraced topic, even admitting that it created an anxiety in him, which caused sleepless nights.

The study of trees emerged as a special interest. Around his house in Quincy he planted both fruit and what he termed forest

trees, preferring to put seeds in the ground rather than trans-
plant young trees. He ended up with almost a forest of his own.
Still, that so many of his plantings failed to grow into healthy
trees both puzzled and distressed him.[64]

Although becoming an amateur tree farmer both exhilarated
and frustrated Adams, he could never totally divorce himself from
his presidential duties. As chief executive of his country, he had
significant responsibilities for domestic as well as foreign affairs.
With the latter he could easily take the initiative, though as the
Panama episode illustrated, he could still need congressional
approval to conclude certain projects. Regarding the former, he
laid out an ambitious agenda in his first message. Realizing it in
the face of serious opposition would require from him enterprise
and determination.

As president, Adams kept as his chief foreign policy goal one
of his two as secretary of state. He wanted to secure the hege-
monic position of his country in the Western Hemisphere that had
been set by the close of Monroe's second administration. Thus
his major purpose became ensuring that no European intervention occurred on his side of the Atlantic Ocean. Keeping Europe
out, he believed, would permit the growth and strengthening of
the republics south of the United States. To that end he strove
to advance the peaceful resolution of remaining conflicts between
Spain and its former colonies. His policy also included insisting
that Colombia and Mexico halt their effort to expand by absorbing Caribbean islands still in Spanish hands. He feared that their
continuing on that path would prompt the European interference
he so wanted to prevent. On these fronts he largely succeeded.
Yet, as the failure of his Panama venture exemplifies, the United
States did not become as active as he had hoped regarding the
development of the new republics.

The second great objective of his tenure in the State Department had been territorial expansion. And in this endeavor he had
remarkable success, making his country a continental nation.
During his presidency, however, expansion became distinctly sec-

John Adams, father

Abigail Adams, mother

Louisa Catherine Adams, wife

James Monroe

John Tyler

James K. Polk

Daniel Webster

Martin Van Buren

Henry Clay

John C. Calhoun

ondary. Three locations occupied his and Secretary of State Clay's attention: the unsettled boundary between Maine and the Canadian province of New Brunswick; Cuba, still Spanish; and Texas, which came under Mexican control in 1821 when that country won independence from Spain. The issue of the Maine boundary had existed since the end of the American Revolution and had not been finalized in the Treaty of Ghent. Even though Adams had no ambition to attach Canadian territory, a lasting settlement escaped him and, in fact, did not occur until 1842.

Regarding Cuba and Texas, Adams had different aims. He had no intention of acquiring Cuba, though the island was just over one hundred miles from southern Florida. Yet he did have a great interest in keeping any other country from replacing Spain as Cuba's master. In his judgment the United Sates could not permit any such change. Should a major European power like England or France attempt to take over, the United States would have to prevent it by whatever means necessary. During his presidency no serious effort to displace Spain took place.[65]

Texas was different, however. Its eastern and northern frontiers abutted the state of Louisiana and the territory of Arkansas, which placed that portion of Texas far from the center of Mexican authority in Mexico City and close to the United States, from which immigrants were already streaming into the territory. The precise location of the boundary had been at issue in the negotiations behind the Adams-Onís Treaty. Moreover, Adams knew that an insecure border like that with Florida had the potential to cause serious problems. Thereupon he and Clay tried to purchase Texas with a border as far south and west as possible, instructing the American minister to Mexico to try and make the deal. In large part because of internal Mexican politics, their attempt failed, once again passing along the Texas issue to reappear in both his and the country's future.[66]

Nothing had been more central in the grand national plan that Adams described in his first annual message than a centrally planned and managed system of internal improvements. Yet, after presenting that soaring vision, he basically backed away, leaving its implementation to Congress. Aside from an almost half-hearted effort to enlist Congressman Daniel Webster as a leader for his legislative program, he all but withdrew. His sense of his role as president evidently did not include active engagement in the legislative process.[67]

Why he took that position is not easily explained, for he certainly believed in and advocated an energetic central government. Perhaps his lack of legislative experience made him reluctant. Two decades earlier, during his brief time in the U.S. Senate, the mechanics of legislation had scarcely interested him. Unquestionably the arrangements, trade-offs, and deals usually necessary to construct congressional majorities he found distasteful. Possibly, his intent to press his oft-praised virtue of harmony motivated him. In February 1828, congratulating himself on the lack of vigorous Senate opposition to his treaties and nominations, he recorded that he had done "everything in my power to avoid a collision, and none has occurred." Whatever the entire explanation, no substantial Adams program ever passed Congress; in fact, none was even specifically proposed and fought for.[68]

His withdrawal did not mean, however, that internal improvements ground to a halt during his administration. On the contrary, more legislation passed and more projects got underway then than during all the previous presidencies. Congress passed many bills, and he signed them. But they were overwhelmingly local projects following no national blueprint. Most members of Congress were eager to support internal improvements, though only for undertakings that benefited their constituents. They had no appetite for a national system planned and directed by the federal government. On this matter Adams clearly did not lead. Rather, he followed as Congress mutilated his grand design.

On another major domestic issue he acted similarly. A protective tariff, a tax on imports to benefit particular sectors of the economy, had been a significant question in national politics since the 1790s. Generally northern states backed such a tariff in order to support their fledgling, but by the 1820s growing, manufacturing interest. In contrast, southern states with an economy devoted mainly to raising staple crops for export, with cotton ascendant by the 1820s, mostly opposed protection. To them a protective tariff meant their agriculture subsidizing northern industry.

In addition, constitutional interpretation became involved. The Constitution clearly empowered Congress to enact tariff legislation with the goal of funding the government. But it did not specifically sanction protection. Strict constructionists accordingly denied the constitutionality of protection, while those championing broad construction, or a more elastic interpretation, found it within the intent of the Constitution. Protection thus got caught up in the disagreement over the size and function of the federal government—strict constructionists wanted it small and limited, whereas the broad constructionists favored a more expansive and active version.

Although Adams certainly aligned himself with the broad constructionists, he also had no difficulty with some form of protection. He would support a tariff policy that assisted manufacturing, but he did not want agricultural interests severely harmed. In the midst of the presidential campaign of 1824, he told a South Carolina congressman that opposing sides on the tariff contest of that year should invoke "a spirit of mutual accommodation and concession" to reach an equitable solution.[69]

Becoming president did not change his opinion. During his administration discussions about the tariff occurred, but he neither took the initiative nor pushed any measure. His policy was to let Congress make its choices, and as president his duty was either to accept by signing or to reject by vetoing legislation sent to him. Congress did act in 1828, passing a new protective tariff, the highest up to that time. In fact, none would exceed it before 1860. Its opponents denounced it as the Tariff of Abominations. Involved and tangled politics connected to the 1828 presidential contest of that year marked its journey through Congress. Standing where he had previously, Adams took no active part in the congressional struggle. He did, however, sign the bill into law.

One other major domestic issue concerned him, a conflict between the state of Georgia and the Creek Indians. The future of the native tribes had occasioned discussion in his cabinet. Secretary of State Clay took a hard line, asserting the impossibility of civilizing the Indians. Anticipating their extinction sometime in the future, he did not believe them worth preserving, though he did favor treating them humanely while they survived. A shocked Secretary of War Barbour could not stand with Clay. He said, however, that he had given up the idea of incorporating Indians into the states where they resided. Instead, he proposed grouping them all into "a great territorial Government west of the Mississippi [River]."

Adams eventually sided with Barbour. He had long held the belief that the natives possessed no God-given right to maintain themselves on their original lands. He felt Clay's views much too severe, though he feared they had more than a little validity. At the same time he could envision "no practicable plan by which they can be organized into a civilized, or half-civilized Government." Still, he approved Barbour's approach because he admitted he had nothing better to suggest.[70]

Any possible long-term solution aside, Adams had to make a timely decision in the clash between Georgia and the Creeks. He had to decide, not turn to Congress or wait for it to act. Following their defeat by Andrew Jackson during the War of 1812, the Creeks had been required to cede the bulk of their land to the United States. Most was located in the area that became Alabama and Mississippi, but a portion fell within Georgia.

Then a treaty with the Creeks in 1825 transferred title to some five million acres to the state of Georgia. In the last days of Monroe's presidency, the Senate ratified it, and upon taking office Adams affixed his signature. He soon learned, however, that to obtain the Creeks' agreement corruption and force had been employed. Adams thereupon suspended that treaty and obtained a more equitable one, which the Senate also ratified.

Refusing to retreat from the original accord, Governor George Troup of Georgia moved quickly to have the Indian land surveyed and made available for settlement by eager white Georgians. News of Georgia's rapid move distressed Adams, who in December 1825 informed his cabinet that the United States could not yield to Georgia. Doing so, in his judgment, would visit a great injustice on the Creeks. Told that opposing Troup would drive Georgia toward his political opposition, Adams averred that potential outcome was inconsequential to him.[71]

When Governor Troup actually sent his surveyors into land not given up by the Creeks in the second treaty, the struggle between the state and the federal government escalated into a full-blown crisis, a precursor to the well-known clash that took place later involving Georgia, the federal government, and the Cherokee Indians. Both Creek and federal authorities challenged the surveyors, with Secretary of War Barbour writing Governor Troup that the president would use all the means in his power to enforce the provisions of the second treaty. On the offensive, Troup responded to Barbour that he would resist any federal military action against his state. Many southerners lined up on Georgia's side, encouraged by the man looming over Adams's reelection chances, Andrew Jackson.

Adams received conflicting advice from his two chief advisers on this matter. Henry Clay wanted him to use force, to send in the army. Barbour preferred dispatching a confidential agent to Troup to warn him against proceeding further. They agreed that all pertinent documents should go to Congress. The president declared he had no doubt about his authority to order troops in as well as the right to take that course. Yet he seriously questioned the wisdom of doing so.[72]

On February 5, 1827, he dispatched to Congress what he deemed "the most momentous message" he had ever sent to that

body. In it he went over the history of the confrontation and contrasted his civil and military choices. While there was cause to
employ the latter, he told the representatives and senators, he had
chosen not to do so. If he had chosen military force, he wrote, "a
conflict *must* have ensued," which would have inflicted a terrible
wound on the Union—one state at war with the rest. At all hazards he wanted to avoid that outcome. Yet he asserted that, should
Georgia persist in illegally encroaching on Creeks, he would have
to reconsider. He never did. He was not ready for combat, believing that the damage done to the Union might result in its demise.
He did not feel the country ready for that eventuality, and he was
certainly not willing to chance the possibility.[73]

While formulating plans to deal with events in Georgia,
Adams faced a mushrooming political opposition. The force that
had initially appeared to oppose Clay's confirmation only intensi-
fied in the succeeding months, until by 1828 it had become a full-
fledged party. As at the outset the two most prominent national
leaders associated with the movement remained Calhoun and
Jackson. Both of them professed that their former admiration for
Adams had ceased because of his own actions. Calhoun wrote
that changing his opinion he counted "one of the great misfor-
tunes of life" because formerly he had thought so highly of his
colleague in Monroe's cabinet. Yet he claimed he had no choice
given Adams's ambition and lack of judgment, which turned him
away from President Monroe's cause, from principles, and led
him to embrace those propounded by his former foes, with Clay
at the forefront.[74]

Jackson concentrated chiefly on his interpretation of the Adams-
Clay connection, insisting that he had always "esteemed [Adams]
as a virtuous, noble and honest man." When first informed that
Adams had made a pact with Clay, he declared, he refused to
believe it. Only Clay's actually receiving the appointment as secretary of state moved Jackson to accept what he deemed Adams's
disgraceful conduct. At that point he halted all exchange with
Adams because his code forbade him to maintain an association

with "those whom we believe corrupt or capable of vice when it ministers to self aggrandizement." Considering Adams captured by Clay, whom he regarded as evil, Jackson concluded that the man he used to admire was now "really to be pitied."[75]

A third man had an equally central, perhaps even more central, role in molding the political union determined to make John Quincy Adams, like his father, a one-term president. A master political manager and strategist, who had risen to leadership of one of the two factions of his state, Senator Martin Van Buren of New York did the difficult work of bringing together disparate groups into an organized unit. In his early forties the short, stocky, always elegantly dressed Van Buren had the ability to ingratiate himself with political friend and enemy alike. With perfect manners and exquisite social skills he cultivated all. Unlike his more notable contemporaries Adams, Calhoun, and Jackson, who could never separate the personal from the political, Van Buren kept personalities out of his political vocabulary. Without name, fame, or outstanding achievement to rely on or to boost him, Van Buren made politics his profession. He had an unmatched political mind.[76]

Though no ideologue, Van Buren did profess loyalty to the classical Jeffersonian doctrine of limited government and strict construction. He wanted to build on an alliance between southerners and northerners who shared his outlook, the hallmark of Jefferson's original Republican party. And he saw the hero Jackson as the vehicle that could make his dream a reality. Behind Jackson's popularity he could bring together those who disliked Adams, those who simply desired office, those who wanted power, and those who held dearly the traditional constitutional and ideological shibboleths. His ultimate goal was to construct a political party that, like the first Republican party, could dominate nationally. In sharp contrast to Adams, he had no aversion to party, either intellectually or practically. Nor did an opposing party concern him; in fact, he saw it as essential for holding his coalition together. A common enemy was as important as common goals.

While Jackson's heroic image and popular appeal were certainly essential to the ultimate success of this new political organization, Adams's opponents employed concrete measures to build up their edifice. Without doubt the South provided a sturdy foundation. Early on Congressman Webster discerned that congressional southerners did not like losing their hold on the executive branch of the federal government. In his judgment they would stand against not only John Quincy but any northern president. On the other side Calhoun confirmed Webster's observation, pointing to an increasing southern unity against Adams. The loss of regional power in 1825, coupled with the almost simultaneous call to regain it, resonated with southerners.[77]

Van Buren understood this fact. In the spring of 1827 he toured the southeastern states, urging all to line up behind Jackson, including those who had backed Crawford, as he had. He especially courted Virginians who had been Crawford stalwarts and who distrusted Jackson's military background. With the heroic general heading their presidential ticket, he prophesied the new party would return victory and power to the South. After all, Jackson was not only a westerner but also a southerner, a slave-owning cotton planter. To this base Van Buren anticipated Jacksonian strength in the West and expected to attach his own New York and other northern states that could be rallied behind the hero to return the country to what he described as constitutional and republican government.

The leaders of the Jackson party did not rely solely on the general's stature to build their following. First, they proclaimed their allegiance to strict construction and limited government; simultaneously they assaulted Adams's eloquent plea for a powerful government. In the hands of Calhoun, Jackson, Van Buren, and their loyalists that goal inevitably meant despotism and tyranny.[78]

They brandished Adams's refusal to stand foursquare with Georgia on the Indian question as a pro-Indian program that would deprive white American farmers of the land they deserved. It did not matter that his cautious policy did not really defend the

Indians. Although this instance referred only to Georgia, opponents presented it as a precedent for what would occur with lands farther west.

For most southerners the tariff of 1828, the infamous Tariff of Abominations, became an exclamation point to the powerful central government they equated with Adams. Even though this bill did not originate with him and he had little influence on its course through Congress, he did sign it into law. It served as another millstone around his neck. In fact, Van Buren adroitly orchestrated the arrangement of legislation intended to bring doubtful states like Pennsylvania to Jackson's side. He discounted southern opposition, aware that the South would never embrace Adams, as he assumed New England would not stray from the president's camp. Still, southerners blamed John Quincy and touted Jackson as their savior from such nefarious measures.

Yet, underlaying the several specific items, Adams's foes repeatedly announced that he had set about to destroy the republic. According to their script the corrupt bargain signaled that his administration began in a cesspool of corruption. American citizens had been robbed of precious rights, and their villainous president did not care. An unending drumbeat of speeches, pamphlets, and editorials underscoring his not caring about the wishes of the people reverberated through the country, with Adams's unfortunate phrase that members of Congress should not permit the will of their constituents to reject his program as the major chord. A rabid pro-Jackson editor summed up this strident cry: "Power is always stealing from the many to the few."[79]

Adams definitely heard the heavy artillery shelling him. In the wake of the Clay confirmation vote, he admitted that his administration would have antagonists, and he acknowledged the growth of their strength over time. Furthermore, he recognized Calhoun and Van Buren as leaders of the forces gathering behind Jackson's banner.[80]

For him their political opposition turned into personal enmity. He could not conceive of friends and those he had supported taking a political stance against him. Thus Calhoun, whom he had once praised for his intellect and ability, had despite his talent been brought down by an overweening ambition, which had made of him a "dupe and the tool of every knave." As for Jackson, he had become a Judas, for in Adams's mind his attention and backing in an earlier time made the general obligated to him. He even understood the key role of Van Buren, whom he evaluated as "the ablest man of them all." Yet he faulted the New Yorker for wasting his talent on political intrigues and machinations instead of championing principles.[81]

At the same time Adams granted Van Buren's ability to retain civil relations with all, including adversaries. He recorded a visit Van Buren made in May upon his return from his southern tour, noting that the two men engaged in friendly conversation. Even Adams, who understood that the goal of his visitor's mission in the South had been to eject him from the presidency, could not rebuff Van Buren's charming manner.[82]

While he identified the chieftains of those against him, Adams was also aware of the weapons they utilized. The floor of Congress became a rostrum for constant, often abrasive, speeches against him and his administration. Perhaps the most vituperative was John Randolph of Roanoke, whom Adams had met during his time in the U.S. Senate. By the late 1820s he had grown to despise the Virginian, so much so that Randolph was barred from all social occasions at the Executive Mansion. Denouncing his nemesis, Adams asserted, "The rancor of this man's soul against me is that which sustains his life." Adams could also count what was happening in Congress. By 1827 a strong majority opposed him, with congressional committees stacked with foes. He comprehended his predicament.[83]

Early in 1826 the Jackson camp took an important step. Major Jackson supporters purchased a Washington newspaper, renamed it, and brought in a Calhoun disciple as editor. The *United States Telegraph* became the organ in the nation's capital of the anti-Adams party. Partisan newspapers had long been a staple of

American politics, and Washington had known its share. The *Telegraph*, however, came into existence with a single mission— to shape national public opinion against Adams and for Jackson. Cries about venality and abuse of power filled its columns. Aware of the purpose of the *Telegraph*, friends asked Adams whether they should take tangible notice of what one called "the declaration of war." He responded negatively. Once again he neither could nor would accept or adapt to the new politics swirling around him, though he understood them.[84]

Adams's refusal to countenance a vigorous, focused response to the establishment of the *United States Telegraph* conformed to his disdain for newspapers that to him had joined the spearhead of election battles delivering mortal wounds to reason. Those who penned articles and editorials attacking him he grouped with the speakers and pamphleteers who wallowed in lies and misrepresentations, terming the lot of them "skunks of party slander." In their bitter contests he saw intelligent, talented men, even those with integrity, surrendering all those qualities to "passions." Defending his position, he asserted that the presidency of the United States was an office neither to be sought nor to be declined. With such opinions he surely considered himself above the ugly fray. He had evidently stored away the memory of the exertions he had made in 1824 and 1825 to secure that office for himself, though he never did engage in public name-calling.[85]

During the campaign his attitude did not change. In different situations he clung to his rejection of active participation in his own behalf. When Daniel Webster urged him to intervene in a struggle for a U.S. Senate seat in New Hampshire, he said no, averring that his doing so would both contravene his principles and probably prove unsuccessful. Told that funds were needed in Kentucky to carry state elections that would be crucial for the outcome of the presidential race there, Adams would not contribute, declaring such an act unprincipled. Exhorted by a Philadelphia supporter to attend the opening of the Pennsylvania Canal, where he could do himself great good by meeting German farmers and speaking with them in their own language, he replied that that form of electioneering violated his taste as well as his principles.[86]

Adams's utter rejection of the political dimension of both his presidency and reelection hopes centered on patronage—the lifeblood of political leaders. Rewarding the faithful with jobs generated enthusiasm and loyalty that could spread through the electorate in any given area. Upon assuming office, he made clear he would remove federal officeholders only for cause, such as malfeasance or misconduct, never for purely political reasons. He maintained that his desire for harmony and conciliation precluded any standard of partisanship for officeholding. Such a criterion "would make the Government a perpetual and unremitting scramble for office," and he could imagine nothing more pernicious. He was emphatic; he would not employ patronage for his political advantage. He seemed to be trying to cling to a political order that no longer pertained in the late 1820s.[87]

He held tenaciously to that creed even when his own stalwarts pushed him to make patronage decisions that could only benefit him. Clay and the cabinet desired that none but friends of the administration be appointed to public office. Specifically, Clay recommended the removal of principal customs officials, whom he branded as antiadministration, in Charleston, New Orleans, and Philadelphia, and their replacement with pro-Adams men. Webster encouraged the president to give a post to a friend of a key Philadelphia editor in an effort to bring that influential newspaperman to the president's side. A Kentuckian reported to Clay that a postmaster appointment in the town of Maysville would seriously harm the administration. He went on to say that he had written Adams on this matter, to no avail. In all these cases Adams refused to act. Neither the importuning of associates nor their criticism for his spurning their advice would move him. Even at the close of 1827, almost three years into his presidency, he held to his conviction that without a substantiated charge of moral or official misconduct he would not remove anyone, thus creating a

situation where his enemies reviled him while dwindling supporters regarded him as pusillanimous or ineffective.[88]

Adams's dealings with Postmaster General John McLean
best illustrate his steadfastness, even stubbornness, on patronage. The Post Office Department controlled more jobs than any
other unit in the federal government; even villages had federally
appointed postmasters. At the same time it was not a cabinet-level
department. And without doubt McLean was a most productive
postmaster general, who made the postal service a model of effi-
ciency and effectiveness. Yet he was no nonpartisan civil servant.
He had gained his appointment in 1823 through the efforts of
John C. Calhoun, and he remained a Calhoun loyalist, though he
followed his benefactor into Jackson's camp.

By spring 1827 Adams recorded in his diary that broad opinion
identified the postmaster general as hostile to his administration;
the warnings about McLean's true allegiance kept coming. In
October, Clay told the president he believed McLean "to be bitterly, though insidiously" opposed. He pointed out that in a recent
New York election almost all postal officials lined up on the opposite political side. Nothing changed in McLean's conduct during
the remainder of Adams's term.

Adams listened, and even heard these alarms. Initially, he
acknowledged that because of McLean's ability he made allow-
ances for the postal chief, unwilling to believe him "willfully
treacherous." But he admitted that McLean masked his war
against the administration. Becoming more apprehensive, he
privately accused McLean of placing Calhoun's minions in office
while professing personal friendship to him. In the spring of 1828
he used the term "double-dealing" to describe McLean's behavior. At the same time, however, he noted that firing the traitorous
officer would be extremely ill considered.

Rendering a final judgment in the summer of 1828, only
months before the presidential election, he condemned McLean
for "deep and treacherous duplicity." He admitted that despite

McLean's protestations of personal friendship and commitment to the administration, the postmaster general had used the extensive patronage at his disposal to advance the president's enemies for three years. Even so, Adams did not let him go. He rationalized, "I can fix no positive act that would justify the removal of him." Fixated on his self-proclaimed ideal of public service and his unwillingness to act on his own identification of a disloyal and even pernicious subordinate, Adams assisted in bringing about his own political destruction. In his inflexible and unrealistic handling of patronage, he committed a form of political suicide.[89]

In one political subject, the choice of a vice-presidential running mate, Adams did become directly involved in deliberations, though without taking charge. The incumbent, Calhoun, who had become a major Jackson figure, would have to be replaced. To that date the vice-presidency had not offered the most favored route to the presidency. The first two vice-presidents, Adams's father and Jefferson, had moved up from the second slot, but since 1800 the secretaryship of state had seemingly provided the preferred path to the presidency. Still, the vice-president occupied a potentially advantageous place for advancement. At the outset of his term Adams indicated that he intended to follow Monroe's course and remain neutral in all matters regarding the succession. In late 1826 Clay spoke of himself as a possibility for the vice-presidency, though he stated the choice should be made solely on the basis of its influence on the election. And John Quincy was told that Clay would be a real asset in the West, where he surely needed help. Much discussion about Clay went on between Adams and other cabinet members, who objected to the secretary of state. By late 1827 numerous other names had been brought up.

Adams finally decided on his general preference, informing supporters that the man should reside south of the Potomac. Yet he never made a great effort to ensure such a selection. Beginning in January 1828 several state conventions, all above the Potomac, nominated Secretary of the Treasury Richard Rush of Pennsylvania. When they did so, Adams signed on and naïvely said he hoped all on his side would accept Rush. He also told Rush that no other person would have pleased him more. Even though Adams engaged in discussions, he did not press his preference for a southerner. Others made the choice for him. In this instance, as in all others, he did not use his office to assert himself as a major player in his own reelection effort.[90]

In the midst of Adams's term two new parties presented themselves to American voters. Recognizing that fact, Clay called their existence an "incontestable truth." He identified them as supporters and opponents of the administration, asserting that any reference to any organizations from the past was solely "for the purpose of fraud and deception." The Jacksonians called themselves by different names—the Democratic party, the Democratic-Republican party, the Republican party, or sometimes the National Republican party. But most often and to most people they were known simply as the Jackson party. The Adams forces spoke of the Republican party, the National Republican party, or occasionally the People's party. Yet, like their foe, they were generally known by their candidate's name, the Adams party. These personal designations would not disappear and be replaced by formal party titles until after the election of 1828.[91]

Although there were two parties, they were not equal. The Jacksonians had more central direction and purpose, from organization to newspapers to speakers. Adams's side did, of course, have newspapers and speakers, but they operated in a more fragmented manner without a driving, forceful single message. Basically, as a political union the Adams men could not match their opponents. They lacked a heroic candidate. In addition, they had no organizational master like Van Buren. Finally, and perhaps more important, they campaigned for a sitting president who would not lead, who, in fact, rejected the entire process.

These two parties, incipient though they might be, did engage in intense partisanship. The charges each flung at the other became vicious. In a widely circulated accusation a Jackson editor charged that while in Russia, Adams had acted as a pimp for the tsar, procuring a young American girl to satisfy His Majesty's lust. An outraged Adams categorized this incendiary accusation as the worst of "the thousand malicious lies which outvenom all the worms of Nile." And he went to some lengths in an attempt to demonstrate its utter falsehood.[92]

His friends wallowed in the same gutter, however. A Cincinnati newspaper printed a malevolent editorial proclaiming that Jackson's mother was a common prostitute brought to this country by British soldiers. Thereupon she married a mulatto man with whom she had several children, among them Andrew Jackson. Apprised of this far-fetched, scandalous tale, Adams thought it absurd, but cynically went on to comment that even if proved true it would probably not hurt Jackson. The course of the campaign seemed to substantiate all Adams's apprehensions that fervent partisanship was demolishing reasonableness, a slugfest of calumny and lies replacing political civility. Vice was triumphing over virtue. And the cynicism expressed in his reaction to the malignant piece regarding Jackson's mother and his birth signaled that he had begun to doubt the probity of the republic and its citizens.[93]

Through all the bombast of the summer and fall of 1827 and early 1828 both sides struggled for votes. Optimism often reigned among Adams's loyalists. Detailing states they hopefully put in his column, Clay and Webster pointed to encouraging signs that Adams would prevail. Adams himself was more circumspect. In November 1826 he recorded in his diary that accidents would surely have a part in the outcome. The final issue, however, rested, as always, with "a wise, unerring hand." By the late summer of the next year, contemplating his return from Quincy to Washington, he could foresee nothing positive about it. By the spring of 1828 he pictured his chances as growing desperate and referred to his presidency as "the wreck," from which certain members of his cabinet wanted to flee.[94]

The results of the 1828 election bore out his fears. Jackson won a resounding victory with 56 percent of the popular vote, the largest margin in the nineteenth century—the totals: Jackson 647,292 and Adams 507,730. Those numbers included every state except Delaware and South Carolina, where the legislature still cast the state's presidential ballot. Adams managed to hold New England along with New Jersey and did well in New York, losing there by just over 5,000 votes out of more than 276,000 cast. Yet in the West and the South, Jackson swamped him; Adams could count only Delaware and barely Maryland in his column. The Electoral College result matched the popular outcome, giving Jackson a crowning 178–83 victory. Adams's numbers included the states he won outright and included 6 of Maryland's 11 and 16 of New York's 20. Fundamentally, the election pitted the Northeast against the rest of the country. Adams as president had not been able to expand his appeal, but he had not really tried.

Still, a closer look at the popular returns reveals a tighter election. With only a slight shift Adams could once again have become a minority president, losing the popular vote, but winning the electoral count. Movement of just over 11,500 popular votes in five states—Indiana, Kentucky, Louisiana, New York, and Ohio— would have given Adams a margin of 132 to 129 in the Electoral College. His opponent would still have enjoyed, however, a sizable popular majority. No such turnabout occurred, of course. Moreover, it is unknowable how the country would have reacted. The historical result made Adams's distance from the political world around him total; he lost the presidency.[95]

His defeat made him only the second president, the other being his father, to be denied a second term as president of the United States. The causes came from several directions. Jackson's military exploits went a long way with most American voters, but his image makes up only part of the story, and not the central part. Adams spurned the political world taking shape during his presidency. Defeating Jackson might have been impossible no matter what he did. Yet, had he accepted the reality of this new universe by acting on patronage and using his office to his advantage, he would surely have improved his chances of winning. In his corner he did have talented politicians like Clay, but the haphazardly organized and fundamentally directionless Adams party was no match for the political behemoth the Jacksonians had created. In 1828 the old political order suffered a vanquishing as unequivocal as Adams's own.

In the aftermath Adams expressed two disparate emotions. Personally, he knew, of course, that he would have to submit to his loss, whatever the pain. And the pain was deeply palpable. To his diary he confided, "The sun of my political life sets in the deepest gloom." And he prayed that he and those dear to him would be sustained. Still, in his melancholy he could rejoice that "[the sun] of my country shines unclouded."[96]

Adams's defeat ended one political era and ushered in another. The advent of Andrew Jackson signaled the beginning of a popular politics buttressed by organized, vigorous political parties. Hereafter, without the latter a presidential contender could not triumph, a truth the Jacksonian opposition would learn through experience. Never again could a presidential candidate claim to wear a mantle that had literally been possessed by the Founding Fathers.

A NEW PATH—TRIBULATION

and CONFIDENCE

CHAMBER OF THE HOUSE OF REPRESENTATIVES,
SCENE OF JOHN QUINCY ADAMS'S FINAL STAND

—

CHAPTER 6

"An Overruling Consciousness of Rectitude"

Departing the presidency just a few months shy of his sixty-second birthday, John Quincy Adams looked out upon an uncertain future. The five men who had previously departed, Founders all, had moved seamlessly into private life, their time in office completed. Initially, Adams assumed he would simply follow their precedent. Once in residence in Quincy—and he never thought that home was anywhere else—he would possibly become the literary man he had always declared his calling of choice. At the same time, after three and a half decades of almost constant public service, he had to wonder whether a quiet scholar-writer's life would satisfy him.

He certainly did not feel sanguine about his country's immediate political future. Much closer in outlook to the presidents who preceded him than to the one who would follow him, Adams considered the campaign that ousted him despicable, even vile. Moreover, according to him, Andrew Jackson and his loyalists wanted to take the country in absolutely the wrong direction. Already they had thwarted his ambitious vision for a grand, powerful nation. He viewed them as little more than fragmenters, who wanted to crumble the nation by curbing, even paring back, national power. Perhaps the opportunity would arise that would permit his regaining the role as a selfless public servant to stand against the Jacksonian hordes in a worthy struggle to return his beloved United States to the right path.

Several hours after the New Year had ushered in 1829, Adams began an entry in his diary, noting that his oil lamp had fluttered out—"self-extinguished," his expression. He went on to observe that this loss of light symbolized his own feelings. He understood that all hope for a second term had vanished and that he had to accept his defeat by Andrew Jackson. And he did so, albeit resignedly. Others who knew him discerned a similar emotion, but no one heard any public complaints.[1]

He had become the second Adams to fall to a southern slave owner proclaiming himself the savior of the people's liberty. Believing that he had been vanquished by means unfair, even immoral, he accented his unhappiness by refusing to attend Jackson's inauguration on March 4. It marked only the second time that an outgoing president had absented himself from his successor's ceremony. His father, who did not appear at Thomas Jefferson's, was the first. And John Quincy's refusal to attend was merely the first gesture that came to reflect an ex-president radically transformed by what he perceived as the indignities and insults, politically motivated, that had defined his presidential tenure.

When the outgoing president left the Executive Mansion on March 3, a British traveler described a man with a careworn and anxious expression—not tall, only five feet seven inches, but stocky, becoming portly at 175 pounds, bald, and clean shaven. As a loyal son of his ancestral home Massachusetts, he planned to return to his native state. He would go back not just to Massachusetts but to his hometown Quincy and even to the house of his late father, which he had inherited and which would become his home for the remainder of his life.[2]

Initially, however, chiefly because of Louisa's health, he moved into a rental house on Meridian Hill in Washington, a mile directly north of the Executive Mansion. She had been ill for some time, a condition that had plagued much of her time as first lady. While he escaped the physical maladies that gripped his wife, Adams admitted to his diary that he was "sick at heart." Together he and Louisa awaited the arrival of their eldest son, George, coming from Boston to assist their removal to Quincy.[3]

On Meridian Hill he mulled over leaving the active life that had stretched over three and a half decades in the public sphere. Pondering his future, he informed his former political partner Henry Clay that he considered that phase of his life closed. He intended to bury himself in retirement, becoming "a silent observer of the passing scene." Yet his ambition still towered as had that of the young college student of nineteen who copied in his diary from Shakespeare:

> If it be a sin to covet Honour
> I am the most offending soul alive.

Later he would similarly confide, "No reputation of a great man can be acquired but by the accomplishment of some great object." His political career had not reached that height.[4]

Now he told himself he could focus on that elusive goal by embracing what he had for years discerned as the pleasures of a scholar's life. While secretary of state, he confided to his diary, "The summit of my ambition would have been by some great work of literature to have done honor to my age and country, and to have lived in the gratitude of future ages." With his considerable learning he could have turned in any one of several directions. A gifted classicist with a profound knowledge of Greek and especially of Latin, he was particularly committed to Cicero and Tacitus. And he often prepared translations of the former. Also fluent in French and German, with some knowledge of Dutch, Italian, and Spanish, he could read the great Continental authors in their own languages. An avid student of the Bible, he regularly read the whole of it, along with commentaries, and at times in various languages. Additionally, he was devoted to scientific studies, notably astronomy and botany. Moreover, while the Boylston Professor of Rhetoric at Harvard, he had already studied and written about that subject. Not even the acclaimed intellectual savant Thomas Jefferson could claim greater learning. Clearly he and Jefferson were the most Renaissance-like presidents in their knowledge about their interests.[5]

Yet even with Renaissance-like erudition and learning, by the time he left the presidency one project stood in the foreground. He informed a friend that his chief desire was to write a life of his father. He often reflected upon preparing a biography of John Adams, a man he considered great, though vastly unappreciated and insufficiently recognized by his countrymen. Adams felt deeply aggrieved that the country had not awarded him a second term as president. In his book he would depict the elder Adams in all his glory and genius. Vindication of the father would redound upon the worthiness of the son.[6]

Family tragedy intruded on those musings, however. Since graduating from Harvard in 1821, George Washington Adams's life had become increasingly troubled. By 1829 the difficulties had piled up. He had mismanaged his father's financial affairs in Massachusetts and was in debt to him. Because he never embraced the Adams ethic of hard work, his law practice was in shambles. He drank far too much, indeed showing alcoholic tendencies. Then, unbeknownst to his parents, he had impregnated a young maidservant in the home where he resided. He clearly had not responded to his father's constant admonitions about duty and upholding the Adams name. Now, with the added burden of having fathered an illegitimate child, he would once again have to come face-to-face with a reproving father.

While expecting George any day, John Quincy on May 2 learned that his distressed, twenty-eight-year-old son had been lost from a steamboat traveling through Long Island Sound from Providence, Rhode Island, to New York City. Whether the young man jumped or fell overboard was not at all clear; there were no eyewitnesses. Fellow passengers did testify, however, to his extremely disturbed state. A distraught father struggled to cope with the calamity that literally prostrated his unwell wife. He called on God to comfort him and his family in their "deep affliction." Months later he still prayed to his God for "fortitude, patience, perseverance, and active energy," but, as always, with the caveat "let thy will by done."[7]

Even before leaving the presidency for his temporary residence on Meridian Hill, Adams had involved himself in a controversy that underscored the impossibility of his separating the personal from the political. It all began seemingly innocently with the publication of 1825 correspondence from a now deceased Thomas Jefferson by a pro-Jackson senator, who had it printed in 1828 as an anti-Adams campaign document. In it Jefferson recounted his recollections of events during his administration relating to Adams—the Embargo Act, New England Federalists, and their possible overtures to Great Britain—in which his conduct could be construed as betraying his Federalist associates for political favor from Republicans. Many politicians would have paid it scant attention, for it dealt with circumstances of long ago and a now dead Federalist party.[8]

A seemingly depressed and now greatly sensitive Adams could not do so, however. He perceived his integrity and patriotism questioned. As a result on October 21 he had an authorized statement placed in the *National Intelligencer,* a major Washington newspaper, restating his version of his entirely proper actions. But he did more than defend himself. He went on to charge that leading members of the Federalist party had indeed pursued British cooperation for the possible formation of a separate confederacy.[9]

A month after the appearance of Adams's communication, a number of former Federalists in Boston struck back. A public letter signed by thirteen of them, many old friends or acquaintances of John Quincy's, demanded that he specify those who had advocated separating from the United States. Indignantly they wanted names named. Those men had a personal more than a political motive, for they saw their own or their kinsmen's reputation tarnished with at the least the implication of disloyalty. Learning about their response, Adams recorded in his diary that once again a bitter controversy now confronted him. Declaring that he would reply, he said he would weigh carefully every word he wrote. With, as he saw it, both his and his family's reputation at stake, he acknowledged his "anxiety to be right upon every point is inexpressible."[10]

While he expected his reply dated December 30 would vindicate himself, he also requested that those he knew and cared about would let go of a topic that, if pushed, could ultimately harm the good name of some who had already died. He claimed that he wanted the past to be past. Yet he did not restrain himself; instead, he denied that the thirteen represented the entire Federalist party. Then he refused to identify anyone publicly, asserting that other people might initiate legal action against him. He would, however, be willing to do so in private, to each man separately.

Before closing he addressed a critical point at issue, the right of a state to hold a law of Congress unconstitutional and declare itself out of the Union. In a mocking tone he denied any such right unless it be the right to commit suicide or the right of a resident of a city to set fire to his own home. At the same time, in an effort to be generous, he admitted that others could disagree and proclaim that each state did possess such a right. And, in his view, the New England Federalists who, from their opposing the Embargo Act to their calling for the Hartford Convention, had only upheld their principles.

Closing, he became demonstrably personal, reflecting a profound personal change that distinguished him from the once more diplomatic secretary of state. According to him he had "waived every scruple" to answer them. He had done so because of his long and sincere friendship with some of them that would last as long as he lived. No more should pass between them and him. He simply could not engage in a continuing argument with them, and he urged, "If you please, let our *joint* correspondence rest." His final words: "With a sentiment of affectionate and unabated regard for some, and of respect for all of you, permit me to subscribe myself your friend and fellow-citizen."[11]

The rough-and-tumble world of 1829 respected no such politesse. The men in Boston had no intention of allowing Adams the last word. At the end of that January they issued a public appeal to all citizens of the United States. In this document they charged that the new ex-president had insulted the state of Massachusetts with his accusation of a plot hatched by certain of its citizens against the Union. Yet the accuser would designate no one; thus his indictment was not credible. They went on to defend the Hartford Convention as no more than an assembly of modern Pilgrims, who like their ancestors deliberated on the best way to preserve their liberty. Defending this installment of the public debate, they declared they could not be expected to remain silent when Adams "from his high station" impugned them, their associates, and in some cases their fathers.[12]

The increasingly argumentative Adams promptly took up the cudgels to reply. He began even before leaving the Executive Mansion and continued at Meridian Hill, usually working early in the morning. In his diary he made clear his motive. He had "been so scandalously abused and misrepresented by so many men of influence and power in this country" that he found "it impossible to purse my own justification without the application of the scourge to them." Becoming longer and longer, his manuscript accompanied him when in midsummer he went back to Massachusetts.[13]

He ended up with a veritable treatise on American politics from the 1790s to the close of the War of 1812, totaling 223 printed pages. He clearly could not hold back. He placed the blame for the political animosity in the country and danger to it on states' rights, in his opinion no more than a "cabalistic watchword." And its origins he found in the southern dislike of those descended from "the Pilgrim Puritans," chief among them his father. Among those stoking "the lurking jealousies of the slave-holders," he placed the now permanently reposing Thomas Jefferson fore-most. Cataloging Jefferson's numerous political sins, John Quincy employed harsh language. In Jefferson he perceived "the heart-less selfishness of a demagogue" who engaged in an "overcharged display of democracy." Asserting that all Federalists shared that view of Jefferson, Adams averred, "such were in a great degree my own feelings toward him, aggravated by a deep sense of his injustice and a profound conviction of perfidy in his personal rela-tions with my father." John Adams's defeat in 1800 was clearly an amazingly fresh memory for the son, who, of course, had just experienced the same fate.

Having placed the South, slavery, Jefferson, and states' rights in a simmering brew of political evil, Adams did not permit a total escape for New England Federalists. Those who had opposed his father and led the way to the Hartford Convention he also exco-riated. Yet their states' rights extremism, which endangered the Union in a time of severe stress, they had learned from the South. With both the Jeffersonian Republicans and the New England Federalists hammered, the Adamses, father and son, stood practi-cally alone as paragons of political probity.

Despite the political chicanery and villainy that had infected both South and North, the right had prevailed. Adams closed with praise for the Union, which had not only survived but prospered since 1815. While he condemned the Hartford Convention of 1814 for considering disunion, he presented it as "a perpetual *memento mori*" to anyone projecting a breakup of the country. And since that event he insisted that no part of the Union had been more dedicated to its development and growth than New England. In fact, embedded in his hymn to the Union is a paean to New England, now its strongest and most dedicated supporter.[14]

Although Adams had completed his lengthy discourse by the end of 1829, he did not have it published. Friends to whom he showed it urged that he withhold it from the public unless he moderated much of the strident tone and even eliminated the most brutal attacks on individuals. Also, though unspoken, the severe onslaught against the South and slaveholders could make impossible any future national political course. At the time Adams did decide against publication; in fact, it remained private throughout his life. Not until 1877 did it appear in a book edited by a grandson, the noted historian Henry Adams, which also contained all the writings by John Quincy Adams and others pertinent to it.

In Quincy, already sad, Adams did not devote all of his thinking and writing time to his ongoing quarrel with old and new antagonists. He also set out on his great mission of preparing the life of his father by turning to the extraordinary trove of John Adams's archives. He had in his possession the documentary history of John's long life, from library to diary along with the voluminous correspondence and letter books. And he had Charles Francis's assistance in organizing this mountainous record.

Adams viewed this assignment as his duty, as almost a religious calling, as he did most things in life. He would become a scholar committed to the holy toil of holding up and illuminating the Adams name. "There is no passion more deeply seated in my bosom," he confided in nineteenth-century rotundness to his diary, "than the longing for posterity worthily to support my own and my father's name." His life would capture the entire range of the man, displaying his emotions with their "pure stream" of morality felt throughout. He desired inspiration and knowledge to make his narrative, but he also wanted it presented in a lively style that would attract and captivate readers.[15]

Despite his professed resolve he discovered his dedication compromised by his inability to stay on task. Lashing himself for his "propensity to fly from the purpose and most urgent duty of the day," to anything else that happened by, even trifles, he acknowledged that he also had to fight what he termed his "habit of procrastination," which he feared he could not overcome. "Shall I never do better?" he asked himself.[16]

His answer appeared to be no, for progress on the biography sputtered. John Quincy did not seem able to propel himself forward on his self-appointed noble mission. Something else—

"digressions" he called them—constantly interfered. Several months later he had made little headway. All his declarations notwithstanding, this obligation did not consume him.[17]

He reached in so many directions. One that took time but gave him distinct pleasure was a different form of composition, poetry. From his collegiate days he had regularly written poems, some quite brief, others longer. They appear at irregular intervals in his diary; occasionally they were published, usually in a newspaper. A continual versifier to whom rhyming came readily, he commented on his composing verses while on his horseback rides and walks.[18]

While ardent about writing poetry, he did recognize his limits. A great poet—Shakespeare, Shelley, or Byron—he knew he was not. He compared writing poems to playing chess and billiards. In all these, he stated, work and practice would enable one to reach a certain level of accomplishment, but beyond that "no vigils and no vows will go."[19]

Shortly after his death a number of his poems were published in a small volume that provides an accessible source for considering his endeavors in verse. This collection demonstrates that he generally adopted traditional poetic forms, with the religious element quite strong. He was influenced almost entirely by the neoclassical era, the eighteenth century. He seemed immune to the currents of his own time.

There is scarcely a hint of the romanticism that by 1800 had become prominent among some English poets like Samuel Taylor Coleridge and William Wordsworth, both of whom had grown popular in the United States early in the nineteenth century. Adams's lack of interest in nature reinforces the absence of romanticism, for embracing nature was central among romantics. Although he had become an avid gardener, his turn to the botanical focused on science, not on the imagination or the emotions.

But enchantment with nature certainly was key for Adams's near neighbor Ralph Waldo Emerson, who lived in Concord, Massachusetts. A generation younger than Adams, Emerson became a major figure in American letters during Adams's lifetime. Also unlike the poets inspired by romanticism, Adams did not permit much personal exposure in his poetry. As in other areas, notably his political outlook, he remained firmly anchored in the commitment to reason and rationality that characterized the Founders of the nation, epitomized by his father, whom he so admired.[20]

Yet during the period in Quincy he devoted most of his poetic effort to two lengthy projects. In the winter and spring of 1831 he composed a long narrative poem he entitled *Dermot MacMorrogh* . . . , which dramatized the English conquest of Ireland in the twelfth century. Although the events he related in verse occurred several hundred years prior to 1831, his contemporary political concerns became central themes. The poem was a hymn to liberty and independence, made clear by Adams's empathy with the Irish, who lost theirs to a foreign tyrant, the invading and oppressive English. That the main character, the Dermot MacMorrogh of the title, was an Irishman who for personal gain and power allied with the English to subdue his countrymen testified to Adams's apprehension about the danger posed to his country by Americans disposed to place what he considered parochial interests, whether state or sectional, above the health and well-being of the whole. Ultimately, for his own safety, Mac-Morrogh had to leave Ireland for England; yet he had already sealed the ruin of his country by assisting the English conquest. As usual, Adams's underlying psychological messages were not difficult to ascertain.[21]

Adams described the completed poem as "at once a work of history, imagination, and poetry." Asserting that writing it took all of his poetic talent, he still wondered whether he should consign it to flames. He did quite the opposite, however, and published it. The reaction to it did not please him. He reconciled himself with this unpleasant outcome by equating it with the public assaults on him arising from politics. In his view readers could not separate the poem from the poet. Moreover, he said no one in American political life had successfully ventured into the field of general literature.[22]

Almost immediately after finishing *Dermot MacMorrogh*, he began rendering the entire Old Testament book of Psalms into his own version of poetry. This endeavor took over a year, between the summer of 1831 and the summer of 1832. Upon concluding this substantial undertaking, which he never published, he announced in his diary the closing of his career as a poet with the benediction "perhaps, it were best, forever."[23]

Yet he never stopped. En route from Quincy to Washington in 1833 to take his seat in Congress, he noted that on both steamboat and railroad his head was filled with verses, which he would write down in evenings. As late as 1841 he recognized that his "passion" for writing in verse remained with him. Even later, just two years before his death, he admitted he could not predict the moment when poetic inspiration would enter his mind. It did until the end.[24]

The time Adams spent on his poetry did not at all curtail his reading. As usual, the Bible and the classics occupied a special place. Noting in both 1830 and 1831 the completion of his usual yearlong trek through the Bible, he feared that he did not profit as much from it as he should. With the classics he concentrated on Cicero, whom he considered the greatest mind of Rome. This time his immersion in his favorite Roman's works prompted a regret. If as a young man, he confided to his diary, he had spent an uninterrupted year studying Cicero in the original Latin, he might have been of more use to his country and fellow man. Despite that lamentation he did not spell out how he would have been more useful.

Though central, the scriptures and the classics certainly did not take up all of his reading list. He gave attention to books and pamphlets on colonial Massachusetts, including some by the eminent Puritan divine Cotton Mather, a largely seventeenth-century figure to whom men like Jackson or Clay would hardly have paid attention. The letters of the eighteenth-century French aristocrat Marie de Vichy-Chamrond, Marquise du Deffand, whose circle included the celebrated philosophe Voltaire, intrigued him—letters of no interest to politicians of his day. He said he found them more interesting than any novel, for they recorded reality. At this time he read Sir Edward Bulwer-Lytton's *Pelham; or, The Adventures of a Gentleman*, which appeared in 1828. To him novels emphasized character and manners more than narrative, which he preferred. He also perused portions of Edward Gibbon's massive history of the Roman Empire. Gibbon, however, he did not admire. While he judged Gibbon's philosophy shallow, he most disliked what he termed the historian's "anti-religious acrimony." Simply noticing the range of Adams's reading confirms his admission that he was "greedy of books."[25]

No matter his inveterate reading and writing, he maintained his commitment to physical exercise. Walking, usually around three miles, and horseback riding, often ten or more, marked many days. And, of course, there was always swimming. Before leaving Washington, he kept up his usual practice of plying the Potomac River. In Quincy he swam in Quincy Bay, which touched shore at the town. Yet, at the end of summer 1830, he related that he had given up bathing in the ocean because of its perceived negative effect on his bronchial problems and coughing.[26]

Although he left the water, at least for a time, his attention to gardening never faltered. He filled his diary with detail on the plantings around his house and his care for them. He even used the word "plantation" when describing the area he used for all that he put in the ground. Trees especially preoccupied him. In May 1831 he cataloged the variety and number he had planted in the previous twelve months—150 apple, 50 pear, 10 peach, 10 cherry, 15 wild cherry, 2 apricot, 4 horse chestnut. That he lost so many of them distressed him, but it made him understand why more people did not, as he did, try to raise trees from seeds, nuts, and acorns. No transplanting for him.[27]

During the summer of 1829 when Adams returned to Quincy, he celebrated his sixty-second birthday. Even his vigorous exercise regimen did not ward off all physical complaints. Over the next two years he battled coughs, sore throats, and bronchial complaints. Still, as earlier, his major worry concerned his eyes;

their inflammation alarmed him, especially in the winter of 1831. That debility affected his reading, writing, and sleeping. Even heroic treatment with leeches failed to bring immediate benefit. Traveling through Philadelphia, he sought out the prominent physician Dr. Philip Syng Physick. Describing his symptoms, Adams spoke of his health as "drooping" and "unremediable." Dr. Physick recommended abstaining form all fermented liquors. On a subsequent consultation later that same year, Dr. Physick could only prescribe patience for an anxious Adams.[28]

Aside from physical ailments, Adams brooded about what he perceived as his general decay, particularly identifying his failing memory. Pondering the impact of this decline, in his diary he wrote that perhaps it would prepare him for a gradual, inevitable deterioration of all his powers. He hoped, however, that he could find "aids and resources" that would mitigate what to him was a certain "calamity." Of course, ultimately the end was the will of heaven. Still, he prayed that his old age might come with both usefulness and pleasures.[29]

While Adams wrestled with anxiety about his decline, combatted his wandering attention, and struggled with his faltering biographical mission, he recognized that he had been a public man since his midtwenties, with but brief interludes. The lure of public life had always tantalized him. Even before his marriage he professed to Louisa that serving his country was "not merely an ambition, but a duty." To a young son he wrote that the patriot must always hold himself ready to serve.[30]

Yet the temptation for office or position, even the desire for it, was severely tempered. A biographical as well as ideological son of a major Founding Father, he had inherited and imbibed a powerful obligatory sense of public service when called upon. And he certainly heeded the call—the U.S. diplomatic representative in the Netherlands, Prussia, Russia, and Great Britain, and a member of the American delegation that negotiated the Treaty of Ghent. In the midst of those assignments there had also been a stint in the U.S. Senate. Those posts he followed with eight years as secretary of state and then four years as president.

Absolutely crucial, however, for Adams from his perspective was that he had been called to each of these positions. He repeated time and time again that he had never angled or campaigned or had anyone else intervene on his behalf for any of them. He did not strive; he was chosen. For his own sense of himself, he had to believe that only his merit and virtue brought him office. He did acknowledge his ambition, but he could never consciously permit that aspiration to result in an overt effort to fulfill it. As he told a political supporter, "The principle of my life had been never to ask for the suffrage of my country, and never to shrink from its call."[31]

Even his service as the sixth president he interpreted as simply acceding to the summons of his countrymen. He prided himself on not emulating his peers in James Monroe's cabinet and in the Congress in seeking the nation's highest office. He filled his diary with the now obligatory derogatory notices of their political greed in contrast with his awaiting the decision of his fellow citizens of the republic. Not only did he denounce them for duplicity; he also castigated them for their constant effort to slander his character and reputation "No conclave of cardinals was ever more caballing," he wrote. Yet, when he received but one-third of both the electoral and popular votes, he did not withdraw. And when the House chose him over Andrew Jackson, who had won a plurality of both, he joyfully and thankfully accepted.[32]

His defeat for reelection in 1828 he attributed chiefly to the nefarious political machinations of his opposition and its lack of either moral or political scruples. To that level he announced he would never descend. He viewed an open appeal to the people for votes as political and republican sin. For an honorable election victory they must come unbidden to him. Usually he had faith in America, but that conviction came with a caveat—the public could be led astray by grasping and untruthful office seekers.

While he continued to think about politics and public life,

inquiries came to him from Massachusetts associates about his political plans. Even before he had completed his presidential term, he had rebuffed a request that he consider allowing his name to be put forward for the U.S. Senate. He declared that he intended to separate himself entirely from all connection with public life. Yet, in the summer of 1830, he was willing to talk about the national House of Representatives. Visitors to Quincy told him that he could easily triumph in his congressional district, the Twelfth, known as the Plymouth District, because it centered on the nearby town of Plymouth celebrated for its association with the Pilgrims.[33]

These men wanted a strong candidate opposed to Andrew Jackson to ensure the defeat of any pro-Jackson hopeful. In the aftermath of the election of 1828, the already fractured Republican party disintegrated. Although agreed-upon new party names did not appear immediately, almost everywhere partisans began to congregate in anti- and pro-Jackson coalitions. In both 1824 and 1828 Massachusetts had sided with its native son. There were always Jackson supporters, however, though a distinct minority. No matter their inferior political status, the Jackson men intended to contest elections. And the anti-Jackson forces, most of whom had been in Adams's camp, wanted at every turn to stymie their opponents.[34]

To these queries Adams responded in character. When asked whether he would accept if elected, he answered that he did not know. To say he would, he informed a questioner, seemed too much like asking for a vote, which he would not do. He wanted the people to act on their own. To all inquiries he made clear that he would never embrace what he still termed unsavory politics. Moreover, he could not face the possibility of another rejection at the polls. Should voters choose him on their own, however, that would be quite different. With that outcome in hand, he could decide yea or nay.[35]

He added two more considerations that would influence his decision. Up to that time no former president had ever subsequently held public office; there was no precedent. Adams would have to decide whether taking office would demean the presidency or himself. Ultimately, he concluded it would not. As he saw it, a career in the House of Representatives could even be noble because he had always preached that serving the people at their behest was an honorable calling.[36]

His conclusion that the absence of precedent posed no problem did not, however, eliminate all his difficulties. He had to confront familial opposition to his returning to the public stage in political office. Louisa Catherine Adams had grown to detest politics, particularly political life in Washington, a city where she had once so gallantly triumphed. Abhorring the nitty-gritty of the political world, she rejoiced when her husband left it. And she firmly opposed his return to it. She worried about the unavoidable bitter opposition he seemed to incur and its distressing impact on him and thus on them. That had certainly contributed to her maladies and social withdrawal during Adams's presidency. Although he shared her distaste for the normal practice of politics and most politicians, his ambition and craving for public approval, which he would interpret as exoneration, still flourished. This elemental drive could be satisfied only when voters unasked reached out to him and gave him their approval and trust.

Charles Francis joined his mother in opposing his father's return to the political world. He regretted his parent's succumbing to what he deemed "the temporary seduction of popular distinction." In addition, he feared the unprecedented departure from the non-officeholding careers of previous ex-presidents would be considered undignified. The son wanted the father's full attention to stay on his great enterprise, the biography of the grandfather.[37]

In spite of the objections of those nearest and dearest to him, Adams gave his blessing to those who wanted to place him in the House of Representatives, though he would neither publicly announce his candidacy nor provide unqualified assurance that he would accept if elected. His acceptance, he informed those who wanted to use his name, would depend upon his judgment about the worth of his opponents and his margin of victory, along with his health. He would not permit any further public humiliation for himself or the Adams name. If he had once more to endure that sensation, it would be purely private.[38]

Even so, for the men eager to use his name that quasi-agreement sufficed. The name John Quincy Adams went before the electorate of the Plymouth District. And in November 1830 those voters gave him an overwhelming victory. He won 1,811 votes, 72 percent of the total. Never before had he known such public approval. Euphoric, he recorded in his diary that not even his election as president had been "half so gratifying to my soul." He went on to note that no previous appointment or election had pleased him so much.[39]

Even in the midst of this exultation, his powerful need to distance himself from his ambition made its usual appearance. For himself, he mourned that he considered this summons to serve the public unfortunate because it deprived him of "the last hope of an old age of quiet and leisure." Yet this same man had described himself during the months since leaving the presidency as living in "a state of apathy," unable to follow any systematic course and disgruntled with himself. Now elected, he foresaw his future as his past, "buffeted with political rancor and personal malignity, with more than equal chances of losing the favor even of those who now think they humor themselves by their suffrages more than me."[40]

Yet no matter his inner turmoil, no matter the lack of precedent, no matter family unhappiness, no matter deferring the holy duty of a loyal son extolling a venerated and underappreciated father, John Quincy Adams marched again, in some sense a Christian soldier, into the political fray. He would become a member of the Twenty-Second Congress.

Although elected in November 1830, Adams would not take his seat in the House until December 1831, when the first session of the Twenty-Second Congress would convene. Yet, even by the time of his election, Massachusetts politics was in turmoil caused by the phenomenon of Antimasonry, which swirled through most northeastern states. To understand this movement requires recognition of what it raged against.[41]

Freemasonry, or the Masonic order, was a fraternal organization that came to this country from England in the eighteenth century. Primarily social in character, Masonry declared itself dedicated to philanthropic goals. Hierarchical in structure, it exacted various oaths from members as they moved up toward higher degrees of membership. At those levels of leadership elaborate dress and titles, such as master, king, and, at the top, general grand high priest, obtained. The most important oath demanded from all members the vow to preserve the secrecy of the order. From its beginnings Masonry attracted many leading Americans, including Benjamin Franklin and George Washington, and in Adams's time his political partner Henry Clay and archfoe Andrew Jackson. By 1825 Masonic lodges existed in every state, and everywhere local elites made up a significant portion of the membership.

Explaining how by 1830 Freemasonry became the target of a popular uprising leads to the change and disarray in American politics accompanying the devolution of the Republican party. A series of events in western New York State in 1826 sparked what became the Antimasonic crusade. In that year a discontented Mason in Batavia, one William Morgan, set out to expose the secrecy central to the order. Failing in their effort to seize Morgan's manuscript or to destroy the printing press intended to print it, Masons had their erstwhile colleague jailed in a nearby town for allegedly failing to pay a two-dollar debt. Then they spirited him out of jail and took him some one hundred miles westward to the Niagara River, where his body was discovered.

Though seemingly a straightforward case of kidnapping and murder, only a summary official investigation occurred. Local authorities appeared to look the other way, if they looked at all. Masons orchestrated a thorough cover-up of an event they hoped would soon be forgotten. Their attempt backfired, however. The

populace in the area rose up, charging that the Masonic order con-
spired not only to obstruct justice but to overthrow it entirely. As
a result Masons found themselves and their organization assailed
as immoral and un-American, as a clique of the elite trampling
upon the rights of the people. Those who quickly became known
as Antimasons shouted for the destruction of Masonry.

The Morgan episode took place amid political uncertainty
and insecurity. The disunity evident in the Republican party with
multiple candidates in 1824 and its further breakdown during
Adams's administration produced a political arena more open
than at any other time since the early 1790s. In western New York
anti-Jackson politicians searching for a unifying issue latched
onto the Morgan abduction, murder, and cover-up. They depicted
the episode as a privileged group mocking the people. Those who
felt themselves economically, politically, or socially on the outside
boarded Antimasonry as a vehicle to attack those they perceived
on the inside. That Andrew Jackson himself was a Mason helped
in their effort to brand the Jackson party as an elite pitted against
the people. Almost without warning, Antimasonry became a rising tide surging through the northeastern states, a movement
that threatened to sweep all before it.

Massachusetts was not exempt. Freemasonry had a long history in the state, and by the late 1820s counted more than 4,500
members, mostly men of prominence. Yet many who lived in the
largely rural southern and western counties, including Adams's
congressional district, shared a dislike inherited from their Puritan forebears for secret organizations with a membership bound
by oaths. They provided fertile ground for the Antimasonic
message.[42]

In Massachusetts, however, the Jacksonians did not provide the
chief enemy for Antimasons. With no significant leadership and
lacking elite adherents, the Jacksonians were weak. The major
enemy of the Antimasonic party became the National Republican,
the political home of the Boston commercial and financial elite,
most of whom had Federalist antecedents. Although they surely

supported Adams against Andrew Jackson, they never warmed to him, nor did they entirely trust him. He, of course, shared those some sentiments; he had never embraced those men. Moreover, he had just been engaged in a heated public war with a number of their leaders.

Still, Antimasons got off to a slow start in the state; they held their first state convention on December 30, 1829, and elected a few state legislators, though they did treat Antimasonry as a party. By 1831, with a second state convention and with a substantial number of legislators, Antimasonry had become a force in the state. In that year a new Antimasonic newspaper was founded, the *Boston Daily Advocate*, which became the leading Antimasonic journal in New England.

By this time Adams identified himself with the new crusading party. He had first learned about the movement while still president. Informed in 1827 by a New York politician of the growing strength of Antimasonry in that state, he was asked whether he belonged to the order. He responded negatively. Then, when he ran for Congress, Antimasons supported him. By his election he understood both the potency and the potential of Antimasonry. At the same time he tried initially to maintain neutrality in the Mason-Antimason fracas because he did not want to alienate anyone.[43]

He soon realized, however, the impossibility of sustaining that posture. Invited to attend the Antimasonic state convention in Boston in May 1831 as a congressman-elect, he said he could see no valid reason for declining. His son Charles Francis advised against attendance, fearing an adverse reaction if his father became involved in the Mason-Antimason controversy. Numerous National Republicans who had supported him while president could interpret his turn toward Antimasonry as betraying them and their party. In contrast, Adams asserted that no public man could forever escape from "political collisions." In his judgment anyone who permitted the possible fallout from an altercation to intimidate him had no place in public life. Admitting he had heretofore abstained from becoming associated with the Antimasons, he avowed there was a time when a good citizen had to take a stand. And now his time had arrived. No matter the conceivable consequences, he declared he would not flinch from openly affirming his allegiance.[44]

Adams became a full-fledged Antimason, the first third party in American history. As a former president, he was the most notable member of the party in the country, and certainly in his state. In 1831 some Antimasons asked him to let his name be proposed for governor. He declined, saying the incumbent, a National Republican, was a friend whom he would not challenge. In the election Antimasonic backing helped the sitting governor gain a resounding victory against the Jacksonian entry.[45]

Nationally, Antimasons determined to contest the presidency in 1832. To select a candidate, they held the first national political convention in American history. Prior to that gathering in Baltimore in September 1831, Adams had been spoken of as the party's nominee. A major New York Antimason, William Henry Seward, visited him in Quincy to consult about the nominee and the election. They discussed possible candidates. As usual, Adams stated that he had no desire for the nomination. Yet he added he would accept if nominated, but he thought he could be more useful to the cause if someone else got the nod. Most important, he concluded, the Antimasons must unite behind a single person. In Baltimore he was never a serious contender; too many connected him with defeat. The delegates finally settled on William Wirt, who had been Adams's colleague in Monroe's cabinet and his own attorney general.[46]

In the election of 1832 Andrew Jackson easily won a second term, besting Henry Clay, the National Republican standard-bearer, as well as Wirt. Wirt did not fare well, carrying only Vermont. But the Antimasons had considerably more impact at the state level, where unity tickets, chiefly with National Republicans, and mutual support between the two parties helped each other.

Adams had expressed no hesitation about aligning with the Antimasons. In the political vacuum of his postpresidency, he found himself a political outsider. For both personal and political reasons, an alliance with the Jackson party, by now commonly called the Democratic, was out of the question. He would never combine with Jackson, certainly not in a subordinate role. Furthermore, he saw Jackson and his loyalists blocking his own agenda for national greatness. But he was not at all comfortable with the National Republican leadership in Massachusetts, even though he and they had been on the same side during his presidency. Yet the Boston elite dominating that party was the same group closely associated with his old Federalist foes. He and they had never really embraced each other. And in a fundamental sense he continued to battle them. Thus he stood alone, outside partisan tents; in many ways that location suited him.

Antimasonry, however, appealed to him. Its overall moral message attracted him, for he believed he had always brought a powerful moralism to his politics. He relished this onslaught against those designated as insiders. Even with his pedigree, he always thought of himself as essentially an outsider, a state of being that was further attenuated by his extraordinary intellectual capacity. The Antimasonic attack on manipulation by the powerful and the resulting political corruption fit with his own outlook. In his view that poisonous mixture had brought down his father and had also thwarted him and his program for national greatness. A more practical consideration was that many of his constituents in the Plymouth District adopted Antimasonry. Accordingly, he would be aligning with a party that could enhance his standing among those who had elected him.

Grasping the basic ideological message of the Antimasons, Adams became a vigorous apostle. The elitism of Masonry masked by secrecy and oaths he condemned as "pernicious." Deriding the pretensions of the order, he often ridiculed the titles such as grand master, grand king, and general grand high priest, the topmost, that Masons awarded to advanced members. He pronounced the entire principle of the organization unjust, specifying its hallmark an injustice. The order itself he branded "a moral ulcer on the Community." It had no place in America, notwithstanding the prestige of its members past or present. Advocating the dissolution of Freemasonry on these shores, he professed that outcome more important to Americans of his day and their posterity than the result of any election.[47]

He took his campaign to the public in numerous lengthy letters and statements, stating that he had "a moral obligation" to contribute as much as he could to the cause. In them he repeated time and again his strictures against an organization he constantly castigated as a blot on his country. By the summer of 1832 he reported spending six hours a day on his Antimasonic writings. Years later he published with a lengthy introduction a collection of his epistles, which totaled almost three hundred pages.[48]

By 1833 it appeared that Antimasonry could provide political advancement to Adams in his state. In that year numerous Antimasons wanted their most luminous colleague to stand for governor. Although he insisted that he really wanted to rebuff this push, he did not completely reject it. And the state convention meeting in Boston in September resolved its preference for him. A committee delivered to him in Quincy the resolution of nomination. Its wording made his refusal almost impossible. Simply put, it announced that the people needed him. Praising his patriotism and devotion to the best interests of the public, the language emphasized that the state needed his particular talents, even at personal sacrifice. Accepting, Adams stipulated that the grounds on which he was nominated left him no honorable way to refuse.[49]

The contest had four candidates—Adams, a National Republican, and a Jacksonian Democrat along with one from the tiny Workingmen's party. Polling 29 percent of the vote, Adams finished second to the National Republican, who garnered 40 percent. With nobody receiving a majority of the popular vote, state law mandated that the legislature select the winner. The procedure directed the house to select two of the four and send those names to the senate, the body that would make the final choice.

The two names that the house intended to forward were those of Adams and John Davis, the National Republican.

Even though his party wanted him to stay the course, Adams dispatched a letter to the speaker of the house withdrawing his name. Earlier, upon learning the result of the election, he considered his situation an "emergency," relating that he faced a delicate task—to make the right decision. In his deliberations he told himself that he must totally focus on where the public good and "patriotic principle" would lead him. To ensure that he made the right choice, he would rely on his "consciousness of rectitude" to guide him. When he finally decided, he recorded that he did so in an effort to spur harmony between Antimasons and National Republicans. Yet more centrally, he did not want to risk public defeat, likely in a senate with a National Republican majority. Thereupon, the house replaced him with the Democrat. Despite his formal withdrawal Adams still received eighteen votes. The Senate elected Davis by thirty to four, with Antimasons mostly supporting him.[50]

In the aftermath Adams worried that his decision to remove himself would make him as unpopular with his own party as he was with the others. Lamenting that his final destiny seemed to be "forsaken by all mankind," he said only "an overruling consciousness of rectitude" could sustain him. He remained an Antimason, however, upon which, he confessed in his diary, he had staked his "reputation, character, and fortune." And in the House of Representatives, where he had already been seated for two years, he placed himself with the minority of other members professing loyalty to the Antimasonic party.[51]

Entering the House in December 1831, Adams was asked by Henry Clay, now representing Kentucky in the U.S. Senate, how he felt "turning boy again." Although he did not feel like a youth, Adams had no doubt about his ability and willingness to do whatever his duties as a congressman required. To Clay's warning that hard labor awaited, the new representative replied that as long as his body and mind held out that prospect did not trouble him.[52]

During congressional sessions Adams would stay in his residence on F Street, which he had retained. Residing at home with his wife, he differed from most representatives and senators. The great majority came to Washington without families and congregated in boardinghouses and hotels. That kind of collegial living meant those men would have daily social interaction with peers, enabling them to come to know one another on a personal level. Adams did not share that experience. But never clubbable, he would not have missed what would have been uncomfortable for him.

Adams did not find the House he joined encrusted with a system in which senior members and seniority dominated. When he took his seat, the House had 213 members, 89 of them newcomers like himself. Most congressmen served for only one or two terms. Of Adams's fellow freshmen, only 26 would return a third time. Even in his second term, when the total membership was up to 240 because of reapportionment, there were 152 first-termers.[53]

At the beginning of Adams's congressional service, the unsettled character of the parties matched the flux in their membership. Because of Andrew Jackson's polarizing personality and policies, almost all counted themselves as pro- or antiadministration men. That lineup did not, however, translate into a firm identity with either the Jacksonian Democrats or the National Republican party. And, of course, the Antimason contingent was there. Party loyalty would strengthen and party lines stiffen, but that phenomenon tended to occur first in states. That kind of partisan allegiance did not appear in Congress until 1834 and 1835, during Adams's second term.

Although Adams did identify with the Antimasons, he still thought of himself as his own man, as fundamentally independent, rejecting blind partisan loyalty. Thus he would take different sides, depending upon the issue at hand. In general, he stood with the antiadministration forces, for supporting any measure connected with Jackson was almost unthinkable. That fact meant he usually sided with Clay, now in the Senate and a major figure in the opposition to Jackson. That stance also entailed his often aligning with Daniel Webster, who had moved into that body. Moreover, Webster had become the chief political spokesman for the Boston commercial, financial, and manufacturing elite that Adams could never embrace, nor they him. Still, in Congress he and Webster were usually in tandem.

Webster would become an important person in the remainder of Adams's public life. A native of New Hampshire, Webster had as a young man moved to Boston, where he became an enormously successful attorney and the most influential politician in his adopted state. Moreover, he was a supremely talented orator. Many thought him the most gifted of his time, noting his ability, as even Adams did, to hold audiences mute, even for lengthy orations. That mastery earned him the sobriquet "the Godlike Daniel."[54]

Originally a Federalist, Webster led the vast majority of his fellows into the National Republican ranks. He did support Adams during his presidency and backed him in 1828. Additionally, his expansive view of the nation and national power, which he enunciated from numerous podiums, and his broad interpretation of the Constitution, which he developed in influential legal arguments, meshed with Adams's.

Yet Adams never united with the throng of Webster's admirers. He disdained Webster for the same reasons he scorned so many other political men. In his judgment the baritone-voiced Webster was consumed with ambition, with a shifting public opinion governing his elastic principles. Even more, Adams found Webster's lust for private financial gain, his greed, appalling. He saw totally absent in Webster the qualities he most prized. His summation pilloried the man. After granting Webster a "gigantic intellect," he could discover only "the envious temper, the ravenous ambition, and the rotten heart."[55]

Adams did not begin his congressional career optimistic about his country's future. Even before his election, in a conversation with his friend and former cabinet member Richard

Rush, he cataloged the reasons for his pessimism. The Indians had already been sacrificed to the white man's greed; industry was being impoverished; the public lands were being given away, strangling internal improvements. Moreover, he predicted that by the middle of the decade Congress would refuse to recharter the Bank of the United States; by then the national debt would also be retired. Those eventualities would deprive the national government of a true mission. The result—national greatness would falter, then stumble, and finally fall. By the time he took the oath as a member of Congress, nothing had happened to change his mind.[56]

In his judgment the sickness afflicting the country started at the top, with the president. From Jackson's opposition to his administration through his defeat in 1828, Adams's animus toward the general-become-president had only grown. For Adams two egregious flaws blemished Jackson. The first was policy. From his perspective, Jackson's major initiatives as chief executive tore the fabric of national greatness. From Indians, because he now so increasingly sided with the oppressed, to the tariff to internal improvements to public lands, Adams located Jackson on the wrong side of every issue. Then Jackson's view, expressed clearly in his annual message to Congress in December 1831, that agriculture took first place among human occupations disgusted him. He believed that relegating commerce and manufacturing to an inferior position squandered the American future.[57]

Adams's personal antipathy matched, perhaps even exceeded, his programmatic dislike. He dismissed Jackson's political advancement as relying solely on his popularity as a general, though he had in the past been most impressed with Jackson's military accomplishments. More importantly, he regarded Jackson as an ingrate who returned Adams's essential actions in his behalf during the Florida crisis with unwarranted animosity. At the time, and until his election as president, Jackson had acknowledged the debt, but now Adams saw an enemy who disdained him. The man headed a party that had slandered him. Even though Jackson owed him much—"obligations of a much higher order"—he had turned on his benefactor. In his diary he used a Latin phrase, *"odisce quem laeseris,"* meaning hatred for the one wronged. He could draw only one conclusion. Jackson's ingratitude revealed a man "as rotten as his own heart."[58]

In March 1832, three months after the opening of Congress, Richard Johnson of Kentucky, a Jackson loyalist whom Adams had long known, approached him wanting to restore good relations between the two. Adams replied that Jackson had suspended personal intercourse without explanation. Johnson responded that Jackson's mind had been poisoned by others, but he now had friendly feelings. To that statement Adams answered that he would kindly receive any positive move by the president.

Johnson then became specific. Would Adams accept an invitation to dine? Saying that was an act of simple courtesy usually paid to all members of Congress, he declined. Johnson next asked whether he would join with a select group of friends. He got the same response. Adams considered neither offer any personal initiative toward reconciliation. Finally, Johnson wanted to know what Adams thought proper. To that query Adams said it was not for him to say. Yet he repeated he would receive in "a spirit of reconciliation" any move Jackson would make in the proper spirit.

Noting that Johnson seemed satisfied, Adams reported that the two men parted. He then told himself that the exchange had put him once more "in a situation of the delicacy of which it is my duty to be profoundly sensible." Although he received a polite follow-up note from Johnson, Adams did not have to concern himself about delicacy. This overture went nowhere. Over time relations between the two men deteriorated even further.[59]

Not only dismissive of the president but fearful about his course, Adams was also distressed about the vice-president, John C. Calhoun. He had the same trepidation about Calhoun's politics as about Jackson's. Furthermore, his personal ill will toward his former cabinet colleague matched his toward Jackson, with a singular exception. He never felt Calhoun beholden to him as he did

Jackson. Rather, in his mind Calhoun had been duplicitous, from back in 1822 when the secretary of war had allowed his name to be put forward as Monroe's successor. Then, of course, his teaming with Jackson during Adams's presidency was unpardonable. Most of all, however, Calhoun disappointed Adams, who had once considered that the South Carolinian would emerge as "an ornament and blessing to his country." On the eve of becoming a congressman, Adams indicated that he expected from his former friend nothing more than "evil." Summarizing, he claimed Calhoun's personal conduct toward him was characterized by "selfish and cold-blooded heartlessness."[60]

In Adams's first winter in Congress, as with Jackson, an attempt at reconciliation occurred. At Calhoun's behest an intermediary came to Adams with words about Calhoun's respect for him and a wish to renew their former relationship. Adams replied that he would do Calhoun justice, though he felt deeply Calhoun's estrangement, especially since the end of his presidency. Yet he would bury harsh feelings and receive Calhoun's call upon him.

Calhoun did visit. His explanation that political considerations underlay his keeping away did not sway Adams. In his diary he stated that he would meet Calhoun in renewing "common civility" because he could not do otherwise. Yet he no longer had any confidence in the qualities of Calhoun's heart. In his view Calhoun's selfish interests governed his personal relationships. The vice-president had the disastrous flaws of altering his politics "to be always before the wind" and, even more damning, of making "his intellect pander to his will."[61]

Even Calhoun's complete break with Jackson did not revive what had been lost. Two incidents had already taken place in 1829 and 1831, which had dissolved both personal and political links between the president and vice-president. Both involved Adams, one as a partial participant, the other as an interested observer.

In the autumn of 1829 friends of William Crawford and Martin Van Buren made available to Jackson correspondence indicating that during the Florida crisis Calhoun had not been as supportive as he had thought. The information exaggerated Calhoun's anti-Jackson posture. Adams correctly detected a plot to oust Calhoun from Jackson's inner circle and certainly as a presidential successor. Jackson, however, discerned only disloyalty and deceit. Demanding absolute fidelity from those surrounding him, Jackson found Calhoun sadly lacking. For Jackson such disloyalty, no matter when it occurred, could not go unnoticed. He demanded that Calhoun explain his action. To counter the charges levied against him, Calhoun asked Adams to provide him with relevant information. Drawing on his diary, Adams did make available to Calhoun pertinent material. In all probability he aided Calhoun because he had long detested Crawford, whom he certainly did not want to assist, and he spied the kind of political scheming he had always deplored. To no avail, however, for Jackson would accept no explanation.[62]

The vice-president also became caught up in a social controversy enveloping Jackson and his first cabinet that also registered with all of Washington society. In addition, it produced substantial political fallout. Jackson had named as his secretary of war an old Tennessee companion, John Eaton. A middle-aged widower, Eaton had recently married Margaret O'Neale Timberlake, the daughter of a Washington tavern keeper. Her first marriage had been to a purser in the navy, who was away at sea for long periods. During those months his wife did not have, euphemistically put, a solitary existence. Among her good friends was John Eaton, then a U.S. senator, who also managed the Timberlake family finances. Abounding rumors, wagging tongues, and questions about the paternity of her two children raced through the city. Many believed Margaret the mistress of Eaton, as well as of others. They certainly thought she had been unfaithful to her husband. Then, in April 1828 while aboard ship, Timberlake died, probably a suicide. Yet the record reveals nothing about the causes of his despair. But on New Year's Day 1829 Margaret Timberlake peremptorily married John Eaton, despite the accepted custom in polite society of a widow's waiting a year before remarriage. In the words of one Washington insider, "Eaton has just married his mistress, or the mistress of eleven doz. others."

Proper Washington ladies led by Mrs. John C. Calhoun defied social custom to ostracize the new Mrs. Eaton, refusing to return her visits. Enraged at what he judged a slur upon his friend and his bride, and even upon himself, for there had been serious questions raised about the president's situation before his marriage with his now deceased wife, Jackson insisted that his cabinet officers as well as the vice-president require their wives to accept Margaret Eaton. When most refused, he turned his cabinet upside down, dismissing the majority, keeping only Eaton and one other, whose wife did welcome her. What become known as the "Eaton malaria" dealt Calhoun a second blow. He never recovered. Jackson banished him from his political family.[63]

Witnessing this turmoil, Adams sided with those who in his judgment had maintained the proper standards of society. As he saw it, this episode provided yet another illustration of the ongoing decline of American morals, personal, social, and political. And, unsurprisingly, he located Andrew Jackson at the center of it all. He certainly expressed support for Mrs. Calhoun and those who stood fast with her despite Jackson's explosion.[64]

Even before assuming office, Adams watched with consternation as he perceived his successor wrecking the country. Jackson's appointment credo appalled him. In his opinion Jackson filled his cabinet with incompetent cronies, with only Van Buren, the new secretary of state, measuring up to any reasonable standard. Then he judged despicable Jackson's widespread removal of incumbents throughout the executive branch. Sounding a familiar theme, he charged the president with dismissing decent, capable civil servants, often replacing them with those Adams described as "the vilest purveyors of slander" during the campaign. In his eyes Jackson appointed far too many newspapermen—"electioneering skunks," he called them. Particularly painful for him was the dismissal of his appointee James Barbour as minister to England for a person whom he considered not only an incompetent but also a political prostitute. It seemed to him that merit as a criterion had disappeared, its place taken by blind partisanship.[65]

Prior to his becoming a congressman more than presidential appointments upset Adams. Jackson's policy toward Indians deeply troubled him. The idea of assimilation, of over time bringing Indians into the American polity, had animated governmental attitudes since George Washington's presidency. Adams's administration had not advanced it, however. With his cabinet divided on the proper approach to the native tribes, he did not take a firm stand for assimilation, though he never completely rejected it. Yet he did not halt Georgia's determination to dispossess the Creeks in spite of federal law, including a treaty. Jackson went even further, however, by actually aligning with Georgia when that state adopted an identical posture toward the Cherokee Indians. Adams would not go there.[66]

Jackson's creed, which was already quite apparent in his actions as a general, Adams abhorred. As was spelled out in the Indian Removal Act of 1830, Jackson intended to take all Indian land east of the Mississippi River for white settlers. For him the possibility of assimilation was dead. The Indians themselves would be removed to enclaves set aside for them west of the great river. Although the law did not mention force, few doubted that the federal government would take whatever steps necessary to ensure the success of removal. And, of course, later during Martin Van Buren's presidency, the U.S. Army would oversee the move westward of Indians who had resisted going voluntarily. Had he been in the House in 1830, Adams would surely have voted against the measure.

Adams's open opposition sparked criticism that he had changed his position, which he had, another reflection of how a "failed" presidency altered his views. His critics charged that whereas earlier he had defended white New Englanders taking Indian territory, he now opposed other white Americans, especially southerners, engaged in the same enterprise in their section— the states of Alabama, Georgia, and Mississippi along with the territory of Florida. Of course, Adams's position on the proper federal stance toward Indians and their place in the country had changed, though he insisted it had not.

In one sense he was correct, for he never recanted the assertion he had made in his Plymouth speech back in 1802 that the Indians, whom he depicted as hunters and gatherers, had no unalterable title to their land. He had maintained that whites, with their superior civilization, had every right to settle in areas previously controlled by Indians. Only settlement by sturdy white farmers could ensure progress. Their advance would spread the culture of New England westward.

By 1830, though, his position was totally different. In his judgment, after 1820 Indians no longer posed any obstacle or threat to the country. That possibility had existed only with support from a foreign power, Spain in the South and England in the North. His treaty of 1819 had pushed a weakened Spain back from near American borders, and after the War of 1812 the British no longer combatted America's westward expansion. In the meantime, however, the tribes in the immediately affected area, the Southwest, had developed agrarian ways, emulating the whites. In addition, extensive contact with the superior whites had led them, he held, to acquire "civilized" ways.

According to Adams, Jackson's drive against the Indians took notice of neither of those fundamental occurrences. He refused to countenance this new direction. In his mind, with the issue of security settled, only white avarice could explain the resolution to displace the Indians. Conversing with a friend and fellow opponent of Jackson's direction, Adams admitted their powerlessness to stop the president. Still, they should publicize their opposition to the "perfidy and tyranny" waged upon the Indians. Punishment for the evil they would have to leave to heaven.[67]

Adams discerned two additional horrors in Jackson's course. First, when a complicit president permitted Georgia to flout federal law, the way was open to anarchy. He feared the parts could dismantle the whole. With the overt backing of the president of the United States, a state mocked the nation. In his condemnation of Jackson he pushed far back in his mind that when he had been president his own dealings with Georgia had allowed the state to do likewise, though, unlike Jackson, he did not endorse what Georgia did.

Second, with Jackson's approach he perceived liberty endangered. The eviction of Indians in the Southwest would mean not only whites coming in their stead, but whites with slaves. Slavery would thus supplant freedom, and more settlers with slaves meant more political power for the slave states and a further diminution of New England in the nation. But even more critical, he foresaw the diminishment of national virtue, which he equated with the values of his section. That endangered his cherished ideal of New England expanded.

Upon entering Congress, Adams immediately became embroiled in another Jackson contretemps. Beginning in his first annual message and continuing onwards, the president inveighed against the Bank of the United States. He described two egregious faults. First, he charged that the institution violated the Constitution. He made that assertion even though James Madison, an original opponent, had latterly endorsed its constitutionality and the U.S. Supreme Court had upheld it. Second, he declared in hollow populist terms the bank, headquartered in Philadelphia, a citadel of privilege that benefited eastern financial elites while it harmed hardworking southerners and westerners. He did not want its charter, which terminated in 1836, renewed. Pushing back, congressional supporters of the bank led by Henry Clay, who expected to oppose Jackson in 1832, wanted an early recharter. In Clay's mind he would either secure the bank's future or have an effective campaign issue. Heeding that advice, the president of the bank, Nicholas Biddle, in January 1832 petitioned Congress for such a renewal.[68]

The Bank of the United States that riled Jackson was the second rendition. Urged by Alexander Hamilton, Congress authorized the first in 1791, with a twenty-year charter. A public-private entity with both the government and the private sector as stockholders and naming directors, the bank was empowered to receive all federal deposits as well as those from nongovernment sources and to handle the government debt. Moreover, the bank could establish branches beyond its central office in Philadelphia.

There was vigorous congressional opposition to the first bank, with Representative James Madison in the lead, by those who in the mid-1790s would coalesce in the Jeffersonian Republican party opposed to the pro-bank Federalist party. Arguing correctly that the Constitution nowhere explicitly authorized such a bank, Madison and his allies condemned it as unconstitutional and a threat to American liberty. Even though the bank functioned as designed, in 1811 the dominant Republicans let its charter lapse.

The desperate fiscal situation the country had confronted in the War of 1812 led to a reconsideration of the bank. In 1816 with broad Republican support, including that of President Madison, who asserted that its previous existence had settled the constitutional question, Congress chartered the second Bank of the United States, this one also for an initial twenty years. It had the same organization and functions as its predecessor, which included issuing banknotes that provided a dependable, stable medium of exchange throughout the country. By 1830 twenty-five branches had been established in all sections of the nation.

Following the demise of the first bank, numerous banks sprang up in the states. They issued substantial quantities of paper banknotes, often without a sufficient reserve of gold or silver to back them. The plethora of these notes in circulation, with widely varying values, made for a confusing business and financial climate. Although the new Bank of the United States could not bar local banks from issuing notes, its financial size and power, enhanced by its designation as the sole federal depository, enabled it to exercise a restraining effect on local banks. It could force them to adopt sound practices, or risk failure. By the time Jackson became president, the bank, which had been since 1823 under Nicholas Biddle's leadership, was operating as a central bank stabilizing a growing economy.

Adams became directly involved when in February 1832 he was named to a House select committee appointed to investigate the bank's operations. Antibank Jacksonians had sponsored legislation creating the committee in hopes of discrediting the bank. To the original bill Adams successfully proposed amendments that more sharply focused the committee's charge to the operation of the main branch in Philadelphia. As a result, he ended up on the seven-man committee.[69]

Adams had never been enthusiastic about banks. Basically a hard-money man, which meant he favored gold and silver coins while distrusting paper notes, he understood little about how banks operated. He had no sophisticated understanding of credit or fiscal matters, and despite his wide reading, he read little about economics or finance. In fact, he suspected bankers of being robbers or swindlers or, even worse, sinners. It was beyond him why banks sometimes had to suspend specie payments or why they refused to redeem paper notes with gold or silver. To him suspension always resulted from bankers' misconduct or nefarious schemes.

Yet when he went to Congress, he was, as he had always been, a steadfast supporter of the second bank. While secretary of state he had told President Monroe that in view of the unlimited power of banks in the states to issue paper money, only a strong central bank could maintain the safety of contracts and property as well as specie payments. Admiring Biddle, whom he often visited when passing through Philadelphia, he believed the bank under Biddle's stewardship acted to curb the excesses of untrustworthy banks spread throughout the country.

For him the second Bank of the United States had become an essential part of the growing and powerful nation he cherished. He rejected both the constitutional objection and the accusation that it favored the rich and hurt the average American. He even owned stock in the bank. Yet on his way to Washington in 1831, he instructed Biddle to sell his few shares. He wanted to eliminate all possibility that anyone could accuse him of having a conflict of interest, should he as a congressman end up dealing with any matter concerning the bank.[70]

The select committee did visit Philadelphia. It spent three weeks interviewing Biddle and investigating the bank's operations, with predictable findings. A divided committee issued three reports. Listing a catalog of alleged misdeeds, the Jacksonian majority called for termination of the bank's charter. The probank minority report refuted those charges as partisan and unfounded. Although Adams signed it, he additionally prepared his own, which went further in defending the bank. In it he hurled the unsubstantiated accusation that local banks hated the Bank of the United States for restricting what Adams considered their unsafe practices.

Back in Congress, a rechartering bill with widespread support made its way through both houses, finally passing in July 1832. A week later President Jackson fired a ringing veto. He castigated the bank as a vehicle used by rich and even evil men to trample upon the rights of ordinary Americans, threating their liberty. As the tribune of those people, he had the duty to protect them. The bank men did not have the votes to override the veto. What became known as the Bank War appeared over.

Although Adams participated in the Bank War, he had a more active role in the dispute over the tariff, which had the potential to spark a frightful collision between the states and national power. Shortly after taking his seat in the Twenty-Second Congress, Adams was named by the Speaker of the House to chair the Committee on Manufactures. He recognized the post as "a station of high responsibility," though he worried about the labor it would require and even more that he could estimate the difficulty. Still, even though he had little respect for the Speaker, a Jacksonian loyalist, he could find no fault with him for the appointment.[71]

Yet almost immediately he asked Speaker Andrew Stevenson of Virginia for a change. He wanted to move to the Committee on Foreign Affairs, which he thought would be more congenial and less controversial, and he had obtained the agreement of a Massachusetts colleague to exchange places with him. The Speaker turned him down, however, citing the rules of the House. Aware they had been previously waived, Adams had hoped that the Speaker would concur with the exchange. His refusal meant that he would remain where he had been assigned. Stevenson tried to mollify Adams by emphasizing to him the centrality of the Committee on Manufactures at this juncture.[72]

Stevenson referred to the tariff, which became the major issue for Adams's committee. The tariff had generated contention since 1828, when then-President Adams had signed it into law. Outraged southern opponents denounced the measure as the Tariff of Abominations. It contained the highest rates to that date, and they would not be exceeded again before 1860. Most southerners condemned it for protecting or subsidizing northern manufacturers at the expense of southern agriculturists. At the end of the same year the *South Carolina Exposition and Protest*, authorized and printed by the South Carolina legislature, laid out a radical remedy. Published anonymously, though secretly written by Calhoun, whose authorship became public only in 1831, the *Exposition and Protest* harked back to the classic Jeffersonian texts on states' rights, the Virginia and Kentucky Resolutions of 1798 and 1799. They maintained that because the states had created the federal government, they retained sovereignty. The *Exposition and Protest* went further, however, asserting that a state could declare a congressional statute unconstitutional, which would make it null and void within the state's borders. This doctrine, which became known as nullification and which seemingly had a state simultaneously in and out of the Union, proved too arcane even for most antitariff southerners. Outside of South Carolina nullification had few adherents. Still, it sparked heated controversy and potentially a major crisis.[73]

Prior to entering Congress, Adams had left no doubt about his opinion both of South Carolina and of the constitutional doctrine undergirding nullification. The state, he opined, had been "potioned and philtered and back-scourged, like an old lecher, into a frenzy of excitement," resulting in an attempt to bully the national government. Regarding sovereignty, he declared in an oration in Quincy in 1831 celebrating July 4 that states sprang from the Union. The Union, he proclaimed, came into existence with the Declaration of Independence, more than a decade prior to the ratification of the Constitution. He defined the United States as "a primitive compact" of union, freedom, and independence in which the people had bound themselves before God. No state could legitimately separate from the whole. He arraigned nullification, charging "its naked nature is an effort to organize insurrection against the laws of the United States."[74]

While he did not camouflage his contempt for the theory of nullification, the issue only deepened his distrust of Calhoun. In an entry in his diary in July 1832 he teasingly referred to a conversation on constitutional questions he had with the author of the nefarious doctrine. The word "teasingly" applies, for he provided nothing substantive about their discussion. A few months later, however, he did not hold back when commenting on a Calhoun speech defending nullification. He diagnosed the man, whom he had formerly admired, to be now afflicted with insanity based on his ingenious deductions from his principles. "His learning is shallow," Adams confided to his diary, "his mind argumentative, and his assumption of principle destitute of discernment."[75]

Regarding the tariff itself, Adams did not have a closed mind. For him it had served two valuable purposes: first, it provided protection for industries in his state, and they, of course, helped propel American economic growth; second, it furnished revenue for his cherished dream of internal improvements. At the same time, however, he had two concerns: first, that Jackson and his congressional legions would demolish protection; second, that paying off the national debt, expected by middecade, would diminish the need for revenue, thus undermining a critical rationale for the tariff. The latter eventuality would devastate his hope for internal improvements.[76]

When he took over the chairmanship, most in government

believed the tariff would come down. Unknown was by how much and whether the principle of protection would be retained. While willing to accept some adjustment downward, Adams saw his mission as resisting too much lowering while holding on to protection. With a committee divided over the appropriate policy, members, with Adams's agreement, decided to work with Jackson's secretary of the treasury to develop legislation that could command widespread support.

In the meantime a second House committee inserted itself into the tariff controversy. The Committee on Ways and Means, headed by a South Carolina nullifier, proposed draconian reductions. Through the winter and spring of 1832, tariff proposals and counterproposals captured the attention of Adams's committee. In this struggle his great goal became to salvage at least five million dollars annually for internal improvements.

In May, Adams presented his committee's recommendations, which unsurprisingly pleased neither the nullifiers nor the ardent protectionists. From this presentation he stayed intimately involved in congressional activity, spending long hours at his desk in the House. Writing his wife, he pictured himself chained there as long as the House debated the tariff bill. Finally, just before the congressional session closed in mid-July, the Tariff of 1832 gained a significant congressional majority. Adams was pleased. He thought the final product a reasonable measure that lowered the tariff, though not by too much, while it retained the principle of protection.[77]

The passage of the Tariff of 1832 did not end the battle, however. Infuriated that it maintained protection, nullifiers vowed stepped-up resistance. In South Carolina nullifiers triumphed in a statewide election. In November a special state convention nullified the tariff act. In Adams's view disaster loomed. He had no doubt that despite Jackson's break with Calhoun, the president was in league with the nullifiers. He predicted the president would surrender protection, thus internal improvements, just as he had the Indians' treaty rights. South Carolina would join Georgia in the victory column of states. Twice the nation had lost. He wrote that as president he had striven to strengthen the bonds of Union, but the current chief executive was endeavoring to weaken them. When Jackson in his annual message to the second session of the Twenty-Second Congress called for additional consideration of the tariff, Adams had no doubt that his fears were justified.[78]

Yet within a week Jackson dropped a bombshell. In a powerful proclamation branding nullifiers as traitors and asserting that he would uphold federal law, with force if necessary, the president broadcast his stalwart support for the Union. Even with this striking pronouncement, a hymn to the Union that enunciated his own values, before the public, Adams had his doubts. He still fretted that Jackson had no intention of standing firm.

At this point Congressman Adams had two goals. He wanted to stand by Jackson on the Nullification Proclamation and to stave off efforts to lower the Tariff of 1832. But he soon lost influence over the tariff question, which was taken over by the unlikely alliance of Clay and Calhoun, now representing his state in the Senate. Although the two men differed sharply on policy—Clay a protectionist and Calhoun a nullifier—and the role of the federal government, they shared an abiding dislike of Jackson. Finding common ground, they constructed a deal to settle the nullification controversy.

What became known as the Compromise of 1833 contained two major parts. The president had requested Congress to go on record supporting his use of force against South Carolina, if necessary. The resulting legislation was quickly dubbed the Force Bill. Meanwhile, Clay and Calhoun jointly backed a tariff bill that would gradually lower duties, though not jettison protection. Congress approved both measures, with members often divided on which one they countenanced. Jackson signed on, and with Calhoun in the lead South Carolina accepted the plan. Yet in a display of bravado the state reasserted devotion to nullification by nullifying the Force Bill. In reality that had no impact, for the compromise defused the crisis.

Each side could claim victory. For the president the attempt to nullify a federal law had been blocked. For South Carolina that law had been adjusted to lower the hated tariff. Moreover, the state suffered no political, much less military, harm. The nullifiers had gone head to head with the federal government and not only survived but in their view came out ahead.

For Adams the affair was a catastrophe. In his judgment South Carolina, like Georgia, had humbled the nation. He saw the tariff coming down and his ideal of a serious internal improvements program glimmering. He certainly did not believe that South Carolina had been subdued. He saw the outcome as part of a larger development. The Indians, the Bank of the United States, the tariff, the public lands, internal improvements—in his view, they all composed a whole. Indians removed, the bank abolished, the tariff lowered, public lands almost given away, internal improvements mortally wounded—it added up to a great nation enervated, with a glowing national future endangered.

And he was confident he knew the why behind this dismal chain of events. Southern politics and values had triumphed over the nation. And he prophetically defined slavery as the root cause. He saw the nation as a fragmenting center that could no longer hold. Even before becoming a congressman he had decried what he judged the attempt of the South to govern the nation as it controlled its slaves. South Carolina was the worst bully, for a slave majority in the population caused "the domineering spirit" of the master to reach "the highest pitch of intenseness." He forecast South Carolina's success because "all the slave-driving interest of the Union" would galvanize on its side.[79]

To his vision of the nation, of the Union, he had a powerful fealty. His own father had been central in its formation. Moreover, he considered himself not only both a biological and ideological son of the glorious product of a creative, patriotic generation but also a guardian and servant of its handiwork. Sustaining and augmenting it had been his touchstone throughout his career. But now he began to doubt whether in its original form it either could or would survive. For the moment he kept these ruminations private, expressing them only in his diary and in private letters and conversations.

In the midst of the congressional debates in the winter of 1832–33, he pondered what he termed "the real question now convulsing the Union." Anticipating Abraham Lincoln's famous house-divided speech by two and half decades, he wondered whether a population spread over such a huge expanse could exist permanently with a great division of freedom and slavery. Thus, to him, the question currently under discussion as well as all other assaults on his conception of the Union had a mighty unifier—slavery.[80]

Earlier, in the fall of 1831, at a small dinner party in Boston, Adams had expounded on that theme. Among the guests was Alexis de Tocqueville, a young French aristocrat traveling in the United States who would later write his classic account of the country in the 1830s, *Democracy in America*. Tocqueville asked Adams—they spoke in French—whether he regarded slavery as the great evil for his country. Absolutely, responded Adams. Slavery, he declared, held "almost all the embarrassments of the present and the fears of the future." When questioned on whether southerners shared his awareness, Adams replied that "at the bottom of their hearts they did," but they refused to reveal that recognition. Summing up, he stated that slavery had so influenced southern society that white southerners could not imagine their world without it.[81]

As Adams viewed the status of the country in the mid-1830s, the South appeared triumphant. The advent of Jackson and the concurrent demise of his Union seemed to herald a new turn. In his reading, "the Sable Genius of the South" apprehended the amazing growth and development in the North. Fearing its "inevitable downfall" before the progressive juggernaut facing it, the South with the battle cry of states' rights struck at its sources of strength, such as the tariff and internal improvements. The result, his great desire for the Union, for the nation, was not to be. He had failed and never expected to see in his lifetime the rise again of what he called "national energies." In a letter to Henry Clay focusing on nullification, which he defined as "organized civil War," he saw only one solution to "the odious nature" of the entire conflict—"at the Cannon's month." In a fundamental sense the last major political figure of the founding generation had become the first of the destroying generation.[82]

Even though Adams was fully engaged in momentous questions and ended up disheartened about the direction of his country, he found time to tend to a congressman's essential duty, constituent service. He presented a petition to the House from citizens in his district requesting a new mail route. He took to the War Department letters from constituents asking for information about Revolutionary War pensions. On one occasion an old Revolutionary soldier from a nearby town came to visit him at Quincy. This veteran wanted to apply for a pension but did not have all the necessary papers. A responsive Adams said he would help obtain the required documents and then place them with the secretary of war. The congressman understood that voters expected him not only to represent their views on larger issues but also to look after their more local private concerns.[83]

While in Washington, Adams was not a hermit, and did, in fact, carry on an active social life, though the prepresidential parlors and soirees hosted by Louisa Catherine had faded into the mists of a bygone era. Louisa Adams now kept her distance from political activity. Her husband often played whist, a card game he savored. On New Year's Day 1833 his open house attracted some one hundred visitors, including members of Congress and foreign diplomats as well as private citizens. He noted they crowded in from noon until after three. In his diary he recorded his presence at dinner parties, but admitted they did not bring out his best. "To *stimulate* conversation" while taking only a small part in it, which he defined as "the art of entertaining," seemed beyond him. In contrast, he said he talked too much.[84]

He also grappled with a heavy volume of mail, which came

alongside the visits. Piles of letters, several newspapers, and two or three pamphlets arrived every day. He said he could not possibly answer more than 10 percent of the letters. Even that took time, for he bemoaned his inability to pen a short response. As an example he pointed to one in which he intended to write just four lines but ended up with four pages.

Keeping his incoming correspondence filed also proved time-consuming. He began to wonder whether he should retain any of it, especially because he considered 90 percent, even 99 percent, not worth saving. Additionally, his determination to continue his practice of making copies of all outgoing letters was becoming a burden. The effort troubled him both because of the hours spent and the physical exertion necessary to do so, given his complaints about lameness in his hand. He even contemplated a status of privilege—having a secretary.[85]

One habit he held on to was regular attendance at public worship services on Sundays. He believed his presence valuable to him. Yet more than habit prompted him, for he continued to ponder what he interpreted as troubling elements in the Christian faith. A sermon in a Presbyterian church in which the minister preached on atonement, the Christian doctrine that Christ died for the sins of humanity, that his death reconciled God and man while providing for salvation, triggered his reflections on that fundamental tenet of orthodox Christianity.

He stated that the minister's discourse left an indelible impression on his mind. The entire idea he discarded as "solemn nonsense and inconceivable absurdity." Condemning it as "an admonition of the weakness of the human intellect," he averred that he not only disbelieved the proposition of atonement but hated it. He found the claim that the death of one man eighteen hundred years ago redeemed him and saved him from damnation simply too preposterous for acceptance. It was "a melancholy monument of mental aberration and impotence." In the service itself his immediate reaction was to decline taking communion because he feared either it would seem he agreed with the concept of atonement or he would intrude on a solemn ritual. His refusal to believe in atonement did not, however, signal his shedding his Christian identity. Rather, as a Christian, just as a politician, he forged his own way.[86]

Upon the adjournment of the second session of the Twenty-Second Congress in March 1833, he returned to Massachusetts. In late August he departed for a sojourn in the White Mountains of New Hampshire, boasting the highest peaks north and east of the Appalachians in North Carolina and Tennessee. Traveling by stage and wagon, he spent several days among the heights and valleys. He reveled in some of New England's finest scenery and vistas. Even so, he turned down a trek on horseback to the summit of Mount Washington, the pinnacle of the range. He feared his health could not handle the rigors of that ride. Yet he judged his visit rewarding. He found especially striking "the contrast between the grandeur of nature and the littleness of man." He did acknowledge a disappointment, however. His journey had not provided the physical reinvigoration he had hoped for.[87]

Although he regretted that the excursion had not rejuvenated him, his reservations about his lost energy never caused him to consider giving up politics. To the contrary, he anticipated returning with gusto to Washington for the opening of the first session of the Twenty-Third Congress in December. Back in April he had been reelected to Congress. Even though his district had been redrawn because of the census of 1830, it retained the same core area. Moreover, not only did he still have the support of the Antimasons; this time the National Republicans made him their nominee. Winning more than 75 percent of the vote, he swamped the Democratic candidate. In his diary he exulted in this outpouring of popular approval, calling it "a subject to me of the most ardent gratitude to Heaven." He had finally found a welcoming political home. Congressman Adams would return for a second time to the House of Representatives.[88]

CHAPTER 7

"The First and Holiest Rights
of Humanity"

JOHN QUINCY ADAMS WOULD BECOME A LUMINARY IN CONGRESS during the middle and late 1830s. As the first former president to join the nation's lawmakers, he automatically received more attention that the average representative. But his rise to prominence in the House coincided with the advent of a fierce slavery-related politics. Since the ratification of the Constitution, the country had previously experienced such a contest only once, the crisis over the admission of Missouri as a state. That wrath passed, however, with the passage of the Missouri Compromise in 1820, a quick and seemingly final solution. But the 1830s did not witness such a quick end to its furor. Although the particulars, actors and issues, might and did change, sectional rancor remained a potent force— a force that never really dissipated. Adams consciously took a leading part in maintaining, and even invigorating, the tension.

From middecade national politicians attempted to utilize political parties as a barrier against sectional battles. Both the Democratic party and the Whig party, which by 1835 had become the chief rival of the Democrats, operated nationally. Thus political success required finding ways to preclude sectional disharmony. This goal provided a cement for the barrier that could at times hold back the sectional tide. But it never ebbed for very long.

With just a tenuous partisan allegiance and in a secure congressional district, Adams had considerable freedom of action. During these years his animosity toward those like Jackson and Calhoun who he judged had unfairly driven him from the presidency meshed with his growing concern about southern influence in the nation. He saw southerners prevailing in his nemesis the Democratic party, which dominated the national government. This especially distressed him because it permitted the southerners to protect the evil of slavery.

He would stand, and fight, for what he defined as the moral purpose and grandeur of his beloved country. Embroiled in that struggle, he became more and more convinced that the nation created by the Founders could not survive without wrenching change. Thus the nationalism of the Founders that he had so cherished and for decades had propounded would perhaps have to be redefined. And he as their lineal disciple would have to lead the way. Congressman Adams was present when the first session of the Twenty-Third Congress convened in early December 1833. The partisanship of pro- and anti-Jackson adherents continued to dominate politics, though with shifting boundaries. Adams still held on to some Antimason affiliations, but that party no longer flourished, for following the election of 1832, Antimasonic leaders in critical states like New York and Pennsylvania realized that their party by itself could no longer seriously contend for statewide office, much less compete nationally.[1]

The demise of Antimasonry signaled the coalescing of partisans into two parties, the Democratic and the National Republican. Yet that lineup lacked stability. Because Jackson's personality and policies generated such vigorous opposition as well as staunch loyalty, major anti-Jackson chieftains, led by Henry Clay, worked to create a political organization that could attract the diverse cast of Jackson opponents, from ardent nationalists who backed the Bank of the United States and a protective tariff to stalwart southern states' righters who opposed both. This hope for inclusion stretched to Antimasons and even all the way to nullifiers.

To succeed, Clay and his allies believed they had to jettison the National Republican brand. The presidential elections of 1828 and 1832 had led to resounding defeats. Moreover, the southern states' righters alarmed by Jackson's claim for executive, thus national, power would never subscribe to its identification with strong nationalist measures like the bank and a protective tariff. To reach this political goal, Clay met in private dinners in the winter of 1833–34 with a wide range of anti-Jackson men, including both Calhoun and Adams. He and his partners were determined to find a different way.

They found it with the creation of the Whig party. This new entity was taking shape across the country in 1834 and 1835. The name Whig came from the English tradition of those opposed to royal power and from the Revolutionary forebears, who embraced it in their struggle against the British crown. Whigs proclaimed their allegiance to the heritage of the American Revolution: liberty versus tyranny. Whigs designated Andrew Jackson the new tyrant, characterizing his executive actions as assaults on the liberty of Americans. Whigs broadcast that only by driving Jackson and his minions from office could Americans secure their precious political heritage. This identification with the glorious legacy of the Revolution gave Whigs legitimacy while permitting the gathering of disparate groups beneath their banner.[2]

In the midst of this evolving scene Adams faced his own decision. Understanding that the Antimasonic party was disappearing, he had consulted with Daniel Webster, with whom he had an often antagonistic relationship, and others to accomplish a merger in Massachusetts of the Antimasons and National Republicans. By then, however, the latter had but a short life span. Although Adams continually commented on his prized political independence, he had often associated himself with a party. In Congress he derided "the bugle-horn of party," which in his view rallied the often unthinking faithful. Yet he almost always voted with the anti-Jacksonians; with the arrival of the Whig party, he usually sided with it as well. But he always insisted he did so on his own terms. Asserting that cherished independence, he indicated he would even back the hated Jackson, when the president stood on the right side of an issue, as with the Nullification Proclamation.[3]

The flux in political alignment offered an opportunity for Adams's political advancement. In November 1834, with both Antimasonic and National Republican endorsement, he won reelection with a staggering 86 percent of the vote. In December the resignation of a sitting U.S. senator opened the possibility of his moving into that seat, which he surely wanted.

Massachusetts law required both chambers of the legislature to vote separately for senator. The choice of Adams seemed likely, for the Antimasons pushed him while the National Republicans moving rapidly into the Whig party agreed. It would be a repeat of the congressional election. Adams had a substantial lead in the Senate and in the House trailed his opponent, the incumbent governor, by only a few votes. It appeared that in his second try for statewide office he would succeed.

Yet what initially looked like an almost certain triumph ended in defeat and disappointment. The reason came from Congress. There Adams found himself allied with President Jackson on a foreign policy issue, the French claims. This matter originated in the French navy's spoliation of American ships during the years leading to the War of 1812. Although France had agreed to pay American claims, the case had languished for a generation. The American government pressed, but not too hard; various French governments resisted, but never repudiated.

Not one to let proverbial bygones be bygones, President Jackson decided the time for resolution had finally arrived. He sent a special envoy to Paris, who obtained an agreement that France would pay. But once more no payment was forthcoming. Thereupon, in his annual message to Congress in December 1834, Jackson asked for legislation permitting reprisals on French property until payment was received. Partisanship governed the congressional response. In the new Whig-controlled Senate, the Foreign Relations Committee, chaired by Clay, refused Jackson's request, asserting the president's posture could lead to war. Clay and his colleagues would give Jackson nothing. In the House, the Foreign Relations Committee made no response. Thus Congress apparently intended no action.

This inaction disturbed Adams. He did not think, perhaps as a former president, that on an important foreign policy question the chief executive should be left standing alone. The honor of the country was at stake, and in that situation politics had to stop at the water's edge. Thereupon he proposed a resolution requiring the House to take a position, not remain silent. According to him, action by the House was more important than precisely what it decided. Ultimately, the House did take a position affirming the country's right to demand payment.

The key outcome for Adams, however, took place in Boston, not in Washington. In the House he had moved toward Jackson. For Clay, Webster, and the newly formed Whig leadership, Adams had gone too far beyond the party's unequivocal anti-Jackson stance. He had disregarded the tightening requirements of this new partisanship. To Clay and his comrades no valid reason existed for them to make other than a political decision—trying to tar Jackson with a warlike policy. Adams had proved himself undependable. Webster sent word up to Massachusetts to block his elevation to the Senate.

Webster's message had the desired result. National Republican–Whigs heeded his call, and Adams was duly set aside. His lead in the Senate evaporated; his strength in the House dissolved. His opponent was elected. Adams's son Charles Francis had no doubt that the French claims dispute had doomed his father, who agreed. For the second time his quest for statewide office had failed. He would not try again. To his diary he confided, "Cautious perseverance, support me!"[*]

That backing Jackson on the French issue cost Adams the Senate seat entailed a certain irony, for he had not altered his opinion on the president. Its harshness remained unabated. Back in the summer of 1833 Jackson had toured New England. During his passage through the Boston area, the authorities at Harvard University decided to award Jackson an honorary doctor of laws degree.

That decision made, Harvard's president, Josiah Quincy, journeyed to nearby Quincy to issue that institution's most notable living alumnus a personal invitation to attend the ceremony. An appalled Adams declined the offer, telling Quincy that the personal relations Jackson had ordained between them made impossible on his part any kind of friendly interaction. Even though he identified himself as "an affectionate child of our Alma Mater," he declared he would not be present "to witness her disgrace in conferring her highest literary honors upon a barbarian who could not write a sentence of grammar and hardly could spell his own name." Replying, Josiah Quincy said he understood Adams's position, but because the people of the United States had chosen Jackson as their chief executive, he and other university officials thought Harvard should honor him as it had his predecessor James Monroe.[5]

While Adams was disgusted with his alma mater's decision and disappointed about his political defeat, neither feeling was his chief distress. In the fall of 1834 his second son, thirty-one-year-old John Adams II, became desperately ill. Like his older brother, George, this young man had never really found himself, though alcohol had not become central for him. Married to a first cousin, his mother's niece, and father of two young children, he had failed to find financial security. After serving as his father's private secretary during the latter's presidency, he took over management of the Columbian Mills, a flour and grits mill on Rock Creek in the District of Columbia that Adams owned. The mill had been a financial burden ever since its purchase in the early 1820s from an uncle of Louisa's. John II's supervision did not improve its fortunes.

Then illness struck. Chills and fever assaulted the young man. The same also sent his wife to bed. Still in Quincy when he received word, Adams departed promptly for Washington. But by the time he reached the city, his son was literally on his death-bed. He died the day after his father's arrival. When he asked the attending physician the precise nature of the fatal disease, the doctor responded honestly that he did not know.

The early death of a second son dealt Adams a heavy blow. In his diary he employed the phrase "the unutterable anguish of my own soul." At the same time he cautioned himself, "Let me not murmur at the will of God." He expressed comfort in his conviction that for all human suffering heaven provided relief, with no sorrow and permanent joy.

Yet the pain abided. A week later he called his daily walking "a melancholy pilgrimmage." Coping with "the bitterness of my misfortune," he found himself compelled to seek safe haven in "earnest triflings." In his diary he turned to bleak images like "dark and gloomy terror," which he said now governed him. He confided that only "divine mercy" provided any relief. That mercy he discerned in his having sufficient health to sustain him in the anguish and shock his son's death had visited upon him.[6]

While struggling to cope with that sad event, he also had to deal with his wife's poor health. Her own illness had prevented her from accompanying him to Washington. Various maladies racked her body—coughing, fever, fainting, and a protracted siege of erysipelas. Whether these afflictions had organic or emotional causes cannot be known. Yet her anxiety and distress were palpable.

Speaking of her pain in both body and mind, Louisa Adams constantly asked God to give her strength to navigate "the labrynth [sic]" in which she felt "doomed to stray." Although she did not detail all the particulars of that labyrinth, she lamented her husband's continuing political career. Aware of the strife, the toil, the "mortified vanity," and the grievous disappointments that marked his life in politics, she longed for his retirement, convinced that it would bring a calmness to him. She was sure that outcome would benefit not only him but also herself. She left no doubt that all the turmoil roiling within him spilled over into their relationship, thus affecting her as well.

Even with that somber diagnosis, she never felt she could push her prescription. Understanding her husband's heart and mind, she feared that taking him out of politics would risk "a total extinction of his life." Or she contemplated what she termed "those powers" even more important than life itself—"a suitable sphere of action." She had observed a man floundering during the period between his leaving the presidency and becoming a congressman. She realized, just as he did, that politics in a fundamental sense gave meaning to his life. Thus she could foresee no future for herself but to accept the situation where life as Mrs. John Quincy Adams had placed her.[7]

The results of the Massachusetts congressional nomination and senatorial election reflected an increasing obstinacy or inability to compromise on political matters, but left the political man John Quincy Adams safely ensconced in his House seat. Moreover, with his failed Senate try behind him, he no longer had any reasonable expectation of any higher office, either statewide or national. That realization plus the security of his House district gave him enormous freedom. He had an open political world with few constraints, other than those self-imposed. The overwhelming support of his local constituents both cheered and moved him. Now, he told himself, only failure to control his temper could hobble his usefulness to causes he embraced.

Jockeying for the presidential election of 1836 dominated the immediate political scene, however. The hated Jacksonians offered little surprise. Jackson himself anointed Martin Van Buren, whom in 1832 he had selected as his vice-president, for the succession. The first Democratic national convention, held in Baltimore in May 1835, dutifully named the New Yorker the party's nominee. In contrast, the disparate groups coming into the new Whig party had not yet sufficiently coalesced to agree upon a single candidate. Whigs did not even hold a national convention, relying instead chiefly on state leaders to promote favorite possibilities.

Eventually the Whigs settled upon three candidates, each with particular regional appeal. The South along with the Mid-

Atlantic and the West as well as New England had their choices. The most astute Whig chieftains did not contemplate a replica of 1824. They evinced little interest in a reprise of forcing the choice of a president upon the House of Representatives. The reek of the alleged corrupt bargain remained too powerful. Instead, they hoped running favorite sons would help build strength in the states.

Most important for Adams, of course, was New England. In his native region the nod went to Daniel Webster, initially put forward by the Massachusetts legislature. Adams would never back Webster, the man who had blocked his Senate hopes. In addition, he distrusted Webster. He did not have to worry, for Webster's candidacy never blossomed. That had little impact on Adams, who following his practice in 1832 took no active role in the campaign. Van Buren's ultimate victory over the Whig troika did not surprise him. From it he had no positive anticipation. Instead, he expected more of the same, just another Jackson term. In fact, he had disparaged all contenders as "demagogues," who had no serious program for governing the Union.[8]

Confident that the Jacksonians were marching the country down the wrong road, Adams did have a clear vision of the correct direction. He provided an excellent map to the signposts along that way in extended eulogies he prepared for two men he greatly respected, James Monroe and James Madison, the last standing titans of the Founding Fathers generation. He honored each in orations he gave in Boston, the former in 1831, the latter five years later. An extensive biography was a feature in both, which were really long essays more than simply speeches. Praising both former presidents for their commitment to the entire country, the Union, he awarded them accolades for their pure patriotism. They placed duty to country and devotion to principle above the desire for office, above personal benefit.

In these discourses Adams made a special effort to insist that the people, not the states, formed the foundation of the Constitution, of the nation. And the nation, one of great energy, would become a magnificent empire if only those following Madison and Monroe would embrace their virtues. Placing Madison within this framework required Adams to treat deftly Madison's opposition to Alexander Hamilton's nationalistic policies and his authorship of the Virginia Resolutions, which underscored the validity of states' rights. He did so by pointing to Madison's difference with Jefferson, whose original Kentucky Resolutions pushed the states' rights doctrine further, even to nullification. He then highlighted Madison's rejection of Calhoun's creed of nullification.

For Adams the ultimate goal of those two notable men corresponded with his sense of the thrust of both the American Revolution and the Constitution—"the improvement of the condition of the human race." The bold and new Revolution took a giant stride to accomplish that goal. The equally bold and new Constitution pressed onward on that heading. Madison and Monroe continued that tradition. For Adams, he and his generation had an indisputable duty—"to preserve, to cherish, to *improve* the inheritance which they have left us—won by their toils—watered by their tears—saddened but fertilized by their blood." He and they must become "worthy sons of worthy sires." To do so their voice must proclaim the incalculable value of harmony and Union.

Strikingly, nowhere in the almost two hundred published pages of the two documents did he bring up the topic of slavery. And as he had made clear in his diary, he depicted that institution as undergirding the political parties and the policies that were turning the country away from the virtues he praised in the lives of Madison and Monroe. Yet both men owned slaves, and neither had taken steps to do away with slavery. Adams was not ready to take up public cudgels against the source that he judged the major threat to his vision of the Union.[9]

Although Adams barely mentioned slavery in his two eulogies, a new, potentially powerful antislavery force surged onto the American scene during the time he wrote and delivered them. Known as abolitionists, these men and women drove to the forefront the future of slavery in the United States. Adams soon became caught up in the political dimension of a crusade determined to destroy the institution in the country.

This manifestation of antislavery heralded the advent of a more ardent generation dedicated to annihilating slavery. That goal was, of course, not original, for an antislavery impulse dated back to the American Revolution. The language of the Declaration of Independence, particularly the assertion concerning the equality of all men, plus the widespread rhetoric calling for resistance to tyranny and oppression led to an attack on slavery, which was legal in all thirteen colonies because the British Empire sanctioned it. This antislavery activity led to the ending of slavery in the states north of Maryland, though a number enacted a program of gradual emancipation. In the southern states, however, from Delaware and Maryland south to Georgia, the home of the vast majority of slaves, antislavery had little impact. In fact, in those states slavery emerged stronger, for the institution had successfully withstood all attempts to terminate it, even gradually.

The abolitionists taking charge of antislavery by 1830 had no interest in gradualism. They cried for immediate emancipation, with no compensation for slave owners. This insurgence in the United States is usually dated from 1831 with the publication of the *Liberator*, an abolitionist newspaper in Boston edited by a young native of Massachusetts, William Lloyd Garrison. Yet, in the late 1820s, Garrison had been influenced by African American opponents of slavery, chiefly Daniel Walker, whose lengthy pamphlet of 1829, *Daniel Walker's Appeal . . .* , had a significant effect on northern blacks and antislavery whites like Garrison. The creation in Philadelphia in 1833 of the American Antislavery Society provided organization and focus for the burgeoning campaign.

The American abolitionists acknowledged their debt to those in Great Britain who for decades had striven to end all connection between the British Empire and slavery. In 1807 they succeeded in halting British involvement in the slave trade, and finally, in

1833, Parliament abolished the institution in the empire, though owners received compensation and four years were allowed for actual termination.

American abolitionists faced a much more daunting challenge than their British forebears and contemporaries. The latter only had to persuade a powerful Parliament that had unquestioned authority to legislate for the entire empire. Moreover, slavery existed on the periphery, chiefly in the West Indies, not in Britain itself. In the United States, Congress did not have comparable power. Furthermore, provisions in the Constitution like the three-fifths clause provided legitimacy for the institution. Additionally, even if so inclined, the federal government could not dictate to the states, which shared sovereignty and constitutional rights. Finally, the political power of the slave states within the federal government made action by it against slavery practically impossible.

Even so, events in the early 1830s gave both impetus and hope to the abolitionists. The Nullification Crisis of 1831 and 1832 posed a potential threat to the Union. And abolitionists along with many others, including Adams of course, saw slavery at its root. Then, in 1831, the largest slave revolt in American history occurred in Virginia. Nat Turner's Revolt, named for its slave leader, caused the deaths of more than sixty whites along with numerous slaves. That sent shivers that extended well beyond Virginia. The next year a massive uprising took place in the British colony of Jamaica. It appeared that race war could engulf slave areas. For abolitionists these events made clear the desperate need to end slavery in order to avoid bloodshed and the dismemberment of the Union.

These abolitionists preached a radical doctrine, far more radical than that which Adams espoused. They rejected any thought of colonization. Proclaiming slavery the great evil besetting the country, they demanded immediate action. An evil so profound permitted no temporizing. Going further, abolitionists also condemned all slave owners as evil. Thus they called not only for instant motion against slavery but also for no compensation for owners. In their judgment no one should profit from involvement with such wickedness. The abolitionists insisted on immediate freedom for over two million slaves, with their owners receiving nothing for their value, which in 1830 reached $577 million (today approximately $15 billion).

This unprecedented assault on both slavery and slave owners had its genesis in two key areas. First, the religious crusade beginning in the 1820s known as the Second Great Awakening caused an evangelical tide to rush over much of New England and spread along the migration track New Englanders followed westward through New York State and even beyond. The ministers trumpeted a message that taught individuals they could perfect themselves by renouncing their sins, but these purified Christians could not rest on their personal perfection. They must drive to rid the nation of all sins, such as alcohol consumption and desecration of the Sabbath. Quickly, however, one sin became the most heinous, that of slavery. No Christian nation could permit it, and no Christian could participate in it. Evangelical abolitionists sermonized that the monstrous scourge must be removed lest God turn his wrath on the United States. Hesitation could not be countenanced.

A second moral incentive had economic origins. Once again Britain led the way. There a free-labor ideology had come to dominate. For its adherents free labor characterized a modernizing economy; it meant progress. It demanded at least the appearance of voluntary choice for workers, a condition symbolized by a contract and the payment of a wage. The symbolism was critical, for often the contract and wage mocked free choice and resulted in "nearly absolute subordination." Free-labor apostles damned slavery as qualitatively different from any other kind of discrimination or domination. The slave by definition had no choice and was certainly not party to any contract. Thus a slave-based economy was backward and nonprogressive.

With the merger of Christian morality and economic modernism fueling their endeavor, abolitionists marched confidently forward. They intended to storm the ramparts of slavery. Garrison spoke for this dedicated band as well as for himself when he wrote in the first issue of the *Liberator,* "I am in earnest—I will not equivocate . . . I will not retreat a single inch—*and I will be heard.*"[10]

Adams's first direct involvement with abolitionists came with petitions. The First Amendment to the Constitution enshrined the right of the people "to petition the Government for a redress of grievances." From the beginning of the national government, citizens had utilized that provision to send petitions to their representatives in Congress. Because the House was considered closer to the people, the great majority went to it. In the House every session dealt with scores of petitions submitted by ordinary people. In that chamber on specified days a routine call for petitions occurred, starting with Maine and heading south. Individual congressmen followed a standard brief procedure: note the subject of their petitions, then identify where they originated and the number of signatures, and finally move that the petitions be assigned to the appropriate committee.[11]

Antislavery petitions were not new. Since George Washington's presidency, Congress had received them. But because of the weakness of the antislavery movement, few members got excited. Nobody wanted to discuss the vexing slavery issue if at all avoidable. Usually no one remarked on the petitions before they went to committee, never to be heard from again.

Shortly after taking his oath as a congressman in early December 1831, Adams presented his first petition. Because all were short and similar, he requested that one be read. After his request was granted, he took up no more than five minutes to make a few remarks, explicitly saying that he did not support the position that asked for the abolition of slavery in the District of Columbia. Speaking for the first time before the House, Adams recorded that the sound of his voice unnerved him more than a little. That his colleagues listened attentively he counted as a real achievement. In the next few years, however, this nervousness would be replaced by an assurance that had eluded him in recent years.[12]

The presentation of petitions he considered a moving experience. Though a tedious procedure, he described the exercise as
exemplifying the "magnificent grandeur" and "sublime principles"
of the nation. When members rose to transmit the "prayers," the
word formally used for petitions, they faced "the colossal emblem
of the Union over the Speaker's chair." The ritual of the documents being carried from the members to the chair, the calling
for the ayes and nays, marked by different accents and tones from
the multitude of voices, the Speaker announcing the results, and
finally the smiles and frowns the outcome produced on the faces
of the members impressed him. For him this tangible illustration
of the people asserting their rights in a ceremony binding them
with their representatives demonstrated the meaning of America's liberty.[13]

Adams's initial presentation of an antislavery petition was certainly not his last. Abolitionists kept sending them, and he kept
presenting them. He did not even require that they come from
his own constituents, asserting that his duty as a congressman
required him to do so, no matter their origins. Many came to him
because of his fame. After all, no other former president sat in
Congress. His willingness to transmit their wishes to the House
brought publicity to the abolitionist cause. Yet he continued to
make clear that he opposed what most petitions requested, abolishing both the slave trade and slavery itself in the District of
Columbia. The petitions focused on the District because the Constitution gave Congress direct power over it, whereas few thought
the national legislature had any authority over slavery in the
states. Even though most abolitionists cheered his willingness to
present their petitions, his public declarations opposing specific
contents caused criticism among certain abolitionists, including
Garrison himself.[14]

Garrison along with others of the faithful wondered about that
opposition. Adams provided an answer in an 1833 letter spelling
out the reasons for his stance. There were three. In his judgment
petitioners had no right to demand changes affecting citizens in

other states and territories. Then he argued that the measures the petitioners kept pressing would surely cause resentment in the South and might even lead to harsher laws governing slavery. Finally, combining the personal and political, he stated that the majority of his constituents did not advocate agitating the issue of slavery. He had no intention of alienating those voters whose broad support gave him such a positive sense of his own worth.[15]

By 1835, however, the abolitionist movement had become substantially different. An infusion of money from a few wealthy adherents plus the advent of mass-production technology permitting cheap printing that vastly increased the activity and scope of abolitionists. They intended to bombard the slave states with pamphlets, with a first run of 175,000, advocating the end of slavery. Reaction to this much broader campaign was immediate and vehement. The pamphlets, dubbed "incendiary publications," sparked outrage in the South. Southerners charged that they aimed at inciting slave insurrection. That June in Charleston, South Carolina, a mob went into the post office, removed the sheets before delivery, and used them to start a bonfire. During the summer similar burnings occurred in other locations.

Not surprisingly, President Andrew Jackson agreed with his fellow southerners. Damning abolitionists attempting destruction of "the dictates of humanity and religion," the president accused them of trying to ignite a race war. According to him they should forfeit their lives for their wickedness. In his message to Congress in December, he called for legislation allowing federal censorship of the mails to halt these inflammatory publications. This effort failed in no small part because southerners led by Calhoun wanted no such power granted to the federal government, recognizing that at some future date it could be used against them. Instead, the administration adopted an informal and surely illegal policy of permitting postmasters in the North to refuse dispatching abolitionist materials to the South. This policy remained in effect until the Civil War.[16]

With the distribution of their pamphlets basically blocked, petitions became more and more central to the abolitionists' effort to arouse Americans to eradicate what they believed the fundamental evil affecting the country. In 1836 some 30,000 petitions arrived in Congress; two years later the number swelled to 400,000.

This explosion of abolitionist activity would not go unmatched. Not only did southerners take direct action against their foes; northerners also landed direct attacks on a movement that both threatened the Union and promoted social equality between the races. In July 1835 an angry band in Boston almost killed William Lloyd Garrison; it took the mayor's jailing him to save his life. Two years later Elijah Lovejoy, a prominent abolitionist and newspaper editor in Illinois, lost his life defending his press from an assaulting pack.[17]

Adams strove to remain apart from the turmoil, informing a correspondent, "With the slave and Abolition whirligig I hope to have no concern." At the same time, unlike many northerners, he did not, it must be emphasized, denounce the abolitionists. He stayed away from meetings like the one in Boston where leading citizens denounced abolitionists and their activities. After all, he could not mind assaults on slave owners, because he had only disdain for them and for what he regarded as their political agent, the Democratic party. Furthermore, he had considered slavery for a long time the great evil in the country and the chief danger to its future, and those views did not escape notice in his diary or in private letters. While he was no card-carrying abolitionist, he could legitimately be described as a fellow traveler. In the mid-1830s no other major political figure even came close to that position.[18]

Race made for a crucial element in anti-abolitionist feelings and actions. An overwhelming majority of white Americans, northern as well as southern, believed in the absolute supremacy of the white race. Suggestions of any kind of racial equality brought forth a heated reaction. In the free states African Americans were hardly strangers to vigorous discrimination. None of the newer western states permitted them to vote, and they lost that right in several older eastern ones. Moreover, job discrimination was rife, and northern mobs often terrorized African Americans. Abolitionists found themselves under assault not only for supporting racial equality but also for favoring miscegenation or "amalgamation," to use the term most common at that time. Not all abolitionists embraced amalgamation, and some even shied away from racial equality, but opponents leveled those charges against all.

Adams shared neither the animus nor the intensity of the ardent racists. Additionally, he deplored the violence directed against blacks. Moreover, he never accepted the contention that African American slaves, as property, had no access to the fundamental rights of man as expressed in the Declaration of Independence. He thought that basing what he termed "the first and holiest rights of humanity" upon skin color was immoral and unchristian. He dismissed the assertion that the principles hallowed by the Declaration applied only to whites. In a letter to the historian George Bancroft, his fellow citizen of Massachusetts and an avid Jacksonian, he wanted to know what Jacksonians meant when they cried, "Government *of the People.*" Did they include free blacks, even slaves? According to him there could be no such government without their inclusion. Relating to Bancroft an incident when as cabinet colleagues he heard Calhoun praise universal education, he contemplated adding "skin deep," but resisted the temptation. He still wondered about the impact universal education for whites and blacks alike would have on the South. While he did not provide an answer, no doubt can exist that in his mind a much improved South would emerge.[19]

Yet he clearly shared the conviction that Anglo-Saxons were superior to all others. In his time an upper-class white in Massachusetts could hardly hold any other opinion. Descendants of Pilgrims and Puritans, they believed, as did their ancestors, that they stood at the forefront of Christian civilization, which was white and Anglo-Saxon. For Adams that was settled truth. And in a fundamental sense amalgamation disgusted him. His discussion of Shakespeare's tragedy *Othello* revealed his opinion on that topic. He found the physical intimacy between Desdemona and Othello appalling. The great moral lesson of the play, he argued, affirmed "that black and white blood cannot be intermingled in marriage without a gross outrage upon the laws of nature, and that in such violation nature will vindicate her laws."[20]

His ultimate stance on amalgamation, however, was more complicated. He noted in his diary that many of his fellow House members felt that even a taint of African American blood should disqualify the swarthy delegate from the Territory of Florida. For Adams this man had a more serious problem, his Jewishness. Whenever referring to David Levy, he employed negatives about his Jewishness and gave no attention to the alleged stain of African blood.[21]

Furthermore, and more important, he envisioned amalgamation as the probable solution to his country's most vexing problem, racial slavery. He perceived slavery itself and the possibility of race war as massively worse than race mixing. Colonization schemes provided no solution; he had long believed them fanciful. With his undoubted preference for a racially homogenous society impossible, amalgamation became for him the least disastrous outcome for the United States. He forecast that eventual consequence because whites so outnumbered blacks that over time blackness would be etiolated, with the white population retaining merely "a dash of African blood," just as he thought he spotted in several southern congressmen.[22]

About slavery itself he was certain. The wicked institution would not survive, though its end would probably come only in the distant future. Before that happened, he surmised, slave owners would leave the Union, fearing emancipation. He predicted that when emancipation ultimately occurred, it would be won by the slaves themselves in a massive slave uprising. For the time being, however, he could only lament the power of the slaveholders.[23]

Yet change marked his own political world, remarkable for a man now in his late sixties. By the middle of the decade abolitionists had become a force in the Twelfth District of Massachusetts, especially among those who had welcomed Antimasonry and in villages, critical sources of his political strength. Some twenty-five antislavery societies had been formed in the district. No longer did his constituents tolerate violence against those advocating abolition. In Plymouth a grand jury brought charges against the sheriff for failing to control the mob that attacked an abolitionist minister at a church. On a national level that shift was matched by Adams's increasing antipathy toward slave owners, chiefly because of their power in the Democratic party, which seemed poised to hold on to the presidency in 1836. He saw himself as watching helplessly while Jackson and his northern abettors, all the handmaidens of slavery, drove the country farther along the road to ruin.[24]

In the midst of this commotion, Adams surveyed what he deemed the devolution of his country. Simultaneously he mused about his own decline and the unfair impediments that he had faced in his public life and that he still confronted. He believed that despite the efforts of those who had tried to ruin him he had overcome all to reach the presidency. Since then, however, he felt his fortunes had declined, leaving him dubious whether he could ever recover public favor beyond his congressional district.

For his past struggle and contemporary predicament, he blamed what he depicted as "sorry pictures of the heart of man." In his diary he made clear to whom he referred. From his old Federalist foes to his current nemeses, including Calhoun, Jackson, and Webster, he listed thirteen names. All of them had employed "base and dirty tricks" to impede his cause and malign his character. This situation he judged especially unfair, for he had only "returned good for evil," never wronging any of them. In fact, he had "even neglected too much of my self-defence against them."[25]

Yet he did not always hold back. While listening in the House to a speech praising Jackson by Representative James K. Polk of Tennessee, Adams noted that the remarks included "some coarse and equally dull invective against me." When Polk finished, Adams indicated he would make no reply, only saying he would not respond when a member's extolling of Jackson contained an attack on him. But he did utter a brief riposte:

> No! let the candied tongue lick absurd pomp,
> And crook the pregnant hinges of the knee, . . .

According to him, those words had the desired effect, for in his diary he noted that Polk quietly "shrunk back abashed into his shell."[26]

That sense of triumph was short-lived, however. On policy the southerners with their western and northern accomplices still got their way. What Adams perceived as the giving away of the public lands particularly distressed him. Their sale at properly appraised prices would fund his dream of internal improvements, which would mark the growing greatness of the American empire. Yet he could only mourn, for he could envision no way to halt the cheap-land juggernaut.[27]

Despite his lamentations about himself and policy, Adams stood once more on the verge of national attention, on the way to becoming at once a beloved and a hated figure. His resurgence had a most unexpected source—the unglamorous practice of presenting petitions to the House.

As did its predecessor, the first session of the Twenty-Fourth Congress began in December 1835 with the presentation of antislavery petitions. Initially it seemed that the past practice of accepting and immediately turning aside those petitions would be followed. But a young, ambitious nullifier from South Carolina quickly broke that pattern. Congressman James H. Hammond proposed rejecting peremptorily all petitions for action against slavery in the District of Columbia without hearing or receiving them. He also declared that Congress had no power to abolish slavery in the District.[28]

Hammond's propositions addressed two constitutional questions. Could Congress abolish slavery in the District of Columbia? And could petitioners be denied their right to be heard? While most southerners answered the first negatively, most northerners, even those like Adams who opposed any such act, thought otherwise. They pointed out correctly that the Constitution gave Congress authority over all matters in the District. On the second, northerners overwhelmingly believed that the Constitution required that Congress at least accept all petitions. In the House debate raged.

The goings-on appalled the Massachusetts sexagenarian. He considered proslavery rhetoric dominant, with the voice of freedom muted. He wrote to his one surviving son that he had been urged to stand up and become that voice. He expressed two fears—that if he did not rise, freedom would be "trampled under foot," but that if he did, he would suffer the same fate. On December 21 he did speak briefly against Hammond's tactic, suggesting instead that the petitions be referred to the Committee on the District of Columbia, where they would surely "sleep the sleep of death."[29]

Although the evidence indicates that Hammond acted on his own, he spoke for many southerners outraged by the abolitionists' assaults not only on slavery but on the character and morality of all slaveholders. Slave owners who identified themselves as moral, Christian, and American took great offense at what they termed scurrilous attacks on them as individuals. While all white southerners detested abolitionists, the most ardent urged a direct strike against them. In Congress the great southern spokesman Senator Calhoun wanted to unite the South in an effort to squelch in direct fashion the abolitionists' goal of bringing their crusade before the national legislature. Although a nullifier and a young follower of Calhoun, Hammond took up the cudgels in the House on his own.

Hammond's initiative had an impact on congressional southerners and the Democratic party. No southern politician could afford to be found wanting in defense of his section's major social and economic institution. Outright opposition to Hammond's move was therefore unthinkable. Democratic partisans had a different perspective. They wanted to prevent a vicious battle over the right of petition that would threaten party unity.

United behind their presidential candidate, Vice-President Van Buren, Democrats wanted to retain that union to ensure that Van Buren would follow Jackson as president. With the Whigs fielding a southern candidate aimed at curbing Van Buren's strength in that section, Van Buren and his adherents wanted to stave off inroads on their southern flank. The Democrats thus wanted a plan that would replace Hammond's radical proposal with a solution that would at the same time maintain the allegiance of southern Democrats and not alienate the northerners.

The quandary that Hammond's foray caused among southerners and Democrats did not at the moment affect Adams's course. The Whig party, which had his tentative allegiance, experienced no similar stress. Still putting together disparate parts and with three sectionally oriented candidates, the former president could act as he saw with ease. Accordingly, he continued to bring antislavery petitions before the House in the new year.[30]

The political jeremiads stirred up by now usual railing among congressmen. As rancor built, the reality of national Democratic politics asserted itself. Searching for a way around their Hammond problem, a number of northern Democrats pressed Van Buren to intervene. At this point another South Carolina congressman stepped forward, Henry L. Pinckney, son of a signer of the Constitution, who hailed from the same radical wing of Carolina politics as did his colleague. Moreover, he, too, had followed Calhoun. Yet he now headed in a different direction. Pinckney had become convinced that hard-line southerners like Hammond were damaging the southern, proslavery cause by dividing southerners while uniting northerners. The evidence does not reveal whether Van Buren directly influenced Pinckney, but his adherents in the House flocked to the Carolinian's side.

Fending off furious intransigent southern members, who castigated him as a traitor to their section, Pinckney in early February 1836 proposed sending all petitions regarding slavery to a select committee instructed to report to the House that Congress had no authority over slavery in the states and should refrain from interfering with the institution in the District of Columbia because doing so would endanger the Union. Pinckney's motion bypassed both contentious constitutional points. Congress would accept the petitions, but would automatically bury them and would take no position on the issue of slavery in the District.

Within a week the House accepted Pinckney's proposition. It sharply split the southerners, with half for it and half, the hotspurs, against it. All northerners but one voted aye. And that lone man was not Adams; he was willing to see what Pinckney would produce. James K. Polk, now Speaker of the House, quickly named a committee of eight pro–Van Buren Democrats and one Whig, a Kentuckian, with Pinckney as chair.[31]

Pinckney's committee deliberated for three months before bringing forth its report, which included three resolutions. The first stipulated what almost all politicians, North and South, had long backed—Congress had no constitutional authority over slavery in the states. The second repeated Pinckney's earlier argument about slavery in the District—Congress would not interfere with slavery in the nation's capital, because doing so would generate divisiveness and endanger the Union. The third broke new ground—Congress would lay upon the table all petitions regarding slavery without printing or referring them and would take no further action whatever on them. This last immediately became known as the gag rule. According to Pinckney, it had a straightforward purpose, to eliminate the discussion of slavery within the House chamber.[32]

A short debate ensued, and with the Jackson administration fully behind the report, Speaker Polk exercised tight control over who spoke. Then the resolutions came up for a vote, each separately. An outraged Adams struggled to gain the floor, exclaiming he had a right to speak before any ballot. Announcing the debate had ended, the Speaker declared Adams out of order. The senior statesman cried out, "Am I gagged or am I not?" Having been ruled out of order, he appealed to the full House. The members upheld the Speaker, with a majority of twenty. When the first resolution came up, Adams responded to the call of his name by asking for five minutes to demonstrate its falsehood. Shouts of order reverberated through the chamber. Once more he was unable to gain the floor.

The voting thus went on. The first resolution passed overwhelmingly, with only nine nay ballots. Adams's, however, was among them. Even though the Speaker had prevented his giving his reasons for objecting to the thrust of that resolution, he lined up with the small minority who rejected the notion that the Constitution forbade congressional action on slavery in the states. This status placed him with the most extreme antislavery men in the House.

The next resolutions also passed with comfortable margins, though the opposition was more significant. Forty-five congressmen voted against the second, and 68 against the third, the gag. Yet, on the last, 117 said aye. Adams was recorded on neither, but hearing the vote called on the gag, he shouted that the resolution violated the Constitution and the rights of his constituents.[33]

The breakdown of the vote on Pinckney's resolutions revealed both a sharp partisan divide and that John Quincy, except in the first instance, had numerous allies in his opposition. Only in the initial one did he belong to a lonely coterie. On all three almost every negative vote came from northern Whigs, those who belonged to the party with which Adams loosely identified himself. Not even 10 percent of the northern Whigs voted with the South on the second and third resolutions, while 80 percent of northern Democrats did so. The outcome was a victory for the coalition that had placed Jackson in the presidency and would soon win that office for Van Buren. The partisan divide also presaged the future—until 1860 northern Democrats remained firmer allies with the South than their political opposition.[34]

Although Adams could not defeat the Pinckney resolutions—he could not even get the floor to speak against them—he had no intention of keeping his objections to himself. Later that same day an occasion arose that permitted him to say openly what no one of his stature had ever done. His opportunity came when the House took up a bill providing relief for residents of Alabama and Georgia who had suffered from Indian depredations. He did not intend to oppose that measure, yet in a long speech, fourteen pages in the *Register of Debates,* he spent much time addressing Congress and the war power. Calls for order often interrupted him, but he did not yield or sit down.

A state of war, he insisted, gave Congress vastly more power, power that it did not possess in peacetime. While he agreed that during times of peace, slavery in the states was off-limits to congressional interference, he argued the onset of war in the slave states heralded dramatic change. Then Congress and the executive, the federal government, could surely intervene. He pointed to examples, such as the U.S. military involved in conflict with Indians or a foreign power like neighboring Mexico or the use of armed force to suppress a slave rebellion, which could lead to civil war. With that assertion he took a stand no major national leader since Alexander Hamilton had taken. And no one had heretofore done so in such a public arena as the House of Representatives. In the instances he had posited, he declared, the federal government could and probably would interfere with slavery in any and every way. A quarter century later Abraham Lincoln invoked the war power for just such an interference. Calling on southern members to recognize this truth, Adams warned them about the dangers for slavery inherent in any future armed contest. As for the southerners themselves, he blistered them as a people who had exterminated Indians (as if New Englanders had not), and as warmongers lusting for even more territory, particularly Texas, which was just emerging victorious from its fight for independence from Mexico.[35]

With this speech Adams took public his harsh view of the South, slavery, and southern political power. Recognizing its importance, he identified it a year and a half later as "by far the most noted speech I ever made." No longer would he confine this outlook to his diary and private correspondence. Confident

in his assessment of those who had thwarted him and certain in
the moral righteousness of his cause, he would now assail those
who in his judgment mocked the holy truths of the Declaration
of Independence while they hindered the noble influences of his
cherished Puritan values emanating from his own New England.
Moreover, his being nominated in 1834 for a third term in the
House assured him that he had a secure political base. To his
diary he confessed that approval provided a "cheering consolation" in the face of "the calamities which oppress me." He would
never permit, however, such calamities to deter him from his
sacred duty to defend his sense of liberty and justice.[36]

Even though Adams relished his participation in political
combat on a question he held dear, his ardor did not extend into
his home. Louisa Adams, who had opposed her husband's reen-
try into politics, had not changed her mind. "How bitterly sick I
am of the nefarious details of political life," she wrote. When the
politics-become-personal entangled her, she doubted her ability
to "endure rationally," fearing that her "reason should give way
under the severity of these inflictions." The onetime bipartisan
hostess witnessed friends turn into enemies. She spoke of "my
desolation" and worried that "despair will rise upon my soul." She
prayed that God would "hear the cry of my desolation" and take
pity upon her. She revealed her disgust in her social withdrawal.
Moreover, the emotional and psychological strain surely com-
pounded the travails of her health.[37]

Not only did Louisa Adams find the political world painful; its
impact on her husband concerned her. She believed the anxiety
inherent in his political life negatively affected his health. In her
diary she cataloged the scourges she defined as the "ill requited
troubles"—"of bitter strife, of endless trial, of mortified vanity,
of disappointed ambition." If he would only give up politics, the
resulting calm would not only benefit him but also rescue his
family from the turmoil that enveloped him. Yet she continued to
worry that retirement might risk "a total extinction of his life; or
perhaps of those powers even more valuable than life," for where

else could he find "a suitable sphere of action"? She could only beseech heaven to grant the strength so that she and he might meet their situation "as becomes Christians."[38]

In addition to her general displeasure with politics and her husband's participation, the issue that had become central for him, slavery and its future in the country, caused Louisa great anguish. While she thought slavery evil, she considered agitating it also iniquitous. Although she was against slavery, her Johnson kin still counted as slave owners. Cherishing them, she did not think of them as immoral. Moreover, the prospect of "losing the love, the friendship and the society of my own nearest and dearest connections" particularly distressed her. At the same time she found it "utterly impossible" not to empathize with Adams, whose motives she knew "to be pure and patriotic." She felt trapped between conflicting loyalties, though she would never turn from her husband. She yearned for him to leave "a fame to posterity."[39]

Not surprisingly for her, discussion of slavery brought with it the perplexity of race. Like her husband, she assumed the superiority of her own race. Her conviction appeared more powerful than his, however, for she envisioned no way to bridge the massive racial chasm. No evidence suggests that she shared his ultimate solution to the race question in the country.[40]

Just as he did, she dreaded what she saw as the final outcome of the conflict over slavery. Because she identified the contest as a "great struggle for power and dominion," between North and South, the result would be civil war. In both sections she perceived passion replacing reason. For that state of affairs she held abolitionists equally accountable with southern hotspurs. In her judgment only God could avert the disaster that she foresaw. And she prayed that "he who rules the hearts of men will now dispense them" to adopt "some wise and temperate course that would lead to peaceful resolution." Thus to Louisa Catherine the horror of civil war exceeded the hideousness of slavery. She discerned nothing sublime in the potential bloodletting.[41]

Even with congressional tumult and domestic stress, Adams

had two old companions that provided at least temporary repose. His almost daily walks remained central for him. Yet, even when walking, his analytical bent came through. He liked to measure the distance he had traversed by time and the number of his paces. On one occasion he counted 1,000 paces to a mile and a second for every pace at seventeen minutes to a mile. On another and in cool weather with a good road, it took him 1,070 paces to the mile. He calculated he was striding at three and a half miles per hour. He had previously covered the distances in sixteen minutes.[42]

While his walks provided mental as well as physical exercise, his garden was a salve. He filled pages in his diary with details on plants and their care, from nursery to adult trees. Nothing escaped his attention, from insect infestation to the difficulty of raising trees from seeds or nuts, to the success of his fruit trees. The grounds around the house in Quincy had literally become his botanical playground, though, as with all else, he also took this play seriously.[43]

Although he maintained an active life, he was cognizant now, in his late sixties, of his age. And he knew he could not arrest what he termed "an erosion upon Time." He found concrete evidence in the maladies that struck his body. Rheumatism affected his hands, at times making it difficult for him to write. Periodically a painful inflammation of the eyes afflicted him, though not so severely as he had previously experienced. But with old age upon him, he knew he would have to cope with whatever impairment it brought.[44]

The older Adams appears in a pair of portraits painted by Asher Brown Durand in the spring of 1835. In both he faces to his left in a three-quarter profile, and in both he wears dark clothing, including a large tie that obscures his shirt and some of his chin. These two paintings depict a more elderly and dour man than do those of Stuart and Harding done a decade earlier. But these two later paintings also differ dramatically from each other. The March portrait is darker, in every sense. From the sharply painted eyebrows to the deep, downward creases by nose and mouth, the artist has depicted a man who appears older and more troubled than the man quietly gazing into the near distance of the bland June rendering.[45]

Still, he would not permit either emotional or physical concern to deter him from his political mission to thwart what he designated as an attempt by southerners and their allies to deny, even abolish, fundamental rights enshrined in the Declaration and guaranteed by the Constitution. He might even overcome what he damned as his lack of accomplishment. When the second session of the Twenty-Fourth Congress convened in December 1836, he would be in his seat for what he would help make a tumultuous and memorable session. This time he would press his cause.[46]

Adams began the session on the offensive. Determined to continue his charge against slavery, he would not attack the hated institution and its political phalanx head-on, however. Such an effort would receive practically no support in the House and little more in the North. Moreover, he did not think immediate abolition either possible or practical. He wanted, instead, to maintain his assault, emphasizing the free-speech right of petition, always hoping to embarrass, even ridicule, slave owners. He expected to prod the more hard-line and excitable southerners to follow Hammond's lead with extreme reaction. And he had in hand scores of petitions for the abolition of either the slave trade or slavery or both in the District of Columbia.[47]

Acting promptly, he could make some headway in spite of the gag rule passed back in the spring. Because the gag originated as a resolution, not a formal House rule, it would have to be imposed anew in the current session. Before that occurred, Adams stood to offer his first petition, from 150 women living in his district, and moved that it be read. Immediately members rose in opposition. Responding, he noted that all have or have had a mother and no human emotion surpassed that which every man felt toward his mother. Then he urged the members to listen to their mothers. These mothers only wanted to abolish slavery on earth, surely a magnificent improvement for mankind.[48]

After having this first petition promptly tabled, Adams presented a second. In spite of vociferous objections, he began to read it, which occasioned interruptions with shouts for order. But he did not stop. Speaker Polk scolded him to be silent and take his seat. Complying slowly, he continued to read as he sat. Finally after extended debate, this one was also tabled. And then on January 18, 1837, the House reinstated the gag rule as Adams expected. Even so, he had made his presence felt.[49]

And he was not finished. He had no intention of allowing the gag to silence him. Less than a month after its reinstatement, he tried to present a petition from nine ladies of Fredericksburg, Virginia, saying they wanted only to end the slave trade in the District, not slavery itself. Speaker Polk refused, announcing it came under the gag. Undeterred, Adams next requested a ruling on another in his possession that supposedly came from slaves. He wanted to know whether it would be in order for him to present it.

This question produced bedlam. Infuriated, southerners tried to outdo each other with screams of outrage at what they deemed Adams's intentionally insulting attempt to bring forth a petition from slaves. Proclaiming that slaves had no right to petition, they called for severe punishment, possibly censure or even expulsion for the man they saw as a malicious troublemaker. Adams had understood how to spark an outburst of raw emotion from his southern opponents. He had them now foaming.

Defending his surprise, Adams asserted that he had indicated the petition purportedly carried the signatures, or scribbles, of slaves, and he had not attempted to introduce it, only asking whether its introduction would be in order. Now he specified slaves as signers, though he thought owners might have required the act from their bondspeople. Then he revealed his second shock. The petition opposed abolition; it wanted Congress to keep its hands off slavery. This revelation caused even greater upset among the southerners. They correctly perceived their nemesis playing with them, manipulating them and the House for his own ends.

In the midst of the uproar a Virginia congressman, a native of Fredericksburg, got a look at the petition, still in Adams's possession, from women of that town. Appalled, he discovered the names of free blacks and mulattoes, one of whom he identified as a prostitute. They were in no way ladies, he thundered. Accusing Adams of misrepresentation, this consternated representative only underscored John Quincy's triumph in offending the slave-state men while he claimed solely to uphold the sacred right of petition. Once again he had succeeded in branding southerners as opponents of free speech and the rights of Americans. All the while, however, he kept saying he intended no disrespect to the House or to any member, much less any interest in disrupting normal proceedings.

It took three days to expend the emotional energy generated by the gentleman from Massachusetts. At that point more level-headed members, northern as well as southern, presented three resolutions to the House. They hoped their proposals would halt the commotion while putting the House on record regarding slaves and petitions. They also wanted to provide finality to the contretemps between Adams and his detractors. The first stigmatized anyone who brought forth a petition from slaves as an enemy of the South and the Union. The second made clear that slaves had no right of petition. The third asserted that because Adams had disclaimed any intention to disrupt the House and had stated he would not present a petition against House rules, there was no need for any proceedings against him. The third could best be described as hopeful, for he had made no such pledge about presentation, nor was he likely to abide by any rule he disapproved. His definition of disrespect and that of the majority of his colleagues differed massively.[50]

Because the third resolution specifically named him, he would have the opportunity to defend himself. The House could deny him that privilege, but in doing so would set a dangerous precedent. In the future that tactic could be used against any congressman when the majority decided to do so. The vast majority of representatives did not want to put in place such a possibility.

On February 9, 1837, Adams got up to make the case for him-self. Beginning disingenuously, he moved that he had but a single goal—to get a ruling on whether the House would accept peti-tions from slaves. Of course, he well knew beforehand the answer to his question. Then he went into a lengthy defense of petitions, calling the right to petition a right of humanity, not just of Amer-icans. The denial of that right for unpopular opinions or political partisanship or any other reason would annihilate the Declara-tion and the Constitution.

He did not neglect slave owners as a group, excoriating what he judged to be their degradation. Referring to the Virginian who spoke of the Fredericksburg women as infamous, he asked whether men of their own color or slave masters made them that way. Scourging the slave owners for having sexual rela-tions with their female slaves, he reported his understanding that many among the colored population in the slave states bore a resemblance to their masters. Thus the charge of infamy should be leveled against masters, not any men or women of color. The reporter noted this intimation caused a "Great sen-sation" in the House.

Adams closed by standing his ground. He would not be intimi-dated. He disdained "the gentlemen from the South [who] pounced upon me like so many eagles upon a dove." No matter their attacks, he would stay his course. Yet he presented himself as a champion and guardian of the House, which he revered as the temple of the people. It must never, however, transgress the principles of the holy writ set forth in the Declaration and the Constitution. Thus he requested exoneration.

Despite his refusal to temper either his charges against the South or his insinuation about the morality of slave owners, his plea for exoneration was heard. Too many of his colleagues feared that censuring him would make it much easier for one of them at some point in the future to suffer an identical fate. Thus a reso-lution exonerating him passed by a lopsided margin of 137 to 21, with Adams excused from voting. He had successfully defended himself without at all backing away from his stance on petitions or slavery.[51]

Wanting to make sure that his constituents were aware of his cause in the House and comprehended why he acted as he did, Adams prepared four lengthy, public letters for them. Eventually grouped together in a pamphlet, they totaled forty printed pages. He provided a detailed account of his battle with southerners over petitions. He also spelled out his conviction about the pernicious impact of slavery. In the letters he presented himself as a man imbued with the higher duty of defending fundamental rights. He identified with his voters, all "Sons of Plymouth Pilgrims" immersed in the struggle to maintain the ideals of the Declaration and the Constitution.[52]

For him the petitions served to highlight the danger slavery and its political power posed to the nation. He knew his pushing that sacred right would cause an explosion among the representatives of slavery, "master members" he called them. Because he did so, "the torrid zone was in commotion." In his description their emotions outstripped their reason, with "blind precipitancy and fury" governing the southern response to his initiative.

At the same time he spoke positively about the handful of southerners who realized their comrades had gone too far in attempting to censure him. These men had nothing but contempt for Adams's petitions, but they recognized that such punishment threatened the independence of all members, including themselves. Their stance broke southern unanimity and led to the withdrawal of the most offensive resolution and eventually to Adams's vindication.

His admitting the decency of these few did not, however, cause him to temper his assault on slavery. He castigated slave owners for classifying one group of native-born Americans as outcasts of human nature, even as brutes, because of their African ancestry. For him slavery already had "too deep and too baleful an influence" upon the history of the country. He asserted that the institution could only operate as "a slow poison to the *morals* of any community infected with it." And, in his opinion, the United States was "infected with it to the vitals."

In slavery's demand for its rights, he discovered a great paradox. The masters in Congress claimed that the national government had no right to interfere with slavery in the states "*in any manner.*" If that is the case, he asked, what right does slavery have to interfere with the free states, with, for example, "the sacred privacy of correspondence by the mail?" How can slavery call on the national government for defense, for "vindication of her pretended and polluted rights?" He answered, of course, that slavery had no such right. Vigilance was essential, and he would be vigilant.

While Adams assailed the South and slave owners, southerners struck back. In the House undaunted congressmen from the slave states accused him of endangering the Union and fomenting slave insurrection. Mail from individuals, overwhelmingly from southerners, brought more dire threats. By the end of the decade, he had received scores. Warnings about bodily harm, even death, were commonplace. One man seemed especially determined. In a second letter affirming his intentions already expressed in a previous one, he said his journey to Washington had been slowed initially by ice in the Ohio River and now by rheumatism, which had struck him in a town in western Maryland. Still, he assured Adams he would reach the capital in a week and would shoot him whether in the House or in the street. Even though Adams did not dismiss these warnings out of hand as false alarms, he refused to be intimidated. He would stand his ground against the potential dangers, just as he did against the imprecations hurled against him in the House.[53]

The slave-state congressmen who attempted to silence him elicited his utter scorn. Not only did he return oratorical fire in the House chamber, but in his diary he displayed his contempt for them individually. He had previously belittled Speaker Polk, whom he battled over the introduction of petitions, as unqualified to be anything more than a county court lawyer. A Virginian he dubbed "a beef headed blunderhead." He lacerated a North Carolinian: "There is not a more cankered or venomous reptile in the country." Of a South Carolinian he wrote that the man's "speeches sound like a tin canister, half filled with stones, rolling down an entry staircase." Another South Carolinian he seared with commonplace epithets, branding him "as cunning as four Yankees, sly as four Quakers." Upon a corpulent Alabamian's election to the Senate, Adams lampooned both his size and energy—his "twenty score of flesh have been transferred from slumber in the House to sleep in the Senate."[54]

At the same time he made an exception for a few southerners, all anti-Jackson and anti–Van Buren men and almost all of them Whigs. Adams's wrath had a distinctly partisan hue. A South Carolina senator, not a follower of Calhoun, he praised for the eloquence, beauty, and wit of his speeches. Four years later he described the solon as "the most accomplished orator" in that chamber. "Oh for his elocution," an envious Adams cried. A second South Carolinian, also not a Calhoun apostle, he considered a polished, educated man and a brilliant scholar. Even so, he found both men morally deficient because they lacked fundamental moral principles in their views of slavery. Adams refused to realize that almost every southerner accepted the necessity of slavery, though it is impossible to know how many truly embraced the institution. He also failed to understand that any southerner overtly opposing slavery faced ostracism, or even expulsion.[55]

Clearly his partial caveat did not apply to every southerner he respected, especially those who openly identified with the Whig party. Although these men regularly joined their Democratic brethren in defending slavery, in Adams's view they had the virtue of steadily siding, as did he, with Whig economic policy, for example, the tariff and a national bank. He applauded a slave-owning senator from Louisiana for his talent, taste, good heart, and classical learning. Adams mourned his death, which he termed a serious loss for the country, for it meant the replacement would be "a stinkard," undoubtedly a Democrat. A young congressman from Georgia received this generous compliment: "a man of talents, of good principles, and gentlemanly manners." After the death of Lewis Williams of North Carolina, the longest-serving member of the House, Adams made brief remarks praising him in the chamber. He spoke of Williams as "the father of the House" and one of the best men, not only in the House but in the world. He even walked arm in arm with a North Carolina colleague, also a Whig, at the head of Williams's funeral procession.[56]

For all his sharply different opinions about southerners in Congress, he did acknowledge that in the House southerners, even Democrats, treated him civilly. He said in a conversation with a Massachusetts friend that all dealt with him as gentlemen, and "most of them with kindness and courtesy." He surmised that the southerners respected him because he did not truckle to them. According to Adams, southerners generally scorned those who did. These trucklers he termed "dough-faces," the sobriquet John Randolph of Roanoke had given northern politicians who did the southerners' bidding. But Adams went on to say that "so marked a difference [existed] between the manners of the South and of the North" that intimacy between members should be quite rare.[57]

An example of the respect Adams referred to concerned Congressmen Francis Pickens of South Carolina, an especially vociferous friend of slavery and foe of Adams on the floor of Congress. In his diary he recorded an occasion when Pickens came to his desk in the House to ask his opinion of a school in the District for young ladies, which his granddaughters had attended.[58]

Adams himself had not the slightest respect for the dough-faces whom he had long reviled. The most notable among them was now president. Even though the New Yorker had reached the presidency, Martin Van Buren in Adams's view had not shed his basic character flaws. Admitting that Van Buren did possess certain good qualities, Adams listed a cordial and calm manner along with discretion. They paled, however, beside "his obsequiousness, his sycophancy, his profound dissimulation and duplicity." Even worse, in Adams's catalog of defects, the president's "fawning servility" formed "the most disgusting part of his character." Adams characteristically besmirched a personality that differed from his own.

Yet, in public, Adams managed a most civil relationship with the man of a diametrically opposite temperament. For Van Buren that kind of relationship was second nature, but for Adams it took effort. Attending a large social gathering, he noticed Van Buren. And he commented on the chief executive's courteousness toward him. Van Buren even gave him a ride home in his carriage, telling his companion he would be glad to see him. Adams replied that he would call very soon. And this he did, dining with the president, along with cabinet officers.[59]

Adams's dealings with certain southerners as well as with Van Buren revealed that he could divorce the personal from the political at least in public, provided those he condemned acted mannerly toward him. With one critical relationship, however, that demonstration of social courtesies never occurred.

Adams's hatred of Andrew Jackson only grew over time, to which the Tennessean responded in kind. Because Jackson never separated the political from the personal, he would never seriously extend public civility toward anyone who in his judgment had wronged him. And in his estimation Adams surely had. Sharing that aggrieved feeling, Adams rained epithets upon the man he had at an earlier time vigorously championed. Jackson was "ravenous of notoriety," for Adams a despicable trait. Jackson was enslaved by his passions, meaning he had no self-control, an equally contemptible attribute in the New Englander's eyes. According to Adams, "insolence and insult" marked President Jackson's relations with Congress. For Adams, Jackson's passions were fueled by a rampaging lust to disparage those like himself whom Jackson without cause had labeled as enemies. Jackson "glutted his revenge" by creating fictitious affronts, which led to "bold, dashing, base, and utterly baseless lies."[60]

Jackson matched Adams's vituperation. No man could outhate Jackson. He battered Adams for supposed vindictiveness in efforts to defame him. Lying had become central in Adams's makeup,

Jackson wrote, asserting he "delights more in falsehood than truth." He summarized this judgment with a dismissive phrase, "that lying old scamp." The former president even suggested that his antagonist was demented, for after all "reckless depravity" marked his conduct. Late in life Jackson concluded that Adams's "wickedness has never been surpassed by any thing in recorded history."[61]

Fierceness of language could not match the ferocity of another practice that reinforced Adams's animus toward the slaveholding South. Dueling was widely condoned in the South as necessary to protect honor. In contrast, Adams had long believed the potentially lethal clash between two men to be a barbaric practice. In the 1830s he connected it to the South's major institution, terming it "an appendage to slavery."[62]

The duel had come to America from class-conscious European officers who crossed the Atlantic to fight in the Revolutionary War. They upheld the tradition of private warfare to vindicate the honor of gentlemen. Their code obviously impressed certain Americans, both North and South. Undoubtedly the most famous duel in American history took place in 1804 in New Jersey when Aaron Burr killed Alexander Hamilton. The Burr-Hamilton clash notwithstanding, the duel more and more became associated with the South. Northerners condemned dueling, and it practically disappeared in the free states. Southern states also outlawed that mode of conduct, mandating various penalties for participants. Although state after state banned dueling, the idea of the duel had penetrated the essence of white southern society. Laws could not eradicate it, and the duel flourished until 1860.

Southerners who counted themselves in the upper order of society fought duels to defend their honor, their reputation, their good name. These qualities became extensions of the southern absorption with liberty and independence. They became two parts of one whole—an independent man was by definition an honorable man; a man who cherished his liberty could not allow anyone to besmirch his reputation. This concept gripped southerners intensely because in the South dependence and dishonor meant slavery. Only slaves had to accept assaults on their reputation, their integrity, their honor. White southerners thus embraced the duel to underscore their distance from slavelike characteristics. That southern legislatures exempted individual duelists from the provisions of antidueling laws just as readily as they passed the laws beautifully illustrates that the duel involved fundamental values. That southern society accepted, even demanded, the practice of personal warfare bolsters that conclusion.[63]

Almost all of Adams's major southern contemporaries adopted the culture of dueling. Even men of the stature of Henry Clay and Andrew Jackson fought duels. Clay, in fact, went to the dueling grounds while serving as Adams's secretary of state. On that occasion he faced John Randolph of Roanoke, at the time one of Virginia's U.S. senators. That engagement ended in the manner most proponents of dueling hoped for. Neither was hurt, but both had affirmed his honor.

The duel leapt into national attention because of one event in February 1838. A dispute arose between two young congressmen—William Graves, a Whig from Kentucky, and Jonathan Cilley, a Democrat from Maine. This quarrel originated in notes passed between the two after Cilley on the floor of the House had vigorously criticized a Whig editor, who was Graves's friend. The exchange quickly became nasty, and Graves challenged Cilley to a duel. Even though he was certainly no southerner, Cilley felt compelled to accept.[64]

The men met at the dueling grounds with rifles as weapons in Bladensburg, Maryland, just beyond the boundary of the District of Columbia. This duel seemed especially uncivilized because Virginian Congressman Henry Wise, one of Graves's seconds, insisted that firing continue even after each combatant had discharged his firearm, not only once but twice. On the third shot Graves killed Cilley.

News of the occurrence caused a national outcry because of what many saw as the barbarity of the event. Even the veteran duelist Andrew Jackson condemned it as murder and called on

Congress to act. The blame was placed on Graves, and especially on Wise. According to the code seconds were supposed to assure after the initial exchange of gunfire left both contestants unhurt that each had satisfied the requirements of honor, and that the affair should end. Wise failed to do so, instead insisting the firing continue. The uproar even had a partisan dimension, with northern Democrats charging that Graves had murdered Cilley.[65]

The vigorous reaction soon ensnared Adams. He had been unwilling to push an antidueling measure because he thought it hopeless. The southerners and their allies had too much strength. Zeal alone, he wrote, could not accomplish the task. Yet in the aftermath of the Graves-Cilley duel, the House resolved to have a special committee look into duels and inform the full House of its findings. The speaker named Adams as one of seven on the committee. In late April the committee provided a lengthy, comprehensive report. After considerable debate, the House tabled it.[66]

In the meantime, an antidueling bill was making headway in the Senate. Introduced shortly after the duel took place, this measure did not gain approval before the second session of the Twenty-Fifth Congress adjourned in July. But upon the convening of the third session in December, the Senate once again took it up, and passed it on January 23, 1839. Its penalty section included possible imprisonment for members of Congress who dueled.

In the House, Adams eagerly supported it. According to him no subject before the House had more importance. Yet he thought its enactment would be difficult. In his diary he posited that his efforts for it would require "above all things, the perfect mastery of my own temper—for which I pray for aid from above."

Tumult reigned when the House considered the bill. Attempts to thwart it, to delay its passage, abounded. Amendments were proposed. Motions for adjournment one after another followed. None succeeded. Some members absented themselves, a number of them remaining just outside the doors. The Speaker then directed the sergeant-at-arms to corral the absentees and bring them back into the chamber, forcibly if necessary. Finally, on February 13, 1837, the House gave its approval to the antidueling bill by the wide margin of 118–18. The southern partisans for the duel had failed to block it. Adams had succeeded. On this occasion the mores of New England had bested those of the southerners.[67]

Despite Adams's new obsession with fighting slavery, he did not spend all of his congressional time on these issues. An unexpected bequest from a wealthy Englishman especially excited him. James Smithson's complicated will left half a million dollars to the U.S. government to found an establishment in Washington that would advance knowledge and be named the Smithsonian Institution. Adjusted for inflation, that sum today would come to approximately thirteen million dollars. Informed of this bounty, President Jackson in a message to Congress in December 1835 stated that the executive had no authority to accept the award. Congress, if it so chose, must enact the measures necessary to obtain it and also decide upon its use.[68]

Both houses of Congress reacted positively, and with scant evidence of partisanship. In the House, Adams was named chair of a special committee to draft a bill that would accomplish that goal. In addition his committee prepared a thorough report that would result in the creation of an institution devoted to research. The House approved his handiwork. The Senate also passed an enabling resolution. In reconciling the two, Adams's blueprint won the endorsement of both chambers. The money arrived in the United States in the form of gold coins.

Adams exulted in the possibilities offered by this bountiful gift. He wanted the fund kept whole and used solely for "the increase and diffusion of knowledge among men." He did not want it connected with any other entity, nor did he desire the new organization in any way to be dependent upon the appropriations of public money. His objective was absolute independence to achieve a noble end. Moreover, he insisted that the endowment itself remain untouched; only the interest should be expended. The consequence for him would be the creation of a major research institution. He opposed the granting of any money to any particular college or school, for what he termed "common education." In his judgment spending the money in that fashion would fritter it away piecemeal and invite political favoritism and jobbery.[69]

He envisioned the Smithsonian Institution as a hallmark of his nation's commitment to expanding man's understanding of his world and the universe, which would surely include his long-held dream of an astronomical observatory. When president, he could never get Congress to join him in this endeavor. But now, with this windfall, the country could place itself in the vanguard of the quest for knowledge. The Smithsonian could become the American counterpart of major European research institutions. To ensure that his inspiration had a chance for success, he strove energetically to bring national leaders to his side. Even though he opposed the Van Buren administration politically, he lobbied the president and several cabinet members, always pressing upon them what he saw as their godsend, and his efforts did not cease after Van Buren left office.[70]

He worried this incredible opportunity would end up like the shattered goals of his own presidency. And the perpetrators of this new travesty would be the same breed of shortsighted and selfish politicians who had wrecked his earlier hopes. He employed vivid language, fearing "the noble and most munificent donation" would be "wasted upon hungry and worthless political jackals." No matter his pessimism, he was determined to do all in his power to thwart all those who aimed to torpedo his design.[71]

He knew that reaching that objective would be neither easy nor quick, but he never flagged. For a decade he remained the House committee chair, always vigilant against all attempts to poach on the Smithsonian preserve. A final decision on the shape of the Smithsonian Institution did not take place until 1846, only two years before his death. The outcome was not exactly what Adams had been advocating. Instead of a thoughtfully organized research body, the congressionally created institution included a museum, laboratory, library, and art gallery. The bequest did remain intact, however, and the institution would be controlled by a nonpolitical board of regents. And an aged Adams did vote for the final bill.

Throughout the nineteenth and twentieth centuries and into the twenty-first, the Smithsonian Institution developed into a depository for national treasures and a variety of educational and research activities. No one was more responsible than Adams himself for guaranteeing that the Smithsonian endowment did not become a piggy bank for self-interested politicians. Moreover, no one else had more impact on placing the institution on the path that led to its current distinction.

Whether grappling with southerners or bugling for the Smithsonian, Adams had to retain his seat in Congress to continue his crusade. In 1836 he won his fourth term by the massive margin of more than 80 percent of the vote, an even larger triumph than his two earlier blowouts, both exceeding 70 percent. In the middle of the following year he commented on his overwhelming strength in his district. "No other voice is heard," he noted in his diary. At the same time he realized that almost miraculous situation could change. After all, he operated in a roily political world.[72]

A slight shift, however, did occur in the next contest. Even though all the state legislators from his congressional district congratulated him for his service in the second session of the Twenty-Fourth Congress, his Democratic opponents did not intend to permit his reelection to pass without a fight. By 1838 united Democratic and Whig parties had developed into national competitors for electoral victory. Though generally a minority in Massachusetts and certainly so in the Twelfth District, Democrats did not want to hand over to Adams an unobstructed path to yet another term.

As a result, Democrats in the district put up an avowed abolitionist, hoping that their loyalists allied with voters of that bent would make the Democratic presence felt. Adams realized that "the whole Van Buren phalanx" now backed his abolitionist opponent. The tactic of the Democrats worked, to a degree. Nevertheless, they remained far behind. Adams's majority slipped to 59 percent, still a landslide by any political calculation.[73]

Before Election Day friends urged him to make a speaking tour of towns in the district. Agreeing to such canvassing, however, was impossible for him. He dismissed it as "the stump eloquence of the Southern and Western States," with which he would have no part. He had never campaigned in this manner and had no intention of starting. Moreover, he felt the practice was beneath the standards of proper New England politics. Although he regretted that the South and the West at the moment might be dominating national affairs, he did not want his beloved New England adopting what he considered their inferior mores, political included.[74]

Reelected in 1838 with more than a comfortable margin for his fifth term, yet not having yielded in his convictions about politicking, Adams could feel confident that his constituency stood solidly behind him. His political independence secure, he could continue to follow his own course in the House as the nation began throttling into an increasingly vicious and raucous political way that would define the mid-nineteenth century.

CHAPTER 8

"On the Edge of a Precipice
Every Step That I Take"

A S JOHN QUINCY ADAMS PASSED HIS SEVENTIETH BIRTHDAY, his determination and zeal in the antislavery cause did not flag. The petitions that had been so central retained their importance, but they did not stand alone. Becoming extensively involved in the *Amistad* case over the capture of alleged African slaves, he argued before the U.S. Supreme Court. Here, as elsewhere, he extolled the justice and humanity propounded by the Declaration of Independence and the American founding while condemning slavery as immoral and un-American.

Even more consequential for him, however, was the frightening linkage between territorial expansion and slavery. Always a champion of American expansion, he viewed that likelihood as nothing short of calamitous. The prospect forced him to rethink and recast his outlook. He judged expanding slavery a desecration of the American founding and mission. And conscious of his intimate ties to the Founders, he had no doubt that he comprehended perfectly the purpose and goals of the nation his father and the other Founders had created.

His connection to the Founders gave him a unique place in his country. As Americans looked back with pride on their country's history, they viewed the elderly gentleman from Massachusetts as a living symbol of that history. Even though not all agreed with his politics, all saw him as a living link, even their link, to their glorious past.

Adams's championing of antislavery petitions never wavered. Each passing year seemed to bring increasing numbers to him. Across the antislavery North, from many locations other than his own congressional district or even state, he had become known as the flag bearer for their communication to Congress. In his diary he recorded the precise numbers that he received for presentation to the House and that he actually presented. The daily total that he cataloged varied, ranging from just over two dozen to almost one hundred. At times he grouped them prior to bringing them before the House; on February 12, 1838, he had 350 ready. They "flew upon me in torrents," he observed. Managing this cascade took an enormous amount of time. When not at his desk in the House, he remarked, the arranging, assorting, and filing occupied him day and night, yet it was clearly something he did not mind, and beginning in 1835 he kept a docket listing every one that came to him.[1]

The capstone of these came early in 1843 with a document, designated the Latimer petition, for one George Latimer, an African American resident of Boston claimed as a slave by a Virginian. It contained 51,863 signatures by citizens of Massachusetts. Adams stated he had it in a frame on his desk in the House. A congressional ally described it standing "on a frame rolled around a shaft," which gave it the shape of "a large cylinder some three feet in diameter." Adams included it in a list of thirty-three petitions he delivered to the clerk of the House and demanded that they be entered in the House journal. He also had the list printed in a major Washington newspaper.[2]

Yet through all Adams's unwavering efforts, the gag rule remained in place, kept in no small part to silence him. At the beginning of every session of the House, from its imposition until the early 1840s, he attempted to get it rescinded. He failed, but with his effort he intended to make a point, which he did. Initially it was a House resolution, which meant it had to be renewed at the commencement of each new session. In 1840 the House turned it into a rule, making it more secure because it would not have to be renewed separately when a new session convened. To eliminate it would require a positive vote. For Adams this transition from resolution to rule was a grave offense. He characterized the change as "the difference between petty larceny and highway-robbery."[3]

Over time his struggle to abolish the hated rule gained strength. In 1842 he lost by only four votes, and the following year by just three. He could legitimately hope that in 1844 he could get it removed. Northern Whigs had been overwhelmingly supportive of his cause; after 1840 more and more northern Democrats joined the anti-gag forces. They were responding to the realization that their foes, the Whigs, were using the gag to win elections by drawing vigorous antislavery voters to their side. The congressional tally became less and less partisan and more and more sectional, reflecting the deepening geographical division that increasingly cleaved the nation into two parts. Through the fight the existence of the rule angered Adams. Yet his chief mortification came from his conviction that the gag epitomized "the disgrace and degradation of my country, trampling in the dust the first principle of human liberty." Confronting that outrage molded the "iron that enters into my soul," he declared.[4]

His prominence in this ongoing political combat brought him a recognition he had not heretofore known, a status in the North that had eluded him as president. Commenting on the flattery filling the multitudinous letters from those who supported his cause, he wrote, "I am in imminent danger of being led by them into presumption and puffed up with vanity." Requests for autograph specimens multiplied. Responding to them, he worried that he spent too much time on what he termed "these trifles." In the House, he noted in his diary, hardly a day passed without a northeastern or western colleague calling him from his seat for introduction to their friends and constituents.[5]

Nothing else so denoted his new status as the voluminous requests from across the free states that poured in for him to attend conventions, give lectures, and make speeches. Almost all he refused. But in this case as with the correspondence he could not hope to answer all. In order to address what he considered the impossibility of replying to each, he had published in a major Washington newspaper what he dubbed his "excusatory letter," expressing his reluctant regrets. He chose his positive responses carefully and politically, with his congressional district foremost.[6]

He absolutely relished what he called "this extension of my fame," admitting it was "more tickling to my vanity than it was to be elected President of the United States." Still, it concerned him that the outpouring of praise would be greater "than my honest nature can endure." More fearfully, he was anxious that it could augur "some deep humiliation awaiting me." Meanwhile, he found himself perilously close to the sin of pride. "I pray to God to forgive me for it," he wrote, "and to preserve me from falling in my last days into the dotage of self-adulation."[7]

One invitation he did feel compelled to accept came from the New-York Historical Society. The society wanted him to deliver an address on the fiftieth anniversary of George Washington's first inauguration as president, on April 30, 1839. He wrote that he simply could not repress his obligation to the society, which had repeatedly invited him. Nor could he resist the opportunity to use the commemoration of what he termed "a real epocha in our history" to proclaim his truth about the country's past and future. The detailed and anguished discussion of his preparation in his diary underscored his conviction about the importance of what he had to say. Wrestling with his speech, which he decided to entitle *The Jubilee of the Constitution*, he bemoaned his inability to compress his thoughts. He had been allotted an hour and a half for his presentation. As a result he told himself he could use only about one-third of what he had written. Afterward, he noted that he had actually spoken for two hours. A printed version ran to 120 pages.[8]

He gave his address in the crowded Middle Dutch Church on the corner of Nassau Street in New York City, a most appropriate location. A church was an especially fitting site, for he basically preached a sermon expounding upon his interpretation of the truth of American history. Through the entire exposition ran a single theme—the whole predominated over the parts. He started with the Declaration of Independence, maintaining that the colonies united, not one or two of them, set out to build a new political entity. And those who signed that sacred document did so as representatives of all the colonies, not just the one in which they resided. Then, with the adoption of the Constitution, the people of the new United States legitimized the Declaration. In their "transcendent sovereignty" the people created a civil government to defend their principles and rights. Claims for state sovereignty he rejected as immoral, dishonest, and despotic. In his judgment neither the Declaration nor the Constitution countenanced that nefarious doctrine.

Bringing his remarks to the present, he denounced the theory of nullification as "too absurd for argument and too odious for discussion." He located "the indissoluble links" between the people and the Union of the Constitution as not only in the right but also in the heart. In his view the Constitution simply retained the principles set forth in the Declaration, both holy writ and the work of "the ONE PEOPLE of the United States."

As for George Washington, he often disappeared in Adams's lengthy commentary. Still, no doubt can exist that for him Washington stood as the indispensable man, who embodied, carried forth, and ultimately glorified the holy principles Adams broadcast. He was certain that he simply followed where the first president had led. Washington as slaveholder did not appear. As in his earlier eulogies of Madison and Monroe, Adams made no mention of slavery. Trying to deal with that vexed and troubling subject would have bemired what he intended to be celebratory occasions.[9]

The letters filled with the accolades that caused Adams both delight and anxiety came from above the Mason-Dixon Line. While his mail did contain numerous missives from below that geographic boundary between free and slave states, they did not contain flattering phrases. In contrast, these writers castigated Adams as an enemy of their section and of their major economic and social institution, at times in vitriolic language. They regularly damned him as an abolitionist, which at that time was a loaded term. In his rejection of them, Adams employed an arsenal of negative adjectives: "treacherous, furious, filthy, and threatening."[10]

Yet these southern detractors oversimplified and even exaggerated Adams's ties to abolition and abolitionists. Without question no other political figure of his stature matched his leadership in the petitions war, in which he fought for the abolitionists' right to present their position to the Congress and the country. Additionally, no doubt can exist about his detestation of slavery and his conviction that ultimately the institution would be overcome. He called the outcome "nothing more nor less than the consummation of the Christian religion."[11]

At the same time Adams refused to back the central demand of abolitionists for immediate, uncompensated emancipation. To him the proposition of immediate emancipation was fanciful. He believed that only a gradual, ordered process could safely and satisfactorily accomplish the great mission of ending slavery. He made clear his position when in February 1834 he offered in the House a proposal for gradual emancipation by constitutional amendment. He would also ban the admission into the Union of any more slave states. As he anticipated, it went nowhere, but he had publicly brought forth the only way he judged that abolition could occur without violence. But even this proposition made no mention of compensation. It is not at all clear what he thought about it.[12]

Moreover, despite his submitting hundreds of petitions for emancipation in the District of Columbia, he declared he would vote against it. That he was convinced Congress had the power to

act in the District but not in the individual states made no difference. Asserting that the Declaration of Independence proclaimed
that the just power of government derived from the consent of the
governed, he would not force emancipation when a great majority
of the citizens of the District opposed it.[13]

Abolitionists understood that he was not one with them. He
refused to attend any of their public meetings. Conversations with
him left leading abolitionists disheartened because he declined to
stand beside them. One described herself as "sick at heart of political morality." For them morality dictated but a single duty—an
immediate end to the sin of slavery. As a corollary, they blan-
keted all slave owners with the opprobrium of sinners, for anyone
involved with the wicked institution could be nothing else.[14]

Many thought political expediency—his craving for office—
kept Adams from going the distance with them. They charged
he had nothing to fear from southerners who chastised him, for
his brand of antislavery never seriously threatened them or their
beloved slavery. Garrison was convinced that Adams's interest in
abolitionists extended no further than their ability to assist him
in his struggle in the petition matter. Another major abolitionist spokesman, James G. Birney, was less charitable. Writing in
1844, Birney judged that Adams's dealings with abolition had
been "eccentric, whimsical, inconsistent." According to Birney,
Adams had defended himself "by weak and inconclusive, not to
say, frivolous arguments." He concluded that Adams's cause was
"unworthy of a statesman of large views and right temper in a
great national conjuncture." Garrison, Birney, and their comrades
wanted a moralist, but Adams was not only a man with a moral
view; he was also a political man.[15]

Adams fully comprehended his complex relationship with those
he viewed as antislavery zealots. At times he used harsh words in
describing them: "these raving abolitionists" and "crack-brained a
set." Still, by the mid-1830s his hatred of slavery matched theirs.
And in 1843 in a public letter addressed to a gathering in Bangor,
Maine, celebrating the abolition of slavery in the British West

Indies almost a decade earlier, he pronounced in ringing terms the evil of slavery. Because "the law of nature and of God" forbade it, no human law could legitimize making any man the property of another man, he declared.

Asserting that slavery had baneful practical repercussions, he tore into an old target, the three-fifths clause of the Constitution, "this radical iniquity in the organization of the government," which gave slave-owning southerners undue and unfair influence throughout the federal government. The free states for too long, he thundered, had allowed the noxious forces of the slave states to run over them. He closed with a prayer that his audience would live to witness universal emancipation. As for himself, he would join the jubilation if his voice could be heard from the grave. In his diary he left no doubt about his goal: "I meant it as a vote of defiance to all the slave-holders, slave-breeders, and slave-traders upon earth."[16]

Still, he struggled with how closely he should align himself with the abolitionist cause. His heart and emotional impulse were with them. Countervailing arguments and forces held sway, however. He could never go all the way. He could not accept the charge that every American who possessed a slave was "a Man-stealer." He had known and still knew, even respected, too many slave owners to accept that universal condemnation. Moreover, he recognized that his wife, Louisa, and son Charles Francis desired to divert him from all connection with abolitionists. Then he feared that his being identified too closely with abolition would weaken and possibly even ruin him politically. Struggling among what he defined as "these adverse impulses," he repeated, "My mind is agitated almost to distraction." No matter the direction, he predicted, "I walk on the edge of a precipice in every step that I take."[17]

That last concern not only reflected his recognition of himself as a political man but also testified that he could go only so far in accepting radical solutions, whether intellectual, social, or political. Fundamentally a son of the eighteenth century, he retained its classical and rational outlook, which shunned the romanticism influencing diverse areas of American life, not just the zealous abolitionists. For example, the British social utopian Robert Dale Owen, who established in 1825 his ideal community in Indiana, Adams dismissed as "a nuisance to society."[18]

He especially had little use for an intellectual and literary movement originating in the 1830s in Concord, Massachusetts, a village a few miles north of Boston and not far from Quincy. Transcendentalists, the appellation embraced by the faithful, envisioned themselves as transcending the old order of the universe and initiating a new direction emphasizing personal freedom and placing in harmony the human and the divine, basically nature.[19]

The luminary of this crusade was Ralph Waldo Emerson, a Harvard-trained Unitarian clergyman. Emerson soon left the church, however, to begin a career as an essayist, poet, and lecturer. John Quincy saw Ralph Waldo, the son of a once dear friend, as trying to found a new sect. That effort only came, in his view, after Emerson had failed in regular avocations. In his opinion Emerson and his crowd had but one goal—to declare "all the old revelations superannuated and worn out," while announcing the "approach of new revelations and prophecy." He ranked transcendentalists with other dissidents "characteristic of the age" aiming "to unsettle all established opinions, and to put into perpetual question all the foundations of human society." Change could come, and with slavery should, but it must be gradual, lest the foundations that upheld civil and religious society founder.[20]

Although Adams had a complex relationship with abolitionists, they found a common cause apart from petitions on one notable occasion. This joint effort originated in a court case involving an alleged mutiny on board a ship transporting Africans between two points in Cuba, the principal Spanish possession remaining on this side of the Atlantic. Slavery was still legal in the Spanish Empire, which made the institution legitimate in Cuba. Spain, however, had followed Great Britain and the United States in outlawing the slave trade from Africa. Thus, while slavery was lawful in Cuba, bringing in additional slaves from Africa was unlawful, identical to the situation in the United States.[21]

Yet the demand for new slaves to work on Cuban sugarcane plantations made trading in them highly profitable, though illegal. With considerable money available, Spanish colonial authorities on the island made little effort to enforce the ban on fresh imports of African people. In fact, many participated in aiding the slave traders to avoid it. These officials provided fake documents specifying that the persons just arrived from Africa had been born in Cuba, making them legally slaves.

Upon arrival in Cuba, the Africans were usually unloaded in secret, then marched to holding pens in Havana, the capital, where they awaited sale. After purchase, they journeyed to the sugarcane plantations of those who had bought them. This travel often occurred by ships that sailed along the Cuban coast.

In June 1839 one such coasting vessel, the *Amistad*, set out with fifty-three falsely authenticated slaves, their two owners, and a crew of three. The captain expected a voyage of three days along the northern shore of the island, but a storm intervened, delaying the trip. During the third night, an African given the name of Cinque freed himself from his lock and did likewise for his companions. Throughout he would be their leader. In the hold where they had been held, the captives discovered knives used for cutting sugarcane. Armed, they burst on deck, killing the surprised captain and one other crew member, but spared the two Cuban purchasers and a slave cabin boy.

In command of the *Amistad*, they ordered the Cubans to sail the ship back to Africa. During the daylight hours the Cubans did as directed, with the sun confirming for the Africans the eastward direction of the *Amistad*. But at night the Cubans steered as much as possible toward the northwest, hoping to strike land or meet a friendly ship. As weeks passed, food and water dwindled. Finally, in late August, with provisions desperately depleted, land was sighted. Cinque led a party ashore searching for supplies and prepared to pay with Spanish gold doubloons found on board.

Unbeknownst to them, they had landed on eastern Long Island in New York State. The *Amistad* had ended its voyage in Long Island Sound, where it was seized by the U.S. Navy. The Africans were taken into custody and incarcerated in New Haven, Connecticut, until the courts could decide their fate.

The Spanish government, not unexpectedly, demanded the return of all persons and property to Cuba. Based on the documents issued in Cuba, Spain insisted the Africans were actually slaves; moreover, their taking over the *Amistad* was a slave rebellion. President Martin Van Buren's administration hurried to accede to the Spanish claim. A presidential election would take place in 1840, and looking to his southern supporters, Van Buren wanted to demonstrate his opposition to anything akin to a slave revolt. That the United States and Spain agreed seemed to ensure the Africans would return to Cuba.

At this point a committee of abolitionists led by a wealthy New York City merchant, Lewis Tappan, intervened. This group assembled a talented legal team to defend the Africans, headed by Roger Baldwin of New Haven. After searching ports in Connecticut and New York, they even found an African-born sailor who could speak the language of the prisoners, facilitating communication. Despite the position of the two national governments, the defense attorneys believed they could succeed.

The trial began in the U.S. District Court in November 1839. Because it was an admiralty case, there was no jury. The federal attorney maintained that treaty provisions between Spain and the United States required the return of the vessel and all its cargo. Furthermore, he asserted that on their face the documents proved the legal enslavement of the Africans. In rebuttal the defense argued for the falsity of those documents. The testimony of Cinque and some of his fellows, provided through an interpreter, buttressed their effort. As a result, the defense maintained that those who prepared the papers had flouted Spanish law. In fact, they insisted the Africans had been brought into Cuba illegally.

In January 1840 the judge, who had been appointed by Van

Buren, decided for the defense. In his ruling he declared not only that the Africans were free but also that their status of freedom justified their resisting their captivity. He ordered the government to return the Africans to their native land in western Africa.

Upon orders from President Van Buren, the U.S. attorney appealed to the federal circuit court, which in May 1840 affirmed the decision of the district court. Again, the federal government appealed, this time to the Supreme Court of the United States. That court agreed to hear the case in January 1841, after the presidential election had been decided. Meanwhile, the Africans remained in jail in New Haven, where they studied English and the Christian religion.

Adams took note of the *Amistad* affair shortly after the ship's seizure. In his judgment the Africans had "execut[ed] the justice of Heaven" and vindicated their liberty by taking over the ship from men he termed oppressive murderers. He saw a clear-cut moral issue. Additionally, he refused to believe that the U.S. government would comply if Spain demanded the return of those held in captivity. The case, then, was not new to him when a member of the Africans' legal team requested his opinion on the applicable law. Before giving his recommendations, he took pains to examine a number of legal authorities.[22]

About a year later, in October 1840, after the case of the *Amistad* captives had been appealed to the U.S. Supreme Court, Lewis Tappan himself along with a defense attorney called on Adams. They wanted him to become assistant counsel to Roger Baldwin, who had been selected to present the Africans' side before the court. Initially Adams refused, pleading his age, his responsibilities in the House, and his not having argued a case in court for more than three decades; in fact, his last effort had been before that same court back in 1809. He would, he said, gladly continue to offer advice. His visitors would not be deterred, however. They pressed, asserting the criticalness of the case, emphasizing it was literally one of life or death, for the death penalty surely awaited the Africans if they ended up back in Cuba.

Facing such ardent pleading, Adams relented. He told the two men that with God's blessing and his health permitting he would stand with Baldwin before the bar of the Supreme Court. When he contemplated the magnitude of this decision, he implored "the mercy of Almighty God" to manage his temper, enlighten his soul, and give him the voice so that he could prove himself up to the assignment he had accepted.[23]

He had almost three months to prepare, until the Supreme Court hearing set for January 1841. And prepare he did, filling his diary with accounts of his striving to absorb pertinent documents, legal treatises, and reports of germane court cases. First, however, in the company of Baldwin and others, he went to see the prisoners. Throughout the process he unsurprisingly questioned his ability to fulfill his role successfully. He moaned, "Oh, how shall I do justice to this case and to these men?" On the eve of his appearance in court, he still felt only partially prepared. On the actual day he described himself as almost unnerved.[24]

In the courtroom he was spared, at least for the moment. Chief Justice Roger B. Taney, a native of the slave state Maryland, postponed the proceedings because one justice had not yet reached Washington, and he wanted a full court to hear the case. Though relieved, Adams still reported himself agonizing over what he defined as an ordeal. He used the delay of several weeks for plunging himself "neck-deep" in more study.[25]

When the new hearing date of February 22 arrived, Adams walked from his home on F Street to the Capitol; the chamber of the Supreme Court was in the basement. Even with the extra time for preparation, his bewilderment prevailed—"so bewildered as to leave me nothing but fervent prayer that presence of mind may not utterly fail me at the trial I am about to go through." Yet he spent that day observing. Baldwin went first for the defense, gaining high marks for his presentation from Adams. On the twenty-third more of the same, as Baldwin completed his remarks. Even though Adams had not directly faced the justices, he was nervous.

He related his coping "with increasing agitation of mind, now little short of agony."[26]

Adams's turn finally came on the next day, February 24. Emotional distress and agitation consumed him until it was time for him to speak. Upon rising, however, he did not falter, recording his delight that "his spirit did not sink." While he thanked his God for assistance, he still experienced humiliation because of what he sensed as "the weakness incident to the limits of my power." He certainly overcame all doubts, for he spoke for no less than four and a half hours. At three-thirty the chief justice announced the court would recess until the next day, when Adams could resume.[27]

He gave a highly critical assessment of his performance. He decried his lack of acuteness and rigor in analysis and argument. Still, he satisfied himself that he had not failed totally. Both the justices and the spectators had paid attention while he spoke. His final words: "God speed me to the end!"[28]

The end would supposedly come on the next day. He indicated that the "agitation of mind" that had plagued him for weeks was finally subsiding. Now exhaustion troubled him, and he pointed to a restless night. Still, he reported waking encouraged and optimistic. When court opened, Chief Justice Taney announced that Justice Philip Barbour had died during the night. Out of respect, Taney said, the court would adjourn until Monday.

On March 1 Adams finally concluded his argument. Although he spoke for another four hours, he felt obliged to omit material he had intended to discuss because including it would have taken too long, as the hour of the Court's usual adjournment was at hand. And he did not want to appear on a third day. Thus he made a brief summary of what he had said and closed on a personal note. Although he did not cover all the ground he had planned to, he would certainly have been pleased with the opinion of Justice Joseph Story, whom Adams knew and respected and who like him hailed from Massachusetts. Writing to his wife after Adams's first day, Story termed Adams's speech "extraordinary." "Extraordinary, I say, for its power and its bitter sarcasm, and its dealing with topics far beyond the records and points of discussion."[29]

Before the court Adams stressed two major, intimately related points—justice and injustice. He opened, however, with an apology, telling the justices he would likely reveal both "the infirmities of age and the inexperience of youth." He then praised Baldwin for his able performance, which left him with little to say. But he moved on promptly to characterize the court as a "Court of JUSTICE," and he trusted that justice would inform the court's ultimate decision. He announced the only law he would present was the law expounded in the document hanging on a pillar in the courtroom, the Declaration of Independence. It extolled "the law of Nature and of Nature's God on which our fathers placed our national existence." Adams insisted that law made clear that in this instance justice mandated freedom for his clients.

In contrast to the holy concept of justice, he lambasted the U.S. government for its injustice. The government, he lectured the court, had rejected justice in favor of sympathy with Spain. That stance entailed affinity with whites and injustice for blacks. According to him, all the proceedings of the Van Buren administration had been wrong from the beginning. Considering the conduct of his own government, Adams had but one response, "I am ashamed!" He excoriated what he designated as "the servile submission" of the American president to the demands of the Spanish. He judged the government's behavior "lawless and tyrannical."

He concluded on a personal and quite religious note. He pointed out that he had last appeared before the court back in 1809, and his appearance this time surprised him. But this case had cried out to him. He went on to call the roll of the justices who had listened on that earlier occasion. They were all now dead, having rendered faithful service to their country. And he hoped they had gone to "the reward of blessedness on high." He closed with a prayer to heaven that the men hearing him this day after their illustrious careers in this world had ended would be received in the next with the greeting—"Well done, good and faithful servant; enter thou into the joy of thy Lord."[30]

The court did not delay its decision. On March 9 Justice Story read the decision of an almost unanimous court. One justice did dissent, but he provided no written opinion. The court upheld the decision of the lower courts and ordered the Africans freed. In deciding for the Africans, the court did not follow Adams's lead and talk about the grand theme of justice as propounded by natural law. Rather, it decided along strictly legal lines. Again, following the district and circuit courts, the decision declared the Africans were never legally enslaved. The Supreme Court did make one change, however. It did not order the government to return the blacks to Africa; it simply ruled for their freedom.

An anxious Adams was in the courtroom when Justice Story read the opinion. He described himself as waiting upon "tenterhooks." He was pleased, of course. And he gave thanks where he thought it due. To Lewis Tappan, he wrote, "Thanks! In the name of humanity and Justice to you." At the same time he thought the government should cover the costs of returning the Africans to their homeland. He told Baldwin to have all friends write to the president and Congress urging that course. He certainly made every effort. Yet, before any final decision in Washington, private donations provided the funds to send the Africans home. They embarked from New York City in November 1841 and reached their homeland in Africa in January 1842.[31]

Shortly before their departure, Adams received "a splendidly bound quarto Bible" signed by Cinque and two of his comrades on behalf of all the remaining Africans. Their present delighted him. But he refused Tappan's request for a public ceremony marking the gift. He declined, he said, "from a clear conviction of its impropriety, and invincible repugnance to exhibit myself as a public raree-show." He continued to disdain a public display of himself in what today would be deemed a "photo op," even when it would mean publicizing a cause in which he deeply believed and in which he had notably participated. His sense of the good public servant meant that acceptable publicity could derive solely from engagement in the struggle for what he would define as proper policy. Any occasion that could be seen as display he shunned.[32]

Before his connection with the *Amistad* case, Adams had already become deeply committed on another matter directly related to his growing concern about slavery—Texas. By the time he entered Congress, American settlers had been pouring into the region, a part of Mexico. And in 1835–36 with their numbers increasing, the Americans—Anglos to the Mexican authorities— led a successful revolt against Mexican control. The leaders of this newly independent Texas looked back to their homeland not only for support but also for incorporation in some form.[33]

Americans, chiefly from nearby southern and western states, began moving into Texas when Mexico was still in the Spanish Empire. Almost immediately, however, Mexico achieved independence from its colonial master. Newly independent Mexican officials were eager to populate the sparsely settled region adjoining the rapidly expanding United States. Accordingly, they offered to the immigrating Anglos generous incentives, such as cheap land and partial self-government. Because most of the settlers hailed from the slave states, many brought slaves with them. By 1830 the Anglos notably outnumbered the natives.

In 1829 and 1830, increasingly concerned about this swelling population, the government, in the far-distant capital of Mexico City, took two steps designed to stem the flood from its powerful northern neighbor. The first abolished slavery, and the second attempted to curb immigration. Neither had much effect; the government was simply too weak to enforce either. The numbers of both American settlers and their slaves increased markedly. By 1836 the Americans totaled some 35,000, a vastly larger figure than the native Mexican population.

The dominant Americans wanted to break free from Mexico. In 1835 fighting broke out between Texan and Mexican troops. It continued in 1836 until a decisive victory by the Texans over the major Mexican force ended the armed combat. Texas declared independence, though Mexico never recognized that status. The American press reported the conflict in detail. Much of the reported news originated in New Orleans, the closest American city to the scene. Newspapers there pressed the case of a slave Texas. Often the struggle was presented as white Americans against lesser Mexicans and Indians. The revolt drew thousands of enthusiastic young men from the South and West who went to Texas to join the fight.

During the military confrontation President Andrew Jackson had proposed official neutrality. Still, he never took steps to halt the surge of arms, men, and money into Texas, whose army was commanded by his longtime friend from Tennessee, Sam Houston. After Texas declared independence, Houston was elected the first president of the new country. Most Texans wanted to become part of the United States, as a territory, or even a state. Jackson was reluctant, however, doing nothing to advance that goal. He wanted no controversial issue to interfere with the election in 1836 of his chosen successor, Martin Van Buren. And Texas could be divisive because many northerners, even in his own Democratic party, questioned the incorporation of any form of a slave Texas. Yet, on Jackson's last day in office, March 3, 1837, he officially recognized the independent republic of Texas and the government headed by Sam Houston.

Adams's introduction to Texas came even before the first American colonists immigrated. In the negotiations with Spain that produced the Transcontinental Treaty of 1819, the boundary between the United States and Spanish Mexico was discussed. Anxious about a growing United States, Spain wanted to maintain the frontier of Texas, the portion of its Mexican colony actually contiguous with the United States, as far to the east as possible. In contrast, Americans pressing westward wanted to push back that boundary as far as possible, certainly farther than the Sabine River, the line separating Spanish territory from the state of Louisiana. In short, a number of Americans, Henry Clay prominent among them, desired at least much, if not all, of Texas.

They were, however, unsuccessful. Despite those efforts the treaty retained the Sabine River as the separation point between the United States and Spanish Mexico. President James Monroe never countenanced acquiring any portion of Texas. Secretary of State John Quincy Adams, who did want the line set farther west, followed his president and settled for the Sabine. Afterwards he asserted that he was the last man in the Monroe administration to agree to that decision.[34]

As president, Adams strove to expand his country into Texas, but he had to deal with Mexico, the new owner of that territory. With presidential backing, Secretary of State Henry Clay made several attempts to obtain Texas by treaty or purchase, but because of missteps by American diplomats along with Mexican politics, he never attained his goal. When Adams left the presidency, Texas remained part of Mexico, though with a steadily increasing flow of American colonists.[35]

Thus, when the Texas issue burst on the American political scene in the mid-1830s, Adams had a record stretching back over a decade and a half of trying to obtain that territory, or at least part of it, for the United States. Yet the arrival of Texan independence with the new republic's potential attachment to his country brought him to adopt a quite different posture.

Adams's departure from the Executive Mansion did not mean that he jettisoned all thoughts of Texas. In fact, in the future Texas would become more important to him than it had heretofore been. He knew that his successor Andrew Jackson desired to acquire the territory. In conversation with a southern senator only a few weeks after he had become a congressman, Adams discussed the difficulties Jackson would confront. Based on his experience as president, he avowed that Mexico would never willingly consent to relinquish Texas by purchase or treaty. Yet he said that, as with Florida, force of circumstances might require Mexico to give it up, as Spain did Florida. That possibility existed because of the burgeoning American presence in Texas; Adams assumed those settlers would eventually prefer attachment to their homeland rather than to Mexico. At the same time he pointed out that Mexico had erected an onerous obstacle to acquisition by abolishing slavery. As a result, Texas could no longer be considered slave territory, but rather free, which told him that a significant opposition would arise against bringing in Texas.[36]

For Adams personally the abolition of slavery by Mexico made joining Texas to the United States an entirely different proposition. When critics attacked him for being for Texas until he was against it, they were correct. But rebutting them, he was also correct when he replied that the situation with slavery in Texas had shifted fundamentally, from legal to illegal. He had not opposed expanding in slave areas such as Louisiana and Florida where slavery had been legitimate. Additionally, his attempts for Texas when secretary of state and president occurred when slavery was permitted there, whether by Spain or by Mexico.

Yet turning a free territory into slave country he believed an abomination. He saw reinstituting slavery in Texas as moral regression and unchristian. In his eyes a slave Texas loomed like a tidal wave that could doom freedom and liberty. Appending Texas would besmirch what he regarded as the basic ideals and values of his country. While no doubt can exist about the sincerity of his stance, he brushed aside an equally undoubted reality. Had his endeavor for Texas been successful, the Americans already in residence there and those coming would have maintained slavery, just as they did in spite of the new Mexican law. Facing such determination, President Adams would have been no more successful in getting Texans to give up slavery than he was in preventing Georgians from taking Indians' land.

Timing was also a factor. The possibility of taking in a slave Texas coincided with the ballooning of the petition controversy. The petitions and especially the vigorous southern antagonism to them had already heightened Adams's sensitivity to the evil of slavery—not only the institution but also the political power its adherents wielded. Adding Texas to the slave column would, he feared, reinforce the power of slavery that imposed the gag rule.

Slavery would be even more powerfully imprinted on his country, to its shame.

That conviction governed his reaction to the Texas Revolution and the possibility that Texas would become part of the United States. By the mid-1830s slavery was firmly fixed in Texas, and a vast majority of American Texans had no intention of giving it up. In a major speech before the House in May 1836, Adams spelled out where he stood and why. He depicted the Texas-Mexico conflict as a civil war between slavery and emancipation. And the Texans wanted to draw the United States in on the side of slavery. He denounced them directly, charging that the Anglos or Texans and their allies in the United States, the same people who had hated and destroyed Indians, now made an identical racial argument in portraying Mexicans as inferior to whites. He presented a straightforward explanation for the cause of the Texans: "aggression, conquest, and the re-establishment of slavery where it had been abolished." He asserted that if the proponents of Texas prevailed with the territory's becoming part of the United States, within a year they would mount a military movement against Cuba. According to this script that action might very well lead to war with Great Britain, and possibly even France.[37]

Although he could not directly influence events on the ground in Texas, he was determined to do all in his power to prevent Texas from becoming American. In the House, he asked whether the country was not "large and unwieldy enough already." Size of the country, however, did not make up his chief argument. As with petitions he became the chief congressional spokesman for those, mostly northerners, adamantly opposed to making Texas part of the country. In a March 1837 public letter to his constituents he vilified his own government for attempting to hang "the millstone of Texas slavery" on their necks. Mexico had eliminated "that curse of God," but now villainous people "usurping the name of freedom" designed to undo what the will of God had ordained.[38]

He urged both that anti-Texas prayers be attached to antislavery petitions and that singular anti-Texas petitions be forwarded. And they, like his fan letters, came in torrents. He willingly spent hours cataloging and listing them. Furthermore, he felt it his duty to provide those who entrusted their petitions with him an account of their disposal, writing a general notice to the first petitioner on every petition.[39]

Adams's anti-Texas campaign had two key components. Denying that Texans were struggling for their liberty from Mexico, he proclaimed the exact opposite. In his scenario they fought to establish slavery. He disavowed any Texan claim for honor or glory; instead, Texans deserved condemnation for turning a land of free men into a land of slavery. Additionally, he insisted on a constitutional point, maintaining that the Constitution did not delegate either to the Congress or the executive authority to annex the residents of a foreign government to the Union. According to him that power was reserved for the people.[40]

The Texas matter so consumed him because he considered it "a question of far deeper root and more overshadowing branches than any or all others that agitate the country." He made that statement in 1837, and in the very next year he repeated that conclusion. "I am oppressed," he admitted, "by the magnitude and weight of the subject, and anxious, even to dejection, with regard to the mode of treating it best suited to the success of the cause." He so wanted to demonstrate candidly and with moderation to his fellow citizens that Texas meant a future for freedom or slavery in his country. Yet he asked: could he or anyone else accomplish that task? He doubted that it could be done.[41]

Adams made his greatest effort on his most public stage, the House of Representatives. He demanded from the administration documents relating to Mexico and Texas. Informed there were none to forward, he commented, "There is a film of obscurity and a squint of duplicity." In addition, he regularly presented petitions against Texas, and defended his position at every opportunity. Pro-Texas congressmen wanted those petitions placed under the gag, for they correctly saw them as fundamentally related to slavery. Opposing their tactic, in the spring of 1838, Adams successfully led an effort to get them, along with other resolutions on Texas, some from state legislatures, referred to the Committee on Foreign Relations with instructions to consider them and report back to the House. Dominated by members from the slave states and Van Buren loyalists, the committee did so with little delay, recommending in mid-June that the House take no action on them because technically Texas was not a subject before the House. The House should just lay them on the table. This dismissive response appalled Adams, who unsuccessfully attempted to get its members to provide specific reasons for the committee's decision. Although he managed to publicize that the committee had not really discussed the contents of the petitions and resolutions, he did not move the House, which adopted the committee's report.[42]

Yet Adams's nonstop campaign did have a significant impact on the Van Buren administration, which did have diplomatic communications with Mexico and conversations with a Texas emissary. Even more than Jackson, Van Buren was wary of the political risk in a vigorous pro-Texas policy. And the outcry against Texas in the North, which Adams had pushed, influenced the always cautious Van Buren to hold back. He would take no pro-Texas initiative. This decision meant that the question of Texas's becoming American was put aside, at least for the moment. Adams could claim much of the credit for that outcome.[43]

Although Adams expended considerable energy on matters like Texas and the *Amistad* trial that captured national attention and enhanced his own image among many northerners, he never forgot that a congressman who wanted to remain a congressman, even one who had been president of the United States, had to maintain contact with his constituents and heed their calls for assistance. And even though in 1837 he gave no indication that he wanted to relinquish his seat in the House, to ensure that voters in his Twelfth District were aware of his activities in Congress, he did not rely solely on newspaper accounts reaching them, although the press in Washington and Massachusetts regularly reported on what he was doing and often printed his speeches. Still, he penned public letters for distribution in the Twelfth. He also compiled and sent packets containing his addresses to his constituents.[44]

When voters came to him for assistance with federal agencies, they found a man who readily took up their cause. Many entries in his diary relate his visits to various offices on behalf of those who sent him to Congress. To the War Department he carried recommendations for applicants to West Point, and for appointments to the Annual Board of Visitors to the Military Academy. A claim for damage to a vessel chartered by the government also took him there. In support of a constituent who wished to become a lighthouse keeper, he went to the Treasury Department. The Pension Office also found him advocating cases. The triumph of the Whig party in the election of 1840 brought him numerous solicitations for office. He regretted that he did not have the power to gratify even 1 percent of the requests. He could, however, place them before the heads of the respective bureaus, which he did.[45]

The year 1840 brought not only a presidential contest but in Massachusetts also elections for the House of Representatives. That meant Adams would have to stand for reelection, should he desire another term. His approach to what would be his sixth appearance before voters did not change from previous ones. When asked whether he would once again become a candidate and attend public meetings, he answered typically that he would attend no meetings, and his candidacy would depend on the people in the district. He would neither offer himself nor in advance decline. Though flattered, he turned down a delegation to his house in Quincy inviting him to have all Whigs in the district gather in his hometown, where he would speak. He also refused the request of an abolitionist that he pledge to support the prohibition of the slave trade in the District of Columbia. He would make no pledge, even though he would be facing energetic Democratic opposition, and he thought if the abolitionists backed the Democrat, he could lose.[46]

He did willingly accept his unanimous nomination for reelection by the Twelfth District Whig Convention. As he saw it, the people called. At the same time he informed the committee bringing him the news that he had not and would not take an active part in the presidential campaign. He stated that should he do so, he feared his exertion would be seen as promoting his own reelection. He made clear he would never promote himself in that fashion. Furthermore, he would never risk the perception that he was so engaged.[47]

He need not have worried; his constituents did not disappoint him. He won easily, with almost 55 percent of the vote. Even a well-organized Democratic party and unhappy abolitionists could not dislodge him. Despite the redistricting following the census of 1840 in which Massachusetts lost two seats, Adams still retained the loyalty of a majority. His district boundary changed a bit, though the core continued in place. He now represented the Eighth. In 1842 voters gave him a seventh term, though his margin narrowed.[48]

Adams's appearance before voters in 1840 was but a small part of the biggest, noisiest campaign America had experienced, the presidential election of that year. For his nemesis, the Democratic party, the incumbent Martin Van Buren carried the banner, striving for a second term. The opposition Whigs, Adams's political home, had new life. For the first time the party in 1839 had held a national convention and decided on and rallied around a single candidate, William Henry Harrison. Harrison's adherents had prevailed over the attempt of the Whigs' congressional leader Henry Clay to get the nod. The Virginia-born Harrison had moved west to Ohio, where he won fame as an Indian fighter. Additionally, from that state he had served in both the House of Representatives and the Senate.

United, enthusiastic Whigs, aided by the slowdown besetting the economy, believed they could throw out Van Buren and the Democrats. Politicking and electioneering spanned the country. From Maine to the Mississippi River, it appeared that a campaign

caravan never stopped rolling. The spectacle did not impress
Adams, however. He thought it disgusting that thousands rallied
to hear the interminable speechifying by luminaries like Clay and
Webster and even lesser political lights. For himself he refused all
invitations to attend such meetings, and he received them aplenty,
from the East Coast to the Ohio Valley.[49]

About the election Adams was of two minds. He had little
regard for Harrison, whom Adams had dismissed as a rabid office
seeker while he was president. And he could barely bring himself
to think the Democrats could lose. After all, a Democrat had been
president since his leaving that office. But when early returns
favored the Whigs, he began to hope, but cautioned himself not to
become too optimistic. Yet the final outcome went far beyond his
expectations.[50]

The Whigs won a resounding victory. Carrying states from
New England to Louisiana, and from the Atlantic to the Great
Lakes, Harrison swamped Van Buren in the Electoral College,
234 to 60. The popular vote was closer, 53 percent to 47 percent,
still, however, a clear triumph. In addition, the Whigs would have
a majority in both houses of Congress. For the first time since the
rise of the Jackson or Democratic party, it would control neither
the executive nor the legislative branch.

Though concerned about the durability of Harrison's extraordinary popularity, Adams envisioned something he had not witnessed since entering Congress, "a liberal administration of the
National Government." The Harrison administration would not
push territorial expansion, certainly not in Texas. Additionally
a Whig Congress could be reasonably expected to pass a tariff that would aid manufacturers and create a new national bank
that would stabilize the currency and contribute to economic
growth. There was even the possibility of reversing the cheap
public land policy of the Democrats in order to fund a proper
internal improvements policy. And President Harrison would
surely affix his signature to all such legislation. For Adams it
was almost heady times.[51]

The Whigs had high hopes when Harrison called for a special session of Congress to meet in late May. They were short-lived, however. After only one month in office, Harrison contracted pneumonia, and on April 4 died. With his death all attention turned to his vice-president, John Tyler of Virginia. Tyler had been placed on the ticket to placate Clay's southern supporters after the Kentuckian lost the nomination to Harrison. Though elected as a Whig, Tyler was not a Whig of the Adams-Clay school that advocated an energetic federal government, including a national bank and a protective tariff. Originally a Jacksonian, Tyler broke with Jackson over the latter's claims for executive and national power. A confirmed states' righter, he had never supported a national bank or a protective tariff. If the Whig Congress enacted the anticipated legislation, the question of how Tyler would react remained open. Should he refuse to accept the expected economic program and the congressional Whigs, with the influential Clay dominating the Senate, stand firm, a devastating political war could ensue.[52]

Although Adams would vigorously back that legislation, he had doubts about the new president. A little over six feet tall, Tyler was lean with a receding forehead, with his most notable facial feature a prominent, curved nose. Because a president had never before died in office, Tyler confronted an unprecedented situation. What title and role should he assume? A number of possibilities were floated, such as acting president. Tyler himself never hesitated. He declared himself president in name and fact. That claim appalled Adams, who felt Tyler should take the title vice-president acting as president. According to Adams, upon the death of a president the Constitution conferred upon the vice-president not the office but only the power and duties. In this instance he appeared to detect a distinction where none existed. If one had the power, one also had the office or title.[53]

His distaste for the title President John Tyler matched his denunciation of the man. He castigated Tyler as a devotee of "the slave-driving, Virginia, Jeffersonian school, principled against all improvement." Furthermore, he asserted that a single root had generated both Tyler's morals and politics, "the interests and passions, and vice of slavery." When President Tyler visited Boston to participate in the celebration of the completion of the Bunker Hill Monument, Adams refused to attend any of the festivities, in the same manner that he had spurned an invitation to attend the ceremony in which Harvard awarded an honorary degree to President Andrew Jackson. He confided to his diary that he did so because he would not be associated with "the mouth-worship of liberty from the lips of the slave-breeder." According to him, the presence of the slaveholding Tyler desecrated a holy shrine of liberty. Aside from that fatal flaw, Adams, by now never willing to moderate his views, regarded him as a mediocrity incapable of measuring up to the office that Providence had thrust upon him.[54]

For the new chief executive's relations with Congress and for the well-being of his party, Adams feared the worst. His dread was soon realized. In the special session, which opened on the last day of May, the Whigs passed a bill creating a new national bank. Having opposed a national bank all his public life, Tyler had no intention of changing his mind because he had become president. Accordingly, he vetoed the bill sent to him by Congress. Through the summer attempts were made to find common ground between the president and the Clay-led Whigs in Congress. Members of the cabinet—Tyler had kept intact Harrison's—with Secretary of State Daniel Webster taking a prominent role, led the effort. It came to naught, however. Creating a bank that both president and congressional Whigs would accept proved impossible. The latter demanded national authority, while the former insisted on state power in some form. In late summer Congress did pass another bank bill, hoping Tyler would sign it. He did not. With that second veto, which came on September 9, the entire cabinet resigned, except for Webster, who was engrossed in negotiations with Britain over the boundary between Maine and Canada. Two days later Whig congressmen caucused and read John Tyler out of the party.

With the convening of the Twenty-Seventh Congress in its regular session in December 1841, some Whigs, both pro-administration and pro-Congress, worked to restore harmony. The implacable opposition of Clay to any serious modification of his plan for a bank made impossible any meaningful reconciliation. Senate Whigs spurned Tyler's recent appointments, and both houses dismissed his legislative proposals. Tyler, in turn, rejected legislation that he opposed.

In this bitter internecine warfare Adams sided with the Clay-led Whig majority. Acknowledging his loyalty, the Whigs in the House made him chair of a special committee created in August 1842 to consider the appropriate response to another presidential veto. A week later Adams presented a violently anti-Tyler report, even declaring that the president's conduct merited impeachment. Political reality intervened, however. The committee recommended against initiating that process because the Democrats had the votes in the Senate to prohibit the president's conviction on impeachment charges. But when an angry Tyler sent a written protest to the House, the Whigs on a party-line vote refused to include it in the House *Journal.*[55]

For Adams this disruption of the Whigs caused great distress. Within two weeks after Harrison's death he had predicted the Clay-Tyler imbroglio and the party's doom. In the aftermath of the special session he noted that he and numerous others "felt that the hour for the requiem of the Whig party was at hand." He foresaw the vanquishing of the party throughout the nation. By the end of 1841 he could only see the Whig party "splitting up into a thousand fragments." Regarding the government, he could envisage only dismal prospects for his country. The political difference over the twelve months was stark—1841 opened with unexpected brightness, only to close in enshrouding darkness. And the new year brought no illumination, a clear sign of things to come. Pondering the why of that bleak course, Adams not surprisingly turned to his religion. He speculated that God to reserve beneficence for Himself and "to baffle and disconcert all human exertion to promote its purpose" obliterated all plans for improving the country by taking Harrison's life when fervent hopes for the right kind of government had been focused on him.[56]

No matter the political weather, Adams when in the capital maintained his active social life. The traditional New Year's Day open house at his residence continued to draw large crowds, as many as five hundred. He remarked that he did not always know everyone congregating within his walls. And despite his vigorous anti-South politics, a number of southern congressmen and senators, Whigs of course, always attended. Their presence surprised an abolitionist acquaintance who had difficulty divining the social connection between them and Adams. Never a grudging host, Adams always provided bountiful fare, with wine from his cellar, which held hundreds of bottles.

These annual affairs proceeded even with the irregular appearance of Louisa Adams. Often ill, but perhaps also uninterested, she simply remained in her chamber. It became so uncommon for her to emerge that her husband would even make a notation in his diary when she joined him. And he also noted when she put on a dinner party to honor Henry Clay. Her social withdrawal included often not accompanying John Quincy when he accepted invitations from other Washington notables.[57]

He attended events at the homes of private citizens, diplomats, cabinet officers, and even presidents. They could be quite grand. One party, with some eight hundred attendees, he compared favorably to what in London would be designated "a rout." He could thoroughly enjoy himself, remarking on the "dissipation of an evening" that resulted in an idle morning. At Executive Mansion dinners he joined in succession Van Buren, Harrison, and Tyler when the company could include such major figures of official Washington as Calhoun, Clay, and Webster. As usual, as long as they took the initiative, he willingly interacted socially with men whose politics, and at times presence, he detested.[58]

Occasions with President Tyler provided exemplary illustrations. During the politically fractious summer of 1841, he went to a performance of the U.S. Marine Corps Band held on a stage at the southern enclosure of the Executive Mansion. The president was observing from the south portico. He asked Adams to join him and his family. Adams accepted and was introduced to Tyler's three grown daughters.

A year later, invited by the president's son, Adams, this time with his wife, attended a reception at the mansion. He recounted that the courtesies shown to the guests by the president and his daughter-in-law acting as his hostess matched "all that the most accomplished European court could have displayed." With an elegant supper and dancing the festivities stretched far into the evening. Adams related not getting home until midnight.[59]

In all this socializing Adams reported his special delight at his introduction to a non-Washingtonian famous man, Charles Dickens, the celebrated English novelist. He attended a dinner honoring Dickens. He also invited Dickens and his wife to dine with him and Louisa Catherine. Although the Dickenses had a prior commitment for dinner, they did come to the Adams house for lunch. To a historian's disappointment, he said little in his diary about Dickens other than commenting on the swarming attention paid the Englishman. Aware of the social pressures on Dickens, Adams was flattered when he appeared. Even more flattering, Dickens requested his autograph, which he gladly provided and had delivered before Dickens left the city. Nowhere did Adams make any observations about Dickens's writing.[60]

While Adams's social life did not lapse during this period of political turbulence, his anxiety about maintaining his diary increased. For some time he had bemoaned the difficulty in keeping the record current. His advancing age, seventy-five in 1842, along with his congressional schedule often meant that he fell behind with his entries. He admitted that arrears were occurring more frequently, noting that it took him about two hours to write up a single day. And he acknowledged the physical impossibility of holding to that schedule despite his striving to do so. He did note when he managed to fill in the empty or incomplete days.

The diary was so critical not only because it provided him with a reference he could trust but also because it would be his legacy. He said that after his death he wanted his son Charles Francis to make use of it as he saw fit. Yet he contemplated its relevance beyond Charles Francis. With God's mercy it could even be passed to a grandson who would be "worthy" of keeping it intact for handing down to future generations. In sum, he saw it as a notable chronicle of his and his country's life, and as a valuable historical source. In his estimation the diary, along with his father's manuscripts, could keep alive not merely the Adams name but also the contributions and values associated with it.[61]

His voluminous correspondence erected a major barrier to his spending the time on the diary he believed essential. His complaining about the quantity of mail and the lack of value in most of it was nothing new. Nor was his statement that he could never answer all of it. Yet the problem did not grow smaller; instead, as he aged, it got larger. Even though he replied to just a tiny percentage, he arranged and filed all, which occupied precious hours. Describing this tedious task, he employed nouns like "drudgery" and verbs like "groan." What most distressed him, however, was the impact on his writing: the important letters, private and public, his addresses, and the diary. And as he told his diary, "writing is the only true labour of life."[62]

In spite of this last assertion, Adams labored mightily to understand his Christian faith. To that end, as he grew older, attending a Christian worship service on Sunday became more and more important to him. As his constant references to the divine attested, he never questioned either the existence of God or His interventions in human affairs. That the resurrection of Jesus Christ was vital to the truth of Christianity he never doubted. He recorded that a powerful sermon he heard in the House chamber on that topic brought tears to his eyes.[63]

At the same time, he expressed difficulty comprehending the doctrine of the Trinity because he found it troubling to give the Father, the Son, and the Holy Spirit separate characteristics. He asked, if

Christ be God, what can be the difference between the love of God the Father and the grace of Christ the Son? Unable to discern a distinction, Adams could only conclude that he venerated Christ as his redeemer and as he could best understand the redeemer of the world. But, he admitted, "this belief is dark and dubious." In sum, he attributed the worship of God to "a tribute of the heart."[64]

On two major tenets of Christianity he was mostly certain, though he had serious misgivings about one while he embraced the other. In a lengthy commentary on a sermon by a Presbyterian minister exhorting members of his congregation to provide for the working out of their own salvation, Adams defined himself as beset with sin, "perhaps by the depravity of the human heart, an unreclaimable sinner." While he wanted to do as Christ did, his spirit was willing, but his flesh weak. Yet he also absolutely believed that God controlled man's deeds, whether for good or evil, which meant that sin was God ordained. He asserted, however, that his reason and his sense of justice would not admit that God would punish a man because of his God-directed actions. Contemplating this theological journey, he decided he did not know whether or not he would be saved. But he avowed that neither did the preacher. Thus the sermon he had pondered did not distress him "nor depress my hopes of better things."[65]

Even though doubt may have powerfully affected his conviction about salvation, he grasped the concept of an afterlife. In 1839, witnessing the agonies of a granddaughter's mortal illness, he confided to his diary his conviction of life after death. For him she had been angelic while on earth, and he was certain about her postdeath existence. He could only pray that upon his own passing, which would surely soon follow, he would join her in "the world of spirits where there is neither sorrow nor mourning and where every tear shall be wiped from every eye."[66]

An old comrade reinforced his commitment to the Christian religion. As had been the case throughout his life, the Bible was always close at hand. According to him no other book in the world spoke so effectively about human nature as did the Bible. In a letter to a literary society in Baltimore, he gave advice to members and students on what books they should read. Not unexpectedly, he gave the place of honor to the Bible.[67]

His own reading followed the priorities of that list. While the Bible reigned above all others, he assigned second place to histories. He often returned to the classics, and the works of his favorites among them. Immersed in a French translation of Plutarch, he described "the hours glid[ing] in liquid lapse away." No matter his reverence for classical writers, he did not restrict himself to the ancients.[68]

He spent time on major works by two contemporary historians, William Prescott and George Bancroft, both like himself Harvard alumni and Massachusetts men. He read both in 1839 and 1840. Prescott's study of King Ferdinand and Queen Isabella of Spain he judged admirable and delightful. For the first volume of Bancroft's history of the United States, he strung together an envious list of superlatives, including perceptive, imaginative, and entertaining, and praised the style as more fascinating than Prescott's or perhaps even that of the best-known American man of letters of the time, the New Yorker Washington Irving. He finally lauded Bancroft for his "transcendent talents and indefatigable industry." Despite such accolades he found Bancroft's book morally defective, though he never specified why. One can speculate it could have been the historian's lavish praise of colonial Virginians.[69]

He told himself, however, that he had to guard against the seductive power in a library of good books. He had to resist the temptation of overindulging in reading because he had so much he wanted to write. "I count all time lost that is not spent in writing," he opined.[70]

Reading for him also, of course, provided relaxation. And though the years kept advancing, he clung to exercises and pursuits he had long favored. In winter he walked and in summer he swam. In Washington he spent hours in the waters of his "old bathing haunt," the Potomac River. In Quincy fishing trips provided respite and his garden occupied much attention. Details about the trees and other plantings pervading the area around his house fill pages in his diary.[71]

Travel had never been central to Adams's rest and recuperation from his political duties. In fact, since his return in 1817 to the United States from England, time away from Boston and Quincy and their environs consisted almost entirely of journeys to and from Washington. Although he had made brief excursions to the White Mountains of neighboring New Hampshire and the Canadian province of Nova Scotia just up the Atlantic coast, such outings were rare. But in the summer of 1843 an unexpected opportunity presented itself. For the health of Charles Francis's wife, her father planned a private tour to Niagara Falls. According to Charles Francis, his father was invited along because he had never seen the falls. Nor had he been anywhere else in what was then designated the West. He readily agreed to join the party.[72]

On July 6 the travelers left by train. Riding through his own state, Adams marveled at the beauty of the countryside, extolling it as "the Garden of Eden." Upon approaching the border with New York, he found the forested mountains delightful. Stopping in a hotel for several days, he toured the countryside. He visited a Shaker village where what most struck him were the astonishingly high prices charged in "a small shop of Shakerism." He took a carriage ride to a tower stretching upward fifty feet atop the highest summit in the area. The view from it impressed him; he could see for fifty miles, including, he observed, the states of New Hampshire, Vermont, New York, and Massachusetts.[73]

Arriving at Albany, New York, the travelers turned north and spent much time exploring historic sites. On July 12 Adams toured the battlefield at Saratoga, where American forces had gained a momentous victory over the British in 1777. A serious student, he had along a published account of the battle to help him identify troop positions on the ground. From Saratoga the group moved on to the ruins of the colonial and Revolutionary strong point

Fort Ticonderoga. From there carriage and lake steamer took him across the Canadian border to Montreal.

From that city he took a steamboat down the St. Lawrence River to Quebec City. There he walked over the Plains of Abraham, location of the great English triumph over the French in 1759 during the French and Indian War. He deemed the old city, the core of French Canada, quite beautiful.

He returned up the St. Lawrence to Montreal, thence via Lake Ontario to Toronto, and then arrived back on American soil at Niagara Falls, New York. He noted that the distance from Montreal totaled 438 miles and required two days, nine hours to traverse. The falls stunned him, and he spent several days in the area viewing them from different perspectives. He was also taken to nearby battlefields where American and British soldiers had fought during the War of 1812.

While at Niagara Falls he received an invitation to visit Buffalo, just down the Niagara River from the falls at the entrance to Lake Erie. He agreed and boarded a steamer for the four-hour run to the city. A demonstrative crowd awaited him at the landing. From there he rode in an open barouche to a park where he heard a welcoming speech filled with compliments, to which he responded briefly. Then came a tour of the city and the pleasurable ordeal of shaking hands with hundreds of well-wishers followed by a firemen's torchlight procession. The festivities ended with a splendid supper and evening party.

That reception heralded what Adams experienced as he journeyed by rail eastward across New York State. The railroad basically followed the route of the Erie Canal, which connected the Hudson River with Lake Erie. That had long been the path westward taken by New Englanders. In a fundamental sense this portion of western New York was an extension of New England. Dubbed "the burned-over district" because of the religious revivals that swept through it, it provided a congenial home for diverse groups who wanted to reform American life and institutions, including antislavery zealots and abolitionists. In no other part of the country, outside of New England, would Adams be more cordially received. Starting in Buffalo and continuing along the rail line, invitations from local dignitaries poured in, all desiring him to stop at their towns. He did so and encountered identical adulatory welcomes. His responses to the stream of praise generated some regret. All of his replies he criticized as "full of inanity and gratitude, shamefaced and awkward." He was simply uncomfortable in the midst of such vocal praises, which required from him an impromptu reaction.[74]

Particularly stirring moments did occur. In Rochester he marveled at the procession in his honor that stretched for a mile with bells ringing and cannons firing. In Utica a committee representing the town's African Americans requested permission to call on him to express their gratitude for his efforts to protect the right of petition and promote abolition. He consented. They came and one made brief remarks, "modest and well delivered," in his assessment. With equal brevity he thanked them, saying he had only done his duty and in the future would gladly serve them to the best of his ability. He closed by commending their protection to the God he and they worshipped in common.[75]

And while in Utica he dropped by a female seminary, where admiring teachers and students greeted him. A trustee welcomed him by reading extracts from his mother's published letters to his father and to him. Adams related that the occasion made him once again a child. Unable to suppress his emotions, the seventy-six-year-old congressman openly sobbed. Totally focused on his mother, he confessed to his diary, "My heart was too full for my head to think." He admitted that he simply lost his presence of mind.[76]

The journey produced one setback. Just outside Schenectady, through an open window of his passenger car the wind deposited a small pebble in his left eye beneath the lower lid. Unaware of what had happened, Adams was soon suffering great pain from an inflamed eye. At a sumptuous dinner in the town, the anguish became so unbearable that he excused himself, went into a private chamber, and washed his eye with cold water, to no avail, however.

Observing Adams's extreme discomfort, a physician at the table followed him. Upon examining the eye, the doctor discovered the offending stone and removed it. Relief was immediate.

After Schenectady, Adams reached Albany and the last celebratory occasion, replete with the by now familiar speeches, city tour, handshaking, and festive dinner. Finally, on August 4, he crossed the Hudson River and boarded a train for Boston. Three days later an exhausted traveler was back home in Quincy. It had been a full month of new sights and experiences. The nonstop adulation from Buffalo to Albany was something quite new and totally unanticipated by the aged traveler. At least some of his fellow citizens saw him as a heroic figure worthy of high praise. While he surely enjoyed the attention, he always told himself he would have to keep up his guard, lest conceit overcome his good sense.

A weary Adams barely had time to settle in before his thoughts once more turned westward. While in Niagara Falls, he had accepted, which he rarely did, an invitation to make an address at the laying of the cornerstone of an observatory in Cincinnati, Ohio, an event set for early November. Shortly after returning to Quincy, he started to work on it. When he complained that the time he spent on his speech interfered with his reading, he had in mind what he had earlier termed his "rash promise" to speak at the Cincinnati event. At the same time he worried about how he would compress his topic, the history of astronomy, into a discourse of three hours. He expressed a definite objective: to turn the momentary enthusiasm for astronomy into a permanent pursuit, not just in Cincinnati but throughout the nation. While he perceived his opportunity as God-given, he was concerned that his performance would not measure up to his goal. He could only pray that the Almighty would provide him with the powers essential for him to succeed.[77]

On October 25 he took a train from Boston. On this occasion he would reverse his summer return from Albany, going west rather than east. Passing through Albany, he continued on to

Buffalo. This time no cheering crowds lined his way, however. An early winter storm provided a snowscape for the entire distance across New York State.[78]

Adams reached Buffalo on the twenty-ninth and there boarded a lake steamer headed for Cleveland, Ohio. No public reception awaited him in Buffalo, though he did see a few men from July. Another snow event interrupted his voyage on Lake Erie, with his vessel forced to seek temporary shelter in a protected cove. When the tempest passed, the boat steamed on. It made an evening tie-up in Erie, Pennsylvania, where for the first time on this trip an assemblage turned out to greet him. There were the usual complimentary words given by a former member of Congress followed by a short response from Adams. Then, surrounded by a military escort, a band, and a firemen's torchlight procession, he returned to the steamer, which immediately continued on to Cleveland.

He landed there on November 1, and his continuing journey provided testimony to the intricate network of canals and railroads that had transformed much of America by the 1840s, a network that had barely existed when he was president. Another round of public honors and salutations marked his short stopover. From Cleveland his road took him southward through the state to Cincinnati. For the initial segment to Columbus, his hosts urged him to go by the Ohio Canal rather than overland. Adams agreed. By this point he had acquired a range of maladies, including a cough, a sore throat, hoarseness, and a temperature. The wintry weather had clearly affected him for the worse.

He was ill when he went aboard, and the canal boat itself did not boost his spirits. It was small, just over eighty feet long and fifteen feet wide, and in that space it carried more than two dozen passengers and crew members. It had no private staterooms. Spared the dormitory where most men slept, the ex-president shared a compartment in which four men slept feet to feet on settee beds. Also, the windows were closed because of the outside cold, keeping the inside uncomfortably warm. Looking over the situation, he did not hold back: "my heart sunk." He certainly did not look forward to the scheduled four days on board. Cramped into such a small space with so many people, he foresaw "a trial such as I had never before experienced."[79]

The journey did not turn out, however, to be quite the horror he had feared. He discovered some interesting fellow travelers; moreover, along the way the boat docked at various locations where passengers could disembark, and at some towns small receptions for him took place. At Akron he went ashore for one such affair, with brief words spoken and some hands shaken. A woman coming through the receiving line, and indeed pretty according to Adams, planted a kiss on his cheek. "I returned the salute on the lip," he reported and proceeded to kiss every other woman who came before him. Although his doing so caused some to make faces, he stated that none rejected his overture.[80]

Just short of Columbus he had to transfer to a stage for the final leg into Ohio's capital city, There, though still ill, he met another round of public welcoming. After the festivities he got into a stage aimed for his final destination. En route, at Dayton and Lebanon, the elderly gentleman witnessed enthusiastic acceptances similar to those he had been shown from Erie onward.

Finally, on November 8, Adams arrived in Cincinnati. More of the same greeted him, only a much larger assembly had gathered to embrace him. After the unrestrained praise, in this case from the mayor, he uttered what he rated a disappointing response; he actually used the words "flat, stale, and unprofitable" in his diary. Even so, the crowd chanted its approval before dispersing. Still, a procession of visitors passed through his hotel room until late in the evening.[81]

The occasion for which he had been preparing for more than two months was finally upon him. Even though utterly worn out and still harboring the effects of his illness, as well as being filled with anxiety, he stayed up until one working on his intended opening remarks. And he was up at four applying the final touches. Yet the day turned out to be almost anticlimactic, for a massive rainstorm altered the plans. Despite the weather a procession did form and move forward through what Adams described as "a sea of mud." Finally, his carriage reached the top of the hill—some 450 feet above the city—selected for the observatory. There he did lay the cornerstone. But when he looked out at the crowd to read his opening statement, he saw umbrellas rather than faces. Still, his reading from his rain-spattered manuscript brought forth three vigorous cheers. His major discourse was postponed until the next day, when his venue would be the largest church in the city.[82]

Before an audience that filled the edifice to overflowing, he spoke for two hours. Thankfully, he had no physical difficulty in getting through his lengthy oration. Beginning with a paean to his country and the unique patriotism it cultivated, he moved into his major theme. Historical in his thrust, he recounted in overwhelming detail his version of the progress humankind had made in observing the heavens. He began with the Greeks and Romans and moved on through the giants Nicolaus Copernicus, Johannes Kepler, and Sir Isaac Newton to his own era. Of course, he thought such efforts should continue, for they would advance knowledge and boost human enlightenment. Because God, he asserted, had given humans faces that looked toward the heavens, He also commanded them to raise their eyes toward the stars. Finishing, he was pleased, feeling that his address had been well received by an attentive audience.[83]

After much more socializing and adulation, he was informed that the summit on which the observatory would stand would henceforth be known as Mount Adams, in his honor. Receptions, meals, parties, and laudatory speeches lasted for two more days.

On November 13 he departed in a steamboat that would transport him up the Ohio River to Pittsburgh, Pennsylvania. But before leaving late that afternoon, he went over to the south bank of the river for a celebration in Covington, Kentucky, where he received a hero's welcome with a praiseworthy speech from the governor of the slave state. During the handshaking another pretty woman, according to Adams, took his hand and whispered in his ear, "The first kiss in Kentucky." He did not turn away.[84]

On the way to Pittsburgh, he made an appearance at several different river ports where he heard still more expressions of gratitude and praise. A particularly grand affair took place in Maysville, Kentucky. Its splendor Adams attributed to friends of Henry Clay. Clay had, in fact, invited Adams to spend some days with him at his home in Lexington. Even before starting west, Adams had declined, citing Louisa Catherine's health and his own infirmities. In his comments at Maysville, however, he praised the man who had served in his cabinet and now led his party.[85]

Pittsburgh provided a replica of the celebratory journey that had characterized Adams's preceding three weeks. But on this occasion there was even a cornerstone for a second observatory, and again heavy rain marred the ceremony. Although he saw a disappointing event, he told himself that by participating he had performed his moral duty. Yet, by this time, almost a month on the road, he felt his stamina failing. As a result he declined some invitations. In truth, he now found all the festivities "inexpressibly irksome."[86]

Leaving Pittsburgh on the twentieth, as the fall weather showed signs of yielding to winter, he traveled by stage and train to Baltimore and thence to Washington, getting to his home on F Street on the twenty-fourth. He made it through the final portion of his monthlong odyssey without the constant celebrating. It had been an eventful journey. The welcoming celebrations during his trek from Erie through Ohio to Pittsburgh matched those he had experienced back in July moving through western New York State. As they had, the more recent ones generated both gratitude and fear. Anxious that he was insufficiently grateful to Divine Providence for the outpouring of kindness and honor shown him, he dreaded even more "the danger of being pampered and elated into vanity by them."[87]

No matter Adams's brooding, thousands of his fellow citizens had trumpeted their delight in his coming among them. For a number, especially in the burned-over district, the rejoicing stemmed in part from his stalwart support of their political positions on expansion, petitions, and slavery. In their eyes no other political figure matched him.

There was more, however. While no polls reveal public opinion on these issues in all the territory through which Adams traveled, it stretched credibility that the huge numbers who turned out to cheer him totally agreed with him, or even with each other, on politics. Yet, for both those who did and those who did not, he represented substantially more than an advocate for political causes. Rather, in him they saw the continuity of their country. This septuagenarian was not only the literal son of a major Founding Father; he had also actually known and spoken with George Washington, Benjamin Franklin, Thomas Jefferson, James Madison, and James Monroe—Founders all. Moreover, Washington, Madison, and Monroe as well as his own father had appointed him to office. No other living political figure possessed such a lineage. All those who came out knew they would never again have the chance to see and hear a man whose public career spanned the life of the nation.

CHAPTER 9

"Our Country . . .
Is No Longer the Same"

As CONGRESSMAN JOHN QUINCY ADAMS CONFRONTED WHAT
he considered a philistine Tyler administration, he contemplated
the character and future of his country. From the advent of the
Jackson presidency, he had watched with growing alarm what he
interpreted as the declension of the United States. In his mind
the grand design of the Founders, which he shared and cherished,
appeared blurrier and blurrier. The prospect of national greatness, with the federal government fostering economic growth and
development, had all but disappeared. For a fleeting moment after
the election of 1840, a renewal of that greatness seemed possible,
but it quickly vanished with William Henry Harrison's sudden
death. Thus for Adams in a fundamental sense, 1829 marked a
significant watershed in American history. When he departed the
Executive Mansion, the nation of the Founders left with him.

In its stead he saw a politics centered on a localism that aimed
to shackle national power. Holding high the banner of states'
rights, its chieftains, mostly southerners with their northern lack-
eys, seemed bent on weaving slavery ever more securely into the
national fabric. To make matters even more distressing, these
men were ardent expansionists, and they strove to expand slavery
along with national boundaries. Of course, in Adams's view much

of the blame for their baleful influence rested on what he had long condemned, the notorious three-fifths clause of the Constitution. He could not know the end result of this reality as well as the potential threat to his vision of the country he esteemed, but he feared it would never be the same.

Even before his triumphant western tours, Adams had attained a conquest in the House that immensely pleased him. It also added to his luster among antislavery advocates. He entered the year 1842 with gusto. He had just been named chairman of the Foreign Relations Committee, for which he rightly, given his experience in foreign diplomatic posts and as secretary of state, believed himself particularly qualified. The rift between President Tyler and the Whig majority in Congress lay behind that assignment. A pro-Clay Speaker of the House replaced the incumbent chair, who had moved toward Tyler, with Adams. This position gave him a post where he could guard against renewed activity for acquiring Texas. His appointment, however, did not please either the pro-Tyler Whigs or Tylerites or the Corporal's Guard, as contemporaries dubbed them, or the Democrats. Their unhappiness, of course, delighted Adams, who now thrived on being unpopular with those whom he considered the right people. Moreover, he prepared to present his customary stack of petitions. A dinner guest, the prominent abolitionist Theodore Dwight Weld, captured his mood. Writing his wife, Weld reported, "The old patriarch talked with as much energy and zeal as a Methodist at a camp meeting."[1]

His presentation of petitions, mostly antislavery in some form, created more excitement than usual. As he foresaw, those dealing with antislavery were promptly gagged. Then he brought forth one that he assumed would be incendiary. He had told Weld that he intended to set the slave-state congressmen ablaze. Allegedly from citizens of a Georgia town, the petition called for his removal as chair of Foreign Relations because of his abolitionist activities and his "monomania" for dealing with darker people like Mexicans.[2]

Adams knew this petition was fictitious, for a Georgia congressman had informed him as well as the House that the individual who wrote it did so as a lark. Adams perceived opportunity, however. In presenting the petition, he claimed he did so only to support the right of petition. Yet he hoped he could incite southern hotheads to call for his removal from the chairmanship. If they did, he would have the right to defend himself before the House, meaning he could strike out at his enemies and generate a commotion.[3]

The cynosure succeeded. Discerning his intention, numerous congressmen cried for points of order, hoping to halt the entire affair. Raising the right of privilege, which overrode all else, Adams took the floor. Now he could make his chairmanship central to the dispute. And immediately he began firing his rhetorical rockets, charging "an alliance between Southern slave traders and Northern democrats" colluded to oust him. Trying to stop him, southerners denounced his charges as falsehoods. A number even left their desks and gathered around him to harass him. Confronting them, he reloaded: "I see where the shoe pinches, Mr. Speaker, it will pinch *more* yet." "If before I get through," he continued, "every slaveholder, slavetrader, and slave breeder on this floor does not get materials for bitter reflection it shall be no fault of mine." When the bedlam ended after a day and a half, Adams retained his chairmanship, but five southern members resigned from the committee. And the speaker had difficulty finding southern replacements. Such political fracas would not bode well for the decades ahead.[4]

Still, Adams retained the floor and with more petitions. One started a firestorm that made the preceding furor seem like no more than a simmering teakettle. Forty-six residents of Haverhill, Massachusetts, signed a petition calling for the dissolution of the Union because it favored the South and thus harmed the North. Presenting it, Adams quickly distanced himself by announcing that he opposed the petitioners' prayer. He said the time for that occurrence had not arrived. Instead, he wanted the petition referred to a special committee appointed to consider the request and report back to the House why it should be denied.

Just as he envisioned, the House erupted. Some southerners, Tylerites and Democratic hotheads, asserted that he had insulted the House. Cries for censure were heard. A resolution to accomplish that end was proposed, then another more draconian. It accused Adams of treason and links with perjury.

Again Adams claimed the privilege of justifying himself. Although he denied the right of the House to try him for any alleged criminal offense, he branded the effort to censure him a trial, declaring he would defend himself accordingly. At this point Whigs, including pro-Clay southerners, spoke against the censure attempt. But they failed to gain sufficient votes. Both northern and southern Democrats, as well as the Corporal's Guard, wanted to proceed. Joined by Adams and a few stridently antislavery northern Whigs, they beat back the effort to halt the action.

The vote underscored that the issue had two dimensions. One was surely sectional—Adams against his southern foes. Yet the southerners were either Democrats or members of the Corporal's Guard, not the majority of southern Whig congressmen. Though divided, during the fracas these men inclined more and more toward tabling the censure resolution. Northern Whigs overwhelmingly took that stance. At the same time northern Democrats almost unanimously lined up with their southern colleagues. Thus, in the Adams trial, partisanship as well as sectionalism had significance.[5]

Adams was caught up in his defense. In preparing his case, he accepted the offer of Weld, who became his research assistant, collecting various materials. Weld, who believed Adams was advancing the abolitionist cause, also joined the crowd in the gallery during sessions of the House and described the goings-on in letters to his wife. Adams felt the pressure of this situation, cataloging anxiety and sleepless nights. The tenseness also enveloped Louisa Adams. She was already physically weakened, and her anxiousness for her husband became more than she could handle.

She suffered what her husband termed "a fainting-fit." Yet, she soon recovered, renewing her solicitude for him.[6]

Determined to justify himself, Adams placed his case in a much broader context. He depicted those against him as aiming "to crush the liberties of the free people of the Union" by disgracing him. He described himself in "the midst of a fiery ordeal" to avert his ruin. "God send me a good deliverance," he prayed. While he prayed, his will never faltered. He told Weld, "I am all ready for another heat." And on the floor, he left no doubt.[7]

The uproar in the House, we can suspect much to Adams's delight, became an oratorical free-for-all. To watch the brouhaha, multitudes jammed the House gallery. Even senators walked across the Capitol to observe the rhetorical gunfire. Adams's southern adversaries compared him to other traitors, notably Benedict Arnold, the most notorious traitor in American history. Returning that attack, Adams thundered that southerners had long threatened to dissolve the Union over antislavery activity. Thus the northerners surely had the right to do so when they deemed the Union proslavery. He went on, castigating the South for trying to enslave the free people of the North, for attempting to destroy freedom of the mails and the press, even for trying to stifle free speech with the gag. Contrasting the slave and the free states, he pictured the former as a benighted region plagued with poor roads and schools, run-down buildings, and a general cultural stagnation, all because of slavery.

Not content with his general condemnation, he became personal and vicious in his onslaught. He denounced a Virginia nemesis as a criminal for his part in the Cilley-Graves duel. In Adams's purplish damnation this miscreant had then entered the House stained with blood from that murder, the blots still upon him. As for the author of the censure resolution, Adams stigmatized him as a drunk, constantly in an alcoholic daze. He should go home, Adams instructed, to learn at least something about the rights of American citizens.

With interruptions to conduct essential House business, this theater lasted for two weeks. In his element, Adams had the upper hand. His enemies could not amass the votes to censure him; neither could the other side obtain the votes for closure. Finally, on February 7, 1842, he informed the Speaker he would stand down, provided the censure resolution received a permanent tabling. A Clay Whig from Virginia so moved, and his motion passed, 106–93. A victorious Adams felt vindicated. The southerners who were ever his most ardent antagonists were impressed. A South Carolinian was direct: "Well, that is the most extraordinary man on God's footstool."[8]

This outcome was also a triumph for the Whig party. A majority of congressional Whigs had backed halting the proceedings. Yet Adams's rhetorical bolts made the entire incident seem sectional. At the same time, as he had always done, he aimed his fusillade at Democrats, whom he seemed to equate with the South. In his judgment the southern Democrats dominated the party. Dominant, and following the lead of their great patron Andrew Jackson, whom Adams even in the general's retirement hated, they had for more than a decade led the country in the wrong direction. At least, however, as Adams sensed, they had goals, all pointed to protecting and advancing slavery. In the supporting northern Democrats, for whom he expressed disdain, he saw only a vulture-like hungering for the spoils of office. In his appraisal the political danger had become even graver because he feared President Tyler and his rump contingent becoming allied with the Democrats. Such an alliance would give the wrong kind of southerners even more power.

Victory over his foes in the House succeeded by the adulation in his western tours combined to create a euphonic tone. Yet any source of jubilation was quickly moderated by President Tyler's new political offensive. That Tyler embraced a policy that Adams deemed perfidious did not surprise him, for he expected nothing positive from the accidental president. In his thrust the president did not adopt any fresh initiatives. Rather, he resurrected Texas.[9]

Just as political calculations caused both Jackson and Van

Buren to turn from any step toward annexing Texas, politics propelled Tyler in the opposite direction. The tenth president enjoyed
being president and saw no reason to retire, certainly not voluntarily. At the least he wanted to leave his mark. After his brutal
divorce from the Whig party, he had but two avenues that could
lead to his election in 1844. He might sweep past the odds-on,
albeit unexciting, Democratic favorite Van Buren to become that
party's nominee, or he might initiate a new party.

At the start either possibility would require stirring up the
South. A Virginian steeped in southern politics, Tyler knew
the kind of issue that could arouse his native section and the
potential political rewards such an arousal could yield. As Tyler
understood, nothing else so impassioned southern voters as the
possibility of outside threats to their control of slavery. Jackson
and Van Buren had backed away because of concern that the effort
to gain a slave Texas might undermine unity among northern
Democrats, threatening the party's electoral success. Tyler had
no such worry. His first task necessitated generating southern
support for himself; only then could he focus his attention on the
North. Tyler and his advisers counted on a vigorous pro-Texas
policy unsettling both men and parties in the slave states. As one
of them put it, they hoped to see southern public opinion "boil
and effervesce . . . more like a volcano than a cider barrel."[10]

Tyler and his circle also persuaded themselves that annexation
was in the national interest. On the basis of information from a
Tyler confidant in London, they had come to believe by the summer of 1843 that Great Britain had designs on Texas. British
intentions, they were convinced, would include abolishing slavery
and challenging the domination of American cotton in the British
market. To the southern-oriented Tyler administration, abolition
in Texas would threaten slavery in the South—Texas bordered
Arkansas and Louisiana—and thus endanger national security. In
fact, the British government did entertain the possibility of aiding
Texas financially and assisting in getting Mexico to recognize
Texan independence, which it had never done. And without doubt

the British government favored ending slavery everywhere just as had been done a decade earlier in its West Indian colonies. Yet it never adopted any such stance toward Texas. Put simply, Tyler's source exaggerated the possibility that Britain would act. The official American minister in London correctly reported that any British action was most unlikely. Even so, the president and his advisers distrusted the British. They honestly perceived a threat, which also coincided with Tyler's political calculus.

To achieve his goal, Tyler moved on two fronts, one public, the other private. His administration began a massive public relations campaign emphasizing both the threat of an abolitionized Texas directed toward the South and the economic opportunity Texas offered to commerce and manufacturing aimed at the North. The Tyler message also denied that expansion into Texas meant expanding slavery. On the contrary, according to the Tyler brief, it meant precisely the opposite. It proclaimed that economic forces would soon cause a transference of slaves from the eastern states to Texas; then those same forces would eventually push slavery from Texas to Mexico and Latin America. Thus Texas would act as a conduit to rid the United States of slaves. In sum, the Tyler campaign tried to present Texas as a national issue, not merely a sectional one.

On the private front Tyler began secret negotiations for annexation with the Texas emissary in Washington. He wanted a treaty that he could take to the Senate as a fait accompli. He had a single objective—to have a treaty in his hand and a public opinion receptive to annexation. Thus the Senate would deliver his handiwork to an accepting country.

In the spring of 1844 Tyler advanced another step, completing the treaty to make Texas part of the United States. For the administration the final discussions were overseen by John C. Calhoun, now sixty-two years old, who had become secretary of state in February. Presenting the treaty to the Senate, the president urged that body to maintain the same secrecy in its deliberations that had governed his negotiations. That was not to be, however. An ardently antislavery senator leaked the treaty, along with other pertinent documents, to the press.

Among the documents were letters from Calhoun to the British minister in Washington. In them Calhoun underscored the prominence of slavery by expressing deep concern over the British interest in abolition. He repeated the Tyler refrain that abolition in Texas would lead inevitably to abolition in the South, which would endanger the security of the United States. For self-preservation the United States had therefore concluded the treaty. He went further by providing a lengthy defense of slavery. Calhoun's pronouncement made slavery, morally and constitutionally, a legitimate part of the United States. That postulation was explicitly what Adams had long despised and as a congressman had more and more publicly decried.

Ever vigilant, Adams kept watch on Tyler and Texas. In 1842 he pushed for the House to call for the administration to furnish all correspondence connected with Texas. The next year in the Committee on Foreign Relations, he proposed two resolutions to be reported to the House. The first stated that the Constitution gave no authority to any department of government to annex any foreign people or country to the Union. The second declared that any attempt, whether by treaty or congressional act, to annex Texas to the Union would violate the Constitution. It went further by proclaiming if such did occur, the free states should refuse to submit to it. On these the committee did not do as he wished.[11]

He also conferred with individual abolitionists, traveling to London seeking British assistance for the elimination of slavery in Texas. While wishing these men Godspeed and hoping for British action, he avowed that the freedom of his country and even of all mankind depended on direct interference by Britain to accomplish abolition in Texas. Yet he had no faith that Britain would act. In fact, he doubted that it would.[12]

The actual delivery of Tyler's Texas treaty to the Senate in April 1844 dismayed Adams. He defined that day in characteristically hyperbolic terms as the end of human freedom. For him

Texas represented nothing less than the great struggle between slavery and freedom in the world. He also recognized Texas as Tyler's bid for "a popular whirlwind" to keep himself president. And even though he hated the prospect, he did give Tyler high marks for his political acumen and determination.[13]

Yet the Senate surprised him. On June 10 it rejected the treaty by a wide margin. Needing a two-thirds majority for ratification, the treaty failed by more than two to one, 35–16. Only slave-state Democrats stood stalwartly for it; only one of their number cast a nay ballot. Taking the exact opposite stance, slave-state Whigs voted no, with a single exception. Northern Whigs were unanimous in their opposition, while the more southern-oriented northern Democrats barely went for it. The treaty had simply become too tied to Tyler and southern Democrats. Moreover, after the publication of Calhoun's letter, it had become inextricably joined to the expansion of slavery. Although sectionalism did affect the outcome, partisanship wrecked it. Whigs stood almost as one against the hated Tyler.

Adams's thrill over the result matched his earlier despair. He interpreted the Senate vote as a delivery from Almighty God for his country and for liberty. He tempered his joy, however, with an uneasiness that the divine delivery might be temporary. Drawing on his knowledge of Roman history, he contemplated the saving of the Roman republic from the Catiline conspiracy, which proved only preliminary. The triumph and dictatorship of Julius Caesar soon ensued. If the United States conformed to that pattern, the annexation of Texas would take place—followed, in Adams's judgment, by the inevitable conquest of Mexico and the West Indies. His country would then become "a maritime, colonizing, slave-tainted monarchy," with freedom extinguished.[14]

Although Tyler's treaty failed, the Texas debate had a massive impact on the presidential election of 1844 and on the national consciousness. Initially, it appeared that Whigs and Democrats would wage battle for the presidency over the tried economic issues like the tariff and a national bank and with their accepted leaders, Clay and Van Buren. Both men shied away from Texas as dangerous and divisive.[15]

Adams certainly shared that view. He had no doubt that for the third time the Democrats would put forward Van Buren. And he was one with the Whig party that championed his old comrade Clay. With his usual gloomy outlook on national politics, he at first expected Van Buren and the Democrats to regain the presidency. But by the spring of 1844 he became more sanguine about Clay's prospects. He absolutely believed that a Clay victory would be best for the country.[16]

Tyler and Texas, however, wreaked havoc on early plans and predictions. Unsurprisingly, the Texas thunderbolt struck the Democrats first. Tyler and his coterie had closer ties with them; additionally, Texas especially excited southern Democrats. This excitement soon turned into a demand that the party choose a pro-Texas nominee. The strength of southerners in the party gave them significant influence, particularly because a party rule required the successful candidate to receive a two-thirds majority in the nominating convention. Southerners could thwart anyone they opposed.

When Van Buren came out publicly against immediate annexation, southerners blocked his nomination. Instead, the nod went to the first dark-horse presidential nominee in American history, James K. Polk. A stalwart Jacksonian from Tennessee, Polk had been a congressman, moving up to Speaker, and a onetime governor of his state. Moreover, the Democratic platform boomed the annexation of Texas, and both to cement the party's favoring expansion and to appeal to the northerners, it also called for America to occupy all of Oregon, which for two and a half decades had been jointly overseen by Britain and the United States.

The Democratic absorption of Texas along with the nomination of the expansionist Polk ended Tyler's quest. With the Democratic party making Texas its own, the president lost his issue. While the Democrats took his cause, they had no interest in him. They wanted a party loyalist, not a man who had shown no lasting allegiance to any political organization. Tyler had left the Jackson party and had broken up with the Whigs. He ultimately endorsed Polk.

Texas did not unhinge the Whigs as it had the Democrats. The Whigs stuck by their paladin, Clay. For the nomination he faced no serious competition. Yet on Texas he had to shift somewhat. Northern Whigs remained unified against annexation, but southern Whigs coping with ferocious pressure from Democrats urged Clay to modify his anti-Texas position. To do so, Clay prepared three public letters in which he ended up declaring that slavery in Texas posed no insuperable obstacle to acquisition, but he wanted prior agreement from Mexico. In advocating the party's economic program, the Whig platform made no mention of Texas.

During the campaign itself Adams held to his long-standing refusal to become involved in presidential contests. As before, he turned down invitations to speak, even in Boston. Although hopeful that Clay would prevail, he expressed concern about the possible baneful influence of the Liberty party. Formed in 1840, the Liberty party was populated by politically active abolitionists. A number of abolitionists, headed by William Lloyd Garrison, shunned politics, while others like James G. Birney thought abolitionists should participate in elections, running and supporting only committed abolitionists. In 1844 Birney himself carried the Liberty banner, as he had in 1840.

Adams had observed their activity in Massachusetts. Opposing the basic premise of the Liberty faithful, he declared that they simply threw away their votes, thus their influence. He believed they should back the candidate closest to them. And in 1844 that was Clay, his former ally whom he respected. In his judgment a vote for Birney was in reality a vote for Polk, a man much more objectionable to abolitionists than Clay.[17]

The results of the election devastated the Whigs. In a close contest Polk bested Clay. He took the popular vote by the thin margin of 38,000 out of the 2,700,000 cast, though he garnered a clear majority in the Electoral College, 170–105. Texas surely mattered, undoubtedly affecting the outcome in some southern states. The Liberty party also made itself felt. In New York State Birney gained 15,814 votes, while Clay lost to Polk by only 5,100, depriving him of the state's electoral votes; they would have given him the presidency. Yet the closest student of the election argues that while both Texas and the Liberty party had a noticeable impact, neither separately nor together did they determine the outcome. More important, the Democrats amassed considerably more new voters, chiefly from the foreign born and Roman Catholics, than the Whigs.[18]

Despair best describes Adams's reaction to Clay's loss. He attributed the defeat to a myriad of causes, among them the fraud of slave representation, the Liberty party, and Irish Catholics. Even so, he placed a singular onus on the Liberty party, averring that it cost Clay New York State and the election. According to him the party had caused irremediable damage and deserved the ruin it had undoubtedly brought upon itself. Of the ultimate meaning there could be no doubt, "the victory of the slavery element in the Constitution of the United States." Convinced that "nothing less than the interposition of Omnipotence" could save the country, a mystified as well as despondent Adams still trusted that Providence "intend[ed] it for wise purposes, and will direct it to good ends."[19]

As for himself, Adams could not clearly see what "the further events" of the election might be. But he mused it might signal his retirement from public life. Anyway, he noted "the doom of nature" would soon accomplish his removal. Yet, acting now, he might, if he could, mount the energy to improve the outcome.[20]

Although the Whig debacle left Adams dispirited, he did achieve two victories in late 1844. Standing for reelection for a seventh term in the House, he faced both Democratic and Liberty opponents. The Liberty adherents in his district worried him. Describing a visit to his home by a committee of the party, he commented on their courtesy and their thanking him for his service. At the same time they announced they would run their own man, for they could only support someone who agreed with them on everything. That affirmation Adams refused to make.[21]

This situation made him anxious about the possibility that he could lose. He just hoped he could meet that contingency, if it came, with the proper spirit. He worried needlessly, however. The great majority in his district stood by him. Easily retaining his seat, he took 57 percent of the popular vote. The Democrat gained 38 percent; the Liberty candidate was far behind with a mere 5 percent. A relieved and thrilled Adams recorded that his emotion almost overcame him.[22]

Just over three weeks after his constituents had handsomely sustained him at the polls, Adams was in Washington for the convening of the second session of the Twenty-Eighth Congress. Almost immediately he once more pushed for the repeal of the gag, the House rule he considered utterly pernicious. Since 1840 he had moved closer to that goal. Over time the congressional lineup on the rule had been getting increasingly sectional. More and more northern Democrats had begun voting with northern Whigs against it rather than with their southern counterparts. After the southerners spurned Van Buren for the presidential nomination, northerners felt even more justified in going against their slave-state colleagues.

On December 3 Adams moved a resolution to repeal the gag, the twenty-fifth standing rule of the House. An effort to lay the motion on the table failed, 81 yeas to 104 nays. The question was then put on the resolution itself. By 108 to 80 the House voted to rescind the gag, with more than three-quarters of the northern Democrats on Adams's side. After a long, arduous endeavor of seven years, he had finally succeeded in eliminating the gag. It had been put in place chiefly because of his insistence on presenting a cascade of antislavery petitions. The struggle to get rid of it had taken almost a decade. Overjoyed, he invoked heaven: "Blessed, forever blessed, be the name of God!"[23]

John Tyler disrupted Adams's new prayer of thanksgiving almost upon his offering it. Still president, Tyler would remain in office until March 4, 1845, during the normal life of the lame-duck second session of the Twenty-Eighth Congress. In that position he could revive his pro-Texas offensive. Interpreting Polk's victory as popular endorsement of annexation, he overlooked or disregarded the myriad forces that determined the electoral outcome. In his message to Congress he articulated that view and urged revisiting Texas. Aware of the impossibility of obtaining the two-thirds majority required for a treaty in the Whig-controlled Senate, he proposed a different path to annexation. He pointed out that the Constitution authorized Congress to admit new states. With that provision in mind, he advocated adding Texas to the Union as a state, which would negate any need for a treaty or a two-thirds majority. Congress could admit a state by resolution. That procedure called for approval by the House as well as the Senate, but only by a simple majority in each chamber.[24]

In addition to giving Tyler a new opportunity to achieve his goal of making Texas part of the United States, Polk's triumph also influenced northern Democrats. The pro-Texas Polk, who had supplanted the anti-Texas Van Buren, had been elected president. With the party platform advocating Texas and a president chosen upon it, the Democrats now stood foursquare behind expansion into Texas. Furthermore, the party's patriarch lent his still potent voice to the cause of Texas. In letters to party leaders, some of which became public, Andrew Jackson, now seventy-eight years old, insisted on annexation, asserting that an American Texas was essential for the safety and security of the United States. Slavery should not be an impediment. For Adams that his hated foe embraced another nefarious cause meant that he acted in character. In sum, Tyler could assume significant congressional support from northern Democrats as well as southern.

Democratic solidarity would be indispensable for Tyler's plan to succeed. The president could count on the House, which the Democrats controlled, for a positive vote. The Senate, however, was a different matter, for it had a Whig majority. And with all northern Whigs and most southern Whigs still against Texas, a

Democratic phalanx was a necessity. Yet, even with it, for a resolution to pass, more than the single slave-state Whig who had
voted for Tyler's treaty would have to come over to the Texas side.

In the midst of this renewed push for Texas, Adams maintained his ground. In fact, in the aftermath of the treaty's failure, he had expressed apprehension about the future. "Moloch and
Mammon have sunk into slumber," he recorded with ripe biblical
imagery in his diary. At the same time, he feared that what he
branded "the Texas treason" had been stopped only temporarily.
He envisioned a continued drive for Texas would transform his
country into "a conquering and warlike nation." He could foresee
a large and costly military establishment and even a "Captain-
General for life." The law of force would replace the Constitution,
and "the skeleton forms of war and slavery will stalk unbridled
over the land." He cried out in typical style to his God to prevent
such a fate.[25]

In an address to his constituents prior to the election, he made
an especially powerful public pronouncement equating Texas
with slavery. He contended that Tyler and Calhoun wanted to for-
tify slavery in the South against worldwide condemnation of the
wicked institution. Declaring Texas and slavery interwoven in
the Democratic flag, he proclaimed to his audience, "Freedom or
death should be inscribed on yours." Going for Texas, he shouted,
would mean "a war for slavery." "Freedom! Peace! Union!" must
be your watchwords, he broadcast. His final exclamation: "If Ato,
hot from Hell, will come and cry Havock—fight—fight and con-
quer, under the banner of universal freedom!"[26]

In the House of Representatives, Tyler's call for Texas generated a flurry of activity. Several congressmen prepared resolutions favoring annexation, each different in details. Adams found
all appalling. According to him Congress was on the verge of jet-
tisoning the Constitution. A pessimism settled over him because
he deemed the contest hopeless. Even so, he confided to his diary
that he could think only of Texas. Yet he could not decide whether
to join the battle. "I am crushed between the upper and the nether

millstone," he wrote, "of the question to speak or not to speak in this debate."[27]

Finally, after gathering reference materials, he addressed the House on January 24. In a labored effort in which he strayed from the chief intention, he recounted the errors of earlier speakers, commented on the Louisiana Purchase, and justified his past conduct. Just as he reached what he considered the crux of his remarks, he found himself checked by the one-hour time limit set for members' speeches. Before closing, however, he made an honest admission, but one that undermined his constitutional argument. He said he would go for Texas tomorrow if slavery were forbidden and Mexico consented.

On the next day he attempted to explain that avowal, which he insisted had been misunderstood. In his words, "the slave mongers" had distorted his statement. He had barely gotten underway when an adversary objected on the grounds that he had already made an explanation. Thus the Speaker should require him to relinquish the floor. "I did not give him time," Adams recorded, "but concluded."[28]

Expansionist fervor now gripped the nation in the mid-1840s, and neither Adams nor anyone else could stop the momentum for Texas. On January 28 the House passed an annexation resolution by the comfortable margin of 120 to 98. Partisanship more than sectionalism governed that result. All southern Democrats and more than half their northern colleagues lined up on the aye side. Only eight slave-state Whigs joined them. Every northern Whig along with a majority of their southern brethren populated the losers' column. In sum, 90 percent of Democrats said yes, while 80 percent of Whigs said no.

In the Senate the partisanship was even more pronounced. With the Whigs dominant, endorsing Texas would entail both Democratic unity and Whig defections. Debate made clear that the House-passed resolution could not gain the necessary support. As the March 4 adjournment neared, an amendment was advanced that would permit the president either to offer Texas statehood under the House plan or to negotiate a new treaty. That provision attracted a few wavering northern Democrats to Texas. The final tally was 27 to 25 for the amended resolution; three slave-state Whigs joined the unified Democrats.

The House quickly gave its assent to what the Senate had done, and on March 1 John Tyler signed the joint resolution. Few in Congress appeared to have anticipated that Tyler would act on the authority granted the president. Most solons assumed he would leave the decision to Polk, who would take office in three days, on March 4. And Polk had certainly led northern Democrats to believe he would opt for renegotiation. The vice-president no one had ever expected to become president, however, had no intention of passing on the opportunity to finish what he had started. On the day before his term expired, he dispatched a courier to Texas with the offer of immediate admission into the Union as a state. The new president did not disavow Tyler's action. On Texas, James K. Polk stood precisely where Tyler did. And Texas responded affirmatively, and admission as a state took place before the year's end.

An aged and increasingly weakened Adams perceived catastrophe. To him the victory of the Texas forces signaled what he had long decried, the power of representatives given to slavery by the Constitution, his detested three-fifths provision. His strenuous opposition for a decade had come to naught. Ruminating about the common American assumption that the voice of the people and the voice of God were one and the same, he could only deduce that the Texas measure enjoyed "the sanction of Almighty God." Yet he did not lose all hope. He refused to accept that any act based on "fraud and rapine," which in his view underlay the Texas enterprise, could forever hold God's blessing. The ultimate outcome, he mused, might mightily disappoint those who embraced Texas. Having sown the wind, he opined, they might reap the whirlwind. For that whirlwind he could look only to the inscrutable ways of God: "The Being who left to the will of man the improvement of his own condition will work it out according to His own good pleasure."[29]

That Polk affirmed Tyler's decision did not surprise Adams. He had been contemptuous of the new president since their time as colleagues in the House. To him Polk was no more than another proslavery, southern Jacksonian. Almost on the eve of Polk's inauguration as president, Adams penned a brutal description—"he is sold soul and body to that grim idol, half albino, half negro, the compound of Democracy and slavery, which, by the slave-representation in Congress, rules and ruins the Union."[30]

Reacting to the inaugural ceremonies, Adams stuck to his opinion. He rejected invitations both to the place assigned him as a former president at the inauguration itself and to the inaugural balls. He proudly commented that he witnessed none of the rites. He could be civil, however, when the occasion warranted. A month after Polk's taking office, the two men—Tennessean and New Englander—saw each other after a church service. Adams recorded that the president walked up to him and courteously shook hands. He reported that he responded with equal politeness.[31]

Nor would their relationship improve. When Polk had a mutual friend invite Adams to dine with him, the congressman informed the intermediary that Andrew Jackson had made a similar offer, which he had declined. Likewise, he sent his decline to Polk. More than two years into his presidency Polk noted that Adams had not called on him. The Lear-like New Englander never would.[32]

Adams loathed the Democratic party in general and Polk along with Tyler in particular because in his judgment they had turned a matter central to him as well as to his country into something evil. Nothing had been more pivotal to him in his political career than territorial expansion. As a freshman U.S. senator he brooked the opposition of the Federalist party that had elected him to support Thomas Jefferson's purchase of Louisiana. Then as secretary of state he had been instrumental in obtaining Florida, which brought all territory east of the Mississippi River under American control. Moreover, that same treaty made the United States a continental nation, giving it for the first time a boundary on the Pacific Ocean. Not least, as president he had tried, albeit unsuccessfully, to add Texas to the national domain.

Now, however, he feared that the annexation of Texas presaged a move by the country, with military force if necessary, toward absorbing at least part of Mexico as well as Caribbean islands. According to him the architects of this territorial extension had one overriding motive, the expansion of slavery. A slave Texas meant more political strength for the southern interests that he charged with the undoing of the country. Bringing in more territory from farther South would only exacerbate that dire situation.

Adams had long envisioned substantial American territorial expansion, but the insertion of slavery altered the situation. The Monroe Doctrine, which he authored, certainly did not preclude what now alarmed him, but in the early 1820s he evidently never seriously contemplated the convergence of slavery and expansion. He apparently did not see the Louisiana Purchase or his Florida treaty as significant precedents.

When Adams condemned the South and southerners, he usually focused on southern Democrats. Southern Whigs never boarded the expansion-bound express. As Adams well knew, on both the Texas treaty and the resolution, most southern Whigs voted as he had. Still, because he perceived the Democratic party as dominating the South, he generally identified southern Democrats and the South as identical.

In an October 1845 letter to a friend he articulated his dismay. Grieving, he wrote, "Our Country if we have a Country is no longer the same." In his view the virtue of the early republic had been corrupted. His words: "The Polar Star of our Foreign Relations at that time was Justice, now it is Conquest." Even worse, "her vital spirit was then Liberty, it is now Slavery."[33]

Yet in his righteous despair he compartmentalized. Both the Louisiana Purchase and the Transcontinental Treaty expanded slavery. While the former had not caused him much concern about slavery, the latter had done so. He had even confided to his diary that had he been a senator from Massachusetts, he would have opposed the treaty he had negotiated because of slavery in Florida. But he rationalized that as secretary of state he served the nation, and the treaty was essential for the nation.

Regarding slavery, Texas fundamentally replicated Louisiana and Florida. Adams could point out that both France and Spain permitted slavery whereas Mexico had outlawed the institution. Yet the American settlers in Texas possessed slaves, whom they had no intention of giving up. In addition, he could note that while France offered Louisiana for sale, Mexico strenuously opposed American annexation of Texas. In Florida, however, he had used Jackson's military exploits and the threat of even more to cajole Spain to accept American terms. Thus for him to lament that the expansion of slavery and the possible implementation of armed force in Texas and potentially beyond exploded American values meant that he had either to rewrite history or, at the least, to whitewash it. He surely would have to expunge his portion of it.

The mission for the historian is to explain why his viewpoint changed so dramatically. There is no single explanation. Since his time in the Senate and even since Monroe's administration, his antipathy toward the South and southern influence in the nation had grown exponentially and continued to grow. His animus toward Jackson and his Democratic party greatly exceeded that which he felt toward Jefferson and his Republican party. Additionally, for a number of years he evidently believed, as did many of the Founders, that a growing United States would eventually jettison slavery. By the 1830s, however, he had concluded that eventuality was in the far-distant future, if it were ever to come. His optimism expired. And slavery, that sinister national boarder who had been restricted to a backyard shed, had now moved into the front parlor. He dreaded it would destroy the Union, and only the sword could kill it—both horrors.

Of course, his shift also involved personal issues. The Jackson party had made him a one-term president. Accordingly, Jackson and his southern legions had ended his national career, just as an earlier southern chieftain and his cohorts had turned out his father. From his perspective, the virtues of character, liberty, freedom, and national aspirations epitomized by father and son had been spurned by representatives of slavery. Not only were both Jefferson and Jackson slave owners, but the three-fifths clause of the Constitution underlay their political power and that of their followers. Thus, as he saw it, the infinite possibilities for American greatness had been and were being blocked by narrow, provincial minds—all to protect slavery. Thus he could no longer anticipate a lengthy life for his country with both slave and free states. The past could not be preface for the future. He hungered for a slave-free America.

The elimination of a national political future also enabled Adams to disregard any interests beyond local boundaries. Even statewide office in Massachusetts was beyond his grasp. His boundaries were thus circumscribed by his own congressional district. Within it he stood as a colossus. With constituents bound to him by a shared heritage and common values along with pride in having an Adams represent them, John Quincy Adams enjoyed enormous political freedom to press personal beliefs, to indulge personal prejudices, and to pursue personal political goals with little fear of repudiation by those who sent him to the House.

Adams's despondency blended with disgust over what he considered the merger of expansion and slavery and did not signal unyielding aversion to the former. He continued to believe in its value, provided it could be severed from slavery. The advent of the Oregon question revealed his loyalty to expansion embedded in his vision of American exceptionalism.

In his Transcontinental Treaty, Adams had acquired from Spain a claim to the Pacific Northwest. The southern line rested on at that time Spanish California; the northern reached all the way to Russian Alaska, 54 degrees 40 minutes of latitude. Yet Britain exercised authority over much of the northern country, or Canada, as far south as the Columbia River, currently separating the states of Oregon and Washington. In 1818 the United States and Britain signed an agreement stipulating joint occupation. During Adams's presidency in 1827 this agreement was renewed, with the provision that each signatory could with a year's notice announce revocation of joint occupation. This huge territory became known as Oregon.

Oregon moved to the fore in the mid-1840s for two reasons. First, by the end of 1844 some five thousand Americans had settled in that portion which became the state of Oregon. That fact changed the dynamic, for previously most whites in the region had been British engaged in the fur trade dominated by a British company, with its headquarters on the northern bank of the Columbia River. Their numbers never exceeded around seven hundred. The American immigrants looked to their homeland for political allegiance, not to Britain. Second, in their election platform in 1844 that called for Texas, the Democrats put themselves on record as demanding all of Oregon, all the way to fifty-four forty, as the slogan decreed. The inclusion of Oregon was designed to appeal to northern Democrats by demonstrating that the party embraced national expansion, not just sectional. The glory and reward of expansion would extend to all Americans, not only southerners.[34]

Accordingly, President Polk could not concentrate solely on Texas, while ignoring Oregon. Without question Texas was paramount for him, for he saw it as essential to reach his ultimate goal, California, which like Texas had come to Mexico after that country successfully rebelled against Spain. Polk had every intention of having the American flag fly over California. To accomplish that end, he was willing to negotiate a purchase price. Yet, if diplomacy and dollars failed to move Mexico, he would not back away from military force. Still, for him to succeed he had to keep both his northern and southern partisans with him. Thus, he had at least to make overtures toward fulfilling his party platform's insistence on an American Oregon.

Even so, in his quest for Oregon, Polk did not display the determination and drive that characterized his avid pursuit of Texas and California. In fact, most scholars agree that he masked his willingness to compromise on Oregon's northern boundary with rhetoric echoing the Democratic platform's cry for all of it. Earlier the Tyler administration had suggested to Britain the extension of the American-Canadian boundary east of the Rocky Mountains, which ran along the forty-ninth parallel, on to the Pacific Ocean, except leaving on the western end all of Vancouver Island in Canada. In the summer of 1845 the British minister in Washington received a similar proposition from the Polk administration, to divide Oregon along the forty-ninth parallel, which he rejected.

In his annual message to Congress in early December of that year, an angry Polk insisted that Congress enact a law notifying Britain that in one year the United States would terminate the joint-occupation agreement. By doing so he energized Democratic expansionists who interpreted his step as the first toward American occupation of the entire territory. In April 1846 Congress did pass a notice of termination, though with an addition encouraging the two countries to reach a peaceful accord.

That provision did not trouble Polk, for he wanted Britain to tender a settlement. He never contemplated going to war with Britain for the far north of Oregon. Even before the congressional act pronouncing the end of joint occupation, he had informed the British that he would entertain a compromise proposal. But before responding, he would put it before the Senate to get its advice. He did not want to stand accused of abandoning on his own the all-Oregon crusade. In May the British did revive the forty-ninth parallel offer. Following the scenario he had provided the British, he referred it to the Senate for its opinion before either agreeing to it or signing it, the usual presidential custom. The Senate quickly gave its consent by 38–12, more than the two-thirds majority required for a treaty. Polk thereupon prepared a treaty partitioning Oregon according to the British plan, had the Senate ratify it, and in June forwarded it to London. The matter was finally settled.

Through the diplomatic maneuvering and congressional debate, Adams stood stalwart for Oregon. Early on, however, he perceived that Polk had no intention of holding fast to any demand for all of Oregon. Within ten days of the president's asking Congress to revoke joint occupation, he correctly predicted that Polk would back down from his advanced position and accept a compromise.[35]

Although Adams expected the president to equivocate, he never did. In the House he intended to vote for termination, but not take an active part in the debate, believing he had to conserve his waning strength. He had no doubt, however, about the validity of American ownership all the way to fifty-four forty, and he stood steadfast for that line. He remained quiet until he was challenged on the legitimacy of the American claim.

On February 9, 1846, Adams, with a visage containing the skin and wrinkles of an old man approaching seventy-nine, rose and addressed the House. He began by requesting members to defer briefly all technical questions about title. Then he had the clerk of the House open the Bible that lay on his table. Thereupon he gave directions on the passages from Genesis and Psalms that he desired read. All had to do with God's giving man dominion over the earth. The final verse he wanted members to hear came from verse eight of the second Psalm: "Ask of me, and I shall give thee the heathen for thine inheritance, and the uttermost parts of the earth for thine possessions."[36]

According to Adams, the Bible gave undisputed authority for his chosen people, the Americans, to possess Oregon. In his interpretation the United States had no natural right under God to Texas, for it legally belonged to Mexico. But his country did have that right to Oregon, once proper notice had been given to Britain, and the one year had passed. Just as his Puritan forebears had thought of their settlement in Massachusetts as a city on a hill, he envisioned his country as that city, provided slavery stayed outside its boundary. Americans would bring civilization and Christianity to a wilderness. His fervor for Oregon matched his earlier zeal while negotiating the Transcontinental Treaty. He, then, remained an evangelist for American expansion, provided slavery was excluded.

Only after this theological lesson did he turn to the historical and juridical evidence that supported the American right to all of Oregon. He put forth a lengthy catalog, which included exploration, treaties, charters, and occupation. In closing, however, he returned to his theme of a special America. "I want the country for our western pioneers," he asserted. They have the qualities essential to make a great nation in Oregon, "which must come to us as a fountain comes from its source, of free, independent sovereign republic instead of hunting grounds for the Buffaloes, braves, and savages of the desert." That very afternoon the House passed the joint resolution of termination, with the conciliatory proviso, by 163–54. Adams cast his vote with the majority.

A few weeks later he repeated his view in a letter to a British acquaintance. He declared that Americans simply desired "to fulfill the commands of Almighty God to increase and multiply, and replenish, and subdue the Earth." Using the word "earth," he made clear that he referred specifically to the land contiguous to the United States. Continuing, he emphasized that Americans intended to civilize and Christianize a wild land populated by "savage hunters." Americans would turn that wilderness into a cultivated garden. In contrast, he depicted Britain as wanting only to stunt American growth and prolong the domination of "the buffalo and the bear." The distinctive character of his country he did not doubt.[37]

Even before final realization of the treaty settling the Oregon dispute, President Polk had launched the country into a war with Mexico. The location of the Texas boundary with Mexico provided the ostensible cause, but in reality his determination to acquire California was paramount. The acquisition of Texas sparked a treacherous relationship between the United States and Mexico. Upon annexation, Mexico as promised broke diplomatic relations with the United States. Not recognizing Texan independence, Mexico still considered the area a Mexican province. Never doubting that

Texas had become an integral part of the United States, the president in the summer of 1845 dispatched units of the U.S. Army there to underscore American sovereignty.[38]

Thereafter Polk moved on two fronts. He instructed the American commander General Zachary Taylor to station his force as close to the Rio Grande as prudence permitted. Proclaiming the Rio Grande as the Mexican-Texan border, Polk backed the position of Texas. In contrast, Mexico insisted that the Nueces River, some 150 miles to the north, was the true dividing line because it had marked the southern frontier of the Mexican province of Texas. Initially, Taylor did halt at the mouth of the Nueces, where it met the Gulf of Mexico, but in January 1846 he received orders to advance all the way to the Rio Grande.

While Polk put American soldiers on the ground in Texas, he also engaged in a diplomatic effort to gain his great ambition, California, along with New Mexico as a land bridge between it and Texas. In the fall of 1845 he sent a minister plenipotentiary to Mexico City with authorization to offer five million dollars for New Mexico and twenty million dollars for California as well as assume the debts owed to Americans. With Mexican politics already unstable, no government could afford to make a pact with the American aggressor. In fact, the government refused to receive Polk's envoy. By early 1846 it became apparent that the attempt to realize the president's goal with dollars had failed.

In spring Polk concluded that no diplomatic overture could succeed. Mexico would sell none of its territory, whereas it was clear that the Oregon matter would be peacefully resolved. The president then determined to use force to gain what he wanted. He prepared a war message, stating that Mexico had rebuffed his minister plenipotentiary and had failed to pay legal debts. Yet, before he could submit it to Congress, a communication reached Washington reporting that a clash between American and Mexican troops resulting in American casualties had occurred on the northern side of the Rio Grande—in Polk's judgment on American soil. Thereupon he revised his call for war to declare that a state of war already existed. Mexico had invaded the United States and killed American soldiers. He asked Congress to declare war, indicating that Mexico had begun it.

The bulk of Congress did not share the president's enthusiasm for hostilities. Many doubted the legitimacy of the president's assertion about a Rio Grande boundary. Whigs generally opposed the contention that Mexico had begun an aggressive war, but they were unwilling to oppose appropriations for Taylor's force. In the House, however, their desire to provide funds without the accompanying proposition that Mexico had initiated hostilities did not succeed, by a tally of 123–67. Then the actual declaration carried, by 174 to 14, with 35 abstentions, mostly northern Democrats. The 14 votes all came from northern Whigs. Among their number was Adams.[39]

For Adams, Polk's militancy came as no surprise. In his judgment the president simply carried on the policy commenced by Tyler of pushing forward the expansion of slavery in whatever manner necessary. He interpreted Polk's insistence on a continental vision of adding California to Oregon to enhance the American presence on the Pacific as little more than a sham. The real motive was to expand slavery. According to him a combative slaveholding president had made the United States a bellicose power. The entire affair tarnished his country. "The nation is plunged into an unjust and wicked war," he lamented.[40]

For Adams the situation had an eerie familiarity. During the War of 1812 numerous New England Federalists, Massachusetts men among the leaders, had been against both the declaration and the prosecution of that conflict. Adams had not been on their side. In contrast, even though he was in Russia, he vigorously supported the necessity to fight Great Britain. And he had no kind words for those with whom he disagreed. In his mind that war defended the honor of his country, whereas this one with Mexico dishonored his homeland. He depicted the two in starkly different terms. War in 1812 was defensive to protect American independence; war in 1846 was offensive to expand slavery.

In the House, however, his votes revealed a divided mind. He did say no to the declaration itself, though he was one of only four congressmen to back the bill of a Massachusetts colleague to have all American troops withdrawn from Mexico and the resulting peace agreement contain no demand for reparations or territory. He also consistently opposed proposals to honor or reward the officers and men serving into Mexico. Yet he never cast a nay ballot on the appropriations measures essential to sustain the war effort. He refused to have American soldiers in a foreign land abandoned, but he would countenance no accolades or rewards for them.[41]

The specter of slavery followed the onset of war. Late in the hot summer of 1846, during the final days of the congressional session, Polk made a surprise request for an additional two million dollars to assist in obtaining California and New Mexico. A small band of northern Democrats decided to stand against their president. Anger over a number of issues, ranging from expanding slavery to patronage, prompted them. They decided to vent their unhappiness by amending the bill to prohibit slavery in any territory gained with the money.

An obscure congressman from Pennsylvania, David Wilmot, presented the no-slavery amendment, which would become famous as the Wilmot Proviso. Coming at the close of the session, it did not generate great excitement at the time. Many thought it represented simply disgruntled Democrats slapping at this president, rather than a serious move against slavery. Adams did, however, speak for it. He said he favored it but did not think it necessary. Because slavery had been outlawed in Mexico, it would remain so in any area that came to the United States. According to him, only a provision in a treaty ceding territory or positive congressional legislation could reinstitute the institution. And he did not expect either to occur.[42]

In congressional voting the Wilmot Proviso smashed through partisan lines. Although it passed the House with Adams in the affirmative, it failed to come up in the Senate before that chamber adjourned. More important, only a handful of House members crossed sectional lines. Northern Whigs and northern Democrats joined together in getting it through, while southern Whigs and southern Democrats found themselves allied in the minority.

The proviso did not disappear, however. Wilmot brought it back during the next congressional session, the second of the Twenty-Ninth. Once more Polk was looking for an additional appropriation; this time he wanted three million dollars to defray unusual expenses in arranging a peace. Because of his health, Adams did not take a central part in the legislative struggle. He did, however, vote for the proviso, which passed the House, again with a sectional divide, as did a separate appropriations bill. This time the Senate rejected the proviso while approving the appropriation. Upon that measure's return to the House, the antislavery forces tried to reinsert the proviso. Once again Adams voted with them, but they failed. By a narrow margin the proviso went down. Party pressure persuaded enough northern Democrats to side with the South to kill it. The three million dollar bill passed, with nothing said about slavery.

Although Adams had succeeded in Congress neither in stemming the march toward war nor in legislating to prohibit slavery in any new territory, he maintained his prowess in his congressional district. Prior to returning to Congress for the second session of the Twenty-Ninth Congress, he had to stand for reelection. In Massachusetts the election for members of the Thirtieth Congress, which would not convene until December 1847, occurred in November 1846.

Despite the attenuation of his physical strength, he welcomed renomination by his fellow Whigs. In fact, when the Whig convention of the Eighth District unanimously gave him its nod, Adams felt honored. That these constituents supported his cause on Oregon and the Mexican-American War as well as expressing general confidence in him delighted their venerable neighbor. At the polls the seventy-nine-year-old congressman won his ninth consecutive election to the House of Representatives. As usual, he amassed a substantial majority, winning 62 percent of the vote against a distant-second Democrat and a far-behind third Liberty man. He would be eighty when the Thirtieth Congress met.[43]

While Adams struggled futilely in Congress against policies he believed disastrous for his country, he had to contend with the physical frailties increasing with his age. In the spring of 1844 he thanked God for granting him partial respite from the inflammation of his eyes and the fluttering of his hands.[44]

But in that same summer an accident brought a severe setback. Returning in July from Washington to Massachusetts, he and Louisa stepped off a train in Jersey City, New Jersey, in order to board a ferry that would carry them across the Hudson River to New York City. Night had fallen, and in the gloaming he fell. He recounted that while falling he had the distinct sensation that he had been killed. Hearing a shriek from his wife, he feared that she too had lost her life. He described these two perceptions as sparking "a thrill of horror of which I knew not that the human frame was susceptible."

Neither of them suffered life-threatening damage, however. Even so, both sustained painful injuries; the sixty-nine-year-old Louisa Adams fainted at the scene. Bruises, cuts, and sprains afflicted their bodies. Although they were able to continue their journey northward, Adams detailed their slow recovery. A week later he declared himself still crippled, though he could get around. By that time his wife could leave her room. Almost a month passed before he felt himself able to walk normally. Yet within a few days he had a second fall, this time at his home in Quincy. Not nearly so severe as the first, it still set him back somewhat. Ten more days went by before he thought himself basically recovered from his injuries.[45]

But more than falls debilitated him. In 1845 he devoted considerable space in his diary to his physical decline. He made particular mention of sciatica giving him a bad time. Because these maladies interfered with his long-standing habit of bathing in rivers or oceans, he ordered a Bates's Chamber Shower Bath from Boston. Its height required that it be set up in a cellar because the ceilings in the regular rooms were too low. Labeling his first use as "startling," he said it jarred his body. Never becoming satisfied, he dispensed with it after two weeks. At that point he moaned that he could probably no longer look forward to bodily comfort on earth.[46]

A year later, at seventy-nine, he gave himself a bleak diagnosis. In July 1846 he lamented that the remainder of his life seemed surely to consist of "a long disease." Yet at times he felt unpredictably stronger and more optimistic.[47]

In late November his physical state took a terrible blow when he suffered a stroke. Walking with a companion in Boston, he suddenly sank to his knees, unable to continue. With that person's assistance he made it back to the home of Charles Francis, whom he was visiting. His physician came and put him to bed, where he remained for several days. He said he felt little pain, though his bodily power had been suspended. At the same time he could barely exercise his mind. Upon getting the news, Louisa Catherine, already in Washington, rushed back to his side. She found him not so invalided as she had dreaded, but still a sick man. She remained with him until he was able to travel to Washington, which did not happen until February 1847.[48]

This event made a powerful impression upon him. He confided to his diary that from the moment of the stroke he dated his decease and believed he was of little use either to himself or to his fellow man. He averred that he would entitle anything further that he might write "a posthumous memoir." Despite that grim lamentation, he never contemplated resigning his seat in the House, which remained a life-sustaining force until the end.[49]

Adams's physical decline affected both his exercise regimen and his tending the garden at his Quincy home. In the summer of 1845 he sadly noted that he could no longer enjoy his seasonal swimming and bath in both river and sea. Yet the next year in Washington he returned sporadically to his favorite spot on the Potomac for a five- to ten-minute swim. Once he saw three young men there; in his hearing one of them said, "There is John Quincy

Adams." His stroke ended this activity. Even before then, he had in the fall of 1845 sharply curtailed his gardening by closing the nursery and basically ending his hands-on involvement.[50]

The diary thus became a casualty of his deteriorating health. By the summer of 1845 his handwriting was becoming increasingly shaky. On September 30 he recorded that he could no longer write with his own hand. Accordingly, he would have to discontinue his daily journal. It went on, however, though with others handling the pen. Beginning in October he employed two granddaughters as amanuenses, taking dictation from him. Even so, their contributions did not extend beyond August 1846.

Contemplating his now interrupted personal record, which since his youth had been fundamentally his most confidential friend, Adams thought about what it might have been. If only his Creator, he mused, had awarded him the intellectual powers given to some individuals, then his diary might have become "next to Holy Scripture, the most precious and valuable book ever written by human hands." That would have put him among the major benefactors to his country, and even to humanity. But, sadly, he did not receive "the conceptive power of mind" that would have enabled him to reach that level. As always, he found himself falling short. He lamented he had not improved the gifts that had been bestowed on him as he "might have and ought to have done."[51]

In that same August of 1846 he once again began making his own entries. Most were quite brief, with a few longer ones interspersed. After the stroke they became mostly fragmentary, and those only at intervals. The final entry is dated January 4, 1848. In sum, after 1846 the forceful narrative that had characterized his personal documentary for some six and a half decades disappeared.[52]

Portraits in the 1840s captured his changing physical appearance. Edward Marchant's of 1843 presents a man without the deep creases and wrinkles of advanced age. Only his head is depicted, with his eyes looking beyond the frame, in seeming contemplation. In contrast, George Caleb Bingham's painting done the next year renders him with a furrowed brow and deep lines by nose and mouth, and a dark gaze, directed straight at the viewer. This portrait conveys him with a more serious or troubled look.

The next two artists found a different man. In 1845 George P. A. Healy painted a more robust-looking Adams, emphasizing plump jaws and broad shoulders. Both his eyes and his mouth appear more relaxed than in the Marchant and Bingham efforts. Moses Billings in 1846 displays a man of less severe mien. The eyebrows are not so dark nor the facial lines so deep. Moreover, Billings captured the same aquiline nose and severe look that Copley did in his famous 1796 portrait of the young Adams. This likeness was clearly completed before his stroke in November.

In the last known portrait of Adams, by William Henry Powell in 1847, one sees an old man with sunken eyes peering into the distance and a mouth turning down at the corners. Here his face clearly reflects the effects of the stroke he suffered the previous year.

In addition to sitting for portraits, the son of a Founding Father also made himself available for the new invention, the daguerreotype. An early image taken in 1843 or 1844 by Philip Haas captures him in stark profile, with his wrinkled face and balding head in outline against a black background. As in some of the later oil portraits, the down-sloping lines beside the nose and mouth leave no doubt of his age. The most familiar daguerreotype of Adams was taken in 1843 by Albert Southworth at home in Quincy. In it he sits informally by a fireplace next to a small table piled with books. His legs crossed, his hands held together, his chin lowered to his chest, he looks downward but far away.

Finally, Matthew Brady, the most famous photographer of his time, had Adams for his subject. The result exists today only in photographic reproductions and an engraving. The presumed date of 1847 places this picture sometime after Adams's stroke. Sympathetic and almost poignant, this likeness has him facing forward with downcast eyes as in the Southworth image. The elderly gentleman seems to be looking inward, contemplating his mortality.[53]

As noted, Adams's illness kept him in Massachusetts past the opening of Congress in December and into the new year of 1847. On January 1 he began taking carriage rides through Boston and by late in the month commenced taking short walks and attending worship services. In early February he felt sufficiently recovered to leave for the capital. On the thirteenth when he entered the House, the congressman speaking suspended his remarks. Thereupon the members rose as one to give him an ovation; even his opponents participated in the cheering welcome. The grand old man had once again joined their number.[54]

Even though he again took his seat, Adams's days as a force in the House were decidedly over. In the debates over the extension of slavery, whether they concerned the Wilmot Proviso or the incorporation of the Missouri Compromise line in the organization of the Oregon Territory, he took practically no part, except to cast his vote consistently against even the suggestion of the hated institution. He could not imagine, however, giving up public office and told his wife so. She was convinced that his doing so would immediately end his life.[55]

Only once did he rise to make extensive remarks. An effort to provide a $50,000 indemnity to the owner of the *Amistad*, in a case that he thought had been settled, brought forth a stinging riposte. No legitimate reason existed, he declared, for the country to make such a payment. It would entail a robbery of Americans to pay slave traders. The proposal went down to a thunderous defeat.[56]

Now his political thoughts often turned to his son. Charles Francis Adams had become active in Massachusetts politics and like his father aligned with the Whig party. In the mid-1840s, however, Whigs in the state began to divide between a more conservative element that became known as the Regular or Cotton Whigs, who wanted to maintain good relations with their southern counterparts, and those designated as Conscience Whigs, who assumed a stern antisouthern stance, including adamant opposition to any extension of slavery. The former group contained the titan Daniel Webster and other old-line stalwarts in their camp, while the latter attracted chiefly younger and more radical men, Charles Francis among them.[57]

The father looked on with pride. He had long considered Webster and those like him as unprincipled. Moreover, he identified one faction with "public principle" and the other with manufacturing and commercial interests. When Charles Francis spoke against Texas in the Massachusetts legislature, Adams worried about the political tribulation awaiting the young man. The elder prayed, "May the God of Justice be his guide and guard, and the God of Mercy protect him." When Charles Francis participated in the outcry against Whigs from his state who had voted to declare war on Mexico, the parent applauded.[58]

Even so, this political bond had its tension. In 1847 when, because of perceived family obligations, Adams supported a leading Regular for Speaker of the national House, a rift occurred. Taking the other side, a distressed Charles Francis urged his mother to try to ensure that his father's opposition ceased. The father-son clash did not linger, however. The two men shared a basic affinity. Just six weeks before his death, Adams penned his son a most affectionate letter, closing, "A stout heart and a clear conscience and never despair." Adams would have been proud, for, upholding his father's legacy, Charles Francis became a substantial figure in national and state antislavery politics.[59]

With Congress adjourned late in the spring, John Quincy and Louisa Catherine again headed north toward Quincy. There on July 11 he observed his eightieth birthday. Just over two weeks later, on the twenty-seventh, he enjoyed a family-arranged celebration for his and Louisa Catherine's fiftieth wedding anniversary. Through much trial he and she had remained stalwart for each other. He stayed in Quincy until November, when he once more made the familiar journey to Washington. The first session of the Thirtieth Congress would convene in early December.[60]

Adams was in his seat on December 6 when Congress began its initial session. His thoughts focused more than anything else on what he saw as the wrong direction his country was headed in and the chief reason for that movement. For some time he had been fulminating about what he stigmatized as "the insolent domination of the Southern slave-breeders." Gloomily for him, he could foresee no breaking of that yoke during his lifetime. In his opinion constant victories by the political forces of slavery had made of the Constitution "waste paper."[61]

With the war in Mexico still raging and more territorial expansion on the horizon, he could envision no change. He expected nothing from the Democrats. According to him the southerners in the party placed the interests of slavery paramount, while their place-greedy northern counterparts were in thrall to their southern masters. Perhaps the Whigs might offer hope. Northern Whigs had been overwhelmingly on his side, almost as a phalanx against the agenda of the slaveholders. Even many of the southern Whigs opposed Texas and the war with Mexico, as well as acquiring territory from Mexico. Moreover, in the elections held in 1846 and 1847, the Whigs had won a majority in the House. The party, in his judgment, needed only a solid antislavery leader for the 1848 campaign. He even told a major northern Whig that if the party would choose an antislavery man as its standard-bearer, he would be "prepared to make my testament."[62]

In this instance, as was his wont, he equated the slavery politics he loathed with southern Democrats, absolving southern Whigs, though many among them owned slaves. That distinction also held in his judgment of individuals; he rarely demonized southern Whigs as he routinely did southern Democrats. Yet, as the votes on the Wilmot Proviso demonstrated, the southerners in his party had no less sectional loyalty when they perceived threats to slavery or southern rights. Adams would surely have been appalled had he lived to see his party's choice for 1848—General Zachary Taylor, a hero from the war he despised and a large slave owner. Although his precise course cannot be known, he would never have supported Taylor.

As for the root cause of the terrible state of the country, Adams had given up his earlier belief that somehow slavery could be peacefully purged from the Union. Dating this judgment precisely is impossible, but it surely occurred at some point in the mid-1830s. He had become persuaded that the South would never willingly give up the evil system. Furthermore, he was convinced the institution would not expire "until it goes down in blood."[63]

He coupled these dire reflections with the accurate premonition that his own life was nearing its close. A few years earlier, while bemoaning the probable natural decline of his hometown of Quincy and his family with it, he wondered, "Will prayer to God preserve the branches and shoots from my father's stock?" That sorrowful pondering triggered an outburst, "What a phantasmagoria is human life!"[64]

During the winter of 1847–48 war still raged in Mexico while both Democratic and Whig politicians coped with issues raised by the Wilmot Proviso as they looked ahead to the presidential election of 1848. During those weeks Adams maintained his regular appearances in the House and his practice of attending worship services on Sundays; at the same time he pondered his perilous condition. His wife reported that he kept telling her that he was a dying man. He did make sketchy entries in his diary and write a few letters. Still, the end was near. On February 20, 1848, he made what would be his final posting in the diary. In a quavering hand he penned a four-line poem:

> Fair Lady, thou of human life
>> Hast yet but little seen.
> The days of sorrow and strife
> Are few and far between.[65]

On the twenty-first he took his carriage from the house on F Street to the Capitol, just as he had done since the first of the year. The members now always treated the generally quiet elder statesman with great respect. That day he once again registered his opposition to the war he blamed on President Polk and on an aggressive slavocracy. The House took up a resolution praising

American soldiers for their performance on the battlefield. It also specified that eight gold medals be struck and presented to generals. Telegraphing his dissent, Adams voted in the negative. That his side lost did not surprise him.[66]

The resolution had barely passed when, at one thirty, his right hand grabbed at the corner of his desk as he sagged to the left. The congressman seated next to him caught the collapsing body. Colleagues rushed to his side. Several members placed him on a sofa and carried him to the rotunda, at the center of the Capitol. This second stroke left him conscious, but unable to move or speak. Four physician members attended him. On the sofa he was moved to the east portico and finally to the Speaker's office, with only physicians and close friends permitted inside. There he briefly regained consciousness, calling for his old foe and then colleague Henry Clay. Clay, ten years younger, came in and wept at the side of the stricken man. Louisa Catherine had been summoned to come quickly from their home. Even though she did so, she arrived too late to hear the final words he ever uttered:

"This is the end of earth, but I am composed." He lingered in a coma for two days, until just past seven in the evening of the twenty-third, when he breathed his last.[67]

CODA

"Proceed—Persevere—
Never Despair"

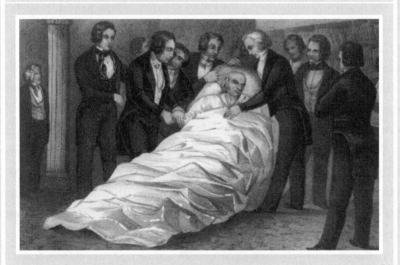

DEATH OF JOHN QUINCY ADAMS IN THE CAPITOL—
LITHOGRAPH, 1848

ONGRESS TOOK PARTICULAR NOTICE OF ADAMS'S
death, much as it did during his life, though on this occasion
in full reverence. When the House convened the following
day, the Speaker made the official announcement to a full
chamber and crowded gallery. Thereupon the senior surviving member of the Massachusetts delegation declared

that a national treasure had been struck down, a man whose public service spanned the history of the country. He then gave a condensed biographical sketch that concluded with a series of resolutions stipulating actions the House should take. But before they could be considered, five more congressmen spoke briefly. Their number included Isaac Holmes of South Carolina, an inveterate opponent during Adams's life. Now, however, Holmes extolled history and memory: "When a great man falls, the nation mourns; when a patriot is removed, people weep." After these statements the House unanimously approved the resolutions detailing the steps it should take to commemorate the deceased. The Senate engaged in an identical process.[1]

The body lay in state in a room in the Capitol. Thousands of mourners passed by the casket. The arrival of Charles Francis from Boston on the twenty-forth interrupted the public viewing. For a short while the sole surviving son remained alone at the bier. Afterwards the long line began once again to move.

On Saturday, February 26, the funeral took place in the House. Just before noon the Speaker called for order. The bell on Capitol Hill began to toll. Led by President Polk, dignitaries filed into the chamber. After him came the justices of the Supreme Court, senior military officers, the diplomatic corps, and the senators. The nation, however briefly, seemed one again. Then Charles Francis along with other family members entered and occupied seats reserved for them. A bereaved Louisa Adams, then seventy-three years old, felt herself unable to attend. Later she cried to her diary: "Thy fiat has gone forth O Lord my God: and I am left a helpless Widow to mourn his loss which nothing on the dreary earth can supply." She would live four more years, dying in Washington at seventy-seven in 1852.[2]

The coffin, adorned with a spread eagle, was brought in and placed on a catafalque directly in front of the speaker. It carried an inscribed plate:

JOHN QUINCY
ADAMS

BORN

An Inhabitant of Massachusetts

July 11, 1767

DIED

A Citizen of the United States,

in the Capitol, at Washington,

February 23, 1848,

HAVING SERVED HIS COUNTRY FOR

HALF A CENTURY, AND ENJOYED

ITS HIGHEST HONORS.

At the behest of the Massachusetts solons, Senator Daniel Webster had written it. The inscription would have pleased Adams, albeit not so much the hand that composed it.

The House chaplain opened the service with prayer. A choir in the ladies' gallery sang a dirge. For his biblical text he chose a passage from the Old Testament book of Job (chapter 11, verse 17 and the first part of 18) that surely befitted Adams: "And thine age shall be clearer than the noonday; thou shalt shine forth, thou shalt be as the morning." Then the chaplain preached a commonplace sermon praising Adams for his virtue and service and thanking God for giving the country such an estimable man. A final hymn ensued.

With the completion of the service, the solemn cortege moved from the chamber to the east front of the Capitol, where a long procession formed to escort the body to the Congressional Cemetery, almost two miles away. Military companies, a band, chaplains of the House and Senate, other clergymen, family members, luminaries from the president onward to judges, diplomats, military officers, and government officials followed by an array of others made up the company. The funeral carriage located near the front of the line was flanked by twelve honorary pallbearers, John C. Calhoun among them. Upon reaching the cemetery, the casket was placed in a vault where it would remain until its transport to Quincy.

President Polk remarked on the impressive ceremony. He described the funeral procession as the longest he had ever seen. "It was a splendid pageant," he recorded.[3]

News of Adams's stroke and death spread rapidly through the nation. Not long before, the telegraph had put the nation's capital in almost instantaneous contact with places as far north as Portland, Maine, as far west as the Ohio River valley, and as far south as Richmond, Virginia. Newspapers promptly pushed the baleful tidings into even farther corners. Throughout the country Americans could share practically simultaneously in events taking place in Washington in a fashion heretofore impossible. Everywhere the press reported on the public funeral at the Capitol.[4]

One week after the temporary internment at the Congressional Cemetery, the casket was loaded onto a funeral train for the trip to Massachusetts. So many times in the preceding decades as a senator, a cabinet officer, a president, Representative Adams had made the journey north to home in Quincy. This time, in addition to the family, the House-appointed Committee of Escort, one member from each state and territory, accompanied the remains.

The grave assemblage appeared to have embarked on a pilgrimage transporting a sacred relic to its final resting place. As the black-draped carriage snaked along the 500-mile course to its destination in Massachusetts, flags flew at half-mast and people stood with heads bowed. At station stops businesses closed. In major cities the committee even had the coffin removed and positioned in a prominent place, such as Independence Hall in Philadelphia, where citizens could view it and honor the memory of the man therein. And multitudes came to pay their last respects. In New York City thousands lined the streets to catch a glimpse of the procession along the four-mile route to city hall, where the body lay in state. The massive outpouring of esteem displayed along the way mightily impressed the Illinois congressman on the Committee of Escort. Later he wrote that no such demonstration had previously occurred and would not again until the death and funeral train of Abraham Lincoln, and in that he would be right.[5]

Finally, after the funeral formalities had riveted the nation, on March 11 the procession arrived in Boston. A heavy rain prevented a planned public agenda, but a local committee met the train and transferred the casket to Faneuil Hall, the temple of city and state politics, where several held forth on the deceased's contributions and merits. For the short ride to Quincy the local and national committees shepherded the remains aboard a special train pulled by a new locomotive, the John Quincy Adams. There in the church long attended by the Adamses, the local pastor and family friend conducted the final service. Truthfully, he informed the congregation, "Mr. Adams' character is no exotic. It is the genuine growth of the American soil." Then his coffin was borne across the street to the simple church graveyard where John Quincy Adams was laid to rest in the family vault.[6]

The respect and honors marking the passage from Washington exceeded those Adams had experienced in life, even compared with the mass outpouring of sentiment on his western tours back in 1843. In this instance as in that, certainly not everyone of those signaling their regard agreed with all his political positions, but they did recognize and take pride in his sovereign status as the one man whose link to the Founding Fathers was most indelible. He had actually known George Washington, Benjamin Franklin, Thomas Jefferson, James Madison, James Monroe, and, of course, his own father. Those men stood foremost among the venerated Founding Fathers, the individuals who had created the United States. Moreover, all of them, Franklin and Jefferson excepted, had appointed him to responsible offices. No other American of that time could match John Quincy's rich lineage. His American contemporaries saw him in the words of a Virginia congressman as "a living bond of connexion [*sic*] between the present and the past."[7]

In expounding upon the meaning of Adams's life, everyone did not send the same message. The intellectual and religious milieu in which his own worldview had been formed and nurtured eulogized him with images and words that would surely have produced his assent, maybe tempered by his mother's reproach of any expression of vanity. Concentrated in the North, especially New England and areas to the west heavily influenced by the New England diaspora, the overwhelmingly Whiggish clerics, academics, and politicians praised him as a Christian patriot. For them he not only provided continuity with the Founding Fathers; just as importantly, he embodied the glories of Puritanism in his commitment to Christian values, liberty, and industry.

In their scenario, as in his, the nation lamentably had rejected their noble way. In contrast, these mourners depicted a country commandeered by men from the backward South stained with vices like slavery, dueling, and indolence. The America of 1848 was only thirteen years away from the shots fired at Fort Sumter, and almost a score of years had passed since Adams had left the presidency. In their judgment the United States had devolved from the heroic founding. These sentiments chorused Adams's own during his later years. And in the 1850s they would become the watchwords of the Republican party.[8]

In the disparaged region, however, Adams's death did not generate sectional recrimination. Mentions of his New England heritage and loyalty did inevitably occur, but assertions quickly followed that even his personal and political enemies admitted that "a great spirit had departed." From Virginia to Texas, Democratic and Whig newspapers alike celebrated him as "eminent a statesman" and a patriotic American. They portrayed him as a great man whose death was "a national calamity." While acknowledging political differences, commentators declared that those disagreements should not preclude recognition of his lengthy public service and his devotion to his country. As "almost the sole existing link" to the colonial and Revolutionary past, his life connected those distant times to the present. In short, with few exceptions, editors, politicians, and correspondents honored his memory.[9]

The encomiums from the slave states would surely have pleased John Quincy Adams because they characterized him as he did himself. Yet they would also have puzzled him, at least somewhat. He would never have backed away from his slashing assault upon what he deemed "the transcendent power of slavery and the slave-representation." While during his later years his unsuccessful onslaught left him pessimistic about the near future, he never lost hope that a just God would not permit the American vessel to capsize.[10]

Somehow under Providence's guidance America would find the way to a slave-free future. Counseling Charles Francis on the ongoing struggle against what he regarded as the menacing navigation of the slavocracy, Adams commanded, "Proceed—Persevere—Never despair—don't give up the ship."[11]

ACKNOWLEDGMENTS

—

THIS BOOK MAY SEEM STRANGE COMING FROM SOMEONE WHO has spent his career writing about the South. For its genesis I claim no credit. That belongs to Aida DiPace Donald, the widow of the eminent historian David Herbert Donald. My teacher and mentor both as an undergraduate and a graduate student, David subsequently became a friend. Some years back, David had committed himself to a study of John Quincy Adams. Unfortunately he passed away before his John Quincy had taken form. Following his death Aida asked me whether I would take on the project. I agreed, with the understanding that I would not begin until the completion of my then manuscript-in-progress, which became *We Have the War Upon Us: The Onset of the Civil War, November 1860–April 1861*, published in 2012. My agreement generated both excitement and trepidation— excitement because working on John Quincy Adams would take me into new and challenging territory, trepidation for the same reason.

Most generously Aida sent me the materials David had gathered in his preparation. There were precious few notes and no specifics on his intended approach, except for the general notion that he expected to focus on character. Yet he had accumulated an impressive body of research materials, including a massive collection of photocopied scholarly articles and contemporary documents, including speeches. That bounty was of incalculable value to me. I hope that, in part, this book stands as a memorial to David.

As it has been throughout the years, my own Louisiana State University, including the Department of History, has liberally supported my research and writing. That generosity has persisted with this book, continuing into my retirement. My chair Victor Stater has been, as usual, most accommodating, even to an emeritus professor. Likewise, Darlene Albritton, who manages the departmental office, never flagged in her willingness to assist. A former LSU undergraduate, Samantha Arcement, ably performed typing duties. Two LSU graduate students, one past, one present, provided indispensable research assistance—Dr. Michael Robinson and Jeff Hobson, who also contributed notably to getting the manuscript ready for publication.

I also want to express my gratitude to the Massachusetts Historical Society for making its Adams manuscripts so accessible. In the 1950s the society made available on microfilm the Adams Family Papers, which the Middleton Library at LSU possesses, and more recently it digitized the diary of John Quincy Adams. Both were essential for me.

I benefited immensely from the aid given by three fellow historians. My colleagues Andy Burstein and Gaines Foster along with my longtime friend Mike Holt all read the manuscript with care. Their critical scrutiny has certainly made this a significantly better book.

My editor at Liveright, Bob Weil, has championed this undertaking and me from the beginning. His amazing editorial astuteness and thoroughness have few, if any, equals. I prize my association with him. Also at Liveright, Marie Pantojan assisted in so many ways to shepherd my manuscript through the publication process. Additionally, I had the immense good fortune to have the services of Otto Sonntag as copy editor and Amy Medeiros as project editor, both extraordinaire. Ike Williams and Hope Denenkamp provided much appreciated help with contractual matters.

My dedication underscores all that I owe to my wife, Patricia Holmes Cooper, who has always been there.

All the people named in these acknowledgments had a hand in the making of this book. Yet it is mine, and I accept full responsibility for it.

NOTES

—

ABBREVIATIONS
USED IN NOTES

AA   Abigail Adams

Adams Papers   Adams Family Papers, Massachusetts Historical Society, Boston, MA

AFC   L. H. Butterfield et al., eds., *Adams Family Correspondence*, 13 vols. (Cambridge, MA, 1963–)

AJ   Andrew Jackson

AJP   Daniel Feller et al., eds., *The Papers of Andrew Jackson*, 10 vols. (Knoxville, TN, 1980–)

BAJ   John S. Bassett, ed., *Correspondence of Andrew Jackson*, 7 vols. (Washington, DC, 1926–35)

Bemis   Samuel Flagg Bemis, *John Quincy Adams*, 2 vols. (New York, 1949, 1956)

CFA   Charles Francis Adams

CFA Diary   Marc Friedlander et al., eds., *Diary of Charles Francis Adams*, 8 vols. (Cambridge, MA, 1964–)

CG   *Congressional Globe*

Clay Papers   Robert Seager II et al., eds., *The Papers of Henry Clay*, 10 vols. and supp. (Lexington, KY, 1959–92)

Diary   Diary of John Quincy Adams, Massachusetts Historical Society, Boston, MA

JA   John Adams

JAW   Charles Francis Adams, ed., *The Works of John Adams . . .* , 10 vols. (Boston, 1850–56)

JCC   John C. Calhoun

JCC Papers   Clyde N. Wilson et al., eds., *The Papers of John C. Calhoun*, 28 vols. (Columbia, SC, 1959–2003)

JQA   John Quincy Adams

JQA Diary   Robert J. Taylor et al., eds., *Diary of John Quincy Adams*, 1779–1788, 2 vols. (Cambridge, MA, 1981)

LCA   Louisa Catherine Adams

LCA   Judith L. Graham et al., eds., *Diary and Autobiographical Writings of Louisa Catherine Adams*, 2 vols. (Cambridge, MA, 2013)

M & P   James D. Richardson, comp., *A Compilation of the Messages and Papers of the Presidents*, 10 vols. (Washington, DC, 1896–99)

Memoirs   Charles Francis Adams, ed., *Memoirs of John Quincy Adams, Comprising Portions of His Diary from 1795 to 1848*, 12 vols. (Philadelphia, 1874–76)

Portraits   Andrew Oliver, *Portraits of John Quincy Adams and His Wife* (Cambridge, MA, 1970)

RD   *Register of Debates*

TJ   Thomas Jefferson

TJ Papers   Julian P. Boyd et al., eds., *The Papers of Thomas Jefferson*, 42 vols. (Princeton, NJ, 1950–)

Webster Papers   Charles M. Wiltse et al., eds., *The Papers of Daniel Webster*, 6 vols. (Hanover, NH, 1974–84)

Writings   Worthington Chauncey Ford, ed., *The Writings of John Quincy Adams*, 7 vols. (New York, 1913–17)

NOTES

PREFACE

1   William H. Seward, *Life and Public Services of John Quincy Adams . . .* (Auburn, NY, 1849).

2   Bemis, *John Quincy Adams and the Foundations of American Foreign Policy* (New York, 1949) and *John Quincy Adams and the Union* (New York, 1956); Charles N. Edel, *Nation Builder: John Quincy Adams and*

the Grand Strategy of the Republic (Cambridge, MA, 2014); and John Lewis Gaddis, *Surprise, Security, and the American Experience* (Cambridge, MA, 2004), chap. 2.

3   Howe, *What Hath God Wrought*... (New York, 2007); also see William Lee Miller, *Arguing about Slavery: The Great Battle in the United States Congress* (New York, 1996).

4   Kaplan, *John Quincy Adams*... (New York, 2014); Traub, *John Quincy Adams*... (New York, 2016). There have also been two recent biographies of John Quincy's wife, Louisa Catherine Adams. Margery M. Heffron's *Louisa Catherine: The Other Mrs. Adams* (New Haven, CT, 2014) includes excellent treatment of the wife's political value to her husband. Unfortunately, because of the author's death, the book stops in 1825. Louisa Thomas's *Louisa: The Extraordinary Life of Mrs. Adams* (New York, 2016) concentrates on the wife's emotional life.

CHAPTER 1: *"To Bring Myself into Notice"*

1   For genealogy consult Paul C. Nagel, *John Quincy Adams: A Public Life, a Private Life* (New York, 1997), 3–7. Robert Middlekauff, *The Glorious Cause: The American Revolution, 1763–1789* (New York, 1985), chaps. 3–12, remains a valid, reliable account of the events leading to the American Revolution.

2   *Memoirs*, I, 5, VII, 325 (quotations), VIII, 545, XII, 203.

3   Ibid., VIII, 156–57; Woody Holton, *Abigail Adams* (New York, 2010), 69.

4   JQA to JA, June 2, 1777, *AFC*, II, 254.

5   JA to JQA, July 27, Aug. 11, 1777, ibid., 289–91, 307.

6   Diary, Sept. 10, 1845.

7   For the American diplomatic mission and the negotiations, see Stacy Schiff, *A Great Improvisation: Franklin, France, and the Birth of America* (New York, 2005). David McCullough in his *John Adams* (New York, 2001), chaps. 4 and 5, focuses sharply on JA.

8   JQA to AA, Sept. 27, 1778, *AFC*, III, 93.

9   JQA to Charles Adams, Oct. 2, 1778, and Charles Adams to Thomas Adams, Oct. 3, 1778, ibid., 102–3; JQA to AA, Sept. 9, 1778, ibid., 88; Bemis, I, 10.

10   AA to JA, March 8, 1778, *AFC*, II, 403.

11   AA to JQA, June 10 [?], 1778, ibid., III, 37–38.

12   JQA to AA, April 12, 1778, ibid., II.

13   JQA to AA, April 20, May 5, Aug. 11, 1778, ibid., 16, 29, 73.

14   JQA to AA, Sept. 27, 1778, ibid., 92–93.

15   JQA to AA, June 5, 1778, ibid., 33.

16   JQA to Arthur Lee, May n.d., 1779, *Writings*, I, 1.

17   JQA to AA, Nov. 6, 1778, June 14, 1779, *AFC*, III, 116, 205; JQA to AA, Feb. 20, 1779, ibid., 176.

18   *JQA Diary*, I, xxxvii; AA to JQA, Jan. 19, 1780, *AFC*, III, 268.

19   *JQA Diary*, I, 2–10, provides some detail on the voyage.

20   Ibid., and *Memoirs* entire.

21   *JQA Diary*, I, 13–34 (quotation 25).

22   JQA to William Cranch, March 17, 1780, *AFC*, III, 309; JQA to JA, March 16, 1780, and JA to JQA, March 17, 1780, ibid., 307–9.

23   AA to JQA, Jan. 19, March 20, 1780, ibid., 268–69, 310–13.

24   JQA to JA, March 21, 1780, and to AA, Sept. 10, 1783, ibid., 314, and V, 244.

25   AA to JQA, May 26, 1781, ibid., IV, 136–37.

26   JA to JQA, Dec. 20, 1780, Feb. 12, 1781, and JQA to JA, Dec. 21, 22, 1780, ibid., 39, 40, 45, 80.

27   JA to JQA, Dec. 28, 1780, May 14, 1781, ibid., 56, 114.

28   *JQA Diary*, I, 66, 70, 72, 75 n.

29   Ibid., 91–101.

30   Ibid., 101–53 passim (ball on 136); JQA to JA, March 4, 1782, *AFC*, IV, 286–87.

31   JA to JQA, Dec. 14, 1781, April 28, 1782, *AFC*, IV, 263, 317.

32   AA to JQA, Nov. 13, 1782, ibid., V, 37–39.

33   JQA to AA, July 30, 1783, ibid., 221.

34   *Portraits*, 17–18; *Memoirs*, II, 649–50 (June 22, 1814); JA to JQA, May 14, 1783, *AFC*, V, 160–61.

35   JA to JQA, May 14, 1783, *AFC*, V, 160–61.

36   JA to JQA, May 19, 1783, ibid., 162–63.

37   JA to JQA, May 14, 1783, ibid., 160–61.

38   *JQA Diary*, I, 187–94.

39   Ibid., 197–207; JQA to Elizabeth Cranch, April 18, 1784, *AFC*, V, 322.

40   JQA to JA, June 6, 15, 18, 1784, *AFC*, V, 339, 343, 347–48.

41   JA to JQA, June 21, 1784, ibid., 351.

42   *JQA Diary*, I, 209–24 passim, 262 (May 4, 1785 quotations 224, 262); TJ to James Monroe, March 18, May 11, 1785, *TJ Papers*, III, 44, 148–49.

43   JQA to William Cranch, Dec. 14, 1784, *AFC*, VI, 32–33.

44   *JQA Diary*, I, 256 (April 26, 1785).

45   JA to Benjamin Waterhouse, April 24, 1785, cited in *Writings*, I, 20 n.; JQA to JA, April 2, 1786, *AFC*, VII, 129.

46   JQA to JA, April 2, 1786, *AFC*, VII, 130; Elizabeth Smith Shaw to AA, March 18, 1786, ibid., 93.

47   JQA to JA, April 2, 1786, ibid., 130; JQA to AA, May 15, 1786, ibid., 163–64; JQA to Elizabeth Cranch, April 9, 1786, and to Thomas Adams, July 2, 1786, ibid., 134–35, 230; *JQA Diary*, II, 48 (June 12, 1786), 317 (Nov. 14, 1787).

48   Mary Smith Cranch to AA, April 22, 1787, *AFC*, VIII, 15–16.

49   JQA to William Cranch, Aug. 20, 1786, ibid., VII, 323–24; *JQA Diary*, II, 196 (April 8, 1787, quotation), 179–81 (March 20, 1787), 250–52 (July 7, 1787).

50   JQA to Elizabeth Cranch, April 9, 1786, *AFC*, VII, 134–35; *JQA Diary*, II, 24, 29 (May 1, 8, 1786).

51   *JQA Diary*, I, 296–338 passim, 339 (Oct. 12, 1785), II, 208 (April 18, 1787), 240 (June 15, 1787, quotation), 245 (June 25, 1787), 303 (Oct. 15, 1787).

52   Ibid., II, 92 (Sept. 7, 1786), 107 (Oct. 2, 1786).

53   JQA to JA, June 30, 1787, *Writings*, I, 30, also 34; *Memoirs*, VI, 77 (Oct. 7, 1822); Mary Smith Cranch to AA, July 21, [1787], *AFC*, VIII, 132.

54   JQA to George Sullivan, Jan. 20, 1821, *Writings*, VII, 89; *Memoirs*, IX, 354 (April 26, 1837); *JQA Diary*, II, 243 (June 20, 1787).

55   *JQA Diary*, II, 104 (Sept. 29, 1786).

56   Ibid., 253 (July 11, 1787).

57   JQA to JA, Aug. 30, 1786, *Writings*, I, 26; JA to JQA, Jan. 10, July 20, 1787, *AFC*, VII, 428, VIII, 130; Cotton Tufts to JA, June 30, 1787, ibid., VII, 101–2.

58   JQA to William Cranch, May 27, 1789, April 7, 1790, *AFC*, VIII, 301 (quotation), IX, 41, 43; *JQA Diary*, II, 331 (Dec. 21, 1787), 372–73 (March 8, 1788).

59   *JQA Diary*, II, 302–3 (Oct. 12, 1787), 357 (Feb. 7, 1788, quotation), 373 (March 8, 1788); JQA to AA, Dec. 5, 1789, *AFC*, VIII, 445–46. For the 1780s Middlekauff, *Glorious Cause*, 603–41, provides solid coverage.

60   *JQA Diary*, I, 356 (Nov. 12, 1785), II, 297 (Oct. 1, 1787), 307 (Oct. 22, 1787), 391–92 (April 16, 1788).

61   Holton, *Abigail*, 278–79; Abigail Adams Smith to JQA, June 6, 1790, *AFC*, IX, 68–69; JQA to AA, Nov. 20, 1790, ibid., 145–46; JQA to William Cranch, April 7, 1790, ibid., 41–42; Diary, Nov. 18, 1838.

62   JQA to AA, Dec. 14, 1790, *AFC*, IX, 161. Abigail Adams Smith to JQA, Feb. 10, Aug. 8, 1788, ibid., VIII, 229, 290; *JQA Diary*, II, 343 (Jan. 12, 1788).

63   *JQA Diary*, II, 343 (Jan. 12, 1788), 427–28 (July 11, 1788), 447–51 (Sept. 5, 1788).

64　JQA to AA, Oct. 17, 1790, *AFC*, IX, 132; JA to JQA, Feb. 9, 19, 1790, ibid., 14, 16.

65　JQA to AA, Oct. 17, 1790, and JA to JQA, Dec. 17, 1790, *Writings*, I, 61 and n. Not until he became a seasoned member of the House of Representatives did he feel comfortable in speaking at the moment.

66　JQA to JA, April 12, 1794, ibid., 185–86; JQA to Thomas Adams, Nov. 20, 1793, *AFC*, IX, 454.

67　JQA to William Cranch, July 12, 1790, *AFC*, IX, 80; JQA to AA, Aug. 29, 1790, ibid., 96.

68　See, e.g., JQA to JA, Oct. 19, 1790, Dec. 8, 10, 1792, Dec. 10, 1793, ibid., 135, 340–41, 348–50, 402–3. For excellent discussion of the origins of partisan politics and the impact of the French Revolution on them, see Andrew Burstein and Nancy Isenberg, *Madison and Jefferson* (New York, 2010), chaps. 7–9, and Gordon S. Wood, *Empire of Liberty: A History of the Early Republic, 1789–1815* (New York, 2009), chaps. 3–5.

69　JQA to JA, April 12, 1794, *Writings*, I, 185–86.

70　Ibid., 65–110, has the Publicola letters; Madison to TJ, July 13, 1791, *TJ Papers*, XX, 298.

71　Fred Kaplan, *John Quincy Adams: American Visionary* (New York, 2014), 112–13; Boston *Independent Chronicle*, Nov. 30, 1792; Boston *Columbian Centinel*, Dec. 19, 1792.

72　*Writings*, I, 48–76, has the Columbus letters.

73　JQA to JA, Jan. 5, 1794, *AFC*, X, 12.

74　JQA to Thomas Adams, June 23, 1793, ibid., IX, 438.

75　Diary, July 4, 1793; *Oration Pronounced July 4, 1793 . . . in Commemoration of the Anniversary of American Independence* (Boston, 1793).

76　JQA to JA, Feb. 10, 1793, *AFC*, IX, 403; JA to JQA, Feb. 19, 1793, Dec. 14, 1793, ibid., 411, 470.

77　*Memoirs*, I, 31–32 (June 3, 5, 8, 10, 1794); JQA to JA, July 27, 1794, *Writings*, I, 194.

CHAPTER 2: *"Only Virtue and Fortitude"*

1　JQA to JA, July 20, 27, 1794, *AFC*, X, 213–14, 218–22 (quotations from this letter).

2　JQA to JA, Oct. 23, 1794, *Writings*, I, 202–3 (quotations); *Memoirs*, I, 47 (Oct. 18, 1794). For the Jay Treaty consult Andrew Burstein and Nancy Isenberg, *Madison and Jefferson* (New York, 2010), 294–96, 301, 307–9, and Gordon S. Wood, *Empire of Liberty: A History of the Early Republic, 1789–1815* (New York, 2009), 196–98.

3   *Writings*, II passim, and *AFC*, X and XI passim; JQA to AA, June 29, 1795, *AFC*, X, 468 (quotation).

4   JQA to Daniel Sargent, Oct. 12, 1795, *Writings*, I, 419 (quotation); JQA to Charles Adams, Dec. 30, 1795, May 10, 1796, *AFC*, XI, 114, 288.

5   *Memoirs*, I, 142 (Dec. 1, 1795); JQA to Charles Adams, June 9, 1796, *AFC*, XI, 311–12.

6   *Memoirs*, I, 170 (June 30, 1796).

7   Ibid., 171 (June 30, 1796), 177 (July 31, 1796); Diary, day following Feb. 28, 1797; JQA to Charles Adams, April 10, July 6, 1795, *AFC*, X, 413, XI, 3.

8   *Memoirs*, I, 130 (Oct. 28, 1795).

9   JQA to JA, June 27, Oct. 31, 1795, *Writings*, I, 371, 425.

10 JQA to JA, Nov. 25, 1796, ibid., II, 44–45.

11 Diary, Feb. 1, April 1, May 1, 1796; *Memoirs*, I, 172–73 (July 11, 1796).

12 Diary, May 1, 1796. On Johnson and his home as social club, see Margery M. Heffron, *Louisa Catherine: The Other Mrs. Adams* (New Haven, CT, 2014), chaps. 2 and 4, and Louisa Thomas, *Louisa: The Extraordinary Life of Mrs. Adams* (New York, 2016), pt. 1.

13 Diary, Feb. 7, 14, 21, 1796.

14 For Johnson and his family consult Heffron, *Louisa*, chaps. 1 and 2, and Thomas, *Louisa*, pt. 1; *LCA*, I, 37–38.

15 *LCA*, I, 37–43; Heffron, *Louisa*, chap. 4.

16 *Portraits*, 37, 39.

17 Diary, April 18, 1796.

18 AA to JQA, Feb. 29, Aug. 10, 1796, *AFC*, XI, 61–62, 356–58; JA to JQA, Aug. 7, 1796, ibid., 354–55.

19 JQA to AA, May 5, 1796, ibid., 286.

20 My discussion of the courtship is based chiefly on numerous letters between JQA and LCA between the summers of 1796 and 1797, printed ibid., 304–578 (specific citations only for quotations). Also see *LCA*, I, 44–47.

21 LCA to JQA, July 24, Sept. 30, 1796, *AFC*, XI, 337–38, 385–86.

22 JQA to LCA, Aug. 13, Nov. 21, 1796, ibid., 358–60, 410–12.

23 Heffron, *Louisa*, 74, 95–102, covers Joshua Johnson's business affairs.

24 *Memoirs*, I, 188 (day at end of Dec. 31, 1796).

25 JQA to LCA, July 9, 1796, *AFC*, XI, 333.

26 JQA to LCA, May 12, 1797, and LCA to JQA, May 26, 1797, Adams Papers.

27 Diary, July 12, 1797; *LCA*, I, 47.

28   JQA to JA, July 22, 1797, Adams Papers; JQA to AA, July 29, 1797, *Writings*, II, 192.

29   JA to JQA, Nov. 3, 1797, *Writings*, II, 173–74 n.

30   *LCA*, I, 50–51, 197; Diary, Oct. 9, 1797.

31   Diary, July 29, Aug. 19, 1797.

32   JA to JQA, June 2, 1797, *JAW*, VIII, 545.

33   JQA to AA, May 25, 1800, *Writings*, II, 456.

34   Diary, Jan. 31, Feb. 10, 1799.

35   Ibid., March 21, July 14, 1798, Nov. 17, 1797, Dec. 31, 1800. Prior to this time the diary has little about religion.

36   *LCA*, I, 55, 84.

37   Ibid., 101–2, 131, 143–44.

38   Ibid., 59, 95.

39   Bemis, I, 95, 96.

40   *Memoirs*, I, 240–41 (editorial comments), 313–14 (Sept. 20, 1804); *Letters on Silesia* . . . (1804; Elibron Classic, 2007); Paul C. Nagel, *John Quincy Adams: A Public Life, a Private Life* (New York, 1997), 122; Diary, July–Sept. 1800.

41   JQA to JA, Nov. 25, 1800, *Writings*, II, 480.

42   JQA to Thomas Adams, Dec. 3, 1800, ibid., 485.

43   Diary, April 12, 1801; *LCA*, I, 154.

44   JQA to Rufus King, Oct. 31, 1801, *Writings*, III, 1.

45   *Memoirs*, I, 247 (Sept. 21, 1801).

46   JQA to LCA, Oct. 8, 1801, Adams Papers; Heffron, *Louisa*, 139.

47   *LCA*, I, 164–65.

48   Diary, Jan. 8, 1802.

49   *LCA*, I, 157.

50   *Memoirs*, I, 249 (Jan. 28, 1802).

51   Ibid., 250 (April 1, 1802).

52   Diary, Nov. 3, 1802.

53   *An Oration Delivered at Plymouth, December 22, 1802* . . . (Plymouth, 1820).

54   Diary, Dec. 31, 1802.

55   Ibid., April 2, 1803.

56   Everett Somerville Brown, ed., *William Plummer's Memorandum of Proceedings in the United States Senate, 1803–1807* (New York, 1923), 114, 126, 250–51. Robert R. Thompson, "John Quincy Adams, Apostate: From 'Outrageous Federalist' to 'Republican Exile,' 1801–1809," *Journal of the Early Republic* 11 (Summer 1991): 161–83, provides an overview of JQA and political partisanship. For the Jefferson administration and Congress, Burstein and Isenberg, *Madison and*

Jefferson, chaps. 11 and 12, provides a detailed, instructive account. Ronald P. Formisano, *The Transformation of Political Culture: Massachusetts Parties 1790s–1840s* (New York, 1983), chaps. 5–7, covers politics in JQA's home state in the early years of the nineteenth century. Samuel Eliot Morison's *Harrison Gray Otis: The Urbane Federalist, 1765–1848* (Boston, 1969) discusses JQA's Federalist opponents from the perspective of a leader among them in Massachusetts.

57　Diary, Dec. 21, 1804.

58　*Memoirs*, I, 269 (day following Oct. 31, 1803), 311 (March, 25, 1804).

59　Ibid., 276 (Dec. 4, 1803).

60　Ibid., 277 (Dec. 5, 1803), 400 (Feb. 3, 1806), 445 (Jan. 22, 1807).

61　Ibid., 447–48 (Jan. 28, 1807).

62　Ibid., 287 (Jan. 31, 1804); Brown, ed., *Plummer's Memorandum*, 445, 643; Theodore Lyman to Timothy Pickering, Jan. 1, 1804, *Writings*, III, 30 n.

63　JQA to Rufus King, Oct. 8, 1802, *Writings*, III, 8.

64　Ibid., 48–77, has the articles. Quotations in order in the following paragraphs come from 70 and 71. For the stillborn address see ibid., 87–100, and n. 1 on 87.

65　JQA to LCA, June 29, 1806, *Writings*, III, 150; *Memoirs*, I, 443 (July 11, 1806). Donald M. Goodfellow, "The First Boylston Professor of Rhetoric and Oratory," *New England Quarterly* 19 (Sept. 1940): 372–89, remains a solid account.

66　Diary, July 31, 1806, June 13, 1807.

67　Ibid., June 13, 1807, May 21, June 14, 1808.

68　*Memoirs*, I, 550–51 (July 15, 28, 1809).

69　Cambridge, MA: Holland and Metacalf, 1810; a two-volume reprint appeared in 1962. JQA to Thomas Adams, Aug. 7, 1809, *Writings*, III, 334–35.

70　*Memoirs*, II, 148 (Aug. 8, 1810).

71　Ibid., 317 (Nov. 23, 1804), 330–31 (Jan. 11, 1805); Brown, ed., *Plummer's Memorandum*, 606 (no specifics provided).

72　*LCA*, I, 204, 215–16.

73　Ibid., 204, 232–33.

74　Ibid., 212.

75　*Memoirs*, I, 359 (Feb. 27, 1805).

76　*LCA*, I, 220, 262, 269.

77　JQA to LCA, June 30, 1806, ibid., 236, n. 262.

78　Ibid., 255.

79　JQA to James Sullivan, Jan. 10, 1808, and to Thomas Adams, July 31, 1811, *Writings*, III, 186, IV, 161.

80   *Memoirs*, I, 510 (Feb. 1, 1808).

81   B. Gardiner to Rufus King, Feb. 26, 1808, *Writings*, III, 232–33 n.; Woody Holton, *Abigail Adams* (New York, 2010), 349, has the quotation from AA.

82   *Writings*, III, 189–223.

83   JQA to JA, Dec. 27, 1807, *LCA*, I, 264, n. 301; *Memoirs*, I, 509 (Jan. 30, 1808), 512 (Feb. 2, 1808).

84   JQA to Massachusetts Legislature, June 8, 1808, *Writings*, III, 237–38 (1st quotation); *Memoirs*, I, 535 (June 23, 1808), VIII, 121 (March 27, 1829, 2d quotation).

85   JQA to JA, Dec. 24, 1804, *Writings*, III, 100–101.

86   *Memoirs*, I, 501 (Jan. 7, 1808); JQA to JA, Jan. 27, 1808, *Writings*, III, 188–89.

87   Diary, Dec. 12, 1808.

CHAPTER 3: *"Let There Be . . . No Deficiency of Earnest Zeal"*

1   *Memoirs*, I, 543 (day following Dec. 12, 1808).

2   Ibid. (March 2, 1809).

3   JQA to LCA, March 9, 1809, *Writings*, III, 291.

4   *Memoirs*, I, 549 (July 5, 1809), II, 5 (Aug. 6, 1809).

5   Ibid., II, 5 (Aug. 6, 1809); JQA to Robert Smith, July 5, 1809, and to William Eustis, July 16, 1809, *Writings*, III, 329, 332.

6   *LCA*, I, 283.

7   Ibid., 284.

8   JQA to JA, April 30, 1810, *Writings*, III, 424.

9   *Memoirs*, II, 420 (Nov. 4, 1812).

10   JQA to AA, Nov. 30, 1812, *Writings*, IV, 413; *Memoirs*, II, 531 (Oct. 10, 1813).

11   Diary, Jan. 14, 1810; *Memoirs*, II, 331 (Dec. 24, 1811).

12   *Memoirs*, II, 141 (July 16, 1810), 454 (April 3, 1813).

13   Ibid., 313 (Oct. 4, 1811), 73 (Jan. 28, 1810); Diary, Feb. 23, 1811.

14   *LCA*, I, 302, 325–26.

15   JQA to AA, Feb. 8, 1810, *Writings*, III, 396.

16   JQA to AA, Dec. 13, 1812, ibid., IV, 423–24.

17   Diary, Oct. 1, 1811; *Memoirs*, II, 185 (Oct. 10, 1810).

18   Diary, April 10, 1811, Dec. 28, 1813 (quotation).

19   Ibid., Jan. 1, 17, 19, 28, 29, and Feb. 14, 25, 29, 1814; *Memoirs*, II, 220 (Jan. 28, 1811), 276 (June 19, 1811), 547 (Nov. 18, 1813), 552–53 (Dec. 30, 1813) (quotation), 566 (Jan. 22, 1814), 579–80 (Feb. 25, 27, 1814).

20   JQA to AA, March 25, 1813, Adams Papers.

21 *Memoirs*, I, 111–12 (April 7, 1810), II, 322 (Oct. 31, 1811).

22 JQA to Thomas Adams, Oct. 27, 1810, April 10, 1811, *Writings*, III, 529, IV, 44; Diary, Sept. 22, 1811.

23 *Memoirs*, II, 8–17 (following Aug. 31, 1809). It is not at all clear that his sons ever saw this document. At their ages they would surely have had extreme difficulty understanding its contents. Still, it reveals much about JQA's conception of fatherhood as well as his sense of himself.

24 JQA to Thomas Adams, Sept. 8, 1810, *Writings*, III, 496–98.

25 Diary, Sept. 18, 1811, March 31, 1813.

26 *Memoirs*, II, 282–83 (July 25, 1811).

27 Ibid., 304–5 (Sept. 9, 1811); *LCA*, I, 351.

28 *LCA*, I, 357, 368.

29 Ibid., 373–55.

30 Diary, Sept. 17, 1812; JQA to AA, Sept. 21, 1812, quoted in Fred Kaplan, *John Quincy Adams: American Visionary* (New York, 2014), 276, and on Oct. 24–25, 1812, quoted in Woody Holton, *Abigail Adams* (New York, 2010), 382–83.

31 *Memoirs*, II, 173–74 (Sept. 26, 1810), 351 (March 13, 1812).

32 *The Bible Lessons of John Quincy Adams for His Son*, intro. by Doug Phillips (San Antonio, TX, 2002), 25. This volume collects all the letters to George. Diary, Nov. 25, 1813. In the Diary on Sept. 1, 1811, JQA noted that he was beginning a series of letters upon "subjects of import."

33 *Bible Lessons*, 21, 30.

34 *Memoirs*, II, 356 (April 12, 1812).

35 Ibid., 356–57 (April 12, 1812).

36 Diary, Jan. 27, 1811.

37 *Bible Lessons*, 59, 61; *Memoirs*, II, 297 (Aug. 16, 1811).

38 *Bible Lessons*, 62, 72.

39 Holton, *Abigail*, 357.

40 AA to Madison, Aug. 1, 1810, J. C. A. Stagg et al., eds., *The Papers of James Madison: Presidential Series*, 8 vols. (Charlottesville, VA, 1984–), II, 455–56.

41 Smith to Madison, Sept. 5, 1810, and Madison to Smith, Sept. 12, 1810, ibid., 528–29, 537.

42 Madison to JQA, Oct. 16, 1810, ibid., 582–83.

43 JQA to Madison, Feb. 8, 1811, ibid., III, 156–58.

44 *Memoirs*, II, 274–75 (June 4, 1811).

45 JQA to Madison, June 3, 1811, *Writings*, IV, 93–94; JQA to JA, Aug. 20, 1811, ibid., 182; Paul C. Nagel, *John Quincy Adams: A Public Life, a Private Life* (New York, 1997), 198.

46   JQA to Madison, June 3, 1811, *Writings*, IV, 94–95.

47   JQA to Thomas Adams, April 10, 1811, ibid., 46–48.

48   JQA to JA, June 7, 1811, ibid., 98, 101.

49   JQA to JA, April 30, 1810, ibid., III, 424. Bemis, I, chaps. 9 and 10, has a full discussion of JQA's diplomatic endeavors.

50   JQA to Madison, Jan. 7, 1811, *Madison Presidential Papers*, III, 103–5.

51   *Memoirs*, II, 158 (Aug. 28, 1810).

52   JQA to AA, Jan. 1, March 30, 1812, and to Thomas Adams, Jan. 31, 1813, *Writings*, IV, 284, 302, 427.

53   JQA to AA, June 30, 1811, and to JA, Aug. 31, 1811, ibid., 128–209.

54   *Memoirs*, II, 205–6 (Dec. 30, 1810), 233 (Feb. 24, 1811).

55   Ibid., 233 (Feb. 24, 1811), 374 (May 31, 1812).

56   Ibid., 379 (June 21, 1812), 333 (Jan. 4, 1812).

57   Ibid., 387 (July 11, 1812).

58   Ibid., 647, 649–50 (July 18, 22, 1814). For Ghent both *Memoirs*, II, 652–62, III, 3–144, and the Diary, July 1814–Jan. 1815, contain a myriad of details. Bemis, I, chap. 10, and Robert V. Remini, *Henry Clay: Statesman for the Union* (New York, 1991), chap. 7, provide excellent coverage. More recently Troy Bickham, *The Weight of Vengeance: The United States, the British Empire, and the War of 1812* (New York, 2012), chap. 8, which treats equally both the American and British sides, has enormous value. Older, but more detailed and still worthy, is Bradford Perkins *Castlereagh and Adams: England and the United States, 1812–1823* (Berkeley and Los Angeles, 1962), chaps. 1–8. My account follows them, with notes provided only for direct quotations.

59   *Memoirs*, I, 444 (Jan. 15, 1807).

60   JQA to JA, July 7, 1814, *Writings*, V, 57 n.

61   *Memoirs*, V, 392 (Nov. 7, 1821).

62   JQA to LCA, July 2, 1814, *Writings*, V, 59.

63   *Memoirs*, II, 656–57 (July 8, 9, 1814).

64   JQA to William Crawford, Aug. 29, 1814, quoted in Perkins, *Castlereagh*, 79; *Memoirs*, III, 20 (Aug. 19, 1814).

65   *Memoirs*, III, 27–28 (Sept. 1, 1814).

66   Ibid., 39 (Sept. 22, 1814).

67   Ibid., 41 (Sept. 25, 1814).

68   JQA to AA, Nov. 23, 1814, *Writings*, V, 207.

69   *Memoirs*, III, 101–2 (Dec. 10, 1814).

70   Ibid., 75 (Nov. 29, 1814).

71   Ibid., 61–62, 78–79 (day following Oct. 31, 1814, and day following Nov. 30, 1814).

72   JQA to LCA, Nov. 15, Dec. 2, 1814, *Writings*, V, 189, 225; *Memoirs*, III, 43–44 (Sept. 29, 1814); Diary, Oct. 15, 1814.

73   *Memoirs*, III, 127 (Dec. 24, 1814); Diary, Dec. 31, 1814; JQA to William Eustis, July 25, 1815, *Writings*, V, 329.

74   *Memoirs*, III, 138 (Jan. 5, 1815).

75   *Portraits*, 50–53. The letter to LCA, Jan. 24, 1815, is quoted on p. 52.

76   *Memoirs*, III, 145 (Jan. 26, 1815).

77   Diary, Dec. 21, 1814.

78   JQA to LCA, Dec. 27, 1814, quoted in Margery M. Heffron, *Louisa Catherine: The Other Mrs. Adams* (New Haven, CT, 2004), 239.

79   *Memoirs*, III, 146–48 (Jan. 30, 1815).

80   JQA to AA, March 4, 1816, *Writings*, V, 522–23.

81   *Memoirs*, III, 154 (Feb. 12, 1815).

82   Ibid., 150–78 passim (March 4–23, 1815); Diary, Feb. 7, 1815.

83   LCA's own account written in 1836 is in *LCA*, I, 375–406. Michael O'Brien's *Mrs. Adams in Winter: A Journey in the Last Days of Napoleon* (New York, 2010) is marvelous.

84   *LCA*, I, 405. In his Diary, March 23, 1815, JQA simply recorded that he was "delighted" to see them.

85   Heffron, *Louisa*, 270–71.

86   *Memoirs*, III, 182, 184, 185 (quotation), (March 29, April 5, 9, 21, 23, 1815).

87   Ibid., 384–85 (June 1, 1819), VIII, 40 (June 22, 1828).

88   Ibid., III, 199 (May 16, 1815).

89   Diary, May 25, 1815.

90   Ibid., day following May 31 and July 11, 1815. Heffron, *Louisa*, chap. 12, covers family activities in England. Notes are provided only for quotations and particular events.

91   For diplomatic details consult Bemis, I, chap. 11, and Perkins, *Castlereagh*, chaps. 9 and 11.

92   *Memoirs*, III, 223, 237, 240–44 (June 19, 30, July 1, 1815).

93   For Ealing and school selection see Heffron, *Louisa*, 274–81, 283–84; AA to JQA, Aug. 15, 1815, quoted ibid., 273–74.

94   Diary, day following Oct. 31, Nov. 15, 1815.

95   Ibid., Oct. 13, 14, day following 31, 1815.

96   Ibid., Oct. 28 (quotation), Oct. 23–31, Nov. 1, 2, 1815.

97   Ibid., Oct. 14, 1815.

98   *Memoirs*, III, 205, 252 (May 29, Aug. 18, 1815).

99   JQA to AA, March 25, 1816, quoted in Bemis, I, 239.

100   *Memoirs*, III, 77 (Nov. 30, 1814).

101   JQA to JA, Oct. 9, 1815, May 29, 1816, *Writings*, V, 408, VI, 38.

102   JQA to AA, June 6, 1816, ibid., VI, 44; *Memoirs*, III, 323 (April 4, 1816).

103   *Memoirs*, III, 379 (June 5, 1816), 372 (June 2, 1816), 217 (June 7, 1815).

104   For JQA and Bentham see ibid., 520–65 passim (May 6–June 8, 1817); Diary, April 29, 1817; Bentham to AJ, June 14, 1830, in *BAJ*, IV, 147.

105   Diary, Oct. 16, 1816.

106   Ibid., June 1, 1816, on Scott and Dec. 5, 1815, on the rhinoceros.

107   Ibid., June 5, 1816; *Memoirs*, III, 320, 407–8, 420, 520 (June 5, July 26, Aug. 13, 1816, May 6, 1817).

108   JQA to AA, Dec. 5, 1815, and to JA, Aug. 31, 1815, Jan. 3, 1817 (long letter), *Writings*, V, 362, 432, VI, 134–36.

109   *Portraits*, 57–63; *Memoirs*, II, 353 (March 20, 1812, for height) and III, 352 (May 3, 1816, for weight).

110   Diary, day following June 30, 1816, April 28, 1817.

111   Heffron, *Louisa*, 294.

112   Diary, day following March 31, 1817; JQA to JA, Jan. 3, 1817, *Writings*, VI, 131–34.

113   *Memoirs*, III, 458–59 (Dec. 24, 1816).

114   Monroe to TJ, Feb. 23, 1817, in Stanislaus Murray Hamilton, ed., *The Writings of James Monroe . . .*, 7 vols. (New York and London, 1898–1903), VI, 3–4; also Monroe to AJ, March 1817, ibid., 5.

115   JQA to AA, n.d., in *Memoirs*, III, 502 (July 17, 1817), and on April 23, 1817, *Writings*, VI, 179; Monroe to JQA, March 6, 1817, ibid., 165–66.

116   JQA to Monroe, April 17, 1817, ibid., 177; Diary, April 26, 1817.

CHAPTER 4: *"Perhaps the Most Important Day of My Life"*

1   Diary, June 25, 28, 1817; Margery M. Heffron, *Louisa Catherine: The Other Mrs. Adams* (New Haven, CT, 2014), 295.

2   Diary, Aug. 8, 1817.

3   JQA to AA, May 16, 1817, *Writings*, VI, 180; Diary, Sept. 20, 1817.

4   JQA to Alexander Everett, March 16, 1816, and to William Eustis, Jan. 13, 1819, *Writings*, V, 538, VI, 138. For Massachusetts and New England Federalists as well as the Hartford Convention, three books provide superb coverage: James Banner Jr., *To the Hartford Convention: The Federalists and the Origins of Party Politics in Massachusetts, 1789–1815* (New York, 1970); Ronald P. Formisano, *The Transformation of Political Culture: Massachusetts Parties, 1790s–1840s* (New York, 1983); Samuel Eliot Morison, *Harrison Gray Otis, 1765–1848: Urbane Federalist* (Boston, 1969).

5   JQA to JA, Aug. 1, 1816, *Writings*, VI, 60.

6   For details on the State Department during JQA's tenure, see Elmer Plischke, *U.S. Department of State: A Reference History* (Westport, CT, 1999), 73–75.

7   *Memoirs*, IV, 100 (May 22, 1818), V, 61 (June 28, 1820).

8   Ibid., V, 233–34 (Jan. 9, 1821).

9   Ibid., 130 (May 24, 1820).

10   Ibid., 173 (Sept. 2, 1820), IV, 368 (May 21, 1819).

11   Ibid., V, 338 (April 4, 1821, quotation), 143 (June 7, 1820), IV, 340 (April 16, 1819).

12   Ibid., IV 367 (May 20, 1819). *Writings*, VI and VII passim, contains lengthy letters on policy and instructions to American and foreign diplomats.

13   *Memoirs*, IV, 527–28 (Feb. 17, 1820), 321 (April 1, 1819).

14   Ibid., V, 238–39 (Jan. 19, 1821).

15   Charles N. Edel, *Nation Builder: John Quincy Adams and the Grand Strategy of the Republic* (Cambridge, MA, 2014), 135.

16   *Memoirs*, II, 137ff (beginning from June 30, 1810), IV, 13 (Oct. 7, 1817), 402–3 (July 25, 1819); JQA to TJ, Dec. 11, 1817, *Writings*, VI, 219–20.

17   The standard biography of Monroe remains Harry Ammon, *James Monroe: The Great National Identity* (New York, 1971). Dependable on his presidency is Noble Cunningham Jr., *The Presidency of James Monroe* (Lawrence, KS, 1996). Though dated, George Dangerfield's *The Era of Good Feelings* (New York, 1952) is still a lively account of the era.

18   *Memoirs*, VI, 128 (Jan. 12, 1823), VI, 497 (Jan. 8, 1820).

19   JQA to AA, April 23, May 16, 1817, *Writings*, IV, 178–82; *Memoirs*, IV, 450 (Nov. 26, 1819), 13 (Oct. 24, 1817).

20   *Memoirs*, IV, 164 (Nov. 6, 1818), 411 (Aug. 16, 1819, quotation), V, 70 (April 15, 1820), 201 (Nov. 12, 1820).

21   Ibid., V, 158 (June 23, 1820), VI, 170 (Aug. 9, 1823).

22   Ibid., IV, 187 (Dec. 7, 1818), 193 (Dec. 16, 1818).

23   Chase C. Mooney's solid *William H. Crawford, 1772–1834* (Lexington, KY, 1974) is the only full biography.

24   For Calhoun, Charles Wiltse's thorough *John C. Calhoun*, 3 vols. (Indianapolis, 1944–51) remains generally authoritative, though more than half a century old. The best one-volume treatment, and a good one, is John Niven, *John C. Calhoun and the Price of Union* (Baton Rouge, 1988).

25   *Memoirs*, IV, 36 (Jan. 6, 1818), 214–15 (Jan. 7, 1819), 241–42 (Feb. 3, 1819).

26   Ibid., 36 (Jan. 6, 1818), 477 (Dec. 13, 1819), V, 221 (Dec. 27, 1820), 361 (Oct. 15, 1821).

27   Ibid., IV, 451–52 (Nov. 27, 1819).

28   Ibid., 429 (Oct. 29, 1819), 451 (Nov. 27, 1819).

29   For JQA on Clay see ibid., 28 (Dec. 6, 1817), V, 52–53 (March 31, 1820). Clay's major biographer agrees: Robert V. Remini, *Henry Clay: Statesman for the Union* (New York, 1991), chap 10.

30   *Memoirs*, IV, 212 (Jan. 5, 1819), 70 (March 28, 1818).

31   Ibid., V, 206 (Nov. 24, 1820).

32   Ibid., 279 (Feb. 14, 1821).

33   Ibid., IV, 157 (Nov. 2, 1818); Diary, Oct. 30, 1818.

34   *Memoirs*, IV, 155, (Nov. 1, 1818).

35   Ibid., 202 (Dec. 1, 1818); JQA to JA, Nov. 2, 1818, *Writings*, VI, 463.

36   Diary, Sept. 1, 1819, Oct. 3, 1840; *Memoirs*, XI, 400 (Aug. 1, 1843).

37   *Memoirs*, III, 516 (May 3, 1817).

38   Ibid., 549 (June 1, 1817).

39   JQA to JA, Aug. 1, 1816, *Writings*, VI, 60–61.

40   *Memoirs*, IV, 438 (Nov. 16, 1819). On JQA as secretary of state, Bemis's magisterial biography provides detailed coverage in I, chaps. 12–27. See also James Lewis, *John Quincy Adams: Policymaker for the Union* (Wilmington, DE, 2001), chaps. 3–4, for a briefer treatment. For broad assessments of JQA's outlook as secretary, emphasizing his focus on power and independent American action, consult especially John Lewis Gaddis, *Surprise, Security, and the American Experience* (Cambridge, MA, 2004), chap. 2, and Edel, *Nation Builder*, 62, 105–6, which stresses his determination to defend American prerogatives by pressing his country's freedom to act on its own. Their perspectives have informed my discussion.

41   For details on relations with Spain between 1817 and 1821, particularly JQA's role, Bemis, I, chaps. 16–17, remains indispensable.

42   Best on AJ is still Robert V. Remini's *Andrew Jackson*, 3 vols. (New York, 1977–84), thorough as well as laudatory. For an excellent account of AJ and Florida, see his much briefer *Andrew Jackson and His Indian Wars* (New York, 2001).

43   In *Memoirs*, IV, June–July 1818 passim, JQA provided a substantive record. Cunningham, *Monroe's Presidency*, chap. 5, is a solid treatment. *Memoirs*, V, 113 (July 19, 1818, quotation); JQA to Monroe, July 8, 1818, *Writings*, VI, 384.

44   *Memoirs*, IV, 115 (July 21, 1818).

45   JQA to George Erving, Nov. 28, 1818, *Writings*, VI, 474–502; also note JQA to Onís, Nov. 30, 1818, ibid., 503–11. *LCA*, II, 407, has the TJ comment. Worthy is William Earl Weeks, "John Quincy

Adams's 'Great Gun' and the Rhetoric of American Empire," *Diplomatic History* 14 (Winter 1990): 25–41.

46   *Memoirs*, IV, 105 (July 8, 1818).

47   Ibid., V, 54 (March 31, 1820), and 67 (April 13, 1820), for his being the last to abandon the Rio Grande.

48   *LCA*, II, 504; *Memoirs*, IV, 274 (Feb. 22, 1819).

49   *Memoirs*, IV, 305 (March 18, 1819), 289 (March 8, 1819).

50   Ibid., V, 54 (March 31, 1820), 67 (April 13, 1820), 289 (Feb. 22, 1821), XII, 78 (Sept. 27, 1844).

51   Ibid., V, 54 (March 31, 1820).

52   On the Missouri crisis, Robert P. Forbes, *The Missouri Compromise and Its Aftermath* (Chapel Hill, NC, 2007), is excellent. John R. Van Atta's *Wolf by the Ears: Missouri Crisis, 1819–1821* (Baltimore, 2015) presents a succinct account based on the most recent scholarship. Glover More, *The Missouri Compromise, 1819–1821* (Lexington, KY, 1953), though more narrowly focused, retains value.

53   *Memoirs*, IV, 398 (July 5, 1819).

54   Ibid., IV and V between Jan. 1820 and March 1821 passim, contains John Quincy's own record of his reaction to the crisis.

55   Ibid., IV, 499 (Jan. 8, 1820), 502–3 (Jan. 10, 1820), 531 (Feb. 24, 1820).

56   Ibid., 528–29 (Feb. 20, 1820), 524–25 (Feb. 11, 1820).

57   Ibid., 517 (Feb. 4, 1820), 531 (Feb. 24, 1820), V, 210 (Nov. 29, 1820).

58   Ibid., IV, 506 (Jan. 16, 1820), 524–25 (Feb. 11, 1820), V, 307 (Feb. 28, 1821).

59   Ibid., IV, 583 (Feb. 27, 1820), 506 (Jan. 16, 1820); also see V, 15 (March 7, 1820).

60   Ibid., IV, 529 (Feb. 20, 1820), V, 11 (March 3, 1820).

61   Ibid., IV, 10–11 (March 3, 1820).

62   Ibid., V, 209 (Nov. 29, 1820).

63   Ibid., VI, 353–54 (May 22, 1824).

64   Ibid., 13–14 (June 7, 1822), 37 (June 29, 1822, quotation).

65   In his *What Hath God Wrought: The Transformation of America, 1815–1848* (New York, 2007), 260–66, Daniel Walker Howe offers an excellent, succinct account of the American Colonization Society.

66   *Memoirs*, IV, 354–55 (April 29, 1819), 294 (March 12, 1819), 476 (Dec. 10, 1819).

67   Ibid., 356 (April 29, 1819).

68   Ibid., VI, 402 (July 31, 1824).

69   Ibid., 229 (Jan. 8, 1824), 373 (June 3, 1824).

70   *An Address Delivered . . . On the Occasion of Reading the Declaration*

of Independence on the Fourth of July, 1821 (Washington, 1821), quotations on 9, 10, 16, 21, 22, 23, 27, 28, 29, 31.

71   *Memoirs*, II, 183–84 (Oct. 9, 1810).

72   For background and context on JQA's negotiations concerning Europe and South America, see Bemis, I, chaps. 15–19; Edel, *Nation Builder*, chap. 3, and Bradford Perkins, *Castlereagh and Adams: England and the United States, 1812–1823* (Berkeley and Los Angeles, 1964), chaps. 15–17. *Memoirs*, IV, V, and much of VI passim (1817–23), contains great detail on what JQA thought and did, from his perspective, of course.

73   *Memoirs*, IV, 186–87 (Dec. 7, 1818).

74   Ibid., VI, 179 (Nov. 7, 1823).

75   Ibid., 200, 212 (Nov. 25, 27, 1823). See Worthington Chauncey Ford, *John Quincy Adams: His Connection with the Monroe Doctrine (1823) . . .* (Cambridge, MA, 1902), which includes pertinent documents, especially regarding Russia. Ford also published the same material in two articles in the *American Historical Review* 7, 8 (July and Oct. 1902): 676–96, 28–52.

76   *Memoirs*, V, 176 (Sept. 19, 1820).

77   *M & P*, II, 209. For JQA on his words consult *Memoirs*, XII, 218 (Dec. 6, 1845).

78   *Memoirs*, VI, 195 (Nov. 21, 1823).

79   Ibid., 140, 157 (March 4, June 24, 1823, for Canning); IV, 330–31 (April 12, 1819, for de Neuville); IV, 305–6 (March 18, 1819, for Onís).

80   Ibid., IV, 339 (April 14, 1819).

81   Ibid., 244 (Feb. 4, 1819), has an example.

82   JQA to LCA, Oct. 7, 1822, *Writings*, VII, 316–17.

83   Diary, Nov. 8, 1819, Dec. 31, 1820; *Memoirs*, V, 171 (Aug. 25, 1820).

84   *Memoirs*, V, 291 (Feb. 22, 1821); *LCA*, II, 540.

85   *Report . . . on Weights and Measures . . .*, 16th Cong., 2d sess., S. Doc. 119 (Serial 45); *Memoirs*, V, 291 (Feb. 22, 1821).

86   Paul C. Nagel, *John Quincy Adams: A Public Life, a Private Life* (New York, 1997), 262–65, has a clear synopsis.

87   *Memoirs*, IV, 62 (March 18, 1818). A superior account of the election of 1824 is Donald Ratcliffe, *The One-Party Contest: Adams, Jackson, and 1824's Five-Horse Race* (Lawrence, KS, 2015). My discussion in this and the following chapter relies on it for background, context, and general treatment.

88   *Memoirs*, IV, 70 (March 28, 1818), V, 152–53 (March 31, 1820), 325 (March 9, 1821, quotation). Remini, *Clay*, chaps. 13–14 passim, covers Clay's positions.

89   *Memoirs*, IV, 241 (Feb. 3, 1819), 428–29 (Oct. 29, 1819).

90   Ibid., 120 (July 28, 1818), V, 304 (Feb. 27, 1821), 476 (Jan. 2, 1822).

91   Ibid., V, 477–78 (Jan. 3, 1822), VI, 42–43 (July 8, 1822); Diary, Nov. 15, 1823. Also see William Plumer Jr. (a New Hampshire congressman) to William Plumer, Jan. 3, 1822, in Everett Somerville Brown, ed., *The Missouri Compromises and Presidential Politics, 1820–1825* (St. Louis, 1926), 70–75, which has a detailed account of Plumer Jr.'s conversations with both JCC and JQA.

92   *Memoirs*, IV, 247–48 (Feb. 9, 1819); AJ to James Gadsden, Dec. 6, 1821, *AJP*, V, 121.

93   *Memoirs*, IV, 64 (March 18, 1818).

94   Ibid., 230–31 (Jan. 25, 1819); JQA to LCA, Aug. 23, 1822, *Writings*, VII, 296.

95   *Memoirs*, V, 297–98 (Feb. 25, 1821).

96   JQA to Robert Walsh, June 21, 1822, *Writings*, VII, 272.

97   On the Russell affair *Memoirs*, V, 240ff., VI, 3ff., has JQA's detailed account. Also see JQA to LCA, July 22, 1822, *Writings*, VII, 284. Bemis, I, 485–509, thoroughly treats the Russell incident, while Remini's *Clay*, 215–18, concentrates on Clay's role; he basically agrees with JQA on Clay's involvement. JQA's tome has a title almost matching the length of the volume: *The Duplicate Letters, the Fisheries and the Mississippi* . . . (Washington, 1822).

98   JQA to LCA, Oct. 7, 1822, *Writings*, VII, 315–18.

99   Ibid. and *Memoirs*, V, 496 (Jan. 2, 1822).

100 *Memoirs*, IV, 477 (Dec. 13, 1819, for Calhoun), V, 323–25 (March 9, 1821, for Clay), VI, 129 (Jan. 2, 1822, for AJ), V, 468–69 (Dec. 31, 1821, for congressmen seeking support). The letters: JQA to John D. Heath, Jan. 7, 1822, *Writings*, VII, 191–95, and JQA to Freeholders . . . , Dec. 28, 1822, *Writings*, VII, 191–95, 335–54.

101 Joseph Hopkinson to LCA [summer 1822], *Memoirs*, VI, 130 (following Jan. 12, 1823); "The MacBeth Policy," *Writings*, VII, 356–62.

102 *LCA*, II, 416; *Memoirs*, IV, 131 (Oct. 12, 1818), 197 (Dec. 22, 1818), 388 (June 4, 1819, quotation), V, 165 (July 15, 1820, quotation), VI, 94 (Nov. 2, 1822).

103 *LCA*, II, 555, 560, 659.

104 Ibid., 658, 425, 669.

105 Ibid., 680 (1st quotation), 634 (2d quotation), 542, 665. For a multitude of references to her events and her as hostess, consult ibid., 413–688 passim. Heffron, *Louisa*, chaps. 13–14, provides inclusive coverage of LCA's social world, while Catherine Allgor's fascinating *Parlor Politics: In Which the Ladies of Washington Help Build a City*

and a Government (Charlottesville, VA, 2000), chap. 4, places LCA in context and assesses her place.

106   *LCA*, II, 457.

107   *Memoirs*, VI, 46 (July 28, 1822).

108   *Portraits*, 73–77, 81, 84–89, 91–95, 102–4, 106, 108–12; the portraits themselves are on 75, 86, 88, 94, 103, 110.

109   Diary, July 30, 1823; *LCA*, II, 541.

110   Diary, Feb. 6, April 12, 1820; *LCA*, II, 465. See also the letters to John, Dec. 17, 1817, and to George, Dec. 26, 1817, *Writings*, VI, 258–59, 279.

111   Diary, Sept. 30, 1821.

112   *LCA*, II, 614–15.

113   Diary, Oct. 1, 1821, Aug., 27, 1823.

114   Ibid., July 30, 1823.

115   *Memoirs*, IV, 425 (Oct. 24, 1819), V, 18 (March 12, 1820).

116   Diary, June 18, 1820, July 14, 1822.

117   Ibid., May 19, 1824.

118   Ibid., June 12, 26, 1818, July 2, 1818, July 17, 1819, Aug. 18, Sept. 6, 12, 1822, June 19, 1823; *Memoirs*, VI, 161 (July 8, 1823, quotation), 162 (July 11, 1823), 169–70 (Aug. 9, 1823), 406 (Aug. 5, 1824), 412 (Aug. 25, 27, 1824).

119   Diary, March 30, 1818, March 31, May 10, 1819, Jan. 10, 1824; *Memoirs*, IV, 11 (Sept. 26, 1817), 361 (May 6, 1819), V, 495 (April 21, 1822); *LCA*, II, 673 and n.; JQA to LCA, Aug. 28, 1822, *Writings*, VII, 298. For the summers see both Diary and *Memoirs* passim for those months between 1817 and 1823.

120   Diary, Oct. 11, 1819.

121   *Memoirs*, IV, 11 (Aug. 26, 1817), V, 484–85 (April 1, 1822); Diary, June 14, 1822 (quotation). The gaps can be readily seen, as can the brief notations, in the Diary passim. In the *Memoirs* the gaps are often simply decisions by the editor, JQA's son CFA, to omit material.

122   *Memoirs*, V, 334 (March 20, 1821), 383 (Nov. 4, 1821), VI, 339, 343 (May 17, 20, 1824), 349 (May 23, 1824).

123   Ibid., V, 334 (March 20, 1821), 219–20 (Dec. 25, 1820).

124   Ibid., 316 (March 3, 1821), VI, 169 (Aug. 6, 1823); JQA to Edward Everett, Jan. 31, 1822, *Writings*, VII, 205.

CHAPTER 5: *"To Meet the Fate to Which I Am Destined"*

1   *LCA*, II, 680–88. For more detailed coverage see Margery M. Heffron, *Louisa Catherine: The Other Mrs. Adams* (New Haven, CT, 2014),

348–50, and Catherine Allgor, *Parlor Politics: In Which the Ladies of Washington Help Build a City and a Government* (Charlottesville, VA, 2000), 176–81.

2   *LCA*, II, 684.

3   Ibid., 681, 685.

4   Quotation from Heffron, *Louisa*, 349; for LCA's rivaling Dolley Madison, James Brown to Henry Clay, June 25, 1825, *Clay Papers*, IV, 465.

5   William Plumer Jr. to William Plumer, Dec. 3, 1823, Everett Somerville Brown, ed., *The Missouri Compromises and Presidential Politics, 1820–1825* (St. Louis, 1926), 84–85, 87.

6   *Memoirs*, VI, 253 (March 11, 1824), 269 (March 27, 1824, quotation), 274 (April 2, 1824), 284–85 (April 9, 1824), 332–33 (May 15, 1824, quotation 333).

7   Ibid., 191 (Nov. 19, 1823), 237 (Jan. 25, 1824, quotation), 244 (Feb. 3, 1824).

8   Chase C. Mooney, *William H. Crawford, 1772–1834* (Lexington, KY, 1974), 240–41, on Crawford's illness; *Memoirs*, VI, 234 (Jan. 17, 1824), 234–35 (Jan. 20, 1824), 237 (Jan. 25, 1824, quotation), 246–47 (Feb. 4, 1824).

9   *Memoirs*, VI, 236 (Jan. 25, 1824), 265 (March 23, 1824), 403 (July 31, 1824).

10 Ibid., 238 (Jan. 26, 1824, quotation), 312–13 (May 1, 1824), 315–16 (May 3, 1824, quotation); Daniel Webster to Jeremiah Mason, May 9, 1824, *Webster Papers*, I, 17.

11 *LCA*, II, 673; *Memoirs*, VI, 261 (March 19, 1824, quotation), 323 (May 8, 1824, long quotation).

12 *Memoirs*, VI, 415 (Aug. 31, 1824).

13 Diary, Sept. 5, 1824; *Memoirs*, VI, 416 (Sept. 8, 1824).

14 *Memoirs*, VI, 418 (Sept. 30, 1824).

15 On the election again consult Donald Ratcliffe's excellent *The One-Party Presidential Contest: Adams, Jackson, and 1824's Five-Horse Race* (Lawrence, KS, 2015), especially chaps. 8 and 9; app. 1 has both the electoral and the popular votes.

16 *Memoirs*, VI, 217 (Nov. 28, 1823, for withdrawal), 448 (Dec. 19, 1824), 466 (Jan. 12, 1825), 468 (Jan. 15, 1825), 470 (Jan. 18, 1825), 472 (Jan. 20, 1825), 474 (Jan. 21, 1825), 476 (Jan. 22–23, 1825), 480 (Jan. 26, 1825), 487 (Jan. 31, 1825), 490 (Feb. 2, 1825), 493 (Feb. 4, 1825); Diary, Dec. 18, 1824.

17 Heffron, *Louisa*, 350; Gaillard Hunt, ed., *The First Forty Years of Washington Society . . .* (New York, 1906), 171 (quotation).

18 William P. Plumer Jr. to William P. Plumer, Dec. 9, 1824, Brown, ed., *Missouri Compromises*, 120–21.

19 Plumer Jr. to William P. Plumer, Dec. 24, 1824, ibid., 123–24; *Memoirs*, VI, 458 (Jan. 1, 1825).

20 *Memoirs*, VI, 447 (Dec. 17, 1824), 452–53 (Dec. 23, 1824), 457 (Jan. 1, 1825).

21 Ratcliffe, *One-Party*, chap. 10; on Clay also see Robert V. Remini, *Henry Clay: Statesman for the Union* (New York, 1991), chap. 15.

22 *Memoirs*, VI, 464–65 (Jan. 9, 1825, quotation), 483 (Jan. 29, 1825).

23 Ibid., 453 (Dec. 23, 1824). I am grateful to my colleague Professor Steven Ross for the translation.

24 Ibid., 392 (June 21, 1824, assessment of Webster), 474 (Jan. 21, 1825), 492–93 (Feb. 3, 1825); Webster to Henry R. Warfield, Feb. 5, 1825, *Webster Papers*, II, 6.

25 *Memoirs*, VI, 478 (Jan. 25, 1825), 491 (Feb. 3, 1825).

26 Ibid., 489–90 (Feb. 2, 1825).

27 Plumer Jr. to William P. Plumer, Feb. 13, 1825, Brown, ed., *Missouri Compromises*, 138–39.

28 *Memoirs*, VI, 501, 503 (Feb. 9, 1825).

29 Ratcliffe, *One-Party*, 253.

30 Webster to Ezekiel Webster, Feb. 26, 1825, *Webster Papers*, II, 11; *Memoirs*, VI, 491 (Feb. 2, 1825); William P. Plumer Jr. to William Plumer, Feb. 16, 1824, Brown, ed., *Missouri Compromises*, 101.

31 *Memoirs*, VI, 508 (Feb. 12, 1825), VIII, 174 (Jan. 18, 1830, list).

32 Ibid., VI, 508–9 (Feb. 12, 1825); Plumer to William Plumer, Feb. 16, 1825, Brown, ed., *Missouri Compromises*, 140–42.

33 *Memoirs*, VI, 513 (Feb. 26, 1825); Ratcliffe, *One-Party*, 253.

34 Ratcliffe, *One-Party*, 255 (Jackson quotation); JCC to J. G. Swift, March 10, 1825, *JCC Papers*, X, 10.

35 *Memoirs*, XI, 431 (Nov. 14, 1843); *Clay Papers*, X, 673. For the most recent scholarly discussion of the corrupt-bargain matter, and one especially judicious, see Ratcliffe, *One-Party*, 253–57.

36 *Memoirs*, VI, 451 (Dec. 22, 1824), 474 (Jan. 21, 1825).

37 Ibid., 518 (March 4, 1825).

38 Plumer Jr. to William Plumer, March 4, 1825, Brown, ed., *Missouri Compromises*, 144; James Fenimore Cooper, *Notions of the Americans: Picked Up by a Travelling Bachelor*, 2 vols. (Philadelphia, 1828), II, 217.

39 *M & P*, II, 294–99.

40 For JQA's administration Mary W. Hargreaves, *The Presidency of John Quincy Adams* (Lawrence, KS, 1985), covers the basic ground; Bemis, II, chaps. 4–7, also provides details, with more focus on JQA

himself. *In What Hath God Wrought: The Transformation of America, 1815–1848* (New York, 2007), 244–60, Daniel Walker Howe fits JQA's presidency into his larger interpretation, emphasizing JQA's vision of what America should be. Charles N. Edel in his *Nation Builder: John Quincy Adams and the Grand Strategy of the Republic* (Cambridge, MA, 2014), chap. 4, again concentrates attention on his view of JQA as a grand strategist. My general discussion of the issues in JQA's presidency draws from them; my citations will focus on quotations and particular references to JQA himself.

41 *Memoirs*, VII, 59 (Nov. 22, 1825).

42 Ibid., 59, 61 (Nov. 23, 1825, quotation 61), 62–65 (Nov. 26, 1825).

43 Ibid., 63 (Nov. 26, 1825).

44 *M & P*, II, 299–317 (quotations 311, 313, 315, 316).

45 AJ to John Branch, March 3, 1826, quoted in Remini, *Clay*, 287.

46 *M & P*, II, 317–20; *Memoirs*, VI, 531 (April 23, 1825), 536–37 (April 27, 1825), 542 (May 7, 1825). Edel, *Nation Builder*, 216–24, has a trenchant analysis of the Panama episode.

47 Webster to John Denison, May 3, 1826, *Webster Papers*, II, 16.

48 *Memoirs*, VII, 104 (Jan. 12, 1826), 111 (Jan. 21, 1826, quotation), 113 (Feb. 7, 1826).

49 Ibid., 120–21, 124 (July 4, Aug. 26, 1826), 125, 128, 129 (July 9, 12, 13, quotation, 1826).

50 Ibid., 125 (July 9, 1826).

51 Diary, May 14, 1830, June 19, 1835, Sept. 30, 1841, quotation.

52 *Memoirs*, IX, 442 (Dec. 6, 1837).

53 Ibid., VII, 147, 149 (Sept. 3, Oct. 1, 1826), 229 (Feb. 18, 1827, quotation).

54 Numerous comments and descriptions ibid. and in Diary detail his presidential schedule and activities. My citations will be illustrative: *Memoirs*, VI, 531–40 (April 30, 1825), VII, 8 (May 18, 1825), 21–22 (May 31, 1825), 66 (Nov. 29, 1825), 97 (Dec. 31, 1825), 202 (Dec. 9, 1826), 235 (March 5, 1827), 344 (Oct. 25, 1827), 365 (Nov. 30, 1827), 419 (Feb. 3, 1828); Diary, June 21, July 3, 13, 14, Nov. 5, 1827, Feb. 11, 15, 23, May 15, 1828.

55 *Memoirs*, VI, 190, 192–93 (Jan. 30, 1826, quotation), 209, 216 (Dec. 16, 21, quotation, 1826); Diary, Nov. 13, 1826.

56 *Memoirs*, VII, 13 (May 24, 1825, quotation), 297 (June 29, 1827).

57 Ibid., 332–33 (Oct. 13, 1827, quotation), VIII, 49–50 (July 4, 1828).

58 Ibid., VII, 95, 103, 184 (Dec. 28, 1825, Jan. 11, 1826, Nov. 23, 1826); Diary, March 4, Dec. 14, 1825, Feb. 28, Dec. 22, 1826, Jan. 9, 1828; *LCA*, II, 664–65 (quotation); Heffron, *Louisa*, 355–56; Allgor, *Parlor Politics*, 191, 193.

59 *CFA Diary,* II, 75, 220.

60 *Portraits,* 122–33, 138–44, especially 130, 133, 142.

61 *Memoirs,* VI, 518 (preface to March 4, 1825, CFA statement), 548 (May 14, 1825), VII, 210 (Dec. 7, 1826, complaints); Diary 1825–29 passim.

62 *Memoirs,* VII, 36 (July 22, 1825), 38 (day following July 30, 1825), 165 (Oct. 31, 1826), 193 (Nov. 30, 1826), 311 (July 31, 1827), 418 (day following Jan. 31, 1828), 531 (May 26, 1828), 542 (May 16, 1828), VIII, 16 (May 28, 1828), 21 (day following May 31, 1828), 52 (July 8, 1828); Diary, Dec. 13, 1825, July 14, 1826, Sept. 30, 1827.

63 *Memoirs,* VII, 37 (July 28, 1825), 248 (March 26, 1827), 258 (April 13, 1827), 273 (May 13, 1827, quotation); Diary, March 29, 1827, Jan. 15, 1828.

64 *Memoirs,* VII, 121 (July 5, 1826), 261 (April 4, 1827), 297 (June 8, 1827), 292 (June 13, 1827), 323 (Aug. 12, 1827), 488 (March 27, 1828); Diary, June 12, 1827.

65 *Memoirs,* VII, 10 (May 19, 1825).

66 Ibid., 239–40 (March 14–15, 1827).

67 Ibid., 84 (Dec. 15, 1825).

68 Ibid., 455–56 (Feb. 29, 1828).

69 Ibid., VI, 353 (May 22, 1824).

70 Ibid., VII, 90, 113 (Dec. 22, 1825, Feb. 7, 1826).

71 Ibid., 92 (Dec. 23, 1825).

72 Ibid., 219–20 (Jan. 27, 29, Feb. 2, 1827).

73 Ibid., 221 (Feb. 4, 1827); *M & P,* II, 370–73, quotation 372.

74 JCC to L. Woodbury, Sept. 21, 1826, and to J. A. Dix, Dec. 6, 1827 (quotation), Oct. 5, 1828, *JCC Papers,* X, 206, 314, 429.

75 AJ to Henry Lee, Oct. 7, 1825 (1st quotation), and to Richard K. Call, March 9, 1826 (2d quotation), *AJP,* VI, 104, 151.

76 On Van Buren and party building Robert V. Remini's *Martin Van Buren and the Making of the Democratic Party* (New York, 1959) and Richard Hofstadter's *The Idea of a Party System: The Rise of Legitimate Opposition in the United States, 1780–1840* (Berkeley and Los Angeles, 1969), chap. 6, remain extremely instructive and valuable. John Niven, *Martin Van Buren and the Romantic Age of American Politics* (New York, 1983), is an excellent biography.

77 Webster to Jeremiah Mason, March 27, 1826, to William Gaston, May 31, 1828, to William Plumer Jr., Feb. 11, 1827, *Webster Papers,* II, 15, 18, 22; JCC to M. Sterling, Dec. 16, 1826, *JCC Papers,* X, 237.

78 For the campaign and election of 1828, Donald B. Cole, *Vindicating Andrew Jackson: The 1828 Election and the Rise of the Two-Party Sys-*

tem (Lawrence, KS, 2009), provides thorough coverage, including organization, message, and voting. Also see Remini, *Clay*, chaps. 18–19, and *Andrew Jackson*, 3 vols. (New York, 1977–84), II, chaps. 6–8, along with Niven, *Van Buren*, chaps. 11–12. My general account follows them, with my notes chiefly for quotations.

79 Quoted in Cole, *Vindicating*, 49.

80 *Memoirs*, VI, 525 (March 6, 1825).

81 Ibid., VII, 447 (Feb. 23, 1828, JCC), VIII, 128 (April 4, 1829, AJ and Van Buren).

82 Ibid., VII, 272 (May 12, 1827).

83 Ibid., 377 (Dec. 10, 1827), 472 (March 11, 1828, quotation).

84 Ibid., 113 (Feb. 7, 1826).

85 Ibid., 14 (May 25, 1825), 241–42 (March 18, 1827), 379 (Dec. 13, 1827, 2d quotation), 431 (Feb. 14, 1828, 1st quotation), 469–70 (March 8, 1828).

86 Ibid., 469–70 (March 8, 1828), 297 (June 29, 1827).

87 Ibid., VI, 510 (Feb. 15, 1825), 521 (March 5, 1825, quotation).

88 Clay to Webster, April 14, 1827, and Webster to JQA, March 27, 1827, *Webster Papers*, II, 29, 24; *Memoirs*, VI, 546 (May 13, 1825), VII, 163–64 (Oct. 28, 1826), 390 (Dec. 28, 1827); Adam Beatty to Clay, June 26, 1828, *Clay Papers*, VII, 401–2.

89 *Memoirs*, VII, 275 (May 23, 1827, 2d quotation), 343–44 (Oct. 22, 1827, 1st quotation), 349 (Nov. 7, 1827), 364 (Nov. 30, 1827), 544 (May 17, 1828, 3d quotation), VIII, 25 (June 3, 1828, 4th quotation), 51 (July 7, 1828, 5th quotation). Richard R. John, *Spreading the News: The American Postal System from Franklin to Morse* (Cambridge, MA, 1995), chap. 3, is superb on McLean and the Post Office.

90 *Memoirs*, VII, 185 (Nov. 25, 1826), 216–17 (Dec. 21, 1826), 351 (Nov. 10, 1827), 352 (Nov. 12, 1827), 374 (Dec. 7, 1827), 378 (Dec. 11, 1827), 380 (Dec. 15, 1827), 400 (Jan. 9, 1828).

91 Clay to Webster, April 14, 1827, *Webster Papers*, II, 27.

92 *Memoirs*, VII, 415–16 (Jan. 30, 1828).

93 For the editorial see Remini, *Clay*, 325; Diary, July 14, 1828.

94 Clay to Webster, June 14, 1826, *Webster Papers*, II, 19; Webster to Jeremiah Mason, April 10, 1827, to Nathaniel Williams, Sept. 5, 1828, to Clay, Oct. 23, 1828, ibid., 26, 46, 47; *Memoirs*, VII, 171 (Nov. 6, 1827, quotation), 525–26 (May 1, 1828); Diary, Aug. 29, 1827.

95 Cole, *Vindicating*, 182–84, has the state-by-state returns and the conjecture about shifting votes.

96 *Memoirs*, VIII, 78 (Dec. 3, 1828).

CHAPTER 6: *"An Overruling Consciousness of Rectitude"*

1 Diary, Jan. 1, 1829; JRR to Dr. John Brockenbrough, Dec. 7, 11, 1828, Kenneth Shorey, ed., *Collected Letters of John Randolph of Roanoke to Dr. John Brockenbrough, 1812–1833* (New Brunswick, NJ, 1988), 111– 12; *Memoirs,* VIII, 78 (Dec. 3, 1828).

2 Mrs. Basil Hall, *The Aristocratic Journey . . .* (New York and London, 1931), 169.

3 Diary, April 27, 1829.

4 JQA to HC, May 11, 1829, *Clay Papers,* IX, 37; *JQA Diary,* II, 104 (Sept. 29, 1786, quotation from *King Henry V*); *Memoirs,* X, 117 (April 25, 1839).

5 *Memoirs,* V, 220 (Dec. 25, 1820).

6 Ibid., VII, 418 (Feb. 2, 1828), IX (Sept. 30, 1833).

7 Diary, May 3–8, 1829; *Memoirs,* VIII, 159–60 (day after Dec. 31, 1829); also see JQA to HC, May [2], 11, 1829, *Clay Papers,* VIII, 37.

8 Henry Adams, ed., *Documents Relating to New England Federalism, 1800–1815* (Boston, 1877), 1–22, for TJ letters and related materials.

9 Ibid., 23–26.

10 Ibid., 43–45; *Memoirs,* VIII, 87 (Dec. 28, 1828).

11 Adams, ed., *Documents,* 46–62 (quotations 61, 62).

12 Ibid., 63–92 (quotation 91).

13 *Memoirs,* VIII, 132 (April 8, 1829).

14 Adams, ed., *Documents,* 107–329 (quotations 140, 153–54, 328).

15 *Memoirs,* VIII, 196 (March 2, 1830).

16 Diary, day following Oct. 31, 1822, day following April 30, 1830.

17 Ibid., Aug. 27, 1829, June 7, 1831, day following Aug. 31, 1829, Sept. 11, 1831.

18 *Memoirs,* VIII, 123 (March 31, 1829), 339 (March 8, 1831).

19 Ibid., 124 (March 31, 1829).

20 *Poems of Religion and Society* (New York, 1848). I am indebted to my colleague Boyd Professor Emeritus Gerald Kennedy of the LSU English Department for his commentary on the poems in this volume.

21 *Dermot MacMorrogh; or, The Conquest of Ireland: An Historical Tale of the Twelfth Century in Four Cantos* (Washington, 1832).

22 *Memoirs,* VIII, 347 (March 17, 1831), 352 (day after March 30, 1831), 354 (April 16, 1831), IX, 23–24 (Oct. 17, 1833).

23 Ibid., VIII, 383 (July 20, 1831), Diary, July 4, 5, 1832.

24 *Memoirs,* IX, 29 (Nov. 7, 1833), Diary, Sept. 29, 1841, March 15, 1846.

25 *Memoirs,* VIII, 235 (Aug. 18, 1830), Diary, Oct. 25, 1831; *Memoirs,*

VIII, 183 (Feb. 1, 1830), 243 (Oct. 24, 1830), 248 (Nov. 8, 1830), Diary, July 15, 1830, Oct. 18, 1830; *Memoirs*, VIII, 120 (March 21, 1829), 155–57 (Sept. 24, 1829), 163 (Jan. 4, 1830, 1st quotation), Diary, Oct. 17, 1829 (2d quotation).

26   Diary, Jan.–Feb., May–June 1829 passim, July 17, 1830, day following Aug. 31, 1830.

27   Ibid., May 4, 1831, Sept. 6, 1832.

28   Ibid., Feb. 2–9, March 1, April 5 (quotation), Nov. 10, 1831, *Memoirs*, VIII, 309–10, 321 (Feb. 2, 19, 1831).

29   Diary, June 14, 1831, *Memoirs*, VIII, 235 (Aug. 18, 1830), 193 (Feb. 24, 1830, quotations), 281 (Jan. 17, 1831).

30   JQA to LCA, Feb. 7, 1795, *Writings*, II, 109 n.; *Memoirs*, II, 14 (Aug. 21, 1809).

31   *Memoirs*, V, 89 (May 2, 1820).

32   Ibid., 475 (Jan. 1, 1822).

33   Ibid., VIII, 81 (Dec. 9, 1828), 241 (Sept. 25, 1830); *CFA Diary*, IV, 321 n.

34   On Massachusetts politics in this period, consult Ronald P. Formisano, *The Transformation of Political Culture: Massachusetts Parties, 1790s–1840s* (New York, 1983), chaps. 8–11 passim, and Leonard L. Richards, *The Life and Times of Congressman John Quincy Adams* (New York, 1986), chap. I.

35   *Memoirs*, VIII, 241 (Sept. 25, 1830).

36   Ibid., 239–40 (Sept. 18, 1830), 246–47 (Nov. 7, 1830).

37   *CFA Diary*, IV, 175, 328–29, 352.

38   *Memoirs*, VIII, 240 (Sept. 18, 1830).

39   Ibid., 245 (Nov. 6, 1830), 247 (Nov. 17, 1830); Michael J. Dubin, *United States Congressional Elections, 1788–1977: The Official Results . . .* (Jefferson, NC, 1998), 97. JQA gave his total as 1,812, only one vote more than the official total reported in Dubin.

40   Diary, Dec. 9, 1829; *Memoirs*, VIII, 246 (Nov. 7, 1830).

41   The standard treatment of the Antimasons is William Preston Vaughn's solid *The Anti-Masonic Party in the United States, 1826–1843* (Lexington, KY, 1983); Michael F. Holt's incisive analysis in his *Political Parties and American Political Development from the Age of Jackson to the Age of Lincoln* (Baton Rouge, LA, 1992), 88–111, is also essential. My general account follows them.

42   Vaughn, *Anti-Masonic Party*, chap. 9, has detailed coverage of Massachusetts.

43   *Memoirs*, VII, 345, 410, 416 (Oct. 25, 1827, Jan. 22, 30, 1828); Diary, Nov. 28, 1830.

44   *Memoirs*, VIII, 363, 364 (quotation) (May 20, 31, 1831).

45 Ibid., 413, 414 (Sept. 18, Oct. 5, 1831); Daniel Webster to HC, Oct. 5, 1831, *Webster Papers*, III, 2.

46 *Memoirs*, VIII, 412–13 (Sept. 14, 1831).

47 Ibid., 368, 428 (1st quotation) (June 10, Nov. 22, 1831); Diary, Aug. 13, 1832 (2d quotation).

48 Diary, Aug. 13, 1832; *Letters on Freemasonry* (1847; Austin, TX, 2001); Frederick W. Seward, *William H. Seward*, 3 vols. (New York, 1891), I, 145.

49 *Memoirs*, VIII, 535 (March 6, 1833), IX, 6, 14, 15 (July 10, Aug. 20, Sept. 12, 1833); *CFA Diary*, III, 168 n.; Edward Everett to Daniel Webster, Aug. 9, 1833, *Webster Papers*, III, 8.

50 *Memoirs*, IX, 19, 33 (quotation), 58–59 (Oct. 4, Nov. 15, Dec. 22, 1833).

51 Ibid., 58–59 (Dec. 22, 1833).

52 Ibid., VIII, 443 (Dec. 26, 1831).

53 Richards, *Congressman Adams*, provides an excellent overview. My basic comments on JQA and Congress rely on it; p. 57 has the numbers. For a fascinating investigation into the living arrangements and informal social contacts among congressmen, consult Rachel A. Shelden, *Washington Brotherhood: Politics, Social Life, and the Coming of the Civil War* (Chapel Hill, NC, 2013).

54 On Webster consult Robert V. Remini's superb biography, *Daniel Webster: The Man and His Time* (New York, 1997).

55 *Memoirs*, VII, 139–40 (Aug. 2, 1826), XI, 20 (Sept. 17, 1841, quotation), 47–48 (Dec. 31, 1841), 347 (March 25, 1843), XII, 214 (Sept. 18, 1845).

56 Ibid., VIII, 229 (May 22, 1830).

57 For detail on the initiatives see below; *M & P*, II, 545, for AJ on agriculture.

58 *Memoirs*, VIII, 128 (April 4, 1829, 1st and 2d quotations), 232 (June 22, 1830), 274–75 (Jan. 14, 1831), 404 (Aug. 30, 1831, 3d quotation).

59 Ibid., 484–85 (March 2, 1832).

60 Ibid., 274–75 (Jan. 14, 1831), 277 (Jan. 15, 1831), 323–24 (Feb. 20, 1831), 411 (July 5, 1831, quotations).

61 Ibid., 323–24 (Feb. 20, 1831).

62 Ibid., 274–75 (Jan. 14, 1831), 277 (Jan. 15, 1831). John Niven's *John C. Calhoun and the Price of Union* (Baton Rouge, LA, 1988), 174–75, has a solid, succinct discussion.

63 The standard monograph is John F. Marzalek, *The Petticoat Affair: Manners, Mating, and Sex in Andrew Jackson's White House* (New York, 1997). For an excellent brief account see Catherine Allgor,

Parlor Politics: In Which the Ladies of Washington Help Build a City and a Government (Charlottesville, VA, 2000), 198–210 (quotation on 200).

64 Diary, July 5, 1831.

65 *Memoirs*, VIII, 138 (April 16, 1829), 215 (April 6, 1830).

66 On Indian policy generally consult Ronald N. Satz's solid *American Indian Policy in the Jacksonian Era* (Lincoln, NE, 1975). A more recent succinct and incisive account is Daniel Walker Howe, *What Hath God Wrought: The Transformation of America, 1815–1848* (New York, 2007), 342–57. Lynn Hudson Parson focuses on JQA's views in "John Quincy Adams and the American Indian," *New England Quarterly* 46 (Sept. 1973): 339–79. My treatment relies on them.

67 *Memoirs*, VIII, 206 (March 22, 1830).

68 For an excellent brief account of the Bank War, see Howe, *What Hath God Wrought*, 373–83. Bray Hammond, *Banks and Politics in America: From the Revolution to the Civil War* (Princeton, NJ, 1957), chaps. 5–12, has detail on banking from the first Bank of the United States to Jackson's war.

69 Richards, *Congressman Adams*, 76–81, covers JQA and banks.

70 *Memoirs*, IV, 499 (Jan. 8, 1820), VIII, 425 (Nov. 9, 1831), 493–96 (March 13, 1832).

71 Ibid., VIII, 433–34 (Dec. 12, 1831).

72 Ibid., 436–37 (Dec. 13, 1831).

73 On the Nullification Crisis the classic treatment is William W. Freehling, *Prelude to the Civil War: The Nullification Controversy in South Carolina, 1816–1836* (New York, 1966). Richard E. Ellis, *The Union at Risk: Jacksonian Democracy, States' Rights, and the Nullification Crisis* (New York, 1987), emphasizes the positive outcome for South Carolina. Merrill Peterson's *Olive Branch and Sword: The Compromise of 1833* (Baton Rouge, LA, 1982) concentrates on the making of the compromise. Also see my *We Have the War Upon Us: The Onset of the Civil War, November 1860–April 1861* (New York, 2012), 119–20. My general account relies on them.

74 *Memoirs*, VIII, 226–27 (May 13, 1830), on South Carolina; JQA, *An Oration Addressed to the Citizens of the Town of Quincy, on the Fourth of July, 1831* . . . (Boston, 1831), quotations on 17–18, 35.

75 Diary, June 24, 1832; *Memoirs*, VIII, 536 (March 7, 1833, quotation).

76 Richards, *Congressman Adams*, 65–75, has more detail on JQA and the tariff; *Memoirs*, VIII, 460 (Jan. 25, 1832).

77 JQA to LCA, June 11, 1832, Adams Papers.

78 JQA to Robert Walsh, Dec. 26, 1830, ibid.

79   *Memoirs*, VIII, 229–30 (June 1, 1830).

80   Ibid., 510 (Dec. 24, 1832).

81   George Wilson Pierson, *Tocqueville and Beaumont in America* (New York, 1938), 417–19.

82   JQA to Rev. Charles W. Upham, Feb. 2, 1837, in Henry Adams, *The Degradation of the Democratic Dogma* (New York, 1920), 24–25; JQA to HC, Sept. 7, 1831, *Clay Papers*, IX, 397. Previously some southerners had brought up the possibility of secession because of perceived or potential antislavery acts, but none of them was a major figure. Certainly none came close to matching JQA's stature. Moreover, their scenarios were conditional; something adverse would have to happen to spark secession. JQA, on the other hand, posited his conviction.

83   Diary, Feb. 4, March 12, 30, May 3, 1833.

84   Ibid., Jan. 1, 1833, and 1833 passim; *Memoirs*, VIII, 470 (Feb. 11, 1832, quotation).

85   Diary, Oct. 20, 1829, April 6, Aug. 16, Dec. 27, 1833, June 8, July 1, 1834.

86   *Memoirs*, VIII, 353 (April 3, 1831).

87   Diary, Aug. 23–Sept. 8, 1833 (quotation Sept. 2).

88   *Memoirs*, VIII, 538–39 (April 2, 8 quotation, 1833); Dubin, *Congressional Elections*, 105, has the official returns; JQA had 78.4 percent.

CHAPTER 7: *"The First and Holiest Rights of Humanity"*

1   *Memoirs*, IX, 114–15 (March 27, 1834).

2   On the formation of the Whig party, Michael F. Holt, *The Rise and Fall of the American Whig Party: Jacksonian Politics and the Onset of the Civil War* (New York, 1999), chap. 2, is authoritative. See especially pp. 25–30.

3   *Memoirs*, IX, 75 (Jan. 13, 1834), 78 (Jan. 17, 1834, quotation), 184 (Sept. 6, 1834), 217 (March 7, 1835); JQA to Solomon Lincoln, Nov. 8, 1834, Adams Papers; Webster to Levi Lincoln, Jan. 18, 1834, *Webster Papers*, III, 9.

4   Michael J. Dubin, *United States Congressional Elections, 1788–1997: The Official Results . . .* (Jefferson, NC, 1998), 110; *Memoirs*, IX, 207–8 n. (Feb. 22, 1835, quotation), 212 (March 2, 1835), 238 (May 26, 1835); *CFA Diary*, VI, 73–74 n. Bemis, II, 306–17, has an excellent account of the spoliation issue.

5   *Memoirs*, VIII, 546 (June 18, 1833).

6   Diary, Oct. 23 (1st quotation), 24 (2d quotation), 26, 30 (remaining quotation), 1834.

7   *LCA*, II, 700 (1st and 2d quotations), 702 (remaining quotation).

8   On the election, see Holt, *Whig Party*, 38–49; *Memoirs*, IX, 187 (Oct. 9, 1834).

9   *An Eulogy: On the Life and Character of James Monroe* . . . (Boston, 1831); *An Eulogy on the Life and Character of James Madison* . . . (Boston, 1836), quotations 84, 86. In Madison's case he did discuss an address in 1829 before the Virginia constitutional convention considering the basis of representation in the Virginia legislature. That convention debated a proposal to eliminate slavery from the formula allocating members, Virginia's version of the three-fifths clause. JQA quoted and lauded the portion of Madison's remarks advocating and praising compromise between the two great principles of the rights of property and the rights of persons. The property referred to was slave property. Even though this provided an opportunity for JQA to weigh in against slave representation, he did not. Doing so would have meant finding fault with Madison, which he would not do. On the convention itself see Alison Goodyear Freehling, *Drift toward Dissolution: The Virginia Slavery Debate of 1831–1832* (Baton Rouge, LA, 1982), chap. 3, and William G. Shade, *Democratizing the Old Dominion: Virginia and the Second Party System, 1824–1861* (Charlottesville, VA, 1996), 65–76.

10   James Brewer Stewart, *Holy Warriors: The Abolitionists and American Slavery*, rev. ed. (New York, 1996), provides a sterling overview. More recently, in her detailed and celebratory account of abolitionism, *The Slaves' Cause: A History of Abolition* (New Haven, CT, 2016), Manisha Sinha claims that slave resistance propelled the movement. In his *The Problem of Slavery in the Age of Revolution, 1770–1823* (Ithaca, NY, 1975), David Brian Davis has a suggestive discussion of the origins of the free-labor ideology, 489–501 (quotation on 492). *Historical Statistics of the United States: Earliest Times to the Present*, 5 vols. (New York, 2006), II, 378, 381, gives the slave population and value in 1830. The Garrison quotation is from the *Liberator*, Jan. 1, 1831.

11   Leonard L. Richards, *The Life and Times of Congressman John Quincy Adams* (New York, 1986), 89–90.

12   *Memoirs*, VIII, 434 (Dec. 12, 1831).

13   Ibid., 475 (Feb. 20, 1832).

14   *Liberator*, Jan. 28, 1832; Garrison to JQA, Jan. 21, 1832, Walter M.

Merrill et al., eds., *The Letters of William Lloyd Garrison*, 6 vols. (Cambridge, MA, 1971–81), I, 142–43.

15   JQA to Moses Brown, Dec. 9, 1833, Adams Papers.

16   Daniel Walker Howe, *What Hath God Wrought: The Transformation of America, 1815–1848* (New York, 2007), 428–30; *M & P*, III, 175–76.

17   The standard treatment on anti-abolition violence remains Leonard L. Richards, *"Gentlemen of Property and Standing": Anti-Abolition Mobs in Jacksonian America* (New York, 1970).

18   JQA to Dr. Benjamin Waterhouse, Oct. 15, 1835, Adams Papers.

19   *Memoirs*, V, 11 (March 3, 1820, 1st quotation); JQA to E. Wright Jr., April 16, 1837, and to Bancroft, Oct. 25, 1835 (2d quotation), Adams Papers. On race generally William Jerry MacLean, "Othello Scorned: The Racial Thought of John Quincy Adams," *Journal of the Early Republic* 4 (Summer 1984): 143–60, offers a helpful overview.

20   JQA to Dr. George Parkman, Dec. 31, 1835, Adams Papers; also see *Memoirs*, VIII, 423–24 (Nov. 5, 1831).

21   *Memoirs*, XI, 155, 162, 294, 502 (Nov. 16, 26, 1842, Jan. 14, 1843, Feb. 5, 1844). Born in the West Indies, David Levy served from 1841 to 1845 as the delegate to Congress from the Territory of Florida. In 1846 he took the ancestral patronymic of Yulee and thereafter was known as David L. Yulee. In that same year he married a Christian and adopted that faith. Twice, 1845–51 and 1855–61, he represented the state of Florida in the U.S. Senate. Upon Florida's secession, in Jan. 1861, he resigned his seat.

22   *Memoirs*, IV, 531 (Feb. 24, 1820), X, 483 (June 21, 1841).

23   Ibid., IX, 259 (Aug. 22, 1835).

24   Richards, *Congressman Adams*, 106.

25   *Memoirs*, IX, 263 (Nov. 23, 1835).

26   Ibid., 111 (March 17, 1834); *RD*, 23d Cong., 1st sess., 3014.

27   Diary, Dec. 12, 1834; *Memoirs*, IX, 162 (July 30, 1834).

28   On the initial congressional struggle on the gag rule, three titles provide detail: George C. Rable, "Slavery, Politics, and the South: The Gag Rule as a Case Study," *Capitol Studies* 3 (Fall 1975): 69–87; William W. Freehling, *The Road to Disunion: Secessionists at Bay, 1776–1854* (New York, 1990), chaps. 17–18; William Lee Miller, *Arguing about Slavery: The Great Battle in the United States Congress* (New York, 1996), chap. 12. They inform my general account.

29   JQA to CFA, Dec. 19, 1835, Adams Papers; *RD*, 24th Cong., 1st sess., 2001.

30   *Memoirs*, IX, 266 (Jan. 4, 1836).

31   Richards, *Congressman Adams*, 119–20.

32 *RD*, 24th Cong., 1st sess., 3756–63, 3772–78, 3811, 3903, 4009–31; *Appendix*, 104–14, has the report itself.

33 *RD*, 24th Cong., 1st sess., 4027–31 ("gagged" quotation on 4030); for the votes, ibid., 4031, 4051–54. The Senate passed its own, quite similar gag with fewer rhetorical fireworks; see Freehling, *Road*, 324–27.

34 Richardson, *Congressman Adams*, 124.

35 *RD*, 24th Cong., 1st sess., 4036–49. JQA had earlier expressed the same view of the war power in a letter to Solomon L. Lincoln, April 4, 1836, Adams Papers. For more on the war power question, see John Fabian Witt's superb *Lincoln's Code: The Laws of War in American History* (New York, 2012), 78, 204, chaps. 7–8.

36 *Memoirs*, IX, 431 (Nov. 20, 1837, 1st quotation); Diary, Oct. 27, 1834 (2d quotation).

37 *LCA*, II, 693 (1st quotation), 694, 696 (remaining quotations).

38 Ibid., 702.

39 Ibid., 694 (1st quotation), 700 (2d and 3d quotations), 701 (final quotation).

40 For more on LCA and race see Louisa Thomas, *Louisa: The Extraordinary Life of Mrs. Adams* (New York, 2016), 423–26.

41 *LCA*, II, 696–97 (quotation on 697).

42 Diary, Sept. 29, Oct. 3, 1834, June–Nov. 1835 passim.

43 Ibid., July–Oct. 1834 passim, June–Nov. 1835 passim.

44 Ibid., Aug. 16, 1833, May 2, 1835 (quotation), Sept. 7, 1836.

45 *Portraits*, 168–81, especially 172–73.

46 Diary, Nov. 25, 1836.

47 Ibid., Jan. 23, Feb. 15, 1837.

48 *RD*, 24th Cong., 2d sess., 1314–16.

49 Ibid., 1317–21, 1411–12.

50 Ibid., 1587–734.

51 Ibid., 1673–83, for speech (quotation on 1676, 1677), 1685 for exoneration. The speech is also included in *Letters of John Quincy Adams to His Constituents* . . . (Boston, 1837), 44–65. Because two different reporters recorded the speech, the wording in the two versions differs slightly.

52 *Letters . . . to His Constituents*, 5–44 (quotations in order on 41, 12, 15, 42, 43). The letters are dated March 3, 8, 13, 20, 1837.

53 *Memoirs*, X, 94–95 (Jan. 9, 1839); see also ibid., 81 (Dec. 31, 1838), and Richards, *Congressman Adams*, 131.

54 *Memoirs*, IX, 64 (Jan. 2, 1834), XII, 240 (Jan. 31, 1846, 1st quotation), XI, 197 (July 4, 1842, 2d quotation), X, 517 (July 29, 1841, 3d quota-

tion), XII, 68 (July 6, 1844, 4th quotation), ibid., 25 (May 10, 1844, 5th quotation).

55   Ibid., IX, 399 (Oct. 10, 1837), X, 396 (Jan. 13, 1841, 1st quotation), IX, 433 (Nov. 23, 1837), XI, 500 (Feb. 2, 1844, 2d quotation).

56   Ibid., XI, 500 (Feb. 2, 1844, 1st quotation), 99 (Feb. 24, 1842, 3d quotation); Diary, June 18, 1846 (2d quotation); Theodore Weld to Angelina Grimké, Feb. 27, 1842, Gilbert H. Barnes and Dwight L. Dumond, eds., *Letters of Theodore Dwight Weld, Angelina Grimké, and Sarah Grimké, 1822– 1844*, 2 vols. (New York, 1934), II, 935.

57   *Memoirs*, X, 41 (Nov. 12, 1838); Diary, April 2, 1838.

58   Diary, April 2, 1838. Also see Craig M. Simpson, *A Good Southerner: The Life of Henry A. Wise of Virginia* (Chapel Hill, NC, 1985), 43.

59   *Memoirs*, IX, 369 (Sept. 9, 1837, quotation), 425–26 (Nov. 4, 1837); Diary, March 16, 1838.

60   *Memoirs*, IX, 5 (June 27, 1833, 1st quotation), XII, 101 (Nov. 5, 1844), IX, 51 (Dec. 12, 1833, 2d quotation), XII, 210 (Sept. 1, 1845, 3d quotation), ibid., 93 (Oct. 19, 1844, 4th quotation).

61   AJ to Martin Van Buren, Jan. 23, 1838, *BAJ*, V, 529; AJ to Brigadier General Benjamin C. Howard, Aug. 2, 1838, ibid., 560 (1st quotation); AJ to Francis P. Blair, Nov. 29, 1844, ibid., VI, 332 (2d quotation); AJ to Francis P. Blair, July 19, 1838, ibid., V, 557 (3d and 4th quotations).

62   *Memoirs*, IV, 246 (Feb. 6, 1819), X, 502 (March 6, 1838, quotation).

63   The most thorough treatment of the culture of honor is Bertram Wyatt-Brown's imaginative *Southern Honor: Ethics & Behavior in the Old South* (New York, 1982), though I think he underplays the importance of slavery as formative. On that point consult my *Liberty and Slavery: Southern Politics to 1860* (New York, 1983). For the duel particularly see 117–19.

64   Myra L. Spaulding, "Dueling in the District of Columbia," *Records of the Columbia Historical Society*, 29–30 (1928): 186–201, contains a detailed account of the duel, with pertinent congressional documents. It informed my discussion.

65   Ibid., 193, for the AJ reaction.

66   *Memoirs*, IX, 500 (March 4, 1838); JQA to CFA, March 19, 1838, and to Dr. Benjamin Waterhouse, May 14, 1838, Adams Papers.

67   *Memoirs*, X, 52 (Dec. 5, 1838); *CG*, 25th Cong., 3d sess., 180–82.

68   Bemis, II, 503–13, 522–23, has a full account of the Smithsonian bequest and subsequent congressional activity. For a voluminous documentary record, see *Smithsonian Miscellaneous Records*, vol. 17 (1880). My discussion is based on them.

69   *Memoirs*, IX, 270 (Jan. 12, 1836), X, 45 (Nov. 29, 1838).

70   Ibid., X, 25 (June 24, 1838), 44–45 (Nov. 29, 1838), XI, 22 (Sept. 18, 1841).

71   Ibid., X, 88 (Jan. 5, 1839, quotation), XI, 173–74 (June 11, 1842).

72   Dubin, *Congressional Elections*, 97, 105, 115; Diary, Aug. 28, 1837.

73   Dubin, *Congressional Elections*, 121; Diary, Nov. 13, 1838.

74   Diary, Oct. 23, 1838.

CHAPTER 8: *"On the Edge of a Precipice Every Step That I Take"*

1   E.g., *Memoirs*, IX, 377 (Sept. 15, 1837, quotation), 479 (Jan. 28, 1838), 493 (Feb. 12, 1838), 508 (March 12, 1838), 536 (May 21, 1838); Diary, Nov. 30, 1844.

2   *Memoirs*, XI, 265 (Oct. 24, 1842), 324 (Feb. 20, 1843), 326–27 (Feb. 22, 1843); Joshua R. Giddings to Theodore Dwight Weld, Feb. 21, 1843, Gilbert H. Barnes and Dwight L. Dumond, eds., *Letters of Theodore Dwight Weld, Angelina Grimké Weld, and Sarah Grimké, 1822–1844*, 2 vols. (New York, 1934), II, 976.

3   *Memoirs*, X, 206 (Jan. 29, 1840).

4   Ibid., 206 (Jan. 29, 1840), XI, 35 (Dec. 8, 1841, quotation), 278 (Dec. 12, 1842), 449–50 (Dec. 16, 1843); Leonard L. Richards, *The Life and Times of Congressman John Quincy Adams* (New York, 1986), 175–77.

5   *Memoirs*, IX, 479 (Jan. 28, 1838, 1st quotation), X, 302 (June 4, 1840, 2d quotation), XI, 94 (Feb. 17, 1842), 159 (May 21, 1842).

6   Ibid., XI, 24 (Sept. 25, 1841); Diary, Sept. 20, Oct. 20, 1840.

7   *Memoirs*, X, 138 (Oct. 6, 1839), 365 (Dec. 3, 1840, quotations intermixed).

8   Ibid., 108 (March 23, 1839, quotation), 111–12 (April 3, 1839), 116 (April 20, 1839), 118 (April 30, 1839); Diary, April 1, 10, 12, June 12, 1839.

9   JQA, *Jubilee of the Constitution* . . . (New York, 1839), quotations 16, 68, 69, 116.

10   *Memoirs*, XI, 159 (May 21, 1842).

11   *Niles' National Register*, Aug. 26, 1845.

12   *CG*, 25th Cong., 3d sess., 205.

13   *Liberator*, June 11, 1841.

14   *Memoirs*, IX, 302 (July 9, 1836), X, 128 (July 14, 1839); Diary, June 6, 1837; Sarah Grimké to Theodore Dwight Weld, June 11, 1837, Barnes and Dumond, eds., *Weld Letters*, II, 403.

15   Garrison to JQA, Feb. 8, 1839, and to Francis Jackson, Aug. 16, 1843, Walter M. Merrill et al., eds., *The Letters of William Lloyd Garrison*, 6 vols. (Cambridge, MA, 1971–81), II, 427, and III, 196; Birney to Leicester King, Jan. 1, 1844, Dwight L. Dumond, ed., *The Let-*

ters of James Gillespie Birney, 1831–1857, 2 vols. (New York, 1938), II, 767–68.

16   Diary, Nov. 16, 1839 (1st quotation); William Lloyd Garrison to Francis Jackson, Aug. 16, 1843, Merrill et al., eds., *Garrison Letters,* III, 196 (2d quotation); *Memoirs,* XI, 408 (Aug. 12, 1843, final quotation). For the letter see *Niles' National Register,* Aug. 26, 1843 (all other quotations).

17   *Memoirs,* X, 128 (July 14, 1839, 1st quotation), IX, 365 (Sept. 1, 1837, remaining quotations).

18   Diary, July 14, 1839.

19   Daniel Walker Howe, *What Hath God Wrought: The Transformation of America, 1815–1848* (New York, 2007), 617–26, has a good brief discussion of transcendentalism.

20   Diary, Oct. 6, 1838; *Memoirs,* X, 345 (Aug. 2, 1840, 1st quotation), 350 (Aug. 23, 1840, remaining quotations).

21   Based on wide-ranging research, Howard Jones's evenhanded *Mutiny on the Amistad: The Saga of a Slave Revolt and Its Impact on American Abolition, Law, and Diplomacy* (New York, 1987) remains the standard account. My general discussion follows it.

22   *Memoirs,* X, 133–35 (Oct. 1, 2, 1839).

23   Ibid., 358 (Oct. 27, 1840).

24   Ibid., 360 (Nov. 17, 1840), 372–73 (Dec. 11, 1840), 383 (Dec. 27, 1840, quotation), 396–97 (Jan. 14, 1841), 398–99 (Jan. 16, 1841), 401 (Jan. 19, 1841), 407 (Jan. 27, 1841), 415 (Feb. 8, 1841).

25   Ibid., 398–99 (Jan. 16, 1841), 407 (Jan. 27, 1841), 415 (Feb. 8, 1841, quotation).

26   Ibid., 429–30 (Feb. 22, 23, 1841).

27   Ibid., 430–31 (Feb. 24, 1841).

28   Ibid., 431 (Feb. 24, 1841).

29   Ibid., 431–32 (Feb. 25, 1841), 435 (March 1, 1841); Story to his Wife, Feb. 28, 1841, quoted in Charles Warren, *The Supreme Court in United States History,* 3 vols. (Boston, 1922), II, 350.

30   JQA, *Argument before the Supreme Court of the United States in the Case of the United States, Appellants, vs Cinque and Other Africans Captured in the Schooner* Amistad (New York, 1841), quotations on 1, 8, 75, 80, 83, 135. JQA's argument did not appear in the *Supreme Court Reports,* because he failed to get his manuscript to the court reporter on time. Jones, *Amistad,* 250, n. 17.

31   *Memoirs,* X, 441 (March 6, 9, 1841); JQA to Tappan, March 9, 1841, quoted in Jones, *Amistad,* 194; JQA to Roger Baldwin, March 17, 1841, Adams Papers.

32 *Memoirs*, XI, 29 (Nov. 19, 1841).

33 Howe, *What Hath God Wrought*, 658–71, has an excellent brief account of early American immigration to Texas and the Texas Revolution.

34 For JQA and the Transcontinental Treaty, see chap. 4 herein.

35 Robert V. Remini discusses Clay's overtures and problems in *Henry Clay: Statesman for the Union* (New York, 1991), 303–5.

36 *Memoirs*, VIII, 464–65 (Jan. 1, 1832).

37 *RD*, 24th Cong., 1st sess., 4041–47 (quotations on 4042).

38 Ibid., 4044; *Letters of John Quincy Adams to His Constituents* . . . (Boston, 1837), 43–44.

39 Diary, Sept. 7, 1839.

40 *Memoirs*, IX, 333 (Dec. 24, 1836), 378 (Sept. 18, 1837), X, 11–12 (June 6, 1838), 20ff. (June 15, 1838); *Letters to Constituents*, 43–44.

41 *Memoirs*, IX 333 (Dec. 24, 1836), 431 (Nov. 20, 1837, 1st quotation), X, 22 (June 16, 1838, 2d quotation).

42 Ibid., IX, 420 (Oct. 24, 1837, quotation), X, 50 (Dec. 4, 1838); Washington *Madisonian*, Dec. 19, 1837. William Lee Miller, *Arguing about Slavery: The Great Battle in the United States Congress* (New York, 1995), 287–98, has a spirited account, with extensive quotations of participants, of the committee and the reception of its report.

43 On the Van Buren administration and Texas, consult John Niven, *Martin Van Buren: The Romantic Age of American Politics* (New York, 1983), 443–47.

44 E.g., *Letter to His Constituents*; Diary, Sept. 1, 1838, Nov. 20, 1842.

45 *Memoirs*, IX, 491 (Feb. 2, 1838), XI, 277 (Dec. 10, 1842); Diary, Jan. 27, Feb. 10, 1838, Oct. 16, 1839, Feb. 1, March 24, 1840, March 27, Aug. 31, 1841, April 29, Dec. 1, 1847.

46 *Memoirs*, X, 349 (Aug. 20, 1840), 351 (Aug. 26, 1840); Diary, Oct. 13, 1840.

47 *Memoirs*, X, 357 (Oct. 17, 1840).

48 Michael J. Dubin, *United States Congressional Elections, 1788–1997: The Official Results* . . . (Jefferson, NC, 1998), 127, 132; Diary, Dec. 6, 1842.

49 On the Whig convention and the election of 1840, consult Michael F. Holt's masterful *The Rise and Fall of the American Whig Party: Jacksonian Politics and the Onset of the Civil War* (New York, 1999), 89–113; I base my account on it. For JQA's displeasure see *Memoirs*, X, 352 (Aug. 29, 1840).

50 *Memoirs*, VII, 530 (May 6, 1828); Diary, Oct. 11, 1840.

51 *Memoirs*, X, 366 (Dec. 4, 1840), XI, 29 (Nov. 5, 1841, quotation).

52   On Tyler, see my *The South and the Politics of Slavery, 1828–1856* (Baton Rouge, LA, 1978), 50–51, 150–52; Holt, *Whig Party*, 104. The most recent biographical treatment of Tyler is Edward P. Crapol, *John Tyler: The Accidental President* (Chapel Hill, NC, 2006), which concentrates heavily on his presidency. More detailed about both the pre- and post-presidential years as well as personal life is the older but still valuable Roger Seager II, *And Tyler Too: A Biography of John and Julia Gardiner Tyler* (New York, 1963). A new, comprehensive biography of Tyler would be most welcome.

53   *Memoirs*, X, 456 (April 4, 1841).

54   Ibid., 457 (April 4, 1841); XI, 382–83, (June 13, 2d quotation, 16, 1843).

55   On Tyler and Congress, including JQA, see Holt, *Whig Party*, 124–49, 1004–5, n. 75.

56   *Memoirs*, X, 465 (April 20, 1841), XI, 14 (Sept. 11, 1841, 1st quotation), 28–29 (Nov. 5, 1841, 2d and 3d quotations).

57   Ibid., X, 82 (Jan. 1, 1839), 181 (Jan. 1, 1840), 386–87 (Jan. 1, 1841), XI, 48 (Jan. 1, 1842), 467 (Jan. 1, 1844); Diary, Jan. 1, 1838, April 19, Aug. 17, 1842, Oct. 17, 1843, Jan. 22, 1844; Theodore Weld to Angelina Weld, Jan. 2, 1842, Jan. 1, 1843, Barnes and Dumond, eds., *Weld Letters*, II, 885, 954; Louisa Thomas, *Louisa: The Extraordinary Life of Mrs. Adams* (New York, 2016), 439.

58   Diary, March 16, 1838, Feb. 1, 1843 (1st quotation); *Memoirs*, X, 444 (March 13, 1841), 496 (July 5, 1841), XI, 133 (April 13, 1842), 156 (May 17, 1842), 172 (June 10, 1842, 2d quotation).

59   *Memoirs*, X, 535–36 (Aug. 18, 1841), XI, 174–75 (June 12, 1842, quotation).

60   Ibid., XI, 109 (March 14, 1842); Diary, March 13, 16 1842.

61   Diary, June 27, 1840, Nov. 25, Dec. 24, 1842, March 8, Oct. 3, 1843; *Memoirs*, X, 126 (June 28, 1839), XI, 243 (Aug. 26, 1842), 267 (Nov. 7, 1842, quotation).

62   Diary, June 18, 1839, Aug. 31, 1840 (3d quotation), Oct. 30, 1841, March 31, 1842; *Memoirs*, X, 341 (July 25, 1840, 1st quotation), 449–50 (March 21, 1841, 2d quotation), XI, 275–76 (Dec. 9, 1842), 280 (Dec. 16, 1842).

63   Diary, Sept. 4, 1842; *Memoirs*, X, 259 (April 12, 1840), XI, 340–41 (March 19, 1843).

64   Diary, Sept. 4, 1842 (quotations); *Memoirs*, IX, 507 (March 11, 1838).

65   *Memoirs*, IX, 340–41 (Jan. 1, 1837, quotation), XI, 341 (March 19, 1843).

66   Diary, Nov. 11 (quotation), 20, 1839.

67   Ibid., Aug. 26, 1838; Washington *Madisonian*, Nov. 28, 1838.

68 *Memoirs*, X, 124 (May 24, 1839).

69 Ibid., 355 (Sept. 27, 1840); Diary, Aug. 30, Sept. 13, 25, 1839. Prescott's history of the Spanish monarchs appeared in 1838. Bancroft's first volume came out in 1834, the second in 1837, the third in 1840, and the final one of the original edition not until after the Civil War. I suggest its praise of Virginians as plausible because in volume I, Bancroft gives much adulation to seventeenth-century Virginians.

70 *Memoirs*, X, 123 (May 24, 1839).

71 Both the *Memoirs* and the Diary between 1838 and 1843 contain copious references to those exercises and pursuits—e.g., Diary, Aug. 2, 1838, Aug. 2, 1839, June 5, 8, 9, July 1, 2, 3, 16, 1841.

72 *Memoirs*, XI, 390–405 (July 6–Aug. 7, 1843), provides a detailed account. For the origins see 390 n. There is a notable exception, however. The *Memoirs* entirely omit the journey from Albany north to Canada and thence westward to Niagara Falls. For that portion one must turn to the Diary. My account is based on the two. I will specify only quotations.

73 *Memoirs*, XI, 393 (Aug. 8, 1843).

74 Ibid., 398 (July 28, 1843). Whitney R. Cross, *The Burned-Over District* (New York, 1950), remains standard.

75 *Memoirs*, XI, 400 (July 30, 1843).

76 Ibid.

77 Ibid., 394 (July 25, 1843, quotation), 409 (Sept. 19, 1843).

78 Ibid., 411–43 (Oct. 25–Nov. 23, 1843), details the trip from Massachusetts to Ohio and the return to Washington. Repeating my practice from the earlier western trip, I will specify only quotations. On the Ohio portion George W. Paulson, "Lighthouse of the Sky: John Quincy Adams Visits Cincinnati," *Timeline* 18 (July–Aug. 2001): 2–15, is informative.

79 *Memoirs*, XI, 419 (Nov. 2, 1843).

80 Ibid.

81 Ibid., 425 (Nov. 8, 1843).

82 Ibid., 426 (Nov. 9, 1843).

83 JQA, *An Oration Delivered before the Cincinnati Astronomical Society* . . . (Cincinnati, 1843).

84 *Memoirs*, XI, 430 (Nov. 13, 1843).

85 Clay to JQA, Sept. 21, 1843, and JQA to Clay, Oct. 17, 1843, *Clay Papers*, IX, 358–59.

86 *Memoirs*, XI, 437 (Nov. 20, 1843). For details on his stay in Pittsburgh, see Donald M. Goodfellow, "'Old Man Eloquent' Visits

Pittsburgh," *Western Pennsylvania Historical Magazine* 28 (Sept.–Dec. 1945): 99–110.

87   *Memoirs*, XI, 425–26 (Nov. 8, 1843).

CHAPTER 9: *"Our Country . . . Is No Longer the Same"*

1   Weld to Angelina Weld, Jan. 9, 1842, Gilbert H. Barnes and Dwight L. Dumond, eds., *Letters of Theodore Dwight Weld, Angelina Grimké Weld, and Sarah Grimké, 1822–1844*, 2 vols. (New York, 1934), II, 889.

2   Weld to Angelina Weld, Jan. 23, 1842, ibid., 899; *CG*, 27th Cong., 2d sess., 157–59.

3   *CG*, 27th Cong., 2d sess., 158; *Memoirs*, XI, 98–99 (Feb. 23, 1842).

4   *CG*, 27th Cong., 2d sess., 161–67; *Memoirs*, XI, 68, 70 (Jan. 22, 24, 1842); Theodore Dwight Weld to Angelina Weld, Jan. [23], 1842, Barnes and Dumond, eds., *Weld Letters*, II, 900.

5   *CG*, 27th Cong., 2d sess., 168–215 (I will not provide individual citations). The critical votes are conveniently tabulated in Lynn Hudson Parsons, "Censuring Old Man Eloquent: Foreign Policy and Disunion, 1842," *Capitol Studies* 3 (Fall 1975): 93.

6   *Memoirs*, XI, 74–75 (quotation 75), 79 (Jan. 26, 31, 1842); Weld to Angelina Weld, Jan. 30, 1841[42], Barnes and Dumond, eds., *Weld Letters*, II, 905–6.

7   *Memoirs*, XI, 80 (day following Jan. 31, 1842, 1st quotation); Weld to Angelina Weld, Jan. 30, 1841[42], Barnes and Dumond, eds., *Weld Letters*, II, 905 (2d quotation).

8   *Memoirs*, XI, 87 (Feb. 7, 1842); Theodore Dwight Weld to Angelina Weld, Feb. 6, 1842, Barnes and Dumond, eds., *Weld Letters*, II, 911 (quotation).

9   For Texas consult Joel H. Silbey's thorough *Storm over Texas: Annexation Controversy and the Road to Civil War* (New York, 2005). Also see my *The South and the Politics of Slavery, 1828–1856* (Baton Rouge, LA, 1978), chap. 6; Edward P. Crapol, *John Tyler: The Accidental President* (Chapel Hill, NC, 2006), chap. 6; William W. Freehling, *The Road to Disunion: Secessionists at Bay, 1776–1854* (New York, 1990), pt. 6; Matthew Karp, *This Vast Southern Empire: Slaveholders at the Helm of American Foreign Policy* (Cambridge, MA, 2016), 90–102. They inform my account; I will cite an individual source only for a direct quotation.

10   Cooper, *Politics of Slavery*, 194.

11 *Memoirs*, XI, 206–7 (July 13, 1842), 330 (Feb. 28, 1843).

12 Ibid., 374 (May 8, 1843), 380 (May 31, 1843).

13 Ibid., XII, 13–14 (April 22, 1844), 22 (May 4, 1844, quotation).

14 Ibid., 49 (June 10, 1844).

15 For the election of 1844, Michael F. Holt, *The Rise and Fall of the American Whig Party: Jacksonian Politics and the Onset of Civil War* (New York, 1999), chap. 7, provides a thorough account, albeit focused on the Whigs. For the South see also Cooper, *Politics of Slavery*, 189–219. My discussion is based on them.

16 *Memoirs*, XI, 352 (April 3, 1843), XII, 26 (May 12, 1844).

17 Diary, Aug. 27, Sept. 13, 1844. On the Liberty party Reinhard O. Johnson, *The Liberty Party, 1840–1848: Antislavery Third Party Politics in the United States* (Baton Rouge, LA, 2009), gives detailed treatment.

18 Holt, *Whig Party*, 194–206.

19 *Memoirs*, XII, 103 (Nov. 8, 1844, 1st and 3d quotations), 110 (Nov. 25, 1844, 2d quotation), 118 (Dec. 7, 1844).

20 Ibid., 103 (Nov. 8, 1844).

21 Ibid., 79–80 (Oct. 1–2, 1844).

22 Ibid., 97 (Oct. 26, 1844), 106 (Nov. 12, 1844); Michael J. Dubin, *United States Congressional Elections, 1788–1997: The Official Results* . . . (Jefferson, NC, 1998), 139.

23 Leonard L. Richards, *The Life and Times of Congressman John Quincy Adams* (New York, 1986), 175–79; *CG*, 28th Cong., 2d sess., 115–16; *Memoirs*, XII, 115–16 (Dec. 3, 1844).

24 For the renewal of Texas see the same sources cited herein n. 9, with the addition of Holt, *Whig Party*, 218–22.

25 *Memoirs*, XII, 57 (June 16–17, 1844).

26 *Boston Atlas*, Nov. 2, 1844. Ato was a cacodemon in a cosmology created by John Dee, a sixteenth- and early seventeenth-century English mathematician, alchemist, astrologer, and conjuror, who also advised Queen Elizabeth I on science. A contemporary, Edward Kelley, worked with him in his magical investigations. On Dee consult R. Julian Roberts, "John Dee," *Oxford Dictionary of National Biography*, 60 vols. (Oxford, Eng., 2004), XV, 667–75. For assistance with Dee, I am grateful to my colleague Professor Victor Stater.

27 *Memoirs*, XII, 144 (Jan. 10, 1845), 150–51 (Jan. 22, 1845, quotation).

28 Ibid., 152–53 (Jan. 25, 1842, quotation); *CG*, 28th Cong., 2d sess., 188–89, 190.

29 *Memoirs*, XII, 173 (Feb. 27, 1845), 201–2 (July 7, 1845, quotation).

30 Ibid., 168 (Feb. 14, 1845).

31 Ibid., 172 (Feb. 22, 1845), 178–79 (March 4, 1845), 193 (April 6, 1845).

32 Milo Milton Quaife, ed., *The Diary of James K. Polk during His Presidency*, 4 vols. (Chicago, 1910), I, 128–31, II, 493–94.

33 JQA to Richard Rush, Oct. 16, 1845, Adams Papers. For a more general discussion of this topic, see Charles N. Edel, *Nation Builder: John Quincy Adams and the Grand Strategy of the Republic* (Cambridge, MA, 2014), chap. 5.

34 On Polk and expansion see the discussion by his leading biographer, Charles Sellers, *James K. Polk: Continentalist, 1843–1846* (Princeton, NJ, 1966), chaps. 6, 8, 9, 10. On Oregon, Daniel Walker Howe, *What Hath God Wrought: The Transformation of America, 1815–1848* (New York, 2007), 711–22, provides an excellent brief account.

35 *Memoirs*, XII, 221 (Dec. 21, 1845).

36 Ibid., 242–46 (Feb. 9, 1846); *CG*, 29th Cong., 1st sess., 339–42, has the speech. The vote is on 349.

37 JQA to Joseph Sturge, April, n.d., 1846, Adams Papers.

38 On Polk and the advent of the Mexican-American War, see Sellers, *Polk*, 229–30, 336–40, 398–426. Again, Howe, *What Hath God Wrought*, 731–43, has a first-rate brief treatment.

39 *CG*, 29th Cong., 1st sess., 794–95.

40 Diary, July 28, 1846.

41 Richards, *Congressman Adams*, 193.

42 *CG*, 29th Cong., 1st sess., 1215–16, has JQA's speech; Chaplain W. Morrison's still superb monograph, *Democratic Politics and Sectionalism: The Wilmot Proviso Controversy* (Chapel Hill, NC, 1967), chaps. 1–2, covers the proviso and Congress.

43 *Memoirs*, XII, 275–76 (Oct., 5, 12, 1846); Dubin, *Congressional Elections*, 146.

44 Diary, March 28, 1844.

45 Ibid., July 14, 17, 18, 26, Aug. 6, 13, 16, 22, 24, 26, Sept. 3, 1844; *Memoirs*, XII, 70–71 (July 11, 12, 1844, quotation).

46 Diary, June–July passim, Aug. 6, 9 (quotation), Sept. 16, 20, 21, 1845.

47 Ibid., July 28 (quotation), Aug. 17, 1846.

48 *Memoirs*, XII, 279 (Nov. 20, 1846, heading Posthumous Memoir); Louisa Thomas, *Louisa: The Extraordinary Life of Mrs. Adams* (New York, 2016), 449–50.

49 *Memoirs*, XII, 279 (Nov. 20, 1846, heading Posthumous Memoir).

50 Ibid., 213 (Sept. 17, 1845), 268 (July 13, 1846, quotation); Diary, July 14, 1846, summer 1845 passim (gardening).

51 *Memoirs*, XII, 277 (Oct. 31, 1846).

52 Diary, summer 1845–Jan. 1848 passim; also consult *Memoirs*, XII, 271, 281 (editor's insertions). These citations refer to this paragraph as well as the two above it.

53 *Portraits*, 203–11, 231–35, 250–69, 270–71, 273–74, 282–87, 295–302; for the likenesses themselves, see 205, 232, 255, 271, 275, 283, 286, 294.

54 *Memoirs*, XII, 280 (Posthumous Memoirs); *CG* 29th Cong., 2d sess., 418.

55 Thomas, *Louisa*, 450; *CG*, 29th Cong., 2d sess., Feb. 13–March 4, 1847 passim.

56 Bemis, II, 450.

57 On the split in the Massachusetts Whig party, see Martin Duberman, *Charles Francis Adams, 1807–1886* (1961; Stanford, CA, 1968), 110–22, and Robert V. Remini, *Daniel Webster: The Man and His Time* (New York, 1997), 624–25.

58 *Memoirs*, XI, 518 (Feb. 23, 1844, 1st quotation), XII, 274 (Aug. 23, 1846); JQA to CFA, June 29, 1846, Adams Papers (2d quotation); Duberman, *Charles Francis*, 111–13.

59 On the rift consult Duberman, *Charles Francis*, 130–32, and Richards, *Congressman Adams*, 190–91; JQA to CFA, Jan. 1, 1848, Adams Papers. Later CFA became the vice-presidential candidate on the Free Soil party ticket in 1848, in the 1850s a leader in the Republican party in his state, a congressman, and during the Civil War his country's minister to Great Britain.

60 *Memoirs*, XII, 281, editorial note.

61 Ibid., XI, 65 (Jan. 18, 1842, 1st quotation); Diary, July 3, 1846, 2d quotation); *CG*, 30th Cong., 1st sess., 1–2.

62 William Henry Seward to Thurlow Weed, Feb. 29(?), 1847, Frederick Seward, *William H. Seward*, 3 vols. (New York, 1891), II, 38.

63 Ibid., I, 672.

64 *Memoirs*, XII, 97 (Oct. 25, 1844).

65 LCA to William Henry Seward, March 21, 1848, William Henry Seward Papers, Rush Rhees Library, University of Rochester, Rochester, NY; Diary, Feb. 20, 1848.

66 *CG*, 30th Cong., 1st sess., 380–81.

67 *Token of a Nation's Sorrow* . . . (Washington, 1848), 3–5; Bemis, II, 535–37. In n. 45 on p. 536, Bemis presents a persuasive argument for the version of the final words I have quoted rather than the oft-quoted ones that have two sentences, omitting the conjunction.

CODA: *"Proceed—Persevere—Never Despair"*

1   For the funeral in Washington and the subsequent train trip to Massachusetts and events there, consult *Token of Sorrow . . .* (Washington, 1848), quotation in this paragraph on 13; Bemis, II, 537–43; also see James Traub, *John Quincy Adams: Militant Spirit* (New York: 2016), 528–31. They inform my account. I will make separate citations only for particular items.

2   *LCA*, II, 770.

3   Milo Milton Quaife, ed., *The Diary of James K. Polk during His Presidency, 1845–1849*, 4 vols. (Chicago, 1910), III, 362–63.

4   Lynn Hudson Parsons, "The 'Splendid Pageant': Observations on the Death of John Quincy Adams," *New England Quarterly* 53 (Dec. 1980): 456–66.

5   John Wentworth, *Congressional Reminiscences . . .* (Chicago, 1882), 14–15.

6   William P. Lunt, *A Discourse Delivered in Quincy, March 11, 1848 . . .* (Boston, 1848), 35. Following Louisa's death in 1852, Charles Francis placed her and his father's relics in a crypt beneath the family church. Since then they have lain there in company with those of John and Abigail.

7   *Token of a Nation's Sorrow*, 18.

8   The closest student of this material states that most extant funeral sermons came from northern Congregational and Unitarian ministers. Parsons, "Splendid Pageant," 473–81.

9   This paragraph is based on coverage within the first month of his death in the following newspapers. Quotations are noted with specific dates: Richmond, VA *Enquirer*, Richmond, VA *Whig*, Raleigh, NC *Register* (March 1, 1848, 3d quotation), Raleigh, NC *Standard*, Charleston, SC *Mercury*, Milledgeville, GA *Southern Recorder*, Jackson, MS *Mississippian* (March 3, 1848, 1st quotation), Vicksburg, MS *Daily Whig*, New Orleans, LA *Daily Picayune* (March 1, 1848, 2d quotation), Little Rock, AK *Gazette* (March 9, 1848, final quotation), Houston, TX *Democratic Telegraph and Texas Register*.

10 *Memoirs*, XII, 37 (May 29, 1844).

11 JQA to CFA, June 29, 1846, Adams Papers.

ILLUSTRATION CREDITS

—

Frontispiece

John Quincy Adams. Photo courtesy of Prints and Photographs Division /
Library of Congress / LC-B5-950060.

Part One

John Quincy Adams. Photo courtesy of Prints and Photographs Division /
Library of Congress / LC-D416-509.

Part Two

Andrew Jackson. Photo courtesy of Prints and Photographs Division /
Library of Congress / LC-DIG-pga-02501.

Part Three

Chamber of the House of Representatives. Photo courtesy of the author.

Coda

Death of John Quincy Adams at the U.S. Capitol. Prints and Photographs
Division / Library of Congress / LC-USZC4-5802.

INDEX

—

Note: Page numbers in italics indicate figures.

A. B. Club, *25*

abolitionist newspapers, 318

abolitionists/abolitionist movement, 317–23, 328–30, 337–40, 351–54, 358–62, 388, 395, 397–99; doctrine of, 319–20; election of 1840 and, 376–77; genesis of, 320–21; in Great Britain, 318–19, 320–21, 402–3; growing support for, 327; growth of, 323; John Quincy and, 359–62, 399–400, 404; John Quincy's trial in the House and, 399–400; Liberty party and, 407; in New York, 388–89; pamphlets of, 323–24; postmasters permitted not to distribute, 323–24; printing technology and, 323; send anti-slavery petitions to Congress, 321–22; Twelfth Congressional District and, 326–27; in the United States, 317–19; U.S. House of Representatives and, 321–22

Adams, Abigail (sister), 22, 31–32, 33

Adams, Abigail Smith (mother), 3–5, 7, 12–13, 30–31, 90, 98, 129; arrives in England, 22; buried in family crypt, 490n6; consents to let John Quincy accompany father to France, 8, 10; correspondence with Elizabeth Shaw, 24; correspondence with John Quincy, 10–11, 15–16, 18–19, 31–32, 93, 95, 101–2, 105, 125, 135–36, 139; death of, 158–59, 231; expectations of John Quincy, 111, 218–19; failing health of, 63; financial setbacks suffered by, 67–68; John Quincy's nomination and confirmation to the Supreme Court and, 106–7; learns of John Quincy's engagement, 47–48; objection to John Quincy's relationship with Mary Frazier, 31; in Paris, France, 22; published letters of, 389; publishes John Quincy's letters in Boston newspapers without his permission, 105; Unitarianism and, 136; writes to Madison about financial problems of John Quincy in Russia, 105–6

Adams, Charles (brother), 13, 43

Adams, Charles Francis (son), 90–91, 99, 199, 281, 312, 490n6; abolitionist movement and, 335;

WILLIAM J. COOPER is a Boyd Professor Emeritus at Louisiana State University. A native of Kingstree, South Carolina, he received his AB degree from Princeton University and his PhD from Johns Hopkins University. Professor Cooper spent his entire professional career at Louisiana State University, where he also served as dean of the Graduate School from 1982 to 1989. He has held fellowships from the Institute of Southern History at Johns Hopkins, the Charles Warren Center for Studies in American History at Harvard, the Guggenheim Foundation, and the National Endowment for the Humanities. He is a past president of the Southern Historical Association and a fellow of the Society of American Historians.

He is the author of *The Conservative Regime: South Carolina, 1877–1890* (1968); *The South and the Politics of Slavery, 1828–1856* (1978); *Liberty and Slavery: Southern Politics to 1860* (1983); *Jefferson Davis, American* (2000, recipient of the *Los Angeles Times* Book Prize for Biography and the Jefferson Davis Award); *Jefferson Davis and the Civil War Era* (2008); and *We Have the War Upon Us: The Onset of the Civil War, November 1860–April 1861* (2012, recipient of the Jefferson Davis Award). He is co-author of *The American South: A History* (2017, 5th edition). He has also edited five books and written numerous articles.

He now lives in Atlanta.